D0041106

Managing Networks of Twenty-First Century Organisations

Managing Networks of Twenty-First Century Organisations

Perri 6,
College of Business, Law & Social Sciences,
Nottingham Trent University, UK

Nick Goodwin,
Health Services Research Unit,
London School of Hygiene and Tropical Medicine, UK

Edward Peck,
Health Services Management Centre, School of Public Policy
University of Birmingham, UK

and

Tim Freeman,
Health Services Management Centre, School of Public Policy
University of Birmingham, UK

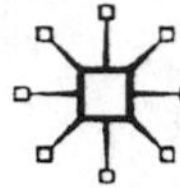

First published in 2006 by
PALGRAVE MACMILLAN
Houndmills, Basingstoke, Hampshire RG21 6XS and
175 Fifth Avenue, New York, N.Y. 10010
Companies and representatives throughout the world.

PALGRAVE MACMILLAN is the global academic imprint of the Palgrave Macmillan division of St. Martin's Press, LLC and of Palgrave Macmillan Ltd. Macmillan® is a registered trademark in the United States, United Kingdom and other countries. Palgrave is a registered trademark in the European Union and other countries.

ISBN-13: 978–1–4039–9609–1 hardback
ISBN-10: 1–4039–9609–1 hardback

This book is printed on paper suitable for recycling and made from fully managed and sustained forest sources.

A catalogue record for this book is available from the British Library.

Library of Congress Cataloging-in-Publication Data

Managing networks of twenty-first century organisations / Perri 6 ... [et al.].
p. cm.
Includes bibliographical references and index.
ISBN 1–4039–9609–1 (cloth)
1. Business networks – Management. 2. Strategic alliances (Business) – Management. 3. Interorganizational relations. 4. Organizational behavior. I. 6, Perri, 1960–

HD69.S8M3272 2006
658′.044—dc22 2005045609

10 9 8 7 6 5 4 3 2 1
15 14 13 12 11 10 09 08 07 06

Printed and bound in Great Britain by
Antony Rowe Ltd, Chippenham and Eastbourne

Contents

List of Figures

List of Tables

List of Boxes

Preface

This book offers what we believe is a distinctive and novel theory of how networks of relationships between organisations operate. It will, we hope, be of interest to practising managers looking for some assistance in responding to the challenges of leading public and private enterprises through the complexities of partnerships, joint ventures and the like. Within the academic field of the social sciences, it will appeal to business and management scholars (and their students) active in both commercial and public management fields, to organisational sociologists and to policy scientists.

Building upon the achievements of a very large body of both empirical and theoretical work, we develop an integrated theory of the factors that shape networks and how they are interrelated. This theory incorporates accounts of the variety of elementary forms that inter-organisational relations can take, of the nature of inter-organisational trust and of the scope for managers and leaders to shape and influence these relationships. In the later chapters, we offer some evidence for the theory by reanalysing four extensive bodies of empirical studies in the social science and management research literatures on networks in four industries; we treat these literatures as case studies to show how our theory makes good sense of the data and, indeed, generally makes better sense of them than the existing theories. Finally, we bring together the argument by comparing the case studies and answering some of the lines of criticism that we can anticipate being offered.

The theory on offer in this book is grounded in the approach bequeathed to social science by one of its founders, Émile Durkheim, but its most immediate progenitor is the work of the anthropologist and social theorist, Mary Douglas, who reinterpreted and recast the central arch of Durkheim's thought. We also draw upon the work of Michael Thompson, Gerry Mars, Steve Rayner, Aaron Wildavsky and Christopher Hood, who have developed a series of applications of her work to organisational processes. However, to the best of our knowledge, this tradition has not previously been applied in a systematic way to understanding the dynamics of inter-organisational relations.

We recognise that readers may come to this book with differing concerns and we feel it is incumbent upon us to provide some directions to our distinct audiences. We think that most readers would probably find it helpful to read the introduction, not least because it tries to bring some clarity and sobriety to the discussion of networks and also provides a brief synopsis of each chapter. We hope that Chapter 2 will be of benefit to managers and students alike, although scholars familiar with the field who are principally interested in the development of theory will find Chapters 3, 4, 5 and 6 of greatest interest. After completing Chapter 2, managers and students may also find that the first third of both Chapter 3 and Chapter 4 are helpful background in order to understand the basics of our approach that informs the chapters that will probably appeal most to them; in particular, readers who want to know more about the scope for practical managerial action arising out of the theory will find Chapters 6 and 7 most rewarding. Given their breadth, we hope that every reader will have an interest in at least one of the empirical case studies that constitute Chapters 8 through 11.

In the course of our work on this book, we have accumulated a great many debts. Our greatest debt is to the Service Development and Organisation programme within Britain's National Health Service Research and Development Programme, administered by a team at the London School of Hygiene and Tropical Medicine. The programme commissioned us to undertake a widely ranging review of the literature on inter-organisational networks, and it was this research that provided the initial basis for the book. We are grateful both to the board which approved the grant and to the staff who worked with us on that project for their support.

The universities of Birmingham, Nottingham Trent and the London School of Hygiene and Tropical Medicine provided supportive and congenial settings for our work.

We are particularly grateful to Rachel Posaner, Pat Metcalfe and Sally Harbison for their unstinting help in tracking down texts, providing us with access to a plethora of online databases, and undertaking searches for us. Wendy Spurr showed great patience in helping us to compile the references and Anne van der Salm was her usual calm and methodical self as we prepared the final manuscript.

Jennifer Nelson at Palgrave has been as understanding a publisher as any author could hope for.

A number of prominent scholars gave us comments on drafts at various stages of our work, and we are very grateful to them for their time and astuteness; they include Chris Bellamy, Nick Gould, Bob Hudson, Gerry Stoker and an anonymous reviewer for Palgrave.

A paper based on our work was presented at the Economic and Social Research Council international expert colloquium, *Governance and performance: how do modes of governance affect public service performance?*, 15–16 March 2004, School of Public Policy, University of Birmingham. We are grateful to Chris Skelcher for commissioning that paper and giving us comments upon it. We also thank those taking part in the discussion of that paper for their helpful comments.

The authors would like to thank the following who kindly gave permission for the use of copyright material for the following figures, which appear in Chapter 8:

MIT Press, for Figure 8.1 from Gansler JS, 1995, *Defense conversion: Transforming the arsenal of democracy*.

Pergamon Press, for Figures 8.2 and 8.3 from Kelley MR and Watkins TA, 1998, Are defense and non-defense manufacturing practices all that different?, in Susman GI and O'Keefe S, 1998, eds, *The defense industry in the post-cold war era*.

Palgrave Macmillan for Figure 8.4 from Creasey P and May S, 1988, *The European armaments market and procurement cooperation*.

Finally, although the book is fully jointly authored, Perri 6 took initial responsibility for the theoretical chapters 1–7, the conclusion and the biotechnology case study; the case studies on defence contracting, crime and disorder and health care were undertaken respectively by Edward Peck, Tim Freeman and Nick Goodwin. The final edit of the manuscript was undertaken by Edward Peck.

Biographical details

Perri 6

Perri 6 is Professor of Social Policy in the Graduate School in the College of Business, Law and Social Sciences at Nottingham Trent University. He worked previously at the Health Services Management Centre at the University of Birmingham, at King's College London, at Strathclyde University and the University of Bath. He spent several years in the 1990s as Director of Policy and Research at the independent London-based think-tank, Demos. He has been a consultant to the Prime Minister's Strategy Unit and conducted work for the OECD, for the Information Commissioner, the Local Government Association and many government departments, local authorities and major businesses. He is the author, co-author or editor of over twenty books, and many more articles. Best known for his work on joined-up government, on privacy and on public policy personal social networks, he has also published extensively on consumer choice in public services, and has made important contributions to the development of neo-Durkheimian institutional theory. His recent books for Palgrave Macmillan include *E-governance: styles of political judgment in the information age polity* (2004) and *Towards holistic governance: the new reform agenda* (2002). He is currently working with Edward Peck on a book for Palgrave entitled *Beyond delivery* about organisational process and policy implementation and another with Christine Bellamy, Charles Raab and others about the relationship between inter-agency collaboration, information sharing and confidentiality in information-age governance.

Tim Freeman

Dr. Tim Freeman is lecturer in health policy at the Health Services Management Centre, University of Birmingham, where he is responsible for the department's doctoral student programme. He teaches and publishes widely on topics related to governance, performance management and quality improvement.

Nick Goodwin

Dr. Nick Goodwin is Senior Lecturer in Health Services Delivery and Organisational Research at the Health Services Research Unit, London School of Hygiene and Tropical Medicine. Nick completed his PhD thesis on the privatisation of public services in 1994 and has since followed a career in health services research. Nick joined the Health Services Research Unit in January 2004 having previously worked as a research officer at the King's Fund (1994–7) and lecturer at the Health Services Management Centre,

University of Birmingham (1997–2003). Nick's key research interests lie in the organisation and management of primary care, integrated care systems and care networks, and international health management and development. Nick has recently completed research into the management of health and social care networks and the effectiveness of different approaches to commissioning in a project funded by The Health Foundation. Nick is the Chair of the International Network of Integrated Care and a member of the International Council of Healthcare Advisors.

Edward Peck
Edward Peck is Professor of Healthcare Partnerships in the School of Public Policy at the University of Birmingham and Director of the Health Services Management Centre. Previously, he combined research, teaching and organisational consultancy in his various roles at King's College London before which he spent over ten years as a manager in the British National Health Service. He is especially interested in the theory and practice of organisational development – and Radcliffe published his *Organisational Development in Healthcare: Approaches, innovations, achievements* in 2005 – in particular in the context of emerging partnerships between both the NHS and local government and the public and private sector. The other major focus of his academic study – policy implementation – will be reflected in his next book for Palgrave entitled *Beyond delivery* to be co-authored with Perri 6.

1
Introduction

After the goldrush: why we need a new account of networks of organisations?

During the 1990s, writers on both public and private sector organisations converged on the claim that 'networks' represented a distinctive trend in their management and governance. They argued that networks were the most promising solution to the dilemmas of designing structures for improved performance, almost regardless of the measures used (e.g. effectiveness of interventions to users or financial outturns).

In the public management literature, American scholars focusing on arguments about implementation as an inter-organisational problem and opportunity (O'Toole, 1988, 1993) were joined by Dutch researchers interested in policy networks (Kickert et al., 1997) and British analysts concerned with the idea of declining capacity for command and control in national government (Rhodes, 1997). In the study of private sector inter-organisational relations, US theorists celebrated 'network' forms in their own industries as uniquely flexible, innovative and trusting. Many of these commentators argued that networks were unlike markets and hierarchies and claimed that they were steadily replacing other forms of inter-organisational relations (Bradach and Eccles, 1989; Powell, 1990; Alter and Hage, 1993). British management analysts quickly followed this trend (e.g. Thompson G et al., 1991; Huxham, 1996). Prior to the Japanese economic stagnation of the late twentieth century, and the more general east Asian financial crises of the late 1990s, there was a great deal of interest in models of inter-organisational relations in Japanese keiretsu and south Korean chaebols as 'networks' (e.g. Best, 1990; Orrú et al., 1991; Westney, 2001). Overall, these arguments tended to eclipse the earlier traditions of scepticism in public administration (Challis et al., 1988) and business studies (Williamson, 1975) that stressed the costs, difficulties and limitations of inter-organisational collaboration.

In the conventional view, inter-organisational arrangements can be divided into three types – hierarchies, markets and networks (Thompson G et al., 1991;

Jones et al., 1997; Domingues, 2002; Kümpers et al., 2002; Hakansson and Lind, 2004; Hudson, 2004 a, b).

A hierarchy is typically taken to be a single organisation which has vertically integrated the supply chain, using internal administrative regulation to govern the movement of services and resources on a co-operative and long-term basis. Large bureaucracies are usually presented as hierarchies, often persisting over decades.

Markets consist of multiple organisations exchanging services and resources using price mechanisms and powers of exit from relationships to manage relations vertically along supply chains. There is also competition between horizontally related organisations. Markets are often perceived as focusing on short-term investment horizons.

Networks are supposed to lie between these two forms. They resemble markets in being multi-organisational and relying on voluntary choice around participation, but resemble hierarchies in that integration is supported to some degree, relations horizontally are co-operative and price mechanisms are attenuated permitting long-term relations of commitment.

Those hostile to network arrangements may regard them either as aberrations within markets, in which case they will be criticised as cartels, restrictive practices or oligopolies, or aberrations within hierarchies, in which case they are condemned as deviant, informal arrangements marked, for example, by producer capture. In contrast, advocates sometimes claim that networks are distinguished by more trusting relations than markets offer and by greater flexibility than hierarchies afford (Bradach and Eccles, 1989; Powell, 1990; Carney, 1998). Transaction cost theory, which was originally developed to explain in a manner consistent with economic orthodoxy the conditions under which hierarchies might prove superior to markets (Williamson, 1975, 1985), later came to be adapted to explain networks as well (Williamson, 1994).

The conventional view has a number of limitations, and much of this book can be read as a critique of this established framework and as an attempt to set out a superior one. It will be argued that the three forms – hierarchies, markets and networks – are not necessarily distinctive and that this simple taxonomy leaves too many cases lumped together in overly inclusive categories where a more finely-grained analysis is needed. Moreover, each form has been excessively lauded for merits that they do not necessarily possess.

At the outset, it is important to acknowledge that a wide variety of empirical research has undermined the claim that these forms are distinctive. For example, Stinchcombe's (1990; Stinchcombe and Heimer, 1985) study of 'contracts as hierarchical documents', in such fields as the aeroplane and automobile industries, shows that functional equivalents of each of five basic elements of hierarchical accountability can be found in the patterned relationships between organisations which are expressed in contracts and settled in markets. The five basic elements are: authoritative control of labour; financial relations; incentive structures organised around status; standard operating procedures with sanctions; and meetings with governance roles. Furthermore, many studies of relational contracting have also shown that there are genuinely market-like forms in many networks, despite the appearance of commitments and accountabilities that are not characteristic of typical market forms (Macneil, 1974, 1980; Williamson, 1985).

Least satisfactory, though, in the conventional view, is the presentation of networks themselves. At its most extreme, O'Toole and Meier (1999) define anything that is not a hierarchy or a market as a network! In the management literature, it is common to find talk of a 'swollen middle' of organisational forms between market and hierarchy (Hennart, 1993), but this is hardly satisfactory for it effectively abandons even the modest aim of describing and distinguishing forms, and certainly gives up on hopes for explanation. As Hennart (1993) points out, this characterisation leaves the concept too capacious to pick out anything in particular. Even those who believe networks to be a useful conceptualisation of relationships have recently begun to explore different types of networks. For example, the recent volume edited by DiMaggio (2001) distinguishes continental dominant types; the authors regard east Asian network types as being distinguished by their hierarchical structure as well as by their culture orientation from the looser and less stable types found in the United States or the mix of types found in post-socialist economies in east central Europe.

The claim that 'networks' are both distinct from markets and hierarchies, and that they are superior in flexibility, trust and innovation, has not gone unchallenged. This is especially true in the business studies literature on strategic management which exhibits interest in recognising network failures, different types of networks, and the fact that networks are often creatures of market relations or of hierarchical regulation (e.g. Stinchcombe and Heimer, 1985; Kogut, 1989; Anderson, 1990; Miles and Snow, 1992; Gulati, 1995, 1998; Doz and Hamel, 1998; Podolny and Page, 1998; Reuer and Koza, 2000).

However, these reservations have hardly dented the popularity of networks in the minds of scholars and practitioners of management. Even recent theoretical studies, the titles of which promise to explore the varieties and limits of networks, pay much more attention to stressing the benefit or the inevitability of network arrangements than to establishing clear taxonomies of network forms and to exploring the studies on failures (e.g. Thompson G, 2003). In the practitioner-oriented literature, 'networks' are still being propounded as the organisational solution in many fields of public services (e.g. Hargreaves, 2003).

At the very least, then, it is immediately apparent that there are 'hierarchical networks' and 'market-like networks' rather than networks being distinct from either hierarchies or markets as forms of organisation. As a consequence, networks do not form a single distinct category of inter-organisational relations, with features shared by all and only those forms properly classified as 'networks' and which can be marked off clearly from 'markets' or 'hierarchies'. This argument suggests that the basic nature of the accountabilities involved in both inter-organisational and in single organisational systems may not be fundamentally different in character. This book builds upon these fundamental insights.

Moreover, there is no research evidence to support the view that all and only those patterns of inter-organisational relations that can be called networks exhibit common or consistent impact upon organisational performance. Indeed, it is only possible to understand the relationship between network structure and organisational performance by examining the biases that *particular* types of relations might have to support certain kinds of performance at the expense of undermining others. In these circumstances, a classification of these types is required. The articulation of such a classification – and its testing in a diverse range of organisational settings – is attempted in the following chapters.

The purpose of this book is to present a balanced account of inter-organisational relations. It does not advocate for networks as a panacea to the problems of organising in the public and private sectors any more than it dismisses them. It contends that networks are neither a novel nor a distinct form of social organisation to be contrasted with markets and hierarchies. Building on this premise, it constructs a typology of networks with greater explanatory power than most of the now standard theories and models. It is in this sense that the book is positioned after the goldrush, when the initial burst of enthusiasm for networks from academics, policy-makers and managers needs to be turned into a robust and sustainable contribution to the literature on organisations and organising.

The core questions that the book will address are:

What are inter-organisational networks?
What varieties of networks are there?
What are their relative strengths and weaknesses?
How can the origins, trajectories, merits and problems of these types best be explained?
What strategies are available to individuals and to organisations seeking to exercise leverage over or within networks?
In what contexts can we speak of trust between organisations and what can be expected of such trust?

Key terms

It is now necessary to begin to set out definitions of some of the key concepts that will be used in the course of the book. First, the term 'network' is considered, drawing on the main theories of networks in the social science literature. Then, the concepts of management within and governance of networks are distinguished. Finally, the implications for management and governance of the identified theories are established.

So, what is an inter-organisational 'network'? For the present, the following broad definition will serve to mark out the general terrain. An inter-organisational or multi-organisational network is

> any moderately stable pattern of ties or links between organisations or between organisations and individuals, where those ties represent some form of recognisable accountability (however etiolated and overridden), whether formal or informal in character, whether weak or strong, loose or tight, bounded or unbounded.

This distinction deliberately makes no distinction between network forms in general and specific patterns of inter-organisational relations. The merit of this, in affording a full account of the variety of institutional forms of networks, will become clear as the argument progresses. Nonetheless, as the argument unfolds in subsequent chapters, this initial account of a network will be progressively refined.

Next, a distinction has to be made between the *governance of* and management *within* networks. These can be defined as follows:

- *Governance of a network*. An activity by organisations which, and/or individuals who are *not* themselves members of the network in question and which is designed to exercise control, regulation, inducement, incentive or persuasive influence over the whole network. The purpose of such governance is to influence the structure of the network, the nature and range of ties between its members, its capacity for collective action, its openness to new members, its commitment to existing functions, or its ability or willingness to shoulder new tasks.
- *Management within a network*. An activity by organisations which, and/or individuals who *are* themselves members of the network. The objective of such management is to exercise control, regulation, inducement, incentive or persuasion over some but not necessarily all other members of the network. It will succeed to the extent that enables the organisation or individual: to change their particular position within the network; to shift the nature or range of ties with other members; to alter that organisation's or individual's role in any function or collective action; and/or to amend its own membership status.

In neither the practitioner literature nor the academic research is there a generally accepted and entirely stable taxonomy of the kinds of more or less formal arrangements that can be entered into by organisations. Terms such as 'partnership', 'alliance', 'strategic alliance', 'joint venture', 'consortium', 'coalition', 'group' are often used interchangeably. They cover arrangements with different financial liabilities, variations in the extent of mutual involvement in decision-making or exchange of personnel and divergent durations and liabilities. Among practitioners, of course, there are good strategic reasons for this instability of vocabulary; representing an arrangement to potential shareholders, for instance, as looser or tighter than is really the case may have important competitive advantages. There have been some scholarly attempts to fix the definitions of a wide range of terms (e.g. Grandori and Soda,1995; Grandori, 1997; Gulati and Singh, 1998), but these have not been widely successful in disciplining the practice of other researchers. However, for present purposes (and without any realistic hope of influencing the general usage), it is helpful to offer some clear distinctions between the kinds of formal instruments that are available to be used in the creation of 'networks' and Table 1.1 offers one way of tidying up the vocabulary.

Arrangements can be distinguished that define liabilities for a single *transaction* (which, in some cases might last for some time), those which govern involvement in a *project* and those which define commitment to a new *organisation*. A transaction is the simplest form of exchange, in which one organisation provides goods or services for a consideration (in the simplest case, for a monetary price). Projects are more protracted endeavours in which two or more parties commit resources other than the simple transfer of payment to the development, production or operation of goods or services. An organisation is a distinct structural form capable of entering into new transactions and projects independently of the 'parent' collaborating organisations which may retain some kind of indirect influence or control over its decisions (e.g. through ownership).

On a second dimension, Table 1.1 distinguishes between arrangements on the basis of the projected duration for which these formal instruments may be required. One set are for a defined and limited set of activities, typically (although not necessarily) bounded in time. The other set are those which are to cover an indefinite range of activities, often (but not necessarily) indefinite in time, and where the instrument cannot or is not intended to set boundaries around those activities. Cross-tabulating these two dimensions provide us with a way of defining how some of the key terms will be used from now on.

Two further points can be made here. First, those activities which are to be the subject of joint action by two or more organisations may relate only to a single function (such as research and development, service delivery, marketing and sales, market research or publishing) or they may range over several of these functions. This distinction is of most importance for consideration of projects because, by definition, a transaction may relate to a single function (such as the purchase of market research) and an organisation is involved in many functions (or must enter into arrangements with others for acquisition of those functions which it will not undertake internally). It is possible that this distinction may also be relevant for longer term, more

Table 1.1 Key types of formal instrument for the specification of types of liabilities entered into between organisations

	Scope	
Level	**Specific in purpose/ bounded in time**	**Generic in purpose/ indefinite in time**
Arrangement for dyadic relations		
1. Transaction	Spot contract	Relational contract
2. Project		
single function	Collaboration / joint venture	Partnership
several function	Alliance	Strategic alliance
3. Organisation	Joint subsidiary	Merger or acquisition
Arrangements for multiple relations		
1. Transaction	Consortium	Coalition
2. Project	Alliance block	Partnership
3. Organisation	Joint subsidiary	Business group

open-ended or 'relational', contracts. Second, it is important to distinguish between arrangements requiring instruments which are between two organisations – a dyad – and those which are between three or more organisations. In these latter cases, the challenges to collective action often become greater and the institutional arrangements required for ensuring compliance are thus more complex and, as a consequence, the more formal kinds of instrument may become necessary.

The allocation of the terms deployed in Table 1.1. is not arbitrary. The distinction between spot or 'one-off' contracts and relational contracts is well established in the literature (see e.g. Macneil, 1974, 1980, 1985; Williamson, 1985). A distinction between a simple alliance and a strategic alliance should surely relate to the scope of purposes for which it is entered into. The concepts of a joint subsidiary and a merger and acquisition are readily understood. In general, the term 'consortium' is used for a group of organisations greater in number than two which, for example, bids collectively for a major contract in one case but where the members might well compete with each other on other contracts. In contrast, 'consortium' would hardly be used for a group that regularly and routinely works together on a wide range of activities and functions over a protracted period; for this, the term 'coalition' seems well suited. Granovetter (1994) defined the concept of a business group to cover everything from the whole nexus of companies within, say, the General Motors empire or the Virgin system, through to Japanese *keiretsu* and Korean *chaebol* structures. The concept of alliance blocks has been developed in academic research to explain the patterns of interfirm collaborations in industries where rival standards emerge and firms cluster in groups according to the standard to which they cleave for as long as the prevailing technology requires them to adapt their products to that standard; Vanhaverbeke and Noorderhaven (2001) use the term to explore the structure of the computing industry working with rival standards of RISC (reduced instruction set computing) microprocessors.

The more problematic terms are 'partnership', 'joint venture' and 'alliance'. Although many arrangements described as partnerships are dyadic, many 'partnership firms' of lawyers, accountants and architects have multiple partners. Some arrangements described as 'joint ventures' are projects and some are subsidiary organisations. However, for time being, it is sufficient to be aware of these relatively minor ambiguities.

Outline of chapters

For ease of reading, following this chapter, this book is divided into four distinct parts (and the Preface contains a brief map to the ways in which different categories of reader – managers, scholars and students – might want to approach the text). Part 1 of the book – Chapters 2 through 5 – presents the elements of an overarching theory of inter-organisational networks. The two chapters in Part II, and perhaps that of most interest to managers, look at what the theory reveals about governing and managing across networks and learning and leading across networks. In Part III, Chapters 8–11, this theory is explored empirically. Part IV consists of a conclusion which compares and contrasts the case studies and tries to anticipate some criticisms of the theory. This next section provides a summary of the contents of each individual chapter.

Chapter 2 summarises, contrasts and critically appraises the main theories offered in the various disciplinary literatures which attempt to answer the core questions identified earlier and discusses their implications for the governance of, and management of and in, networks.

Chapter 3 introduces a number of ways of classifying networks. These taxonomies are examined and the most elementary structural forms within them are identified. This enables the original taxonomy presented in this book both to draw upon and to be comparable with general network theory. The specific social science elements of the approach to classification of networks adopted here are then introduced, rooted in Durkheimian sociology and anthropology. This new classification is then compared with alternative approaches and the main strengths of these other accounts are shown to be captured within it. The chapter goes on to present a theory of the respective strengths, weaknesses and distinctive features of the elementary forms of networks contained in the classification and then proceeds to set out an account of the scope for hybrid forms, including a dynamic theory of their formation, institutionalisation, disorganisation and dissolution.

Chapter 4 is devoted to setting out in more depth an integrated theory of networks. We argue that the most important insights of many of the major competing theories of networks available in the literature on organisational sociology, institutional economics and political science are not only captured by but also specifically enriched in the neo-Durkheimian institutional theory of networks developed in this book. In particular, it is argued that the theory offers a richer account than do conventional institutional economic theories of which transaction costs will turn out to be most salient in the perception of organisation members. The chapter also examines the various ways in which networks can fail. The chapter concludes by presenting a synthesis of the theory, enriched by the insights from other traditions and a simplified model of the dynamics of network institutionalisation and de-institutionalisation is presented in the form of a flow chart.

The final theoretical chapter of Part I, Chapter 5, develops a new and innovative theory of inter-organisational trust. The now extensive literature on trust is reviewed, and the key categories derived from it are used to provide an account of the range of reasons for which anyone may place trust in others (and, therefore, by extrapolation, the range of reasons to which those who wish or need to present themselves as trustworthy must appeal by investing in particular attitudes and/or behaviours). We show that empirical types of trust can be explained institutionally using the theory set out in Chapter 4. Finally, the dynamics of developing and breaking trust in different sorts of networks are first distinguished theoretically and then supported by reference to examples from the recent literature.

In Part II of the book, we examine the challenges of managing across networks of each of the major types introduced in the classification, and explore the strengths and weaknesses of each type in the light of theoretical arguments offered in Part I. Governance and management are distinguished, tools and strategies are considered and forms of leadership are discussed.

Chapter 6 explores the implications of the theory developed in the previous two chapters for the scope for governance of, and management of and in, networks. The implications of the various theories in the literature for governance and management are examined. The activities and goals of network governance, management in and management of networks are distinguished. Management strategies for securing critical positions in networks (such as those of high centrality and betweenness) are identified and analysed, and the scope for management to influence the institutional form or type of networks is appraised, setting out hypotheses from the theory and also supporting evidence from a review of empirical literatures. A classification is presented of the main basic activities of management in networks based on a wide review of the empirical literature. These activities are shown to be built specifically on the available instruments or tools by which power quite generally can be leveraged within and between organisations; the argument draws upon the 'tools of government' literature as well as on the literature on power in order to make this argument. This review of activities is used to argue that the differences between management within a single organisation and management across organisational boundaries in networks have been much exaggerated. That these differences are not so great as some management theories imply is shown as implied in the neo-Durkheimian institutional theory. It argued that this is because this theory proposes that the variation available in the institutional forms of networks is fundamentally the same range of variation that is available in the informal institutional character of organisations, considered singly; that is, there is limited variety in human organising quite generally and this fact is critically significant in defining the scope for and nature of management within and between organisations.

The next chapter – Chapter 7 – argues that the theory presented here offers a subtler account of leadership possibilities than do many standard typological approaches as well as a better grounded account of the role of information conditions and organisational learning than many mainstream theories in management and organisation behaviour studies.

In Part III, the theory of, and management challenges of and in, networks developed in the first and second parts of the book are evidenced empirically by way of four case studies (in defence contracting, biotechnology, combating crime and disorder, and in health care). In each of these case studies, the literature in a particular industry over a recent period – defined slightly differently in each case – is examined in some detail. The data are interpreted to identify distinct types, and hybrids between types, of networks exhibited in each case study. The empirical findings in the literature are interpreted to show that the overarching theory put forward in the earlier chapters of the book makes good sense of them. In many cases, it is argued, the present theory makes better sense than do most of the other theories in the networks literature.

Chapter 8 examines the experience of inter-organisational networks – both vertically along the supply chain and horizontally between firms that might otherwise be competitors in the defence materiel contracting – in the United States and in the European Union during the period 1990–2000 (i.e. is, after the end of the 'Cold War' but before the beginning of the 'War on Terror'). During this period, the main goal of policy makers in exercising governance over the networks in the industry was to ensure downsizing in ways that minimised the losses of jobs, especially in geographical areas that are heavily dependent on defence related industries. This review of the literature, it is argued, shows that the structure of the networks in the industry has become increasingly dense and dominated by a small number of 'flagship firms' around which flotillas of smaller subcontractors cluster and over which the flagships have developed growing authority. This is shown to have been partly influenced by the governance strategies of national governments seeking to promote mergers in the industry and, in some cases, to protect national champion firms. The nature of the network ties between national public defence procurement agencies is examined and found to be sparse and with limited co-operative capacity, despite the aspirations of at least some in NATO for more co-ordinated procurement. The findings are analysed using the categories offered by the present theory and the empirically reported strengths and weaknesses of the emerging network forms are revealed to be as expected.

The dedicated biotechnology sector in the United States from the late 1980s to the late 1990s was especially closely examined by leading network scholars such as Powell and Kogut and their respective collaborators and used to lay out arguments about the emergence of collaborative, horizontal, socially embedded relationships becoming increasingly dominant in science-based industries. In Chapter 9, the literature on the industry is re-examined in order to show that interpretation of these findings in the light of the present theory provides a much more nuanced account of the nature of the network process than is suggested by generic social embeddedness theory or by transaction cost or by resource based theories. Furthermore, it suggests that clearer distinctions between the effects of different kinds of increasing density can be distinguished and trade-offs between network forms more clearly analysed.

In the late 1990s, with the election of a Labour government in Britain there was a change in public policy whereby local police forces, local authorities, probation services and other agencies were mandated – rather than just advised or encouraged – to create joint partnership structures for monitoring, analysing, predicting, and preventing crime and disorder and for co-ordinating a variety of special inter-agency initiatives around particular groups, such as young people. The empirical literature on this case is examined in Chapter 10 in order to explore the effect of this authoritative intervention on the network forms that had emerged and on their strengths and weaknesses. Again, it is shown that the findings are exactly those predicted by the theory set out in Parts I and II.

In the field of health care, there has been growing interest internationally in developing vertically integrated clinical networks. These are intended to institutionalise closer collaboration along the 'supply chain', either as mapped by 'pathways of patient care' or via detailed protocols that describe the flow of patients between services. Furthermore, various approaches to horizontal integration between hospitals and between primary care organisations in different geographical areas have also been developed in order to promote a more coherent division of labour and allocation of resources than that produced by market-based solutions in those fields in which negotiated procurement is thought to have unacceptably high transaction costs. Studies in the health care field are found to distinguish a number of different network types, in effect between networks to promote information sharing and knowledge transfer, those based on the commissioning or procurement of services, and those seeking to better co-ordinate service provision. Typically, these networks in health care exhibit distinct institutional forms that can be explained using the taxonomy offered in this book. The literature on these networks in health care is reviewed in Chapter 11 from the United States, Canada, the United Kingdom and continental western Europe, with occasional reference to other countries. The chapter examines the different types of network in health systems and the relative strengths and weaknesses of these networks in performance on various dimensions and are appraised and shown to be as predicted by the theory.

This sample provides variety by sector as the first two are dominated by private companies while the latter two exhibit extensive public and non-profit sector participation in most countries considered. It also exhibits variety by style of regulation. For example, biotechnology is subject to indirect regulation of pharmaceutical and agronomic products, longstop regulation in competition policy as well as some subsidy for new technology developments and perhaps some assistance in land use planning or zoning, but in general it is much less closely regulated than the crime and disorder field. In defence and health care, states are the main purchasers, while in biotechnology commercial demand is more important. In crime and disorder collaboration is mandated, while in biotechnology collaboration is a strategy chosen voluntarily. Biotechnology and defence are fields marked by very long supply chains, whereas health care and combating crime and disorder are fields with relatively short chains. The sample varies sufficiently on these dimensions that we can regard it as adequate one with which to explore the power of the theory.

Part IV of the book, consisting of a single chapter, brings together the argument of the book as a whole. Chapter 12 presents a structured comparison between the four case studies and shows how they provide support for the original taxonomy of types of networks and for the underlying theory. Finally, there is a complete set of references.

Part I

2 Theories of Inter-organisational Relations

Theories of networks

In this chapter, we summarise, contrast and critically appraise the main theories offered in the various literatures which attempt to answer the core questions identified in the introduction. There are a number of traditions represented in these literatures and they each provide rival accounts of 'networks'. At their most basic, these rivals differ in what they define as a network. For example, strict sociometric accounts allow any system of linkages between nodes to be a network (White, 1981, 2001; Knoke, 1990). Others define a network in ways that specifically exclude certain forms – such as hierarchical relationships – in favour of internally egalitarian relations (Bradach and Eccles, 1989; Powell, 1990). Broadly, the definitions vary in whether links in the network are seen as loose or tight, weak or strong, bounded or unbounded, and formal or informal.

Theories of networks may also address somewhat different questions. Many are silent on at least some of the key questions identified in the introduction. Nonetheless, most seek to offer explanations of the following issues:

- What different forms of inter-organisational relations are available?
- Why do these forms emerge, get sustained, become institutionalised, die away?
- To what extent, and in what particular conditions, are these forms efficient, effective, or, at least, intelligent, strategies?
- How much scope is there for human agency in the form of management and governance to choose, influence or shape the forms of inter-organisational relations in particular situations?

Different theories of inter-organisational network forms posit different forces as fundamental to their existence and so argue that different taxonomies of types of networks are more basic. Moreover, some theories regard certain types that may be distinguished by rival taxonomies as either empirically unimportant or else as normatively undesirable. The following are the nine main schools of theoretical traditions that can be derived from the literatures. Each of them brings important perspectives to the consideration of the origins, purposes and forms of networks. To some extent, they also reflect the broader range of organisational theory (so that learning theories in (ii) below, for example, are associated with wider accounts of organisations which are characterised, in Morgan's (1986) terms, as 'organisations as brains').

(i) *Transaction cost theories* (e.g. Commons, 1934; Coase, 1937; Williamson, 1985; Aoki *et al.*, 1990). These argue that the form of a network is shaped by the maximisation of individual utility subject to the balance of transaction costs. In economic theory, transaction costs are distinguished from direct costs. Whereas direct costs relate to the production, exchange and delivery of goods and/or services, transaction costs are the costs of searching for transaction partners, negotiating with them, coming to agreements, recording and storing the nature of the agreements, monitoring the performance of the other parties for the duration of the relationship, enforcing the agreements and so on. Transaction cost theories of networks argue that inter-organisational forms are driven by factors that are predominantly negative, that is by the pressure to reduce such costs and by the imperative to avoid failures in transactions (such as market failure).

Most economic theories argue that, at least in the medium term, the results of individuals and organisations rationally pursuing their own interests will typically be efficient in financial terms (Williamson, 1994). Within this shoal of theories, transaction cost models are but one type of rational choice theory which, overall, argue that only individual level interests or utilities explain action. Rational choice theory thus rejects, for instance, the idea that the presence of non-economic ties between individuals can have any independent causal force on network form (Dowding, 1995).

So, Williamson (1985) argues that individuals – and by extrapolation organisations – can be assumed to be exploiting networks to maximise their interests and minimise their transaction costs, subject to the constraints that their rationality is bounded and that they can be assumed to behave in opportunistic or guileful ways when the occasion arises. On this account, network forms – voluntary co-operative inter-organisational relations – would be adopted where they efficiently economise both (a) on the costs of negotiating and enforcing contracts under strictly competitive conditions as is the case in pure markets, and (b) on the costs of legitimating and sustaining authority-based relations as the case in pure hierarchies.

(ii) *Organisation competency and learning theories; resource-based view(s).* These two groups of theories assume that individuals and organisations are driven less by negative factors (such as the minimisation of transaction costs) and more by positive ones such as the maximisation of benefits, and, especially, the benefits of enhanced competencies and capabilities. Competency and resource-based theories derived ultimately from Schumpeter (1934), who insisted on the dynamic characteristics of markets and, in particular, their pursuit of competitive advantage through the shaping of strategic capabilities.

The first group of such theories, concerned with learning (Prahalad and Hamel, 1990; Kogut *et al.*, 1993; Powell and Smith-Doerr, 1994; Powell *et al.*, 1996; Colombo, 1998), argues that, to the extent that firms make astute and intelligent judgements of the competence requirements of their field, the links they will seek to form with other firms will be ones that enable them to enhance their own core competencies. Such links will seek to generate efficient and effective divisions of labour between partners in order to secure the competencies and capabilities that the firms do not have the ability, need or wish to cultivate internally. One recent development in this tradition is work on the concept of communities of practice, that is networks explicitly created to share learning (Wenger, 1998; Tsoukas, 2002), which is informing current policy in the NHS (Bate and Robert, 2002; McNulty, 2002).

Resource-based theories are also based around the tendency of individuals or organisations to pursue both competitive and comparative advantage and therefore market power (Penrose, 1959). They do so by configuring their tangible and intangible assets, skills, resources and relationships (Conner, 1991) in order to optimise their benefits. As a consequence, ties to other organisations are chosen instrumentally and internal and external structural characteristics – such as network membership – are manipulated in order to generate appropriate flexibility in strategic options (Kyläheiko *et al.*, 2002). Whereas mainstream economic theories argue that market conditions of competition are critical in explaining which organisations will link with which others, institutionalist and ecological theories point to the influence of factors external to the organisation and technology based views stress the requirements of the prevailing techniques, the resource based view argues that it is internally generated strategy that is key. The theory allows the chosen ties to be for the short or long term, dense or sparse, according to the strategies and capabilities of the participants.

(iii) *Personalistic perspectives* (e.g. Granovetter, 1985; Burt, 1992, 1997). These regard the interactions of organisations as being the consequence of relationships between social individuals (Tilly, 1998 1–73); as a result, influencing organisational networks depends on influencing networks of persons. This outlook should perhaps be traced back to one of the founding figures of sociology, Georg Simmel (e.g. 1971, originally 1907), who argued that the patterns of transactions across organisations should be explained by looking at the inter-personal relationships in which exchange (and other) relations are embedded. He argued that methodical analysis of these relationships (starting with one to one connections) could build an account of how the social structures of networks could be measured by the pattern of interactions between persons. Such an analysis would in turn shape expectations of the extent to which organisations could influence individuals. On this view, the ties between organisations need to be understood by reference to these individuals, perhaps acting as 'boundary spanners' who, subject to organisational and resource constraints, seek to manipulate the opportunities available to them for forming, sustaining and ending ties to other individuals in other organisations. This manipulation may, at least partly, be for private purposes except where institutional constraints are successful in aligning organisational goals and individual motivations.

(iv) *New institutionalist perspectives* (e.g. Orrú *et al.*, 1991; Powell and DiMaggio, 1991; Scott W *et al.*, 1994; Fligstein, 2001). These propose that the possible forms of networks are fixed by organisational constraints, such as institutionalised patterns of authority, path dependence and historical period. Path dependence is the phenomenon by which the historical starting point limits, and in extreme case prescribes, subsequent development; once having committed to a certain style networks are then constrained to continue, and over time, reinforce that style. These constraints leave limited scope for flexibility in, and precious little opportunity for macro-management of, network design. Work by British political scientists on 'policy networks' in the governance of healthcare is often of this type. This view does not need to delineate any sharp distinction between particular forms of inter-organisational relations.

(v) *Ecological perspectives* (e.g. White, 1981, 2001; Hannan and Freeman, 1989). These argue that network forms are selected in 'niches'. These 'niches' are temporarily combined clusters of resources. Changing the structure of such 'niches' is the key to managing networks. Like transaction cost theories, these accounts propose that networking is fundamentally driven by the organisational need to optimise outputs from such clusters at minimum cost. These two views share the assumption that, in the long run, the eventually emergent forms will be efficient; indeed they will have emerged and proven sustainable for precisely that reason. However, the ecological perspective approach also has to take path-dependence seriously, for the available means by which organisations can secure their positions are more tightly limited by both the internal patterns of their inherited behaviour and the evolutions in their external environment than would be the case for rational choice theories (within which the transaction cost account is nested).

(vi) *Problem/technology contingency perspectives* (e.g. Galbraith, 1973; Perrow 1999 [1984]). These contend that network forms would ideally be shaped – were it not for institutional forces and bounded rationality – to solve particular problems in the production of goods and services. On this view, the structures and capabilities of different forms of inter-organisational relations are shaped most by the prevailing technologies of production that require (or do not require) particular inter-organisational links with other organisations possessing access to other specific technologies. The argument suggests that once the nature of the task and the nature of the technologies necessary for undertaking that task have been established, then the structure, form of accountability and efficacy of the network forms that will most suit those conditions can, at least in principle, be identified. Perrow (1999 [1984]), for example, would emphasise the importance of the tightness or looseness of the coupling of particular technologies – for example, magnetic resonance imaging and telemedicine in hospitals – as key determinants of the requisite structure of relationships, and hence of the types of risks of failure that those ties might exhibit. Whereas 1960s contingency theorists – such as Thompson, JD (1967) – were rather optimistic that a reasonably effective fit might be found between technology and task on the one hand and types of inter-organisational relations on the other, Perrow's (1999 [1984]) account is much more pessimistic. He argues that some technological and task niches, for all that they may be occupied by rational organisations, will call for organisational relations that must always be prone to failure for structural reasons.

(vii) *Macro-economic and technological determinist perspectives.* Castells (1996) claims that network forms are consequent on the forces and relationships of production. When these forces and relationships change, so do the network forms (and, as an illustration of this account, the information economy is calling for a new dominant network form). Castells' (1996) argument is ultimately quasi-Marxist in its claim that the present dominance of network forms of economic organisation amounts to something akin to a distinct historical 'mode of production'. Thus, the form of these networks is driven ultimately by the collective interests of fractions of capital, and to a lesser extent by social movements and by innovations in technology. This contrasts with the impact on network form of the individual interests which are the focus of transaction cost theories.

(viii) *Weberian perspectives* (Weber, 1978/1968 [1922]; Mann, 1986; Simon, 1997 [1945]). These argue that macro-social rationalisation produces steadily more efficient, but also more transparent, organisational forms; management of networks consists in the constant reconstitution of authority through ever more routinised, less charismatic institutions: the process of rationalisation is one in which the ideas that justify and legitimate hierarchical forms are steadily undermined by rational argument. In Weberian theory, social organisation is driven fundamentally by interests and by changes in climates of ideas, but strongly mediated by institutions which are in turn the product of prevailing climates of ideas and especially worldviews (Schluchter, 1981; in this respect, Weberian theory converges with new institutionalist approaches: Biggart, 1991). However, interests are defined at very high levels of aggregation, rather than by particular vectors of resources. Logically, therefore, Weberian theories must classify network forms according to their different institutional forms, defining institutions at a level appropriate to distinct worldviews.

(ix) *Socio-technological perspectives, and especially actor network theory* (e.g. Bijker and Law, 1992; Law and Hassard, 1999). These regard artefacts, technologies, persons and organisations as nodes in 'actor networks'. Networks are ever present and ubiquitous features of social life rather than a distinct form. In one version of this account, networks are not to be explained but themselves explain most other interesting variables in organisational life. Alternatively, an argument is put forward where network structures and other relevant factors all affect each other in ways that make it impossible to disentangle the impact of network form from the consequences of, for example, resource constraints; at this point, some of the theorists seem to lose interest entirely in trying to suggest causal explanations. This leaves rather limited scope for discussion, for instance, of approaches to management of inter-organisational relations. A recent review of the limited number of applications of these approaches to inter-organisational relations by Thompson G (2003) finds that those applying the theory tend to resort to qualitative descriptions of networks rather than attempting explanations.

Some readers might have expected to see 'social capital' theory as the tenth framework in this summary list. 'Social capital' is a term popular in many branches of academic endeavour – with sociologists such as Bourdieu (1986) and Coleman (1988, 1990), with economic analysts such as Fukuyama (1995) and with political scientists such as Putnam (2000) – to describe the networks of relationships between individuals, and specifically those which involve a significant degree of trust and reciprocity between those individuals. These relationships are held by some of these writers to be independently important in explaining, for example, patterns of political and economic development or social cohesion (notwithstanding that some theorists identify attitudinal variables as nebulous as views about strangers as important components in constituting social capital (Halpern, 2005)).

However, consideration of the nine theoretical traditions summarised earlier suggests that each provides a quite distinct theory of what social capital is and why it might matter. For example, Lin's (2001) model of social capital is, like Burt's (1997), essentially personalistic; Bourdieu's (1986) conception lies somewhere between the institutionalist and the macro-economic; Putnam's theory has become steadily more Weberian (compare Putnam *et al.*, 1993 with Putnam, 2000). Some of these theories thus focus on the contemporary individual (such as some of the personalistic theories) while others are historical and sociological in character (such as the Weberian, macro-technological and economic theories). For this reason, 'social capital' is not discussed as a separate category of theory.

The nine theories are not necessarily to be regarded as incompatible alternatives to each other. Indeed, there are ways of combining some of these perspectives. For example, there was a rapprochement during the 1990s between those transaction cost approaches – such as North's (1998) – which do not claim the inevitable efficiency of whatever network forms actually emerge, the new institutionalist approaches in sociology (Neef, 1998) and some personalistic approaches. Several attempts have been made to combine transaction cost and resource-based views, of which Noteboom (2004) is the best known. From the resource-based view he takes the idea of strategy as central, while transaction costs considerations provide the key constraints within which strategy is pursued. Unfortunately, working with just these two traditions fails both to capture the insights of the others and to provide a clear typology of the institutional constraints under which organisations can sustain ties. A different strategy is pursued by Weick (2001) who combines a new institutionalist stress on the ways in which informal institutions within organisations shape the ways in which people can make sense of their environment with a technological contingency view of the problems in relations between organisations. This combination can, if sense-making is not very well matched to the complex requirements of tasks involving co-ordination, lead to disaster.

The most sensible way forward seems to be to try and identify further possibilities for rapprochement, first at the level of taxonomy and then by synthesis of multiple accounts of causation; this will be the strategy adopted in this book. To begin this process, Table 2.1 summarises the answers that the theories offer to each of the main questions set out at the beginning

Table 2.1 Theories of networks compared

	Forms, if any typology is used	**Key drivers**	**Conditions when forms are efficient or otherwise desirable**	**Scope for agency**
Rational choice and transaction cost	Market, hierarchy, network	Minimising transaction costs; avoiding types of failure	When they enable transaction cost minimisation	High
Organisational competence and learning; resource based		Pursuit of comparative advantage and market power	When they are open to intrumental manipulation by organisations	High
Personalistic	Strong tie, weak tie	Pursuit of individual advantage under constraints	When they support a mix of strong and weak ties appropriate to the pursuit of individual goals	High
New institutionalist		Adaptation to prior institutional constraints and imperatives	Efficiency is not likely to be achieved because of path dependency	Low

Continued

Table 2.1 Continued

	Forms, if any typology is used	Key drivers	Conditions when forms are efficient or otherwise desirable	Scope for agency
Ecological		Adaptation to particular resource niche conditions	When they allow smooth exploitation of resources and release of resources when niche dissolve	Moderate
Problem/ technology contingency	Tightly/loosely coupled	Adaptation to task and technology conditions	When they permit efficient linkage of technologies to undertake tasks	Disputed
Macro-economic/ technological determinist	Under informational capitalism: markets, hierarchies, networks	Enabled by the prevailing mode of production	Efficiency and other criteria are limited by the institutional conditions of the prevailing mode of production	High within the limits to available forms set by the mode of production, low between forms specified by distinct modes
Weberian	Instrumental, value-based	Driven by different types of rationalisation specified by particular worldviews	Efficiency can be expected to grow over time due to rationalisation, but it may be at the expense of other goals (the 'iron cage' of bureaucracy)	Limited by institutionalisation of worldviews and interests
Socio-technical		Networks of people and things as causes rather than caused	Efficiency question do not arise: network forms are at once fluid and also simply inevitable	Moderate

of this chapter about the typologies of, key drivers shaping, efficiency conditions of and scope for agency (e.g. proactive management) afforded by inter-organisational networks.

Limitations of the standard theories

All of these nine standard bodies of theory have some limitations. At the same time, each captures something of real importance that ought to be retained in a soundly based account of the typology, causation, efficacy and agency of networks. In this section, we consider some of these main weaknesses. Taken together, they argue the need for a richer theory which can address some of these weaknesses and yet also capture and synthesise the strengths.

Transaction cost theories have been criticised on a number of grounds. One central criticism has long focused on the claim that over the medium term – and certainly in the long run – arrangements will neither be adopted nor sustained if they prove inefficient; as a consequence, therefore, the prevailing pattern to which inter-organisational relations tend will be one that is broadly, and economically, efficient. This seems not to recognise the importance of a number of factors that will undermine such efficiency (and in some situations actually mandate arrangements that are inefficient in economic terms): these include path-dependency; lock in to specific technologies of production; institutional constraints of law or generally accepted norms of the best way to operate; weak competitive pressures; public acceptability imperatives; interest group power; and many other factors. If the efficiency claim is scaled back to adjust for these factors, however, then the claim made by this theory becomes banal, for it amounts to little more than that however efficient or inefficient existing arrangements are then that is as good as they can be made.

Williamson's claim that guileful opportunism is the default assumption about motivation when efficiency is apparently absent seems implausible. In practice, opportunism and guile seem to be better treated as variables, the values of which can be influenced by a range of institutional and other factors, rather than as constants (Ghoshal and Moran, 1996). Moreover, starting with such an assumption about motivation leads rather too readily to Williamson's argument that hierarchical solutions are more likely to be the most efficient in many situations precisely because they can control opportunism and constrain guile. Attribution of a wider range of motivational bases might enable a greater range of responses to be considered intelligent solutions to the problems of organising. In this respect Ouchi's (1980) theory – considered in more detail later – does not make the same generalised assumptions and, as a result, is a more plausible application of transaction cost theory.

In the same way, it can be questioned whether the negative character of the theory, which sees inter-organisational relations as driven by avoidance of particular forms of failure, is not also an unwarranted generalisation from one type of case. There seem to be plenty of cases in which people form, sustain and drop ties between organisations in pursuit of gains rather than in flight from losses.

There remains a critical problem about the ways in which transaction costs represent incentives for behaviour in the theory. In Williamson's approach, the causal connection appears to be expected to be largely straightforward and to work in much the same way that direct costs function. It is assumed that even if the costs of transacting are not at the forefront of the minds of individual actors when they make their decisions, then in the medium term the effect of incurring those costs will lead people to adjust their behaviour to minimise the transaction costs they incur (or else to go out of business). However, transaction costs are importantly different from direct costs in that some of them may never in fact be expressed in monetary terms (or indeed in any scale). As a consequence, everyday organisational perceptions of the significance, urgency or impact of transaction costs may diverge significantly from research-based assessments of these factors. This may explain the differences between individuals and organisations in the speed, direction and content of their responses and what might be regarded by economists as prudent behaviour in the face of apparently high transaction costs. If this is accepted, then the simple idea of minimising transaction costs as the sole basis for organisational relations must surely be abandoned.

Furthermore, many studies (e.g. Dasborough and Sue-Chan, 2002) have suggested that the effects of institutions are more profound in shaping decision-making than transaction cost theory allows. This theory proposes that institutional arrangements are themselves selected for their transaction cost minimising features. These studies suggest that the tide of influence runs more strongly in the opposite direction: path-dependency limits the scope for transaction cost efficiency; and institutional norms mould the frames through which transaction costs are perceived.

Finally, a critical problem for transaction cost theory is that often it is very difficult to know whether certain types of network ties represent costs of transacting that ought to be minimised, because they might be regarded as redundant, or constitute important resources that can enable people to secure legitimacy for other ties. Different actors may perceive the same types of ties differently depending on their institutional setting (Poza *et al.*, 2004).

The resource-based view of the organisation appears to capture more of the ways in which practising managers actually think about their motivations, interests and behaviours. However, it too has certain weaknesses. A critical limitation is its indeterminacy; it offers an explanation of why particular ties may be sought – because they provide access to beneficial capabilities – but it has little to say about why these particular capabilities came to be seen as beneficial in the first place.

The key problem with the communities of practice account of organisational learning is that it takes a far too normative, and, even within the typically rose-tinted world of many normative perspectives, too romantic and egalitarian a view of the process of sharing knowledge. There are many inter-organisational arrangements through which knowledge can be effectively generated, distributed and cultivated. The strongly boundaried and densely bonded structure of the community of practice is but one, and perhaps one only suitable for certain types of context and for certain types of knowledge.

The personalistic outlook contributes something of real importance in its focus on the role of interpersonal networks in providing part of the foundations on which relationships at the inter-organisational level are constructed. Nonetheless, even its best known advocates accept its incompleteness, for it is not really possible to account for the structure of inter-personal relations without making reference to the organisational level itself. It is these organisations which provide both constraints upon the range of available and useful ties and also give specific spurs, by way of incentives and acculturation, for the cultivation of particular ties that might not otherwise be developed. Not even the most determined advocates of individualistic analyses of interpersonal networks have tried to reduce all inter-organisational relations to simple aggregates of individual networking choices. Although the inter-personal level remains significant – especially in understanding boundary spanning roles, reticulists, brokers, and entrepreneurs – it cannot suffice on its own as an explanation of network form.

'New' institutionalist theories of network structure have compensated for some of the features missing in the simplest kinds of personalistic accounts. However, the 'new' institutionalism in sociology is a diverse and varied ensemble of perspectives. In particular, they differ according to whether they stress the role of organisations in constraining networks to exhibit greater homogeneity over time (DiMaggio and Powell, 1983) or whether they favour institutional forces as drivers for divergence and distinctiveness whether in national or regional traditions (Steinmo *et al.*, 1992; DiMaggio, 2001) (or, in some cases, allow either, e.g. Brinton and Nee, 1998). Although this variety creates a certain indeterminacy in this overall tradition, both strands are essentially driven by an account of change in networks as the result of positive feedback processes. These processes mean that specific tendencies in organisations reproduce and reinforce themselves over time and these shape the structures of – and the outcomes from – network forms. This is clearly incomplete; any theory that relies upon positive feedback has also to allow for the possibility of negative feedback, where processes of conflict and conciliation will be brought in play. However, allowing for both sorts of feedback effectively transforms institutional theory into something more akin to systems theory, in which broader processes of feedback (e.g. from the external environment) are important drivers of change (e.g. Deutsch, 1966; Dunsire, 1993). In systems theory, much more is involved in shaping networks than the simple weight of the inheritance of the past.

A more common criticism of institutionalist theories is that, by their very nature, they allow insufficient role for human agency, just as neo-Simmelian theories are criticised for allowing too much. The rational choice institutionalist tradition (e.g. Ostrom, 1990, 1998) offers a kind of compromise in which organisational forms are shown to emerge from the rational choices of individuals under the partial constraints of earlier organisations that were, in their turn, the product of the same kind of interaction of human agency and social structure. It is not clear that the result really offers a distinctive explanation of network types; indeed, in general, Ostrom's work contrasts markets and hierarchies with more or less egalitarian groups acting collectively whilst underpinned by individual voluntary choice.

Organisational ecology theories are a fruitful extension of resource dependency approaches to organisational theory, viewing them through the lens of the evolution of populations. They help explain commonly observed features such as entrepreneurial risk-taking, competitive behaviour and exits from markets. However, they have been insufficiently specific about the kinds of inter-organisational linkages that might thrive, survive or perish under the conditions that population ecology methods might be capable of exploring. Although, for example, Talmud and Mesch (1997) show that aggregate social ties within markets affect individual firm level outcomes, this kind of ecological research tells us little about what kinds of ties perform what functions, or how, or why.

Task and contingency theory (e.g. Emerson 1972a,b) appears at first sight to provide a promising enrichment of resource dependency and classical economic exchange theory. It does so by describing some features of the task environment and the prevailing technology that might call for particular adaptations of inter-personal or inter-organisational network ties in order to make the best use of these contingencies for enhanced managerial performance. On further examination, unfortunately, the precise linkages have yet to be specified convincingly. Despite the initially plausible idea that tightly and loosely coupled technologies might require particular – and distinct – forms of social ties, the evidence from studies in the field of technology appear to suggest that most technologies are sufficiently generic – standard information technologies, for example – that they can be used in different ways by different people configured in different types of networks.

In his well-known (1999 [1984]) analysis of the organisational and technological conditions under which organisational–technological failures occur, Charles Perrow argued that the nature of the problem to be tackled, including the technology to be operated, should lead to the avoidance of certain organisational forms as undesirable. This general approach can, of course, be applied to forms of networks as much as to single organisations (indeed, some of Perrow's original cases, such as marine accidents, do involve more than one organisation). Essentially, Perrow's account is a version of contingency theory in the organisational behaviour tradition; that is, the form of organisational arrangements should be, to the extent that people are rational and capable of effective action in institutional design, selected to meet the contingencies of the environment and the problem (Lawrence and Lorsch, 1967; Galbraith, 1973). Contingency theorists stress the degree of complexity and uncertainty in the environment. As the element of complexity rises, the number of divisions within a single organisation or the number of functionally specialised members should also rise. As the element of uncertainty increases, a preference for more flexible and generalist organisations with some potential to deploy uncommitted resources in response to unforeseeable events should increase. Perrow developed the argument by cross-tabulating the complexity of interactions and the looseness or tightness of the coupling of particular relationships to define a space in which to classify types of tasks and technologies to be managed. His punchline was that the combination which runs the highest risk of failures and accidents, but for which the set of well-suited organisational and inter-organisational forms is tragically null, is that of high complexity and tight coupling. More recently, this hypothesis has been refuted in studies on 'high-reliability organisations' (La Porte and Consolini, 1991; Roberts, 1993; Schulman, 1993; Weick and Roberts, 1993, Roberts *et al.*, 1994; Rochlin, 1996) although by and large the 'high reliability' theorists have neither followed the strict logic of contingency theory logic nor focused their attention on inter-organisational structures.

However, as Scott's (1992) review makes clear, empirical studies within the tradition have not unambiguously borne out contingency theory approaches on their own terms. A key problem is that people are only likely to create the forms of organisations or networks that the theory would predict if they can readily obtain information about just how complex and uncertain the environment actually is. As the work of organisational complexity and chaos theorists has sought to show over recent years (e.g. Stacey, 1999), the environment is much more unpredictable than most earlier theorists of organisations would have us believe. Any contingency-based response to such complexity and uncertainty would require the ability to obtain reliable and unambiguous indications about how other people and organisations will act in these circumstances. Moreover, without an appreciation of the biases that people bring to the perception of their environment, it is very difficult to make contingency approaches very powerful in predicting – or even explaining – the organisational and inter-organisational forms that emerge in particular contexts.

Historicist accounts – those that assume distinct and consecutive periods in human endeavour – posit networks as generally replacing markets and hierarchies. They suggest that the prevalence of networks point to changing modes of production. These accounts have certainly attracted widespread attention and interest, as claims about the novel character of the current age typically have at every point in history. Yet it is far from obvious that the empirical claim is true; that is, that hierarchical and competitive structures are giving way in most industries to co-operative ones. Indeed, some of Castells' (1996) argument trades on the very different senses in which the technical characteristics of the internet can be described as a network, or in which business groups can be. For example, the development of the internet relies upon compliance with a set of specified technical standards which are set centrally by a body – the Internet Engineering Task Force – which has developed an essentially hierarchical relationship with a wide variety of telecommunications and information systems industries, and which sustains the perception in the eyes of most users that there is now but one internet. By contrast, business groups may be internally co-operative but are typically highly competitive with each other. Even historicists arguing the case for a general trend towards networks, such as DiMaggio (2001), acknowledge the marked variety – by political and economic geography and by industry – in what is meant by the term. Moreover, once this variety is accepted, then the link between the mode of production at, for example, the level of political economy and the structure of inter-organisational relations in particular cases is much looser than the underlying neo-Marxist logic of Castells' theory would require. Whatever one's views about whether capitalism has changed in its fundamental characteristics to something even more dependent upon the production, organisation and consumption of information than in previous historical periods, it is very difficult to see that this has produced any greater convergence in the patterns of inter-organisational relations than could have been observed, for example, in the post-Second World War period or in the mid-nineteenth century.

Weberian theories are also essentially historicist in character, predicting the growth in rationalisation and technical efficiency, whether for good or (as in the case of the 'iron cage' hypothesis) for ill. Whatever its merits in the history of sociology, it is far from clear that the tradition has developed adequately specified accounts of distinct patterns of inter-organisational relations that can be shown to be markedly more rational than their predecessors. Indeed, typically, its leading writers have had to borrow accounts of networks from elsewhere in order to complete their own theories. The leading Weberian economic sociologist, Swedberg (1998), for example, has found it necessary to adopt concepts of 'networks of innovation' from work done in the Schumpeterian tradition of non-competitive and politically organised structures for innovation (Schroeder and Swedberg, 2002). While sociologically insightful, this adds very little to the causal and typological understanding of inter-organisational relations.

Actor Network Theory (or ANT), deriving from the work of Latour (1987) and Callon and Law (1989), proposes that networks should be understood as comprising both human agents and inanimate objects as actors; that networks should be understood as causes rather than themselves being caused by other phenomena; that they are ubiquitous, fluid and constantly changing; and that, therefore, both agency and structure are emergent properties of networks and best understood by being dissolved back into their constituent network relational characteristics. Although ANT has acquired an enthusiastic following, in particular in science and technology studies, it has some crucial limitations. The refusal to offer any explanation for the forms that networks might take and the reluctance to distinguish networks from anything else make it very difficult to use. The absence of both typology and of distinct causal processes leads many of its practitioners to engage in a kind of theory-rich 'thick description' of particular cases, in which we finally discover that everything comes back to networks without really learning much about the nature of the network dynamics beyond the fact that they are indeed dynamic (for a related critique, see Thompson G 2003: 72–85).

It is important to stress again that each of these bodies of theory captures something of real importance that any good theory of inter-organisational relations ought to encompass. No one would deny that the costs of transacting matter, even if the way in which they matter may require more input from sociology than economic theory allows. Resources, competences and strategies must be central to any account of how and why organisations form ties. The relationship between inter-organisational and inter-personal ties is of critical importance, especially in understanding the roles of brokers, boundary spanners and reticulists (and the informal routes by which such people circumvent formal procedures). The shadow of the past that institutionalists emphasise is at least as important to the prospects for the future patterns, structures, capabilities and vulnerabilities of network forms as the factors that resource-based and competency views stress. Resource 'niches' provide an essential material basis for understanding the role of networks of organisations at the aggregate and population level. The interaction of task and technology within social organisations may be much less deterministic than contingency and neo-Marxist theories allow, but a robust theory ought to be capable of showing what kinds of relationships are possible between these variables. The nature of rationality may be more varied than contemporary Weberians such as Swedberg recognise, but it remains important to show how and why adoption of divergent network forms are rational and intelligent strategies in response to particular conditions. Further, it must be acknowledged that the environmental circumstances within which these forms are created and maintained may be complex and/or uncertain. The ANT tradition may be vague, but its recognition of the consequentiality and ubiquity of inter-organisational relations, and of the weaving together of the social and the physical in their design, remain important. The challenge for this book is to develop an account that can synthesise the valuable elements of these theories while avoiding some of their limitations. It is to this challenge that we turn in Chapters 3 & 4.

3
Types of Networks

Classifying Forms of Networks: Theories and Strategies

One of the central arguments of this book is that the development of a taxonomy of network forms is more useful than any simple definition of networks. Such a taxonomy offers the chance to distinguish between network forms in respect of the opportunities around, constraints on and resources for management within, management affecting and governance of networks. Moreover, each network form has a different context for sense-making around these management activities since all networks exhibit divergent patterns of relationships between the member organisations or individuals (despite the claims of some writers and theorists).

This first part of the chapter sets out the main approaches that are used in the literature for classifying types of networks, and considers each in turn. These classifications are derived from the basic claims of the main theories, for each theory argues that networks should be classified on the basis of those variables that it considers to be causally most important. Just as each of the main theories takes a distinct view about the 'manageability' of networks and the nature of the management challenge that they evoke, so each also adopts a different principle or basis for classifying the types of networks available. This is because each takes disparate features of networks to be significant. Table 3.1 summarises the ways in which the theories seem to proceed.

Taken at face value, Tables 2.1 and 3.1 suggest that there is very substantial disagreement in and between the social sciences about what kinds of networks there are, how they are structured and how amenable they are to being influenced. However, there is a broad mass of empirical findings in the literature that is not in dispute between the theories, even if the interpretation of these findings is the subject of some disagreement.

There are many ways in which we might classify types of networks. At the simplest level, we need to distinguish between different elements, nodes or actors. For example, networks can either comprise of individuals or can

Table 3.1 Theories and their approaches to classifying types of networks

Theory	**Driving force shaping networks**	**Classify distinct forms of networks on the basis of**
Transaction cost	Individual interests, in securing and optimising efficient use of resources	*Content*, or resources exchanged, because interests are concerned with what passes along ties, limited by the costs of agreeing to exchange
Organisational competence and learning	Interests in securing competences and knowledge	*Content*, especially competencies and items of knowledge
Personalistic	Ties between individuals (and thus organisations)	*Structure*, or the overall pattern formed by ties
New institutionalist	Institutions	*Institutions*, at the particular, empirical level
Ecological	Interests, in controlling clusters of resources	*Content*, but limited by path dependence
Problem/technology contingency	Environment, structures of resources and institutions	*Institutions*, at the level of institutional characteristics of problems
Macro-economic/ technological determinist	Collective interests	*Content*
Weberian	Ideas, as shaped by and themselves shaping institutions	*Institutions*, general institutions selected by worldviews
Socio-technical	Unclear	Unclear

comprise of organisations (or – provided that the nature of the ties between them are quite tightly specified – both). Within these general types, however, a relatively small number of ways of classifying types of networks are normally used when trying to understand networks in the context of their management. For these purposes, we might classify them:

- by internal *structure* – that is, by degree of centralisation, by degree of *density* (the number of potential ties between members where there are actual ties), the strength of ties, the extent of structural equivalence between different segments of the network, the extent to which the network is organised into distinct clusters of high density ties which are themselves linked by sparser ties across the gaps between them (where individuals can perhaps broker relationships between *cliques*, etc.);

- by *content* – that is, by the nature of what is passed along the ties that make up the network (information, capabilities, money, authorisation, emotional support, even hostility) where a tie between two organisations or individuals is deemed *multiplex* if more than one kind of thing is passed along the same tie;
- by *symmetricality* – that is, by the sense in which there is equality or inequality in the net value of the content passed from A to B and back from B to A;
- by *functions* – that is, by the extent to which common tasks can be and actually are undertaken by members of the network across ties;
- by *institutional form* – that is, by the degree to which structure, content and function are prescribed by either formal or informal rules, norms, established or sanctioned expectations, where such rules define structure they will probably specify the *boundaries* of officially recognised cliques and hence of a local concept of 'membership' (which may or may not correspond to the actual boundaries of informal ties);
- by styles of *learning* – that is, by the nature of the learning and management of knowledge that organisations either seek to pursue through their external ties or actually practice through those ties (even if incidental to the principal purpose or driving force behind those ties being established); and/or
- by types of *activity* conducted with partner organisations – that is, by the stages in the production process jointly engaged in, acquired or accessed through ties.

Some of the most important and interesting questions about the types of networks – and the scope for their management and governance – arise from the relationship between forms as defined by:

Node – the characteristics of the organisations between which the network represents the links;
Structure – the abstract but geometrically representable pattern of relations;
Content – the kinds of resource exchanged or gifted between people along the ties shown in the structure;
Function – the purpose served, explicitly or implicitly, by the tie; or
Institution – the type of accountability which the ties describe between people.

These five features – node, structure, content, function and institution – can be thought of as key differentiators in the various descriptions and explanations of network forms.

Each of the available taxonomies is often (though not necessarily) directly associated with one of the types of theory discussed in Chapter 2. Classification by network structure – as measured by sociometric techniques of network mapping and mathematical representation (Wasserman and Faust, 1994) – is often associated with something like Granovetter's (1985) personalist claim that the most important things in organisational life are embedded in the structure of social relations between individuals. A taxonomy of organisational networks based on function might well work with a functional explanation of the emergence of those types, deriving from Merton's 1968 [1949] account of manifest and latent functions; the claim would be that the explicit or manifest form of the network serves to further implicitly strengthen the institutional imperatives to which it responds. Equally, a classification grounded in the types of resource passed along ties could readily be used together with a framework such as Pfeffer and Salancik's (1978) resource dependence theory which argues that the shape of inter-organisational networks is driven by the reliance of particular organisations on others for finance, skilled labour, regulatory approval and so on. A taxonomy by institutional form is commonly used by those committed to institutionalist theories to explain the emergence and persistence of network forms (such as that offered by Scott *et al.*, (1994)). However, the next part of this chapter will argue that, in practice, there may be more convergence between these different approaches than first meet the eye.

Node typologies

The most straightforward way to classify types of networks is by looking at the characteristics of the organisations (or individuals) which constitute the members, where each of these forms a single node within the overall network.

Rudberg and Olhager (2003) use just such an approach. They argue that among the most important dimensions which can be used to distinguish types of network are the number of organisations involved and the extent of internal differentiation between them, the latter being operationalised by establishing the number of sites on which an organisation carries significant investment. They propose the following cross-tabulation of these dimensions as the basis for their taxonomy (Table 3.2).

Table 3.2 Rudberg and Olhager's (2003) operations management typology of networks

	Single site per organisation	**Multiple sites per organisation**
Single organisation	*Plant* Co-ordination by optimising productive utilisation of resources	*Intra-firm network* Co-ordination by optimisation of allocation of productive resources
Multiple organisations	*Supply chain* Co-ordination by synchronisation of flow of resources between organisations/ sites	*Inter-firm network* Co-ordination by harmonisation of wider range of resources than just direct production,including financing, human rsources and management systems

Source: Adapted from Rudberg and Olhager, 2003: 35–36.

However, this is a classification of rather limited application because it tells us little about why these differences are of general importance for the ways in which organisations will behave. Moreover, the claims made by Rudberg and Olhager about how co-ordination will be undertaken in each cell neither flow from the classification nor are they are particularly convincing. There are good reasons to suspect, for example, that resource optimisation is unlikely to provide an exhaustive account of co-ordination within multi-site organisations.

Content typologies

Many kinds of things can pass along the ties that link the organisations or individuals in a network. Tangible resources can be shared, such as payments of money, the provision of physical goods and practical assistance. Furthermore, less tangible resources such as emotional support or information (both tacit know-how and explicit knowledge) can also be transported.

One fundamental distinction in this sort of typology is that between ties that are used to pass resources of value only to the individual actors in the networks and those across which resources are passed that are of value to others within organisations. For example, the weakly tied network structures through which Granovetter's (1973, 1995 [1974]) job seekers pursued their strategies for employment are an example of the former. The latter can be exemplified by the activity of organisational boundary spanners – such as procurement managers – who acquire inputs or distribute outputs which are of value to the organisation, and ultimately to the shareholders, rather than to themselves (Birkinshaw *et al.*, 2000).

Another basic distinction is that between networks predominantly defined by trade ties of purchase of inputs and sales of outputs and those where typical ties are either of a non-traded kind or else the ties are to organisations or individuals who neither supply inputs nor consume outputs. The first of these types can be described as a *vertical* network because when the boundaries of one organisation expand to encompass more of such a network this is known as vertical integration. In contrast, the second can be seen as varieties of *horizontal network*. More strictly, and encompassing sub-species that are not always of major interest for the current argument, these distinctions yield four types, and Table 3.3 gives examples of each type.

Moreover, it is important to distinguish between transactions made across ties that are priced as between any two nodes and transactions made across ties that are not priced between two nodes, although all nodes may pay for services from other kinds of organisation to make these transactions possible.

In practice, of course, it is not always straightforward to draw the distinction between the vertical and the horizontal that underpins Table 3.3. There are many cases, in both the public and commercial sectors, in which organisations in broadly the same business enter into bilateral strategic alliances with one another or form multilateral consortia. Within these alliances there is a more or less clear division of labour, though some partners can be more dominant than others. In these cases, it might be debated whether the model of a vertical or a horizontal structure is the more appropriate.

A variant of this approach is offered by Burlat *et al.* (2003). They argue that networks can be classified by the degree to which the services provided by each member are complementary to each other and the degree to which the organisations possess similar competences. Cross-tabulating these dimensions yields the basic typology summarised in Table 3.4.

Table 3.3 A role and financial content taxonomy of networks by tie content

Financial and Organisational content	Priced transactions	Non-priced transactions
Vertical ties		
Transactions made across ties are for the acquisition of inputs or the distribution of outputs, with organisations or individuals whose role in the network vis-à-vis a focal organisation is to do one or both these things	Conventional supply chain network, outsourcing, procurement and distribution or account management	Supply of volunteer labour, gift of outputs, *pro bono* work
Horizontal ties		
Transactions made across ties are for the exchange of resources, where the focal organisation and the others occupy similar roles in the network	Licensing of patented knowledge between companies that might otherwise be rivals (e.g. strategic alliances between companies in the same industry for joint research and development at pre-competitive stage)	Professional networks, trade associations, information sharing groups

Table 3.4 Typology from Burlat *et al.* (2003) by competence and activity

	Non-complementary activities	Complementary activities
Dissimilar competences	Market	Proactive network
Similar competences	Defensive network	Single organisation (i.e. hierarchy)

Source: Adapted from Burlat *et al.* (2003): 402.

The prediction that the presence of similar competences and complementary activities should lead to hierarchical integration can be challenged; indeed, it is challenged by some of the studies in the empirical literature. For example, where there is a need to capture economies of scale but organisational politics prevent merger or acquisition, some other form of collaboration is possible (and if it is accepted that such political factors trump the criterion of efficiency then it is far from obvious that this is inappropriate). Burlat and his colleagues argue that where organisations have different capabilities but work in related areas they have a bias towards anticipating opportunities (proactive network), whereas where they work in different areas but have similar competences they tend to possess a bias for risk anticipation and may ally in order to form bulwarks against perceived threats (defensive network). They go on to trace the various developmental paths according to changes in the similarity of competences and the complementarity of activities. Considering the various stages of development – and introducing other measures – allows them to add detail to the basic typology. However, it is not entirely clear that the characteristics of activities and competences alone suffice to explain biases in perceptions of opportunity and risk.

Functional typologies

Functions are not the same as activities; a function is a purpose, explicitly or implicitly served, while activities are simply behaviours or tasks entrusted to particular organisations, teams or individuals. In the strictest 'functional' definition, the underlying (though not necessarily intentional) outcomes of these activities are typically located at the level of the social organisation involved in the network rather than at the level of individuals, who may nonetheless gain personally from co-operation (Merton, 1968 [1949]; Elster, 1983; Douglas, 1986; Stinchcombe, 1986). Because functions usually take forms which reinforce the explicit or implicit (and these latter are often not fully appreciated even by participants, hence 'latent' (Merton 1968 [1949]) purposes of organisations, functional classifications of networks tend to be closely aligned with institutional ones. However, some commentators identify functions of networks that may convey benefits of a more individual nature. These include the transfer of trust, esteem or emotional support; the transfer of specific knowledge and the transfer of information. For example, high quality of personal performance may be signalled by someone being associated with high prestige individuals or organisations (Audretsch and Stephan, 1996). On the whole, though, whereas content typologies focus on what gets done through networks by examining what is passed along particular and perhaps individual ties, functional typologies move the discussion to the level of collective action. Hence, functional typologies look at the specific tasks that bind together the network over time through holding its members accountable for the performance of shared tasks. Here, the term 'function' is used loosely to cover both true latent functions of organisation, where actors are unaware of consequences, and action where consequences are recognised and perhaps even intended (Stinchcombe, 1986). For example, Podolny and Page (1998) distinguish functions of learning, legitimation and status, economic benefits and insuring against risk; this account effectively equates the concept of a function with that of a benefit, consciously sought or otherwise.

A key distinction between functions that networks perform is that which distinguishes those which are created for the purpose of *risk management* from those that are directed at *opportunity management*. Risk management is the defensive activity of protecting existing resources possessed by at least some members of a network against events or processes that might erode the value of those resources. Opportunity management is concerned with the offensive activity of garnering additional resources to the additional benefit of at least some of the members. For example, many of the studies of networks in the business and management science literature are concerned with practices of 'knowledge management'. This work focuses on the types of network links that are used to access knowledge not possessed within the boundaries of the organisation, but which can be accessed through alliances with other organisations where that knowledge is possessed. This is a case of networking for opportunity management. The literature on networks among biotechnology firms (e.g. Powell *et al.*, 1996), for instance, is largely devoted to the analysis of networks of opportunity management, in which the key content of the ties is the in-licensing of new biotechnology procedures, complex molecules, compounds with potential pharmaceutical or agronomic applications and so on.

By contrast, some of the studies on the roles adopted by the Japanese *keiretsu* suggest that the internal networking among the companies within each *keiretsu* is often undertaken in order to manage certain kinds of risk by hoarding resources within the business group (Westney, 2001). Thus, assets are transferred for optimisation of tax treatment and managers and other skilled staff moved for career development and for staff retention purposes; these exchanges between member enterprises are pursued in order to protect the resource base of the business group as a whole. In another example, Granovetter's (1994) review of the literature on business groups across several continents suggests that one important rationale for their development is the protection of the existing power of influential families or individuals against political risk arising from changes in governmental priorities. Equally, many of the studies on informal networks of individuals within organisations have shown that the rationale for such networking is often the protection of resources that might be threatened by management action (Roethlisberger and Dickson, 1939). For example, by providing lobbying routes for subordinates that are not otherwise available through formal channels and by providing advance intelligence on management intentions, such networks are used for the protection of status.

Overall, since most networks perform multiple functions at this organisational level, and since these functions are not especially associated with any particular structural form or with any particular type of content, functional analysis is generally more useful in explaining behaviour than in developing a specific taxonomy of its own.

Institutional typologies

Up to this point, we have tended to use 'organisation' and 'institution' interchangeably. At this stage, however, it is necessary to define a more precise meaning of institution, where not all aspects of this definition will always apply to formal organisations. Although there are many ways to define the term (Peters, BG, 1999), an institution can be defined as that which

- constrains social rules, conventions or norms (North, 1990),
- may be formal or informal (Douglas, 1986),
- gives structure to the ways in which people interact,
- is more or less recognised by those subject to it (Knight, 1992), and
- leads to the forming of more or less stable social patterns of, for example, social and organisational ties (Jepperson, 1991).

In essence, however, an institution is something which creates an *accountability* (Douglas, 1986). On these terms, the local voluntary activity of the Ledbury Pony Club is just as much institutionalised as Microsoft, albeit that the nature of the accountabilities created differ markedly between them.

Many institutional forces are identified in the literature as shaping networks. However, a few have been given particular attention. Institutions that might shape networks can be defined at the empirical level. Examples include constitutions, religious prescriptions, systems of widely recognised roles that structure the division of labour, quasi-mandatory roles or responsibilities attached to membership of a class or group. This is broadly the level of institutions stressed by 'new institutionalist' theories. Alternatively, institutions can be conceived as 'socially expressed' and possessing more or less entrenched prescriptions that flow from particular worldviews. This is the Weberian approach (consider for example, Weber's 1976 account of entrepreneurial networks as the product of the institutional processes that internalise practices of saving, deferred gratification and risk-taking investment which he believed to be derived from particular religious outlooks).

It is common in this strand of the network literature to distinguish between formality and informality in the nature of the accountabilities between individuals in networks (or 'formal and informal networks' for short). For example, informal networks of individuals – who are employees within the same organisation – have been documented at least since Roethlisberger and Dickson (1939). Table 3.5 presents a synthesis of the concepts of formality and informality in mainstream social science literatures.

Table 3.5 Definitions of formality and informality for ties, institutions and organisations

	Formal	Informal
Social ties	Links of acquaintance or friendship between persons, which are specified and approved by some explicit rule of recognition and some kind of accountability for activities . undertaken jointly. Dedicated to the performance of a specific task or function or set of them; not readily applicable to other tasks or functions (*fungible*) for example, consultants or researchers who occasionally collaborate, write references for each other, occasionally socialise together.	Links of acquaintance or friendship between persons, which are not (i.e. no longer or not yet) subject to any specification or external accountability for the existence of the ties or of activities undertaken together. Not dedicated to the performance of specific tasks or functions (O'Neill, 1996: 195). May be fungible up to a point (depending on form, origin, type) for example, casual acquaintances who only meet at a sports club.
Institutions	Explicit, if abstractly codified, normative rules, readily transmissible, exercising control over decision-making and oversight of execution of some defined sphere of social action (Stinchcombe, 2001) for example, marriage, accreditation criteria.	Implicit, non-codified rules or norms, transmitted by incomplete oral suggestion (for example, hint), by example, emotion (for example, embarrassment at non-performance), which can be to some degree tacit, concrete and particularistic in nature, and which singly exercise only incomplete control over a sphere of social action (Misztal, 2000) for example, norms on acceptable kinds of jokes, unspoken codes for the conduct of supposedly informal meetings.
Organisations	Defined bounded cluster of abstract, codified institutional rules (Aoki *et al.*, 1990), which include a rule of membership for individuals bound by those rules, explicitly defined powers and authorities, and accountability for the use of resources to underpin those powers for example, rules on what defence contractors' and subcontractors' staff can talk about with people outside the firm.	Cluster of institutional rules that are incompletely codified, partially implicit, in which rules of membership defining those persons bound by those rules, and powers and accountability for resources are not (i.e. no longer or not yet) fully explicit and codified, but where there is still a shared understanding of general rules, roles and norms, membership criteria, and others, for example, the code governing who is counted as a project manager, or an appropriate person to nominate for membership of a dinner party circle.

It is also common to distinguish types of networks according to the tightness of the control exercised by the prevailing institutions over their structure, over the functions, tasks and contents of ties, over the actors' behaviour and their attempts to exercise powers of management within the network and so on.

For example, sometimes networks are only created because their existence is mandated by some formal rule (Doreian and Woodward, 1999), while others are created more or less voluntarily by the actors. Some networks are held tightly accountable for their performance of certain functions or tasks, while others are not. In the terms introduced earlier in this book, this spectrum is concerned with the relative weight of governance of the network. While weightier governance may be associated with greater formality, this is not necessarily the case. Tight accountability can, in some circumstances and with certain kinds of institutions, be exercised relatively informally.

Structural typologies

The basic measures of structural characteristics used in the network analysis literature are those of:

Density: the proportion of logically possible ties between members of a population that are actually active;
Clique: a densely tied, bounded cluster;
Centrality: the degree to which the structure of ties enables actor or organisation A to reach every other actor or organisation using the least number of secondary ties;
Betweenness: the degree of exclusivity of control over a route between B and C that is possessed by A;
Structural holes between cliques: the relative lack of alternative routes between B and C that would, if A can become a broker between them, enable A to exploit high betweenness by spanning those holes;
Core and periphery: a structure exhibiting a 'core' cluster with both high centrality and high betweenness, and an unstructured collection of less densely tied actors or organisations; and
Structural equivalence: two actors or organisations are structurally equivalent if they have the same pattern of relationships as each other with all the other actors in the population (Scott J, 1991; Wassermann and Faust, 1994).

Figure 3.1 provides some simple sociogram illustrations of some important types of network cases exhibiting some of these features.

Bringing together archetypal forms of these structural measures in this way shows that there are clear relationships between them; for example, high density is incompatible with the existence of a periphery; centralisation of the whole network is inversely related to the presence of cliques. This approach to classification is potentially rich – and is certainly more visually arresting than Tables 3.1–3.5 – but until it can be shown that these structural forms correspond with or connect to types that are important for reasons of content, function or institutional order, then it remains

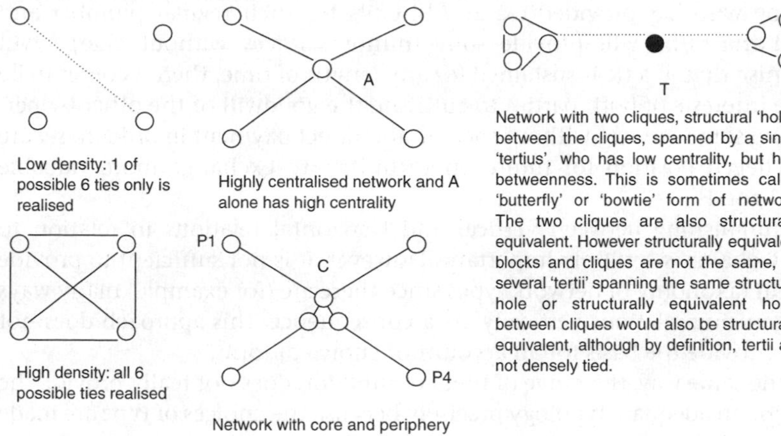

Figure 3.1 Key structural features of networks.

somewhat sterile. In Chapter 4, we shall argue that there are indeed ways of linking these various types within one overarching and original taxonomy.

Limits of these approaches to taxonomy

As with the theories of networks in Chapter 2, each of these typologies illuminates something important. For example, features of the content that is passed along ties, the functions of ties and the institutional character of what drives these ties are all clearly important to an understanding of networks. Indeed, these are all issues that will be discussed in greater detail in later chapters. However, none provides an adequate overall approach to typology. A useful typology should:

- provide the basis for a good account of how choices are made between the types identified; and
- provide the basis for an account of the factors that influence those choices.

Node-based typologies can be useful. However, the most that can really be obtained by examining very generic characteristics of the organisations at each node will be a characterisation of the challenges that may face the functioning of the network. This is really what Rudberg and Olhager (2003) offer. Little can be discerned from such an approach that will help to understand what network forms might be most appropriate to meet those challenges, without supplementing such typologies by additional factors.

The distinction between traded and non-traded goods as resources passed along ties is helpful, but only up to a point as most networks are characterised by ties along which both kinds of transaction are undertaken.

Anyone who has provided tea and biscuits for their regular plumber and found that s/he will provide some minor services without charge will recognise that, if a tie is sustained for any length of time, then it comes to be in the interests of both parties to cultivate the goodwill of the other by performing some services without specific and direct payment in order to secure a privileged position for future opportunities to exchange more valuable traded goods.

Distinguishing between vertical and horizontal relations in relation to supply chains is certainly important. However, it is not sufficient to provide a useful taxonomy of network types since there are (for example) many ways of organising relations vertically. As a consequence, this approach does not really provide the basis for an account of choice of form.

In the same way, the range of types of function does not really provide the basis for an adequate typology precisely because the choices of type are made within rather than between functions.

Institutions are, as we shall argue in Chapter 4, at the heart of the issue. But the degree of formality of member institutions is a matter of preliminary definition rather than the source in itself of a typology for understanding choice of network form.

Structural typologies capture something crucial about the types of network available to choose. The advantage of consideration of measures such as density, strength and weakness of ties and others is that it becomes possible to see fairly readily why different types of network form might be chosen. The structural characteristics alone do not, of course, fully explain the choices; they are, at most, dependent variables, that is, to a significant extent they are shaped by other factors. In Chapter 4, as we begin to develop our own theory, we offer a way to use these structural characteristics – together with some key institutional variables – as a way of synthesising approaches to taxonomy.

4
An Integrated Theory of Networks

In this chapter, we begin to build the theory which will be developed further in later chapters and then explored empirically in Part III. This theory is fundamentally institutionalist, in that it argues that the fundamental causal forces shaping networks are institutional in character. Like institutional theories in general, it suggests that these institutional factors provide marked constraints upon the scope for optimisation in the choice of network form. They impose limitations on the scope for human agency and also exert pressures for the primacy of certain biases in the ways of framing that choice. These limitations and pressures constrain the options available to agents in particular contexts and these can be explained by the institutional factors that the theory emphasises. However, it allows for a wider range of causal dynamics than do many 'new' institutionalist theories.

Approach to taxonomy: institutional factors underpinning structural characteristics

We begin with another taxonomy. This is not only to continue the argument of Chapter 3 but also because the particular institutional forces to which the theory points as causally most important are used in defining the taxonomy of network forms with which it works. Although the theory derives ultimately from the work of the founder of modern sociology, Émile Durkheim (1951), it has been given specific form by the work of the British anthropologist Mary Douglas (e.g. 1970, 1982a,b, 1992; Douglas and Ney, 1998) and her neo-Durkheimian institutionalist school (Thompson M, 1982a,b, 1992, 1996; Thompson M *et al.*, 1990, 1999; Mars, 1982; Gross and Rayner, 1985; Wildavsky, 1998; Hood, 1998; 6, 2003b; 6 *et al.*, 2002).

The neo-Durkheimian approach looks at institutions as connected with deep social structures, and focuses on the more general features of accountabilities. By accountabilities, we mean the pressures, incentives and imperatives that arise from institutionalised features of social organisation for people to act in ways that other people or groups would want. Clearly, such accountabilities are constantly open to rejection, but they only provoke these reactions precisely because they matter greatly. The theory begins with a classification of the basic forms of social accountability that have been found to be of critical importance in any society (and thus, by extension, in and between any sorts of formal organisation).

In *Suicide*, Durkheim (1951 [1897]) first distinguished between two basic institutional dimensions of social organisation which he argued to be causally critical for shaping collective behaviour. In his later lectures on *Moral education* (1961 [1925]), he went on to argue that they are also critical in shaping individual level behaviour and decision making. The first dimension is *social regulation*, or the degree to which social life is governed by and accountable to institutions of rule, role and given fact; he later (1961 [1925])

Table 4.1 The elementary forms of institution (expected to be combined in differing mixes in large-scale units of social organisation)

↑**Social**	→**Social integration**
Isolate *Strong regulation, weak integration*	**Hierarchy** *Strong regulation, strong integration*
Style of organisation: Heavily constrained individuals acting opportunistically, unable to sustain trust save perhaps with close kin	*Style of organisation*: Centrally ordered community – e.g. bureaucratic organisation
Basis of power: Domination	*Basis of power*: Asymmetric status, rule- and role-based authorisation
Strategy: Coping or survival-oriented behaviour, individual withdrawal	*Strategy*: Regulation, counterpoint between vertical and lateral boundaries internally, control through systems of status based on role
Network: Sparse social ties	*Network*: Dense social ties at top; mainly vertical ties at the bottom
Authority: Weak, if any among dominated isolates: at most, temporary celebrity; otherwise, temporary despotism among dominating isolates	*Authority*: Status-based, paternalistic, but with rule-bound discretion (in Weberian terms, bureaucracy)
Allocation of types of contract: Acceptance of balance given externally, as something about which little can be done, with little faith in the efficacy of any of these means	*Allocation of types of contract*: Relational contracting preferred in important functions
Strengths: Enables valuable coping behaviour and survival during adversity, prevents excessive aspiration during periods when this might be destructive	*Strengths*: Enables clarity and complex divisions of labour
Weaknesses: Limited ability to sustain collective action or tackle complex problems	*Weaknesses*: Limited ability to generate prosperity and can undermine it; the system of rule and role can become so Byzantine as to be illegible; risks demotivation of the 'lowerarchy' through denial of access to superior authority and denial of sufficient validation

Continued

Table 4.1 Continued

Individualism	Enclave
Weak regulation, weak integration	*Weak regulation, strong integration*
Style of organisation: Instrumental, entrepreneurial individuals – e.g., markets	*Style of organisation*: Internally egalitarian, but sharply marked boundaries with others; held together by shared commitment to moral principle – e.g., sects, cults, movements, clubs
Basis of power: Personal control of resources	*Basis of power*: Constant personal and collective reaffirmation commitment
Strategy: Brokering, negotiating for control of resources	*Strategy*: Intense mutual support within enclave, confrontation of those outside
Network: Sparse social ties, spanned by brokers	*Network*: Dense social ties
Authority: Power-based: authority derives from ability to define opportunities and bestow rewards (in Weberian terms, merchant adventurer)	*Authority*: In Weberian terms, charismatic, based on personal demonstration of marginally greater commitment to shared principle
Allocation of types of contract: Relational contracting only preferred where previous experience suggests that the balance of risks and transaction costs lies in its favour	*Allocation of types of contract*: Where contract has to be used, preference for spot contracts, in order to mark the boundary between insiders and outsiders more clearly and to minimise the dependence of the enclave on outsiders
Strengths: Unleashes powerful motivations of aspirant self-interest, enables focused instrumental activity	*Strengths*: Empowers passionate principled commitment and supports integrity, unleashes powerful motivations of protection
Weaknesses: Limited ability to define the basic goods and services, rights and duties around which self-interest and instrumental activity are oriented; may eventually undermine the capacity to do so; risks demotivation through insecurity	*Weaknesses*: Focus on distribution can undermine production and prosperity; risks schism; principle of internal equality can undermine level of authority necessary for efficacy; risks demotivation through exhaustion and burn-out, or through schism

called this 'discipline'. The second dimension is *social integration*, or the degree to which social life for an individual is bonded to others and, in particular, to peers, so that accountability is present (or absent) towards bounded collectives or groups; in his later lectures, Durkheim called this 'attachment'. Cross-tabulating these two dimensions (first done in Douglas, 1970) produces four basic types of social organisation, each with distinct structural characteristics (see Table 4.1).

Consider first the strongly regulated and strongly integrated network form. This must have a core which represents the authority of regulation to the periphery, as well as a marked boundary. This gives this network a *hierarchical* form.

The weakly regulated and strongly integrated form will have no core and periphery but instead show an internal pattern in which individuals will be more or less symmetrically located within a boundary marked by the integration; that is, most members will be structurally equivalent to most others. This is likely to mean that the network will exhibit comparatively high density because the boundary will define the network as a *group* or an *enclave*, with sharp inequality between members and non-members but no great inequalities between members themselves.

The weakly integrated and weakly regulated network form will be one that exhibits no group boundary and significant opportunity for exploitation by individuals; these are *individualistic* forms. Individuals will seek to occupy *tertius* (or 'betweenness') positions (Burt, 1992) that link enclaves or hierarchies in order to maximise the opportunities for influence and reward through exploiting control of the ties which enable the passage of resources. This is basically the 'bow tie' or 'butterfly' network, familiar from the ideal typical network form represented in Figure 3.1.

Finally, the strongly socially regulated but weakly socially integrated network form has a periphery with no core, or at least not one that is represented within the network, as the core that imposes regulation is itself outside this form. This leaves only the sparsely bonded individual; the *isolate* may know many other people but has few bonds of accountability to any group.

These basic institutional forms recur in any system of organisations. Table 4.1 summarises the main underlying institutional characteristics (Thompson M *et al.*, 1990; Douglas, 1982a [1978]; Fiske, 1991); Coyle and Ellis, 1994.

As Stinchcombe (1990) showed, the contract is by no means only an individualistic institution. Rather, networks of various types will use contracts but give them different meanings and functions. They serve well as but one example of the institutions that hold distinct network forms together. Table 4.1 summarises the types of bias for contractual relations that will predominate in each type. The argument is that the nature and, more importantly, the *meaning* of a contract will differ according to the underlying institutional and other conditions to which the prevailing form of inter-organisational relationships is a more or less intelligent response. Contracts are essentially institutions that express and define (as far as is found practicable under conditions of uncertainty and unavoidable incompleteness of foresight for contingencies) *accountability* in dyadic contexts, that is, in relationships between two parties. This accountability is shaped in response to a wide range of pressures including current capabilities, past experience, the dominant institutions in the field, the contingencies of the task, and so on. The type of – and meaning attributed to – contracts that are used to exercise some governance over inter-organisational relations therefore exhibit in the most readily measurable form the nature of the accountabilities offered, expected and against which compliance is to be assessed.

Each of these elementary forms of institutions yield, it is now clear, a distinctive 'signature' network form because the forms of accountability specified require particular structural patterns in networks. Figure 4.1 shows these signatures (cf. Mars, 1999, figure 2). The sociograms in Figure 4.1, of course, represent ideal types, although the underlying institutional forms that produce these forces are understood to be substantive social forces. In practice, many networks in the real world exhibit hybridity between two, three or even all four of these stylised sociogrammatic forms. However, any analysis that identifies which basic forms are present also serves to identify

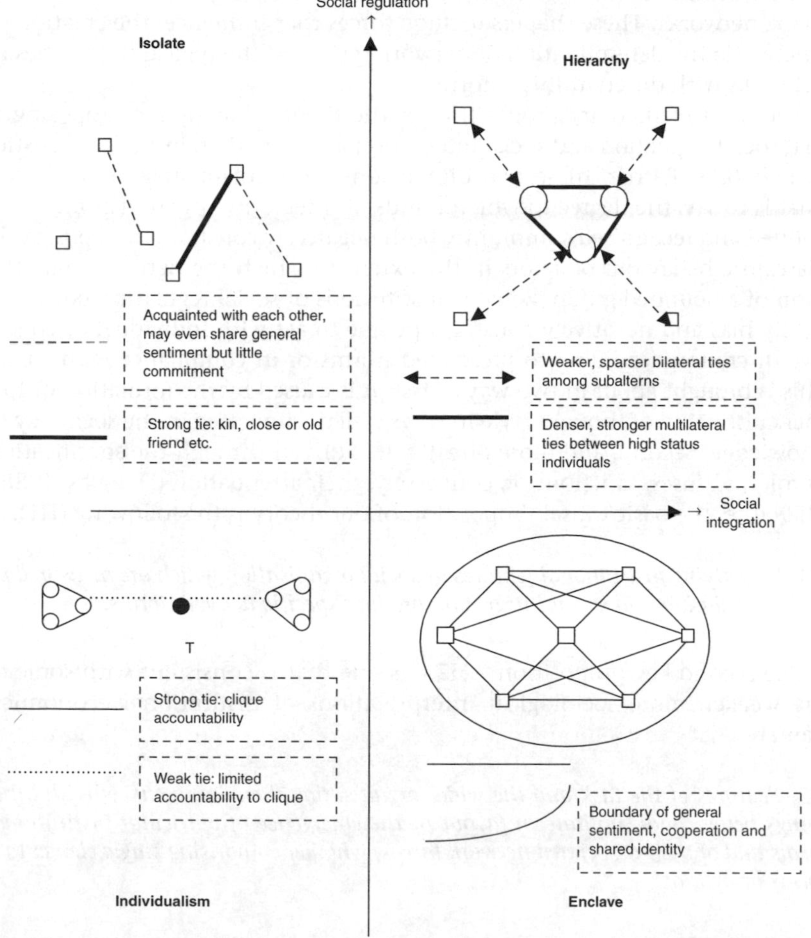

Figure 4.1 A structural typology of networks using the neo-Durkheimian institutional dimensions of social organisation.

the scope for management within the network and – with some further argument yet to be provided – for governance of the network too. To understand the type of hybrid is to understand a good deal; the possibility of hybridity does not undermine the taxonomy. Very often what really matters is to assess the *relative weight* of these four basic institutional imperatives in hybrids.

Causal theory

Having set out the principal ways in which it is possible to distinguish types of networks, it is now necessary to consider the range of forces that can shape networks. These shapers include forces that influence: the creation of a network; the determination of network type; and the typical trajectories of networks with different initial forms.

The most elementary proposition of the theory that we are proposing is that social regulation and social integration are more than just characteristics of networks. Rather, these two dimensions are fundamental causal forces. That is to say, the degree to which bonds of integration in an institutionally defined and recognised community both negatively constrains and positively biases the behaviour of actors in the extent to which the network takes the form of a bounded group. Equally, institutions of social regulation both positively bias and negatively constrain people to act with individual or collective discretion according to prescribed norms or in compliance with them. This is brought about in two ways. First, it is caused by the formation or further cultivation of thought style in ways well documented in the sociology of knowledge. Second, and more directly, it is driven through the specification of roles, statuses, sanctions or, conversely, their attenuation (Douglas, 1986). Therefore, the basic causal proposition of our theory is the following (H1):

H1. *Underlying institutional features of social organisation which are measured by social regulation and social integration produce specific network forms.*

The second key proposition – H2 – is one that is consistent with some of the weaker, more sociological interpretations of institutional economics, namely, that

H2. *Features of the task and the wider organisational environment will, all other things being equal, militate in favour of the emergence of particular institutional forms and of their associated network forms, whether comprising single elementary forms or hybrids.*

By 'militate', we want to suggest a weaker causal relation that the one which is described in the first proposition – H1 – as production. The reason for this weaker relation will become clearer shortly.

The key characteristics of the task and (inter) organisational relations that are relevant here are those of:

- *information* conditions (availability or sparsity, opacity or palpability);
- *task goal* conditions (ambiguity or clarity); and
- *transaction costs* of organising which render some forms of organising easier or more difficult.

The most important set of organisational characteristics concern dynamics. A presentation of dynamics is postponed until a later section of this chapter. However, it is critical to appreciate at this stage in the argument that:

H3. *Processes of organisational dynamics can change and in some cases transform material conditions* (for good and for ill and where material means central to the understanding and undertaking of the task).

Before considering dynamics directly, it is also important to introduce the fourth key proposition that:

H4. *Each of the institutional forms will bias people in their perception of the material and organisational conditions, in more or less systematic ways, and will therefore lead them to act in ways that may be inappropriate to those conditions and which may either realign the institutions to the conditions or further disalign them.*

In particular, each set of institutions can lead people to expect the continuation of material and organisational conditions to which (perhaps) the institutions were originally a response (as in H2), even though those conditions have changed either through modifications in the external environment or as a result of their own actions (and latter is a matter to be addressed under the discussion of dynamics later).

This means that our account is not a typical contingency theory, which would predict that a single network type will emerge, more or less deterministically, in response to a given set of conditions to which it will be uniquely appropriate. There has been a consistent line of criticism of, for example, Williamson's (1985) economic model of institution forms as the product of transaction costs where whatever emerges must be efficient and that people always and almost mechanically produce the right institutions for the prevailing conditions. Any sound theory of networks ought to avoid that consequence. It is important, at the very least, to allow for systematic bias in the ways in which people perceive their circumstances – including the information, task and transaction costs – which can lead them to develop a limited variety of types of institutions from the menu that is conceivable to them. The options on such a menu may well not be especially appropriate or efficient, at least in the medium term and judged against strictly economic criteria.

As a sociological theory, the fundamental causal driver stressed by the neo-Durkheimian institutional approach is the endogenous shaping of preferences by processes of institutionalisation and deinstitutionalisation. This is explained in the next proposition (H5).

H5. *Preferences – including preferences for and against particular network forms – are shaped by informal socialisation, acculturation and (often unconscious) biasing as a result of participation in social organisation under particular patterns of institutions. The endogenous shaping of preferences happens partly indirectly through cognitive biasing (H4), as people cease to be able to imagine either the feasibility or the desirability of alternative institutions. However, it also occurs partly through direct acculturation into support for or rejection of prevailing institutions by such mechanisms as peer reinforcement (enclave), explicit accountability to authorised others (hierarchy), resigned acceptance of the current institutions (isolate) or the institutional salience of opportunities and incentives (individualism).*

H5a. *In the simplest cases, preferences can emerge for the continuation and preservation of the prevailing institutional forms.*

H5b. *In more complex cases, preferences emerge that would react negatively to the continuation or preservation of prevailing institutions.*

The bare bones of this causal theory are, then, described by Figure 4.2.

In the next few sections, we examine these material and organisational conditions in more detail, in order to add richness to the theory. At the end of the chapter, a richer causal flow diagram will be presented, incorporating the more specific account to be presented next. As noted in the preface, readers more interested in this book as a support to network management,

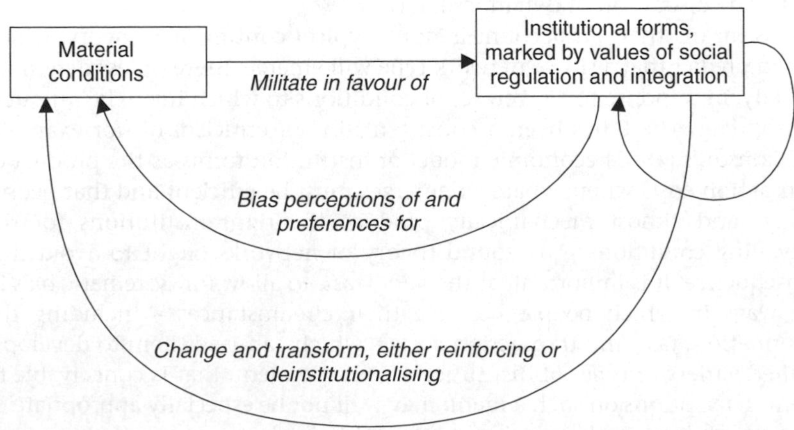

Figure 4.2 The elementary structure of the causal theory.

rather than in the arguments for the original theory that this book presents, may now wish to move onto the section later in this chapter headed 'The neo-Durkheimian cybernetic theory of network dynamics' where some more key hypotheses are proposed. However, it is important for all readers to note one contention contained in the following paragraphs – that is, the suggestion that the four forms of network that are identified in the neo-Durkheimian taxonomy are essentially inter-organisational versions of the same basic repertoire of forms that single organisations can also take. We suggest that the underlying institutional character of inter-organisational networks is not different in nature from the institutional order in the single organisation. This clearly has implications for issues to do with the management styles appropriate for networks explored in Chapter 6.

Goal conditions

Since the 1960s, great stress has been given in organisational behaviour studies to the significance of external environment of organisations, including the 'task environment' or specific features of the problems to be tackled in particular industries. Clearly there are also other environmental features, including institutional and governance power and, indeed, the prevailing prior networks in the organisational field and the larger historical trajectories of development in particular industries.

Over time, the 'new institutional economics' has provided innovative frameworks for analysis of the management and governance of inter-organisational relations. Williamson's (1975, 1985) models build on Coase' (1937) initiating argument about why firms exist at all in market economies. Coase suggested that firms are rationally chosen – rather than being only a system in which individuals interact as solitary producers and consumers – because the costs of negotiating, monitoring and enforcing contracts and of sustaining purely individual approaches to delivering orders for complex goods and services are so high that they would be uneconomic. Williamson extended the argument to suggest that vertical integration of firms might be not only rational but actually superior in many cases. Therefore, the rules in competition and antitrust law which cast suspicion on monopoly may in many cases be misguided because they might force excessively competitive structures upon some industries. Williamson's account of monopoly as sometimes transaction cost-efficient can readily be extended to some forms of oligopolistic and even cartel network forms. This provides a schematic transaction cost account of how network forms that promote horizontal integration both might be justified economically and, to the extent that people act with at least bounded rationality, brought about in response to the perceived balance of costs and benefits.

However, no capitalist economy contains just one big firm. This is explained by the fact that, beyond a certain point, hierarchy also possesses transaction costs as they begin to rise as any company expands. Specifically,

Williamson argued, incentives are impaired, and therefore productivity and innovation begin to fall, beyond a certain point. This then leaves space for a variety of network forms based on contract. In particular, he suggested, networks connected by medium- or long-term high trust relational contracts might well be more efficient in reducing the transaction costs inherent to spot contract; as a consequence, networks based on these forms would often be superior. In this way, Williamson's theory provides a schematic model of how vertical network forms might be justified and, again, given the right sort of rationality, actually emerge in those areas where they would be efficient.

There are two correlated problems with this account, at least in Williamson's particular formulation. One is the danger of the Panglossian view that whatever actually emerges must turn out to be transaction-cost efficient, unless the assumption of universal, or at least general and bounded, rationality is abandoned. The second is the instability in the concept of a transaction cost; if we want to explain why any particular form has come to be adopted, it is always possible to deem whatever negative (i.e. non-benefit) considerations that either could have been or were taken into account to be a kind of transaction cost. In this way, a transaction cost can become almost any opportunity cost that is not measured as a conventional cost of production.

In order to salvage the theory from both Panglossianism and tautology, it is probably necessary to allow greater variety in the forms of rationality than Williamson's economistic model does. One way to do this – which would be resisted in the mainstream economic tradition but is common in sociology (specifically proposed in Durkheimian theory and implied in some readings of Weber's theory) – is to allow rationalities to be determined by the prevailing institutional forms. This introduces a greater degree of inertia and 'stickiness' into the nature of the institutions that define network forms. It allows that, by the standards of one of the rationalities, the recognition of transactions costs by people in other institutions may be regarded as inefficient and *vice versa*. Moreover, Williamson (1994) acknowledges that, in focusing on transactions, the model works best at the level of dyadic analysis of contractual relations. Focusing on this level of analysis, it is by definition not very easy to identify any distinct effects that arise from the different nature of multilateral relationships.

There are some links between the neo-Durkheimian approach to institutional taxonomy of network forms and the institutional form of taxonomy developed within the transaction cost theoretic tradition of new institutional economics that flows from Coase and Williamson (Douglas, 1986). Ouchi (1980) argued, consistently with Williamson's (1985) theory, that the central challenge of all economic and social organisation is to enable agreement to produce goods and services despite the potential opportunism and bounded rationality of individuals. The challenge is either to limit the divergence of potential partners' goals or else to accept that divergence but to work around it, even when it is not always easy to determine providers' trustworthiness or the quality of their performance. Ouchi's thesis was that where performance can be relatively unambiguously evaluated, great divergence in goals can be tolerated in market-like networks. As ambiguity rises, bureaucratic or hierarchical networks have to be adopted in order to deal with market failure. However, above a certain level of ambiguity even these solutions will fail, and it becomes necessary to recruit likeminded people who will share the same goals and commitments and which thus enables economising on the costs of monitoring. The shaded cells in Table 4.2 represent Ouchi's (1980) schema.

However, Ouchi was largely silent about what kinds of organisation, if any, might be available – even if not necessarily fully transaction cost efficient – in cells B, C and F of the matrix. Presumably, organisations requiring co-operation of any kind are likely to be very difficult to sustain in conditions of very high ambiguity. However, cells B and F might sustain some minimal level of organisation because here, at least, just one of these variables presents only moderate difficulties (in contrast to C which has significant challenges on both axes). The neo-Durkheimian argument would be that it is in these two cells that we should expect to find 'isolate' forms, which are to be regarded as plausible, if admittedly minimal, forms of organisation. An isolate is *not* a person or an organisation with no contacts or no ties at all. Rather, the isolate situation is one of impoverished ties that require little accountability to peers and therefore few possibilities for collective action (in Ouchi's terms, moderate or high goal incongruence). Isolates are strongly constrained by external institutions that limit choices or make the environment especially opaque (in Ouchi's terms, at least, this is moderately high performance ambiguity). Isolates have little choice but to be opportunistic and even guileful (Banfield and Banfield, 1958) given the goal incongruence between them and also between them and those with power over them. Trust problems are very serious, therefore, but they can survive

Table 4.2 Ouchi's (1980) schema of organisational forms predicted to be efficient (or at least sustainable) in different conditions of performance ambiguity and goal incongruence

	Low performance ambiguity	**Moderate performance ambiguity**	**High performance ambiguity**
High goal incongruence	A Markets	B [Isolate]	C [No organisation sustainable]
Moderate goal incongruence	D Markets	E Bureaucracy	F [Isolate]
Low goal incongruence	G Markets	H Bureaucracy	J Clan

and exchange some goods and services on a short-term basis and sustain thin networks provided they concentrate their efforts on fairly basic goods and services where performance ambiguity is not excessively high ('survivalism': Thompson *et al.*, 1990). Essentially, the isolate form is a coping style of minimal organisation in conditions where high transaction costs have to be borne but those costs are too high to sustain other forms of organisation. With this addition the two traditions become fully convergent in taxonomy.

The remaining key difference between the two theories then concerns the impact of goal incongruence and ambiguity in the evaluation of performance. The new institutional economics tends to take ambiguity in performance evaluation as a more or less intrinsic feature of particular goods and services; for example, that health care services are intrinsically more difficult for consumers (or even regulators) to monitor. The neo-Durkheimian approach argues (with path-dependence models in other kinds of institutional economics) that the difficulties in evaluating performance are more affected by the current forms of organisation which produce certain biases in perception of performance. Ouchi accepts that, at least at the margin, clans can discipline ('socialise' in his terms) their members into sharing goals, and consequently, in economists' terms, shaping preferences endogenously. This affords some scope for management as an activity within clan-like networks, albeit restricted by the limited differentiation of status and power that means that it is not easy for individuals to secure legitimacy for attempts to monopolise their control of management activity in order to shape preferences and interests.

Transaction cost conditions

A transaction cost account can be rendered of some of the dynamics of the basic forms of organisation identified by the taxonomy in the neo-Durkheimian institutional tradition. This will help provide an understanding of the central role that material factors play in defining the scope for institutional development.

Network forms of each institutional type are both a response to transaction cost conditions created by the task and prior inter-organisational environment and also sources of transaction costs in their own right. Ouchi's account provides a schematic way of thinking about some of the conditions creating transaction costs – or at least risks of transaction costs – to which each of the basic forms might be intelligent but boundedly rational responses. Next, it is important to consider the types of transaction costs that will be minimised, and perhaps increased, under each of the basic institutional network forms.

Table 4.3 recasts the neo-Durkheimian taxonomic matrix by operationalising the two basic dimensions of social regulation and social integration into standard economic measures. The four network forms are then shown as institutional forms recognisable in the institutional economic literature.

Table 4.3 Transaction cost strengths and weaknesses of elementary forms of networks

Fragmented competition ↖	Monopoly/Regulation ↑	Limited competition, contestability ↗	
	Barter market *Network form*: Independent firms with limited co-operation or competition, thin market *Extreme case*: self-production, autarchy *Probabilities of low transaction costs created by the form*: costs of externalisation *Dangers of high transaction costs created by the form*: high costs of any kind of large scale organisation	**Williamson – Coase hierarchy** *Network form*: business group, stable and structured coalition, vertical integration *Extreme case*: single firm *Probabilities of low transaction costs created by the form*: costs of contracting *Dangers of high transaction costs created by the form*: costs of internalising processes and costs of collective decision-making rise over time diminishing returns to organising *Other cost/productivity problems*: Lower productivity and weaker cost control because incentives from property rights are attenuated	
Spot contracting ←	**Hayek–von Mises market** *Network form*: shifting portfolio of strategic alliances *Extreme case*: individuals trading *Probabilities of low transaction costs created by the form*: costs of decision-making, costs of internalisation *Dangers of high transaction costs created by the form*: costs of keeping information proprietary; costs of co-ordinating multiple ties and limiting conflict of interest or commitment; diminishing returns to mainly bilateral ties (alliances); costs of externalisation; costs of negotiation to substitute for collective decision-making *Other cost/productivity problems*: High costs of establishing and enforcing property rights, without risking feud, if not defined externally (e.g. by hierarchy)	**Ouchi 'clan' or Buchanan 'club'** *Network form*: club, trade association, cartel, horizontal integration *Extreme case*: commune *Probabilities of low transaction costs created by the form*: internalising some externalities, economising on need for some (otherwise) public goods *Dangers of high transaction costs created by the form*: exclusion of benefits, esp. as members rise and congestion sets in *Other cost/productivity problems*: Lower productivity and weaker cost control because incentives from property rights are attenuated	→ Relational contracting
↙ Neo-classical competition	↓ Fragmented organisational field/Deregulation	↘ Limited competition: generalised co-operation	

The cells then present the types of transaction and other costs for each form, summarising which are probably reduced in each form and the dangers of which are heightened. At the diagonal extremes are shown the institutional directions to which positive feedback in each cell would tend and which would thus exacerbate the risks of higher transaction costs of each type.

This is a complicated argument, but paying attention to transaction costs in this way brings out a key issue in the theoretical consideration of the determinants of inter-organisational networking. The four forms of network that are identified in the neo-Durkheimian taxonomy are essentially inter-organisational versions of the same basic repertoire of forms that single organisations can also take. In this sense, this particular theory suggests that the underlying institutional character of inter-organisational networks is not different in nature from the institutional order in the single organisation, albeit that there may be disparities in tautness and tightness. For both single organisations and networks are driven by the same dynamics and move to the same few positions on the map of available forms of social organisation in response to the same kinds of pressures.

The transaction cost approach enables us to explore in more depth the constraints and incentives that will tip the choice between separate organisations working within inter-organisational networks, and/or the emergence through merger and acquisition of single organisations to dominate a field. In Table 4.3, it was noted that in each of the four elementary types identified in the neo-Durkheimian theory the limit case might be either a single organisation or very large numbers of organisations. These limit cases are defined on the basis of the conventional theory. However, in each of these institutional situations, an individualistic network, for instance, may be heavily contingent not only on the balance of transaction costs but on the capacity of people working in organisations in each of these institutional settings to recognise, take seriously and act upon different kinds of transaction cost. This requires allowing the stylisation of bounded rationality to be endogenous in the organisational and inter-organisational system. It is in this respect that the neo-Durkheimian theory offers something of real importance with which to supplement and complete Williamson's transaction cost model.

Of central importance, though, is the way in which the consideration of cost dangers in Table 4.3 provides the bridge between the theory of the ways in which institutional forms respond to certain conditions and the discussion in the chapters in Part II of the relative strengths and weaknesses of each form. For the causal basis of these relative strengths and weaknesses can be understood in terms of the risks of creating different categories of transaction cost.

It has been argued already that the institutionalisation and deinstitutionalisation dynamics allow the prospect that people may perceive the same task environment differently, because each institutional form biases people to think about their world in particular ways. In particular, this process will bias people towards taking some kinds of transaction costs more seriously than others, because different costs will become framed as salient in each institutional setting.

Table 4.4 presents a reworking of Table 4.3 to show how this neo-Durkheimian revision of the transaction cost model – taking account of biased perception – would operate. Table 4.4 preserves from Williamson's approach the idea that there are transaction costs which militate in favour of various forms and that these costs emerge from the prevailing institutions. Therefore, each main cell shows the three possible pressures. However, in allowing that the institutions will stylise rationality divergently in each, this version shows how the basic forms of power institutionalised are privileged in each of the elementary forms and therefore will skew outcomes. It also shows that the balance of forces making for these transformations are also likely to be the ones that generate forces for hybridity between institutional forms. This is because the momentum for sustaining either network systems or dominant individual organisations will lead to incentives to incorporate institutional features from the other three.

Information conditions

In recent years, a number of theories have given particular weight to knowledge acquisition and information exchange. An important strand of theorising about how organisational and inter-organisational forms are shaped is concerned with information; with opportunities, resources, benefits, rights and risks, costs, and duties, and about procedures in relation to information. In short, in these discussions, organisational and inter-organisational forms are solutions, of better or worse kinds, to problems around information (Stinchcombe, 1990) and knowledge. Interestingly, competence and learning theories are often presented as being sharply distinguished from information theories of organisations and networks (e.g. Colombo, 1998).

Networks of different types are thus created and used, and over time reshaped, in order to secure access to information that each organisation in its segment of the network finds relevant. The information searched for, the costs of search and the organisational locations in which one must search will therefore heavily influence the type of the network.

In their simplest form, then, information theories of organisation are very much like transaction cost theories. Unsurprisingly, they exhibit some of the same strengths while suffering from some of the same weaknesses. For example, problems of trust arise in principal–agent relationships where the agent possesses more information than the principal about the benefits available to be captured in the course of the relationship; economists refer to these as problems of information asymmetry. One solution to these kinds of problems is vertical integration between principal and agent as a way of overcoming the problem of incentives for agents to keep information from principals. Other solutions include attempts to write ever more detailed

Table 4.4 The balance of forces for inter-organisational networks, separate organisations or a dominant organisation

Fragmented competitition or divide-and-rule ↖	*Exercise and experience of control drives balance between fission or fusion* ↑		↗ *Limited competion, contestability*
Search for access to resources drives balance between fission or fusion ←	**Isolate** *Pressures for multiple separate organisations to exist*: few pressures for collective action, lack of trust coping pushes organisations toward nicheing and autarchy *Pressures for organisations to form ties*: resource dependence *Pressures for a single organisation to emerge*: externally imposed regulation *Transaction costs and benefits most likely to be recognised*, ceteris paribus: in favour of complying with or working within externally imposed (inter-)organisational order	**Hierarchy** *Pressures for multiple separate organisations to exist*: incompatible styles of control *Pressures for organisations to form ties*: greater legitimacy from co-operation: greater access to control enables more legitimate organisations to discipline others into membership of structured-group like network *Pressures for a single organisation to emerge*: aggrandisement in order to exercise control more effectively Where networked form emerges, likely to develop hybrid forms e.g., some individualist elements *Transaction costs and benefits most likely to be recognised*, ceteris paribus: in favour of using or creating or sustaining dominant organisation	→ *Search for legitimacy drives balance between fission or fusion*
	Individualism *Pressures for multiple separate organisations to exist*: inducement-driven competition, innovation, niche-ing *Pressures for organisations to form ties*: resource dependence, competitive pressures select which ties on the basis of inducement *Pressures for a single dominant organisation to emerge*: aggrandisement of organisations with high centrality and betweenness: most powerful organisation is able to accumulate greatest resource base and so exercise greatest inducement Where dominant organisation emerges, likely to develop some hierarchical features (Weber: 'bureaucratisation') *Transaction costs and benefits most likely to be recognised*, ceteris paribus: in favour of vertical network	**Enclave** *Pressures for multiple separate organisations to exist*: fissiparous character of enclave, rival possibilities for suasive influence *Pressures for organisations to form ties*: costs of collective action fall when costs can be pooled for action in the common interest: persuasion is the tool for bringing others into membership of the group-like network *Pressures for a single organisation to emerge*: successful suasive influence achieves cultural hegemony Where dominant organisation emerges, likely to develop some hierarchical features (Weber: 'routinisation of charisma') '*Transaction costs and benefits most likely to be recognised*, ceteris paribus: in favour of separate organisations each pursuing hegemony	
↙ *Neo-classical competition or success leads to monopoly*	↓ *Pursuit of goals under greater voluntary (individual or collective) choice drives balance between fission or fusion*		↘ *Limited competition: schismatic conflict or generalized co-operation*

contracts, a strategy that sooner or later is sure to fail because eventualities will arise that were not foreseen in the contract.

Some theories begin with the nature of the information generated by the problem that the organisations in a given field must work with; for example, information about the opportunities created by the market or the environmental conditions or the intentions of other actors. Most information theories of organisation focus on a limited number of variables to describe the most important features of the information that shape the organisation or an inter-organisational arrangement, such as a type of network, that might arise. March and Olsen (1976) stress the importance of what they call 'ambiguity' – by this, they actually mean 'opacity' – that is, the degree to which the information that an organisation could feasibly obtain about its core challenges, resources and environment is unavoidably uncertain. A situation in which information is typically made explicit – written down, codified, organised in ways that support structured comparisons and analysis – is one in which opacity can be reduced much more easily and at lower cost than one in which information is generally tacit, that is, kept in people's heads, not structured, and represented in the form knowing-how rather than knowing-that.

However, the degree of uncertainty is not the only consideration. The second variable which most theories stress about information is the ease or cost with which it can be kept under proprietary control. Information is often most valuable when other organisations or other groups of organisations cannot readily obtain it. Some information is almost unavoidably public; information about the weather, about last week's stock market trends or recent patterns in the wage levels for clinical or managerial staff is available to almost anyone who wants it. Other kinds of information – who is really committed to doing what, who believes or intends what, whose ties to whom are really important – are much more easily kept under the control of particular organisations, or even individuals within organisations. It is this variable which is most generally stressed by economists interested in information asymmetry and in principal–agent relationships.

Once again, cross-tabulating these two dimensions in the neo-Durkheimian taxonomy presents solutions to the problems that the different combinations of opacity and ease of proprietary control present. The argument behind this matrix (Table 4.5) is that the nature of the information relevant to an organisation or a field of organisations and the difficulty or cost of keeping that information proprietary – which is itself also in part a function of the nature of that information as being either tacit or explicit – in part shape the priorities that organisations will have in trying to make use of that information. Inter-organisational arrangements are as much driven as are single organisations by imperatives to make the best use of scarce information (Stinchombe, 1990).

Clearly, Table 4.5 is not presented as a complete account of the forms that organisations and inter-organisational networks will adopt or develop. Where there are other countervailing institutional or other factors, no doubt these pressures can and are resisted, but they remain, nonetheless, significant.

The converse dynamic is also important; the nature of the organisation or network form also shapes what is counted as a useful nugget. Hierarchical

Table 4.5 Informational conditions to which inter-organisational forms are intelligent solutions

	Information about core problem for the organisation exhibits low ambiguity/opacity – high explicitness ↑		
Low cost of keeping information proprietary ←	**Isolate** priority to secure own access to information that almost anyone can control and use	**Hierarchy** priority to increase proprietary control despite ease of capture and use of information by outsiders	→ *High cost of keeping information proprietary*
	Individualism priority to exploit situations that may only appear to one individual as opportunities	**Enclave** priority to control among insiders, information about 'soft' matters e.g. commitment, belief despite cost of control	
	↓ *Information about the core problem for the organisation exhibits high ambiguity/opacity – high tacitness*		

networks will reject information that would suggest reasons for organising in ways other than in a hierarchy. Individualistic networks will reject information which suggests that, for example, competitive entrepreneurial strategies could be leading to zero-sum outcomes. Enclaved networks will reject information that would lead people to think that internal egalitarianism and democratic decision-making are inefficient or inappropriate in their particular field (Thompson and Wildavsky, 1986). In these ways, network forms institutionalise themselves.

Information is central to the role of trust in networks (see Chapter 5 for a fuller analysis of inter-organisational trust). It is a commonplace in the literature to observe that effective networks are 'high trust' forms. Indeed, many long term strategic alliances that are regarded as 'successful' are indeed ones in which high trust has been built either carefully or in the course of purely practical collaboration. However, this is not always the case. There are many documented examples of looser networks – in neo-Durkheimian terms, less socially integrated ones – in which the form of network is determined by the low levels of trust between each of the nodes. In the absence of powerful reasons for or ability to trust information provided by any one organisation, the other organisation may preserve a variety of linkages to other organisations, all roughly equally loose, in order to secure access information with which to check what is received from each. Many 'issue networks' (Rhodes and Marsh, 1992) identified by political scientists exhibit this character.

Information, expectations and trust

More sophisticated information theories derive from Merton (1968 [1949]), who stressed both the importance of (institutionalised) expectations. These may vary markedly from what might be considered 'accurate' (thereby allowing the theory to avoid the problems of Panglossianism that have weakened transaction cost theories). Moreover, the expectations of *others* matter greatly in shaping the form of social structure. Only where reasonably reliable information about the intentions of others can be obtained, thus enabling stable expectations to be built-up, is sustained trust possible of a kind that can stabilise a network. All forms of organisation and of inter-organisational arrangements require trust to function. Despite the common-place rhetoric, there is nothing special about inter-organisational networks in this regard (however, trust is placed for different reasons in each of the basic different kinds of institutional settings; see Chapter 5. As Ouchi (1980) argued (see earlier), it is wrong to see the cohesion and co-ordination that is achieved in clan-like or enclaved forms of networks as uniquely driven by trust. Rather, trust of a very particular kind is produced by the organisational form of strongly bounded membership, dense ties, and internally egalitarian status system due to a system of distributing rewards connected neither to status nor to individual performance. These institutional–structural factors produce co-ordination only as long as commitment to the 'cause' can provide cohesion, which itself emerges in institutional reaction to the failure of other inter-organisational forms. In the same way, trust of distinct kinds is produced in individualistic and hierarchical networks; people do not enter into contracts and will not sustain status systems without trust. In each case, its latent function is to stabilise expectations.

How, then, are either trusting or non-trusting expectations about the future behaviour of others within networks generated? In part, the institutions within the network that define its form and wider social institutions (sanctions for breaking promises etc.) generate expectations of this kind, at least to the extent that there is reason to think that an individual in question will be bound by them. In economic models, including transaction cost theories, individuals are assumed to be opportunistic and guileful, and to be boundedly rational, and therefore capable of short-term behaviour in violation of institutionalised expectations, unless the institutional forces are of sufficient strength to impose very severe penalties upon them for behaving in this way. At a very schematic level, this might even be sensible. However, the problem arises in trying to work out just which institutions will typically be perceived as imposing such 'very severe' penalties.

The neo-Durkheimian model – as presented here – suggests a way of at least developing some plausible hypotheses about this, for institutions should afford the greatest opportunity for guileful opportunism when they provide the weakest integration (see Chapter 5). In weakly integrated contexts, one's reputation with others is less important because one's accountabilities to those others are most limited.

Second, however, reputation is only one kind of incentive for behaving in a way that acknowledges the long-term benefits of pro-social action within networks of any kind. The possibility of eventual material pay-off as a result of investing in one's position in the network, to secure, for example, a *tertius* position as a broker (Burt 1992) between enclaves, is also a motivation of long-term behaviour. This suggests that weak regulation is not the factor most likely to exacerbate the effect of weak integration. Rather, the institutional setting in which the possibilities of longer term pay-off to investment in network position are most limited is that which combines weak integration with strong regulation; here, strong regulation is not combined with any system of structured status or any system of rules allocating rewards for investment in long-term behaviour. In these isolate settings, it is most difficult to secure reliable information on the basis of which to develop expectations of the behaviour of others, and therefore to trust them, because the external regulation is so strong that their behaviour if often driven by forces over which they have limited control. The opacity problem is therefore most severe here. Moreover, because in weakly integrated settings the costs of keeping information proprietary is low, making guile about one's own intentions a cheaper option. The most Hobbesian opportunists should therefore be expected to be found in networks of isolates (Wildavsky, 1998).

Indeed, there is empirical evidence that this is the case. In the classical ethnographic study of a small town characterised by isolate institutions, Banfield and Banfield (1958) showed that 'amoral familism' does in fact emerge as a perfectly rational strategy of coping for individuals in these conditions. In a study of economic organisation among poor Frafra migrants in Accra, Hart (1988) argues similarly that only with difficulty do a minority achieve collaboration with non-kin in the formation of organisations. In studies of organisational behaviour, the same thing is found. For example, Mayntz (1999) examined the behaviour of science academies in countries in the post-socialist transition of the early 1990s and found that the most opportunistic behaviour was to be found among those in the lands of the former Soviet Union, a finding reinforced by the many studies which have detected low levels of trust in those countries during these periods (e.g. Sztompka, 1999). In the present context, ideally, one would want to test the hypothesis by examining studies of failure to form inter-organisational networks or alliances (e.g. Doz and Hamel, 1998); unfortunately, there are rather few such studies. There are, of course, studies of the breakdown of particular strategic alliances among companies that later go on to form other alliances; this is clearly not a comparable situation.

By contrast, each of the other institutional settings should afford at least some reliable information on which to build some expectations of the behaviour of others (at least as long as these forms have not yet been radicalised to the point that they undermine their own virtues; Thompson M *et al.*, 1990; Wildavsky, 1998).

Network dynamics

Network evolution and change over time

There are some studies which examine the ways in which networks of various kinds evolve and change over time. Van de ven (1992) argues that there are essentially only four basic 'paradigms' – or model mechanisms – for change over time in organisational and inter-organisational studies. These are:

- evolution: non-linear, non-deterministic, driven by adaptation to environmental forces (Darwinian), possibly also incorporating inherited learning (Lamarckian);
- dialectics: non-linear, non-deterministic, driven by conflict between rival forces, catastrophic, oscillatory;
- teleology: linear, deterministic, sequential, progressive; and
- life-cycle: linear, deterministic, sequential, circular.

Some studies are indeed framed in terms of life-cycles, such as Lowndes and Skelcher's (1998) diagnosis of transitions between market, network and hierarchy which are plotted onto something reminiscent of the standard life cycle described in conventional project management terms, with phases corresponding to managerial tasks (criticised as inadequate and too much based on closed system models by Bouchikhi *et al.*, 1998, cited in Faulkner and De Rond, 2000). Others are framed in terms of evolution but in fact boil down to life cycle accounts (e.g. Doz and Baburoglu, 2000). Many life-cycle models are in fact even simpler, and really only have two possible outcomes; continuation at the end of the period studied or else termination: Oliver's (2001) study of life-cycles in networks in the biotechnology industry is of this kind.

There are many happy teleological models in the literature which tell stories of deepening co-operation, leading to greater trust and closer mutual commitment (some of Doz and Hamel's 1998 case studies of successful alliances are of this kind; likewise, Wenger's 2000 arguments about the benefits of communities of practice are also of this type). These are matched by the many dialectical studies of collaborations that have failed (of which, in the public sector, Challis *et al.*, 1988 is perhaps the best known). Of the public sector studies, probably the subtlest of the teleological models of change is offered by Bardach (1998, 2001), who stresses momentum dynamics (positive feedback), albeit allowing for extensive contingency through variations in individual 'managerial craftsmanship' as sources of 'commotion', but nevertheless focuses on models of change in which capacities for deeper collaboration are cultivated and reinforced over time.

All serious models of organisational change allow for important elements of path dependency, and therefore, for institutional limitations on the scope for managerial agency. Prior experience, network inheritance, capabilities already cultivated and so on, heavily constrain the menu of options for change in inter-organisational relations over time (Gulati, 1995). However, the scope for individual managerial agency clearly differs according to the type of network. As the theory set out in Chapter 3 would predict, empirical studies confirm that the more individualistic the network structure, the greater the possibilities for managers to use *tertius* strategies to broker change in inter-organisational relations. This is precisely because both regulation and integration are at their weakest in networks of this type (e.g. Steier and Greenwood, 2000); these are contrasted with the denser, more 'embedded' (in one use of the term) networks, where network structural change certainly occurs – not least as a result of deformation – but less as a direct result of individual managerial manipulation (Hite and Hesterly, 2001).

Teleological models tend to stress positive feedback mechanism of change, except where they allow negative feedback to limit detours from the destination goal. Life-cycle models also describe negative feedback bringing the organisational system back to its starting point, but are often presented as providing for a conflict-free conception of this negative feedback; that is, it is something automatic and homeostatic. The problem with conventional evolutionary models is that, in practice, they can be used to find some environmental circumstance to which almost any change must have been adaptive which tends to produces a Panglossian style of explanation. Narrowly incremental and gradualist evolutionary models therefore fail to encompass high conflict situations of great volatility. However, dialectical models give too limited space for positive feedback because they allow only highly conflictual negative feedback processes.

What are required, then, are more open-ended models, allowing for multiple possibilities, but more clearly specifying the prior conditions that are more likely to elicit particular mixes and imbalances of positive and negative feedback effects and therefore to elicit either gradual or catastrophic change. The neo-Durkheimian theoretical framework, we have shown, offers precisely such a theory of change (Thompson, M, 1982, 1992, 1996).

Path dependence and embeddedness models

An important development within the broad family of institutionalist theories of organisational and inter-organisational forms has been the recognition that prior patterns of development both constrain and define opportunities for future developments. This is a phenomenon generally called 'path dependence', and first given emphasis in the context of technological change (Arthur, 1994) and in the economics of technical innovation as they affect market structure (Nelson and Winter, 1982). It is argued that the irreversibility of history is applied to the forms of networks, the skills and competencies of networking and indeed the actual ties that make up the particular networks. These constrain future abilities, willingness and opportunities for developing ties. Essentially, path dependence stresses positive or self-reinforcing feedback dynamics. This is in contrast to, for example, 'catastrophe' theories and 'punctuated equilibrium' theories (True *et al.*, 1999; Baumgartner and Jones, 2002) which stress negative feedback dynamics or processes whereby one institutional dynamic elicits a correction or check or even reverse on a rival institutional process, or where an institutional dynamic disorganises itself and opens up space for others to supplant it, or at least curb it.

For example, Garcia-Pont and Nohria (2002) show that the network character of the wider industry or organisational field is a key predictor of any propensity to form alliances and thus stress the influence of dyadic relations in the prevailing system. Gulati (1995) gives particular emphasis to the role of prior ties, not only in the instrumental role of providing experience in the skills of managing alliances, but also in defining a structure of constraints and opportunities for present and future tie formation in networks. Again, Kogut *et al.* (1992) and Walker *et al.* (1997) offer a quantitative empirical examination of path dependence in the networks of the US biotechnology industry in the 1980s. They show that first-mover factors were critical, that initial patterns of clustering were steadily reinforced during that decade, and they also find that these cliques steadily increased in density as a result of the reinforcement dynamic.

In the literature on the shaping forces of inter-organisational structures, the path dependence concept has also been expressed using the idea of embeddedness. Originally introduced by Granovetter (1985) to encompass the personalistic idea that organisational action is located within, constrained by and shaped by networks themselves (so stressing inter-organisational and inter-individual ties as independent variables), in more recent work the concept has been used to emphasise that inter-organisational ties are themselves 'embedded' in: (a) wider systems of such ties, following Granovetter's (1985) admonition that Williamson's (1985) transaction cost models still emphasised only dyadic relations; and (b) inherited structures of previous patterns of ties (Uzzi, 1997). Studies such as Uzzi's focus on the balance of benefits and risks for adaptive efficiency arising from embeddedness. To the extent that these benefits can be recognised in advance, or else influence people without recognition, they may be shaping factors for networks. However, Uzzi also identifies the extent to which the constraining process arising from path dependence and the strength of the positive feedback dynamic is a function of the efforts people feel compelled to take in order to reduce their exposure to risk. For in order to assure themselves of the trustworthiness or investment-worthiness of another organisation, they are likely to follow up multiple ties to and from that organisation, in the process reinforcing those ties and adding multiplexity to ties that may hitherto have been less multiplex. In part, Uzzi's is an information-driven explanation; in conditions of key importance of information about risk exposure, it makes sense to work with existing ties along which already trusted indications of the trustworthiness of potential new partners are known already to flow, thus reinforcing those ties. From an economic point of view, the gains in adaptive efficiency are achieved at the price of raised barriers to entry because the path-dependence takes the form of a reputation management network which is costly for a new player to make use of. Uzzi also introduces the notion of 'overembeddedness', meaning the problem for a given organisation of being linked to too narrow a set of cliques or clusters in the wider industry network system, so that if a core organisation in that clique is undermined the focal organisation too is damaged, perhaps irreversibly. This usage has been followed by Grabher (1993). However, the problem with this extension of the concept of embeddedness is that it tends to run together static measures of tie strength and of dependence on resources passed along particular ties with dynamic concepts of the irreversibilities of path dependence.

A problem with path dependence models is that they privilege positive feedback over negative feedback in ways that, while they may be plausible for periods of what might be called, following Kuhn (1970 [1962]), the 'normal science' of inter-organisational relationships (for example, those where the reinforcement dynamics are more heavily influenced by stable task environment and technological lock-in than by other variables), do not envisage important cases of negative feedback (which ultimately occasion Kuhn's scientific revolutions). There are many documented cases of significant change toward more hierarchical or more enclaved (and even on occasions to more isolate forms) of networks after protracted periods of individualistic formation (e.g. Madhavan *et al.*, 1998). Sometimes these are the result of major technological change, but in other cases other factors are more important. In general, however, a theory cannot be convincing which privileges only one of the two basic kinds of feedback system – and its effects – to the exclusion of the other (Jervis, 1997).

The neo-Durkheimian cybernetic theory of network dynamics

The four elementary types of institutions presented in Table 4.1 above are substantial social forms that recur in every social system. The cells in the matrix neither simply describe a continuously differentiable space in which to locate institutions (contrary to Gross and Rayner, 1985) nor yet locate four ideal types (convenient heuristic devices only used mainly for typological taxonomy) but identify four types of real and rivalrous institutional pressure which operate like 'attractors' in non-linear dynamic theory (cf. Kauffman, 1995). In Durkheimian (1984 [1893]) terms, each type is a '*solidarity*', that is, an institutional form of social organisation with a distinct style underpinning many empirical institutions; more specifically, each of these is a 'mechanical solidarity' because each type presses people to be accountable in ways that are internally similar to each other. The theory is *scale-invariant*; the same basic institutional forms will emerge in all units of social organisation from the largest multiples to the smallest dyads and triads.

A key thesis is that of *conflictual interdependence.*

H6: *Each of these four forms arises and asserts itself in reaction to any of the others; in some measure, therefore, all will be present in all but the smallest units of social organisation, however attenuated one of them may be in any particular case.*

The effect of this is that:

H7: *The interactions of these four solidarities will produce a nonlinear disequilibrium system* (Thompson M, 1982a,b, 1992, 1996).

There is no guarantee that, when a enclave revolts in frustration against hierarchical or individualistic institutions or when entrepreneurs begin to use the informal market to undermine a failing over-regulated order, the reaction will be a proportionate one. Quite possibly, the social system will lurch from one extreme to another, and settlements cannot be guaranteed to be indefinitely stable.

This might be thought to present a problem for the theory of institutional viability. For, in the very nature of a disequilibrium system, it is difficult to achieve viability for any one element as it may be buffeted at any time by the forces producing the disequilibrium. The only solution is to look for some process that might moderate the violence of the oscillations and therefore the incoherence of the system, without ever hoping to check or eradicate or postpone the operation of the disequilibrium dynamics. On this account, institutional crafting is understood as the task of seeking to limit incoherence.[1] The neo-Durkheimian theory draws on systems theory to understand the possibilities for dynamic change. Following classical cybernetic theory, social systems theorists distinguish between two kinds of basic force; namely, those of positive and of negative feedback dynamics (e.g. Deutsch, 1963: 182–199; Jervis, 1997; Baumgartner and Jones, 2002).[2]

Positive feedback is the process by which a phenomenon is able to access resources and energy to reinforce its own characteristics. Management literature is replete with hopeful examples of benign positive feedback, in the form of virtuous cycles. For example, there is much discussion of the cycle by which once people trust each other they can work together to their mutual profit and so further reinforce their trust (e.g. Kramer and Tyler, 1996). Senge (1990) applied Beer's (e.g. 1966) organisation systems theory to argue that processes of organisational learning could be self-reinforcing. The process by which organisations with a bureaucratic bias become ever more hidebound by proliferating rules and procedures – what Weber (1978 [1922]) called the advent of the 'iron cage' and Durkheim (1984 [1893]) illustrated in his brief analysis of Byzantine imperial state bureaucracy – is a well-known example of unwelcome positive feedback. Sometimes, positive feedback can be neutral; Arthur's (1994) model of path dependence in technology is a case in which a certain technology having been adopted by a sufficient critical mass becomes a standard and people adapt all sorts of other systems to work with it. The costs for anyone choosing another technology become impossibly high, so reinforcing the commitment to that technology, even if a technically superior one were available. The most famous example is the QWERTY keyboard (David, 1985). What is now the almost ubiquitous keyboard design in the Anglophone world was originally introduced not because it was the most efficient; indeed, it was said to have been introduced to slow down typists who were hitting keys faster than manual typewriters could respond, causing logjams of keys. In the early years of typewriter development, several keyboards were available in competition. However, once a sufficient critical mass of users had bought and installed QWERTY machines, companies were committed to the design, operators had to learn to use it and the technology began to be self-reinforcing.

In other cases, though, positive feedback takes the form of a vicious cycle, in which an entity in a social system reinforces itself to the point either of undermining itself or else of causing wider disorganisation. The canonical studies of the failures of socialist economies suggest that the system of state regulation in the absence of genuine prices proved to be just such a phenomenon (Kornai, 1992). Wilson's (1996) argument that US inner city ghettos suffer as the ablest leave because those left behind are deprived of social ties to aspiring, honest, successful people is another case. In each of these cases, in positive feedback, a phenomenon *radicalises* itself by reinforcement, and, in the vicious cases, this radicalisation is the source of destructive influence.

One of the critical mechanisms by which positive feedback does its work is in the socialisation of individuals and in the moulding of preferences. Under the institutional conditions of, for example, individualism or hierarchy, it steadily becomes more difficult for people to appreciate the force of other ideas, or, as positive feedback proceeds, even to understand other ways of organising. As a consequence, they develop thought styles (Douglas, 1986, 1982a, 1996) and emotional styles (6, 2003a) which are appropriate to the logic of those institutions (March and Olsen, 1989). The steady reinforcement of styles of cognition, affect and conation provides part of the microfoundations for the endogenous generation of institutional expectations, preferences and interests.[3]

By contrast, negative feedback is the phenomenon of resistance by one institutional force against others. For example, loose and voluntarily coordinated individualistic networks coalesce into more formal structures and develop hierarchical forms precisely because people feel frustrated with the particularism and lack of control over resources that such individualistic structures afford. Yet conversely, as formal roles are introduced in the creation of explicit partnerships, very often individualistic and particularistic networks re-emerge to get around the rigidities of the formal institutions. Resistance may take the form of element A being curbed or checked by element B, as when a regulatory body provides a longstop source of correction, for example, to the tendency of some employers to cut occupational health and safety provision in order to compete on price. Homeostatic processes in politics and regulation are of this kind, such as the Bank of England's corrective adjustment of interest rates in response to indications of future inflation or the decisions of national governments to allocate special funds to regions hit by severe economic problems (Baumgartner and Jones, 2002). Alternatively, the resistance may be overwhelming, as when over-regulation begins to drive up business costs to the point of threatening companies' ability to compete. In other situations, the effect of resistance is to produce gridlock, as when the two major parties in Congress are evenly matched and each can effectively veto each other's budget proposals but neither can effectively secure the passage of a coherent, reasonably balanced budget (Wildavsky and Caiden, 2001). Another important form of negative feedback is the 'backlash of the repressed', which is evident in many cases of protest and revolt. In extreme cases, negative feedback can lead to general undermining of systems, as in the case of deep social and political polarisation that produces civil war and undermines many of the possibilities of reconciliation (e.g. Richards, 1996). Negative feedback thus provides the other part of the micro-foundations by which institutions endogeneously generate preferences, but here (to adapt March and Olsen's 1989 terminology) by logics of inappropriateness rather than appropriateness.[4]

In the neo-Durkheimian model, each of these particular cases exemplifies positive and negative feedback dynamics which stem from the underlying solidarities. Solidarities as institutions tend to reinforce themselves and come into conflict in ways that structure particular empirical processes of historical change. Either uncontrolled positive feedback or uncontrolled negative feedback – that is, either phenomenon untempered by the presence of the other – is likely sooner or later to turn vicious and destructive. Either can be sources of institutional failure, that is, erosion of viability.

Positive feedback dynamics by the four solidarities posited in the neo-Durkheimian theory of institutional forms are represented in Figure 4.3, while Figure 4.4 shows the general structure of negative feedback between them. Clearly, the relative strengths of the forces indicated by the arrows will vary according to the case, the history of the disequilibrium dynamic and the forces to which each is most recently reacting. Positive and negative feedback processes are ultimately derived from the same underlying dynamic of institutional self-assertion in reaction against the assertion of other institutions. Uncontrolled positive feedback results when, having been provoked into assertion by another institutional solidarity, no subsequent resistance is encountered. Negative feedback is the consequence of that encounter.

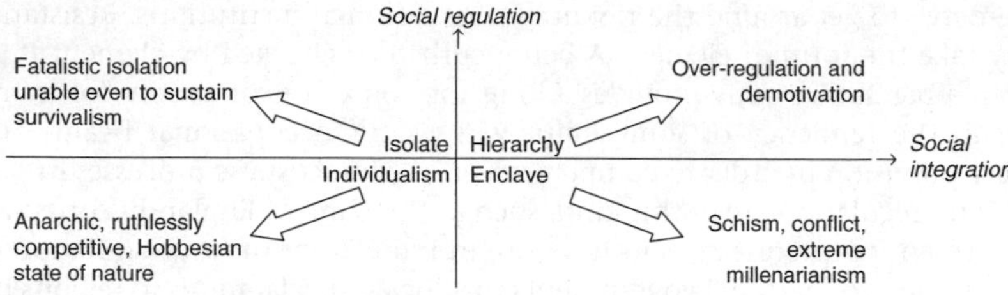

Figure 4.3 The positive feedback dynamics of the four solidarities.

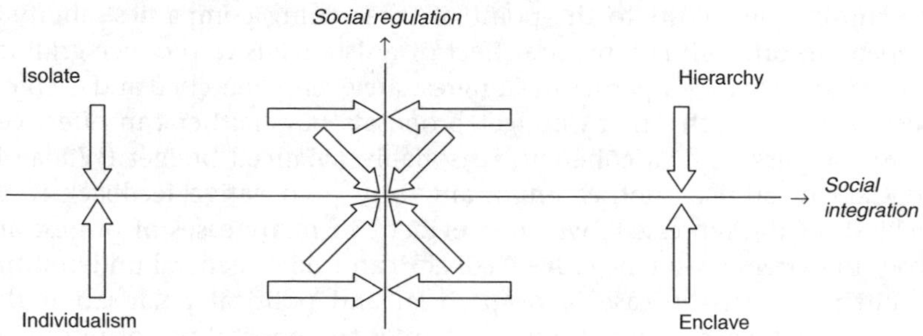

Figure 4.4 Negative feedback between the four solidarities.

Wildavsky (1998) described the dynamic of positive feedback and self-radicalisation within each solidarity as 'curvilinear' with respect to the dimension running from social organisation to social disorganisation. What curvilinearity means is, intuitively, than (a) a little of any form of organisation is beneficial but an excess will lead to disorganisation; but (b) there is not a simple linear transition from one state to the other; but rather there is a notional point at which the trajectory reaches a cusp or a tipping point. Before that tipping point, curvilinearity implies, the net pull of the moderate form could still be greater than the net pull of the end state of disorganisation. That is to say, in moderation, and balanced by the other institutional forms, each form of organisation can stabilise itself. In absence of those conditions, it may go to extremes and eventually disorganise both itself and the wider social system. The cusp is the point at which the positive feedback dynamic shifts from gradual to sudden change, and follows the 'catastrophe theory' form of social change (Thompson M, 1979, 1982, apply the ideas of René Thom to the relationships between forms of social organisation; see also Thompson M, 1992, 1996). Durkheim's two most famous books were devoted to showing that, from different forms of social organisation, this self-reinforcing dynamic could produce quite different sorts of severe ill-being; in particular, suicide (1951 [1897]) and disorganised divisions of labour (1984 [1893]). Both are expressions of strong incoherence of institutions.

Strengths and weaknesses, ways of failing

Structure materially affects strengths and weaknesses in performance in the context of the single organisation (Mintzberg, 1983). That structure affects performance in the context of inter-organisational relations is also generally accepted, but the exact nature and extent of the influence are more difficult to trace. Partly this is due to the limited quantity of research and also the continuing lack of stability in the taxonomies of inter-organisational forms.

Another part of the problem, though, is that different sorts of structures tend to produce better performance in some areas of organisational activity and work, at the expense of worse performance in others. Performance here can be understood broadly as allocative, productive and dynamic efficiency, including the minimisation of transaction costs and subsuming innovation. In these regards, however, all good things do not go together (on dilemmas, conflicts and trade-offs in public management, see Pollitt and Bouckaert, 2000; Hood, 1976).

Before thinking about network performance, consider the case of the specialist agency dedicated to the carrying out of a single task, defined by input or activity, which was widely adopted in the 1980s in the United Kingdom and elsewhere; this was, for example, the model that underpinned the design of the Next Steps agencies (Greer, 1994; Pollitt, 2004). That these agencies were able to achieve greater productive efficiency in the carrying out of their core tasks is widely accepted (see e.g. the review of studies by Pollitt and Bouckaert, 2000: 165). On the other hand, the literature also suggests that these approaches have performed less well on those measures of allocative efficiency, for example, that relate to effective co-ordination with other agencies and services (e.g. Webb, 1991; Richards *et al.*, 1999). Turning from the structure of a single organisation to problems of inter-organisational structure, Provan and Milward (1995; Milward and Provan, 2001) found that a highly structured, integrated and regulated network form in mental health services seemed to be effective in controlling transaction costs of purchasing, contracting and compliance, but many studies of structures that seem to conduce to dynamic efficiency or innovative capacity suggest that such tight regulation and integration is often not the best choice for that goal (e.g. Powell *et al.*, 1996).

What is needed is a richer way of understanding the particular sorts of trade-offs that each type of network faces. We begin this search by examining what is known from recent empirical research about 'network failure'.

Risks and failure

All organisational and inter-organisational arrangements fail, sometimes in different ways and sometimes in much the same way. 'Failure' here denotes several quite distinct phenomena. Failure can mean inadequacy of activity or unwanted activity or unwanted patterns of distribution of goods and services. For example, there is an extensive economic literature on market failure, focusing on such things as the under-provision of high quality public goods because it is difficult to create incentives where access cannot be controlled and charged separately. In practice, many cases of market failure arise from features of inter-organisational relations. For example, where there is under-provision of investment in infrastructure or training by purely commercial entities, this is often due to the highly competitive structure of markets; in some oligopolistic industries, in contrast, such as oil extraction and pharmaceuticals, the inadequacies in commercial investment infrastructure and training are much less significant. Equally, 'government failure' and 'voluntary failure' in the legal and economics literature tend to be cases of inadequate or unwanted activity (Salamon, 1987; Wolf, 1988). That is to say, failure in this sense is measured by public policy concerns about nil or negative impacts on the general public; for this reason, it will be referred to as 'public failure'.

There can also be 'network failure', and each of the kinds of networks identified in this book can exhibit different types of public failure. For example, enclaved networks can be very exclusive and particularistic (cf. Salamon's 1987 account of particularism as a vice of voluntary organisations both separately and collectively). Individualistic networks can exhibit typical symptoms of market failure, and so on. That is to say, essentially the same factors are found to be at work in inter-organisational networks of each kind in explaining public failure as are found to be at work in explaining public failure in single organisation settings.

Failure can also mean simply the perceived unsatisfactory nature of an arrangement – whether the creation of a single organisation or of an inter-organisational structure – to the parties involved, leading to its dissolution prior to their originally expected target date for termination; this can be described as 'private failure'. The literature on strategic networks is full of anecdotal discussions of such private failures (Kogut, 1989; Anderson, 1990; Reuer and Koza, 2000), although it is often difficult empirically to tell terminations on satisfactory completion of task from terminations on recognition of failure (Anderson, 1990), not least because firms have reasons to represent their management as more successful than in fact it may be (Gulati, 1998). Some studies suggest that failure rates for strategic partnerships are higher than failure rates for single firms (Bleeke and Ernst, 1991; Das and Teng, 2000), although these are not based on quantitative analysis of large or representative samples.

There is a large literature on reasons for failure, identifying all the factors that one would intuitively expect to matter – for example, inappropriate selection of partners, mismanaged evolution or response to shocks, lack of capacity, selfish strategic behaviour, inadequate planning, misaligned incentives, incompatible cultures, decisional overreach and excessive ambition and others (see e.g. Doz and Hamel, 1998). Ahern (1993) discusses a case where the advantages of a strategic alliance were not symmetrically appropriated by the members, leading to a worse outcome for one, and raising the possibility of earlier termination than originally planned. Kogut (1989) analyses the 'stability' of strategic alliances in terms of such risks of asymmetric benefits and risks and the possibility of selfish strategic behaviour leading to collapses of trust. Indeed, whole theoretical arguments have been developed in the transaction cost and resource-based traditions to explain private failures of these types (see e.g. Tallman, 2000; Reuer and Koza, 2000).

Most of the factors that explain private failures in inter-organisational relationship structures are structurally very similar to those which are used to explain failures in single organisations. For, when single firms fail, problems of poor information flow, misaligned incentives, overreach, lack of continuity in boundary-spanning personnel are among the key factors that are typically cited (see the studies in Anheier, 1999). There is, however, no general and comprehensive theory of all the factors that might lead to organisational and inter-organisational private failure; the range of relevant contingencies is simply too large, and in any case, perceptions of what counts as private failure can differ widely between different stakeholders, relative to their expectations (Anheier, 1999). Gulati (1998: 306) describes the management literature which seeks to identify the principal causes of private failure – and the kinds of thing that might protect against these factors – as driven by a quest for a 'magic formula' but actually yielding little more than 'wish lists'.

However, some order can be introduced into potentially shapeless lists of factors by distinguishing a number of distinct clusters. At a first cut, we can distinguish between external factors and internal ones. External factors that can create risks of private failure include unanticipatable shocks such as changes in the environment that are beyond the control of the partner organisations and to which any organisational arrangement would be expected to have some difficulty in adapting. Internal factors can be divided further into factors to do with the individual organisations in the network and factors arising from the nature of the arrangement between them. Typically, these must interact before they can represent a significant threat to the stability of the inter-organisational arrangement. Consider the case, for example, of selfish strategic behaviour by one of the parties to the arrangement. This would only be a serious threat to the inter-organisational structure if the incentives, controls, intelligence-gathering and behaviour-revealing institutions put in place by the strategic alliance were insufficient either to deter or discipline such behaviour or to enable automatic adjustment to it. In the same way, a mismatch between the cultures of the organisations, of the kind stressed by Doz and Hamel (1998), only matters if the cultural mediation systems put in place – or *not* put in place – by the alliance are too feeble to broker understanding and adaptation (see Peck *et al.*, 2001). For example, Mohr and Spekman (1994), in a study on the characteristics that make for success in partnerships, identify conflict management institutions in the network system as one of the most important elements.

Types of failure by network type

Each of the institutional types of network identified in Figure 4.1 is associated with particular trajectories of disorganisation which can lead to both public and private failure. These dysfunctions are produced, the neo-Durkheimian cybernetic theory suggests, by positive feedback dynamics, or self-reinforcement, which produces radicalisation, in which people continue to follow the prevailing institutions. The result may be either public failure – in which the network continues but performs poorly in what Seibel (1989) calls 'mellow weakness' or 'successful failure' (1999) and which Meyer and Zucker (1989) call 'permanently failing organisation' – or else private failure, in which the arrangement is abandoned. Table 4.6 contrasts the key strengths of each type of network with the main kinds of failure to which it is peculiarly vulnerable (see e.g. Thompson *et al.*, 1990; Chai and Wildavsky, 1994; Mars, 1994 [1982]; Coyle, 1997).

Isolate networks fail when short-term coping and opportunistic behaviour combine with too casual a pattern of commitments to effectively undermine trust to the point that ties cannot be sustained. Isolate networks are, in any case, close to the most minimal form of organisation. Their activists raise so few and such limited expectations among their fellow 'members' that one could either say that, by the standards of the other forms, they almost represent the form that the failure of those other forms might take. Alternatively, one might say that so little networking is attempted that it is hardly appropriate to speak of success or failure at all. The irony of the isolate situation is that both representations are equally accurate.

Hierarchical networks fail by eroding the very trust that hierarchy is supposed to sustain through its system of rule and role when the process of positive feedback results in baroque, even Byzantine, systems of rules defining membership rights and obligations and systems of decision-making.

Individualistic networks fail when too ruthless strategic exploitation by the stronger of the weaker parties leads to the erosion of trust to the point that the weaker begin to demand protection from the risks to which the power-based networking order exposes them.

Enclave networks tend to fail when they exhaust the motivation of their members, when their reliance upon principle leads to schism over rival interpretation of principles or when rivalry between members focuses on claims by or for individual members that they are more deeply committed to those principles than others. Such networks can be unstable due to insufficient institutionalisation (such as shared resources). Such networks have great value, nonetheless, in creating and developing 'bottom-up' legitimacy and trust between individuals, professionals and organisations to the sharing of information, ideas and strategies and to new ways of working.

Table 4.6 Types of failure to which each type of network is peculiarly prone

Social regulation ↑

Isolate *Strengths*: Enables valuable coping behaviour and survival during adversity, prevents excessive aspiration during periods when this might be destructive *Type of failure*: Limited ability to sustain collective action or tackle complex problems, chronic mistrust, inability to innovate; instability due to simultaneous over- and under-institutionalisation	**Hierarchy** *Strengths*: Enables clarity and complex divisions of labour *Type of failure*: over-regulation and low productivity, limited ability to generate prosperity; gridlock due to baroque procedures; the system of rule and role can become so Byzantine as to be illegible; risks demotivation of the 'lowerarchy' through denial of access to superior authority and denial of sufficient validation; instability due to over-institutionalisation
Individualism *Strengths*: Unleashes powerful motivations of aspirant self-interest, enables focused instrumental activity *Type of failure*: zero-sum competition, instability due to insufficient institutionalisation, high transaction costs esp. in defining and enforcing property rights, severe conflict between powerful individuals, demotivation of weaker groups through insecurity	**Enclave** *Strengths*: Empowers passionate principled commitment and supports integrity, unleashes powerful motivations of protection *Type of failure*: demotivation through exhaustion and burn-out; schism, feud; instability due to insufficient institutionalisation, inability to sustain negotiation with outsiders due to inability to support effective authority internally, poor productivity due to greater emphasis on distributional than productive values

→ *Social integration*

Table 4.6 summarises these differences.

The idea of 'surprises' provides a way to think about what is likely to occur when the peculiar types of failures associated with each style of network organisation begin to set in, especially when these are not anticipated because some members of the network have local organisational styles that do not match the institutional style of the network-wide institutions. Thompson *et al.* (1990) define this situation as one of 'surprise', because the mismatch creates conditions in which the deformations which emerge are ones for which people in local organisational conditions have peculiar blinkers, but where certain kinds of information become palpable even to those with these specified blinkers. Applying the Thompson *et al.* (1990) approach – originally developed for environmental policy conditions – to the situation of network management, we would derive the following taxonomy of types of surprises in private failures of inter-organisational networks (Table 4.7).

Following each type of 'surprise', organisations may be able to act to try to reshape their networks in the light of the information that events have made

Table 4.7 Types of *'surprise'* in network private failure

	Isolate	Enclave	Individualism	Hierarchy
Either network institutions or other members of the network turn out to be ... *Networks are institutionally presumed or assumed to be ...*	*Capricious, short term, casual*	*Factional, schismatic, focused on principle at the expense of either benefit or legitimacy*	*Short-term, opportunistic, focused on benefit at the expense of either principle or legitimacy*	*Rule-bound, pernickety, procedurally baroque, focused on legitimacy at the expense of benefit or principle*
Isolate: Based on *individual, opportunistic coping*		Predict: isolates will peel off, leaving core(s) of enclaves	Predict: Individualists will exploit isolates	Predict: Hierarchy will seek to contain isolates at periphery
Enclave: *Based on equal voluntary commitment of all and only members to each other collectively*			Predict: Enclaves will reject individualists; some may occupy precarious brokerage positions between enclaves	Predict: enclaves will revolt against hierarchical system
Individualism: *Based on sequences of voluntary bilateral transactions between*				Predict: Hierarchy will seek either to co-opt individualists into central positions or else to use as boundary spanners; individualists will exploit position within hierarchy through informal networks
Hierarchy: *Based on regulation of status, role and systems of explicit rules*				

available, even given their initial biases. It is at these points in the dynamics of inter-organisational relations that the use of the available organisational development tools is most likely to be important in managing risks and failures (see Peck *et al.*, 2004).

Toward synthesis

If each of the factors and each of the theories discussed in the first three chapters of this book is capturing something of importance then network forms of inter-organisational relationships are the result of rather complex causal processes. However, from the analysis of network principles using the neo-Durkheimian interpretation, it is possible to identify a range of different network 'types' and to summarise the key characteristics, strengths and weaknesses of them (see Table 4.6); that is to achieve a synthesis of these important insights; that is, it may be possible to introduce some order into the complexity. Whereas previously, the neo-Durkheimian taxonomy was used as a heuristic device and the focus was on statics, in this part of the argument, where the focus has been dynamics, it has been suggested that the neo-Durkheimian institutional approach can be asked to do more work than just this. It can provide a way of mapping the kinds of conditions – encompassing many of the variables identified by other scholars – to which different styles of interorganisational relations appear as intelligent (although not necessarily optimal or efficient) responses.

It has also been argued that, far from the choices of forms being between 'markets, hierarchies and networks', the same types of factors work to determine the form of relations between organisations, within organisations and the choice between single or multi-organisational solutions. In this way, it becomes possible to integrate the transaction costs model of institutional choice into a larger framework. The variables reviewed here – power, costs, rationalities of agency, task environment and technology, information, expectations – are neither unrelated nor randomly related to each other, nor yet in any simple sense equally influencing each other in a dense but symmetric ring; rather they influence each other in more or less intelligible ways. The task of the final part of this chapter is to bring together these key influences into a more comprehensible model.

Each of the principal theories of how network forms are shaped clearly has some merit, but it is equally evident that none is complete. None of the variables posited to be important is irrelevant; equally, theories claiming that only a single type of variable is sufficient to account for the character and forms of inter-organisational relations appear to be invalidly reductionist.

The neo-Durkheimian institutional approach overcomes many of the limitations of the other theories. Unlike conventional transaction cost theory, it does not imply that history is always efficient; it can account for different people's patterns of perception and weighting of transaction costs. It allows both for defensive behaviour, especially but not exclusively in enclaves, and for the kind of entrepreneurial behaviour predicted by some resource-based accounts, especially but not exclusively in individualistic settings. Yet it also integrates the insight of Williamson and Ouchi, that transaction cost conditions do shape the menus of choices of network forms available and perceived to be available. The current theory avoids any romanticising about what gets learned, or its merits, in each setting, and in particular avoids making unwarranted claims for the egalitarian character of communities of practice to share knowledge. Like the personalistic views, the theory particularly emphasises the role of individuals in social networks between organisations, acting in those individualistic niches between enclaved or hierarchical cliques. However, it avoids implausible reductions of institutional influences to individual level factors. By contrast with 'new' institutionalist accounts, the theory encompasses both positive and negative feedback dynamics. Building upon the work of transaction cost, task environment and other contingency theories, the neo-Durkheimian account provides an integrated account of the conditions under which institutional forms can be expected to emerge, but it specifically avoids the weakness of many contingency theories of inferring that the institutions are always rational solutions to problems presented by current conditions. The theory specifically provides for historical change, but without any implausible historicist periodisation of network forms. Unlike ANT, which turns networks into a fetish, it offers clear causal processes.

Broadly, when developing syntheses of theories that seek to avoid invalid reductionism, there is a limited range of approaches one can take. One approach, favoured, for example, by Thompson M (2003), is to identify the 'minimum set' or an (ideally, unique) subset of at least two of the available theories from which one can generate a complete set of all the interactions. However, this requires that all the interactions predicted by all the theories can be fully specified, and it has not proven possible to do this fully with ten clusters of theories. In any case, reconciling that many theories in that manner would only result in a comprehensive set of double-headed arrows, visually arresting no doubt if yielding nothing of interest; rather we need to know which connections, any proposed synthesis claims, are most important for most cases of inter-organisational relations.

The main alternative approach to developing an anti-reductionist compromise is therefore to make the heuristic assumption that the key variables will be treated as being at least partly endogenous. However, it must be emphasised that this is a commitment made only for the present purposes in understanding inter-organisational relations. The next stage is to proceed to try to fill in some of the principal directions of causation between the range of variables posited by the main theories, without seeking to be complete.

Figure 4.5 sets out one plausible result of applying this method using the materials generated so far. The figure shows a simplified model, with a general category of feedback loop between, on the one hand, the basic determining variables and, on the other hand, both the balance of static forms and the dynamics of their interaction. In order for this to be possible, it is necessary to specify two 'periods' (not necessarily literally distinguishable chronologically), one in which the basic causal variables derived from the main theories are taken to be active and a second in which the dynamics they produce are played out in order to shape the conditions for those same variables to determine forms and dynamics in subsequent periods. Before

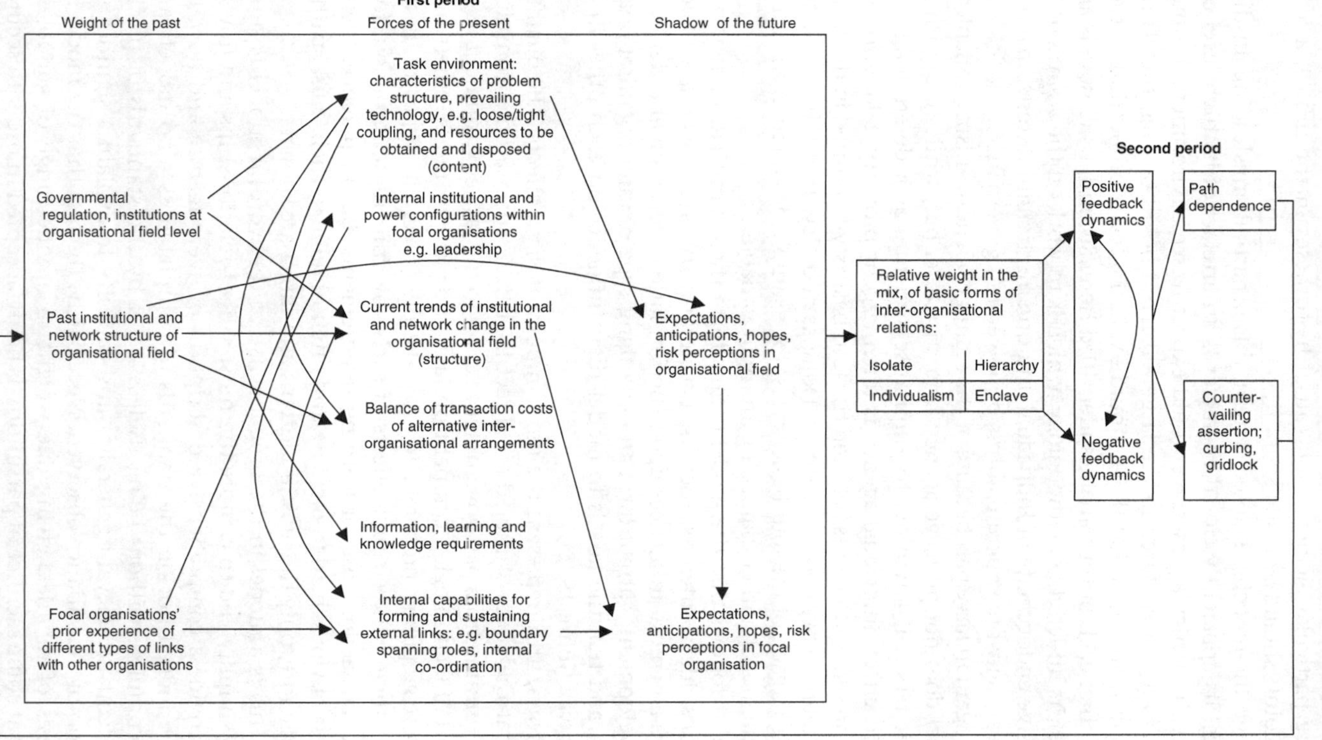

Figure 4.5 The determinants of network forms and dynamics: a simplified model.

discussing particular elements and causal hypotheses in the model, a few general points should be made about it.

Although the model is a closed system, this is partially misleading. In the first place, its apparently closed character is an artefact of its high level of generality. In particular cases, we would expect to see environmental influences that are not captured in the large left hand box; however, the claim behind the synthesis is that these should explain a lesser proportion of the variance than each of the variables identified here. Second, its closure is an artefact of its underlying methodology, which is to work on the assumption of extensive endogeneity of individual and organisational interests, institutions, ideas, network structure, forms of power and governance.

Third, again in large part because of the strategy of endogenising variables, the model does not privilege agency over structure, but, while recognising agency, it tends, if anything, to emphasise structure as a determinant of agency. In effect, individual agency is an emergent property, taking forms which represent settlements between the four basic styles posited in the neo-Durkheimian theory (Douglas, 1982c; Douglas and Ney, 1998). In the same way, trust in each of the four basic styles, for example, is an emergent variable of the model, rather than being an input variable.

Fourth, it follows that the model begins from the claim that, in general, institutions, ideas, interests, social structure and styles of governance and power are all crucial influences upon the formation, development, destruction, development, current form and changing type of inter-organisational relations, and that the task is to model their influence on each other in a dynamic way (John, 1998).

The arrows, fifth, represent the most important *direct* effects. The qualification that the effects captured are direct is critical. For example, consider the lines running from past government action to the task environment (e.g. regulation of technologies, competition law) and current trends in network structure (e.g. public procurement, mandation of certain types of ties). Certainly, there will be subtle effects of such government action upon, for instance, transaction costs or learning requirements, but in practice, these will be less obvious, hard to measure and often oblique in their causal pathways. Therefore, only the most important and direct are shown.

Sixth, this is a model in the proper sense of the word. A model is supposed to simplify and to capture the most salient relationships and flows, not to provide a comprehensive description of every feature and flow. It should be judged not on the standards of completeness – no model can ever be complete without being useless – but by the standards of parsimony, adequacy, relevant generality and capacity to explain a significant proportion of the variance observed. Necessarily, the fact that the model is a synthesis of theories, giving due weight to a wide range of variables, means that some sacrifice of parsimony is being accepted in order to secure greater generality.

The underlying theses that the model represented in Figure 4.5 seeks to capture are the following:

1. Network forms represent influences that exhibit both 'weight of the past' and 'shadow of the future' effects, in the form of inheritance leading to constraints from the past and expectation, aspiration and fear for the future (H4, H5).
2. In general, the more readily measurable and 'material' the nature of a given input variable, the more likely it will be that its most important causal effects will be upon other variables of a similarly 'material' (or otherwise) character. Thus, the system-critical effects of regulation upon task environments are likely to be greater than those of regulation by more oblique routes, for example, upon expectations.
3. Both cost- and risk-minimisation on the one hand and the pursuit of benefits (including competencies and learning) on the other are both variables that are likely to be of great importance.
4. Each of the four basic solidarities is likely to produce positive feedback dynamics or self-reinforcement, at the next stage but at some point each of these will tend to disorganisation, thus opening the space for others (H6, H7).
5. Moreover, each solidarity is provoked by the assertion of the others, producing negative feedback (H6).
6. Settlements between these competing types of pressures are those that determine the character of the input variables in the next (i.e. the third) period (H7).

In the particular flows identified, the model therefore provides embeddedness theorists with the path dependence they require, including the effect of previous network structure. However, it denies their claim that positive feedback dynamics will generally trump negative feedback ones; it is quite common that certain styles of inter-organisational relationship prove too individualistic or too enclaved or too hierarchical for some people who cleave to other institutions. Again, the model grants institutionalists much of what they want, because it specifically acknowledges both the regulatory role of formal institutions and the informal structuring role of local institutions within the network environment and within the focal organisations. For contingency theorists, there is a clear recognition of the importance of the task environment. Transaction costs and competence theories too are given a clear role. Cognitivists, concerned about culture in shaping networks, are recognised in the shaping role of expectations.

It has to be acknowledged, of course, that the model has not been tested empirically using quantitative data. Indeed, it would be a tall demand of a quantitative data set that it would be rich enough to supply sufficient information on all these kinds of variables on a sufficiently large sample to enable it to be tested in any conventional way. However, it does capture many of the central arguments of the main theories reviewed. It also accommodates some of the criticisms offered of their limitations. These two facts provide some preliminary and indirect indication of its plausibility. In the empirical chapters of this book, we begin to explore the theory using existing literature as data.

5
Trust between Organisations

Trust and trustworthiness have long been regarded as essential characteristics of inter-organisational networks. Indeed, it is commonplace within the social sciences for trust between organisations to be regarded as a positive attribute in alliances, partnerships, networks, and joint ventures. Trust, it is argued, helps to manage uncertainty (Glückler and Armbrüster, 2003); make co-operation easier (Doucette and Wiederholt, 1997); enable organisational learning (Ingham and Mothe, 1998); sustain accountability (Tomkins, 2001); encourage effective joint project management (Holt *et al.*, 2000); secure commitment between parties (Geyskens *et al.*, 1996) including those who have very different degrees of power (e.g. Kim, 2000); and support industrial districts (Sabel, 1992; Boschma and Lambooy, 2001) and economic development in developing countries (Murphy, 2003). Unsurprisingly, the crucial importance of trust has seeped into the literature aimed at managers involved in partnership (e.g. Greig and Poxton, 2001). Perhaps more surprisingly, most of these propositions about the general benefits of trust were already well known to social scientists more than 30 years ago (see Akerlof, 1970; Arrow, 1974; Fox, 1976; Barber, 1983; and Zucker, 1986).

At the same time, trust is regarded as not straightforward to achieve, especially where the weight of past betrayals hangs heavy (Rothstein, 2000). However, trust is also made possible precisely because of the legacy of the past (Putnam with Leonardi and Nanetti, 1993; Fisman and Khanna, 1999). Trust is especially challenging to develop between peers by comparison with upstream suppliers and downstream customers (Rindfleisch, 2000), is more difficult to cultivate in some countries than others (Dahlstrom and Nygaard, 1995; Fukuyama, 1995) and is most challenging to sustain in periods of social upheaval (Sztompka, 1999). As with the benefits, the problems of achieving trust between organisations were documented for the public sector many years ago by Challis *et al.* (1988), for the private sector by Williamson (1975) and for organisations generally by Thompson JD (1967).

However, although these studies represent an extensive body of work on the beneficial consequences of, and obstacles to, creating trust, they are hardly satisfactory. For, even when there is convergence on definitions of what is meant by trust, most commentators take trust to be something that is best treated in a series of levels or degrees. The literature does not adequately connect suggested determinants of trust with the wider institutional (and, for our purposes, network) structural forces that sustain different formations of trust. For all this recent work, we still lack a synthesis of the writings on the understanding of trust with the theories of the dynamic processes by which inter-organisational interactions work.

As we have indicated earlier, there is a vast literature on inter-organisational trust and this chapter cannot hope to do descriptive justice to it all, as well as offering a distinctive interpretation and application of the literature. Therefore, the aims of the chapter are: to introduce some clarity about the definitions and types of trust; to distinguish the main bodies of theory; and then to present an account of how different forms of inter-organisational trust can emerge (and be undermined) in different institutional and network settings. The focus of the chapter is not on questions about the consequences of trust – whether benign or malign – but on its roots and determinants. Part of the argument will be critical of some of the earlier literature, showing, for instance, that it is facile to claim, as some leading writers did at the turn of the 1980s and 1990s, that networks are uniquely trust-enhancing; this view suggests that networks are a single category, trust a single phenomenon and both unambiguously good. The argument will be devoted primarily to demonstrating the positive case that trust of different kinds can be found in all the main institutional contexts for inter-organisational relations and that understanding the roots of these differences will assist in assessing the strengths, weaknesses and scope for intervention to influence each of them.

The next section introduces the basic concepts of trust and trustworthiness. The following sections then show how the two main strands of theory of inter-organisational trust have offered contrasting definitions of the concept, rooted in divergent epistemologies. It then suggests that, in recent years, a more catholic approach to epistemology has allowed the emergence, not of a synthesis exactly, but of a willingness to recognise the merits of both of these theoretical approaches in identifying divergent empirical types. A short section follows which refutes the claim that there is something special about networks; that they alone elicit and cultivate trust between organisations. Then, the substantive argument of the chapter takes up the whole of the second half, in which each of the basic types of institutional setting and network structure are shown to generate distinct patterns of trust between organisations. Finally, a short section takes the argument on from the static comparison of forms to a consideration of dynamics.

Trust and trustworthiness: basic ideas and importance

The literature on trust and trustworthiness in inter-organisational relations spans many disciplines and several decades. Major works on the subject – still cited today – were written in the early 1960s and some traditions even have their roots in human relations approaches developed in the 1940s and 1950s. Detailed definitions of our key terms can be postponed to the next section because they are contested between theoretical and empirical traditions. However, even without settling upon exact definitions, it is important to distinguish between trust and trustworthiness for their roles are quite different (Hardin, 2000).

At this stage, it will suffice to characterise these concepts quite generally. It is helpful to think in terms of principal–agent relations (Jensen and Meckling, 1976; Fama, 1980). In a transaction, we can distinguish two actors (individuals or organisations), one of whom (or which) puts significant resources at risk, initiates a transaction and requires a service, and one who puts fewer resources at risk, responds to the initiation and provides services (in special cases of reciprocal relations, both parties play both roles). Even contextually, profound forms of trust cannot be explained without reference to some kind of agency model, even if one which allows for richer contextual specification than conventional institutional economics approaches would (Sztompka, 1999).

Understood in these terms, trust is the attitude or strategy of a principal who or which must assess (among others things to be discussed later) the reliability of an agent, and to speak of trustworthiness as to do with the characteristics of an agent that make for reliability. Of course, principals can, and often do, make wrong judgements about agents, so that perceived or subjective and actual or objective trustworthiness can diverge sharply.

Trustworthiness

Trustworthiness is best thought of as task-specific (or at least role-specific where roles might encompass a range of tasks). For example, we might trust our GP for advice on in-growing toe nails but not to perform any surgery that same toe nail might require, and certainly not for financial advice about pension arrangements. In the same way, organisations are typically trustworthy to others, for example, in the provision of some goods and services but not others.[1]

That trustworthiness is important for the possibility of co-operative relations is hardly news. For when people are routinely untrustworthy, social organisation cannot be sustained; Turnbull's famous (1972) anthropological study of the Ik, a tribe in rural Uganda as they were in the 1960s, shows how dramatic can be the consequences of the erosion of trustworthiness among significant proportions of populations (briefly, Turnbull found that institutions for the cultivation of trustworthiness had all but wholly eroded among the Ik, with disastrous consequences for familial commitment, moral behaviour, trust between friends, capacity for investment, saving and trade and relations with neighbours). Although the details of Turnbull's empirical findings have been contested, the general argument about the consequences of the decay of trustworthiness is widely accepted. Banfield's and Banfield's (1958) ethnographic study of a village in southern Italy found that in conditions in which significant proportions of the population were not trustworthy, albeit there remained just a few institutions to limit the worst aspects of untrustworthiness found among the Ik, social organisation fell back to guileful opportunism with commitment only among the closest kin. The argument has been reinforced by journalistic and academic studies on the decay of social organisation in societies that have experienced catastrophic collapse in core social institutions such as Somalia, Albania and, more recently, Iraq.

Trustworthiness is also important for stable competitive relationships; markets are complex systems of social order which depend on competitors respecting certain rules. For example, most firms in the USA can reasonably expect that their competitors will be sufficiently trustworthy that they will not resort to assassination, sabotage or arson in order to further their business strategies. In post-socialist Russia, to say nothing of failed states, no such trustworthiness can be relied upon, with consequences for the levels of domestic and foreign investment in such countries.

Trust

Trustworthiness is important for co-ordination. It also possesses quite a general claim to high moral status; not only is it useful that people and organisations are trustworthy, but, in general, they ought to be. It is in exceptional circumstances that we expect people and organisations to be untrustworthy on moral grounds. For example, as Arendt (1963) famously argued following the principle adopted at the Nuremburg trials, it follows from the principle that obeying evil orders is no defence to a prosecution for an evil act, that, if agents cannot openly defy those orders or simply resign their roles without facing unacceptable sanctions, then, at the very least, they should be untrustworthy in the execution of their roles in order to undermine the evil process of which they are a part. This argument presumably applies to organisational and business ethics as well as to individual morality. The fact that this is a special case is implied by the fact that, as Arendt stressed, we expect people to know when this exception to the duty of trustworthiness is mandatory and to limit their untrustworthiness strictly to those cases.

By contrast, the placing of trust in others hardly has the same kind of moral status. Although there are still a few heavily moralistic discussions of trust in the literature, the recent tendency has been to accept that there is no *general* merit in people and organisations being casual in the placing of their trust, if only for the simple prudential reason that some people and organisations are not trustworthy and self-interest calls for caution. Further, there is the ethical reason that is wrong to put people and valuable resources at hazard by trusting them to agents too lightly and without sufficient investigation. Moreover, whereas social organisation fails when trustworthiness decays in general, the decay of trusting is the concomitant and consequence of that erosion of trustworthiness not an independent cause of social collapse; indeed, where few if any are trustworthy, it is still both rational – and often moral – not to place trust.

Certainly, trust between organisations is not something to be welcomed in every case. Private failures of trust are common; that is, trust may be misplaced and lead to unwelcome outcomes for the organisations themselves. There are also many obvious cases of public failure, in which, for example, trust and trustworthiness between organisations sustains cartels, anti-competitive practices, collusion, cover-up, lack of accountability. In so doing, trust produces unwelcome outcomes for consumers and citizens.

If the placing of trust is beneficial in its consequences, then it is derivative in two ways upon the benign effects of trustworthiness. First, where agents are available who are trustworthy, it is prudent and often sensible or right to trust them because this conduces to the positive benefits of trustworthiness. Second, and more indirectly and contingently, it is possible that in the presence of background conditions of a reasonable initial presumption of trustworthiness of at least some identifiable agents, placing trust in them might reinforce their trustworthiness by giving them the feeling that their merits are being recognised by principals.

Organisational trust and trustworthiness

Trust in an organisation as an agent or trust by an organisation as a principal are not straightforward matters to analyse. The observable behaviour of organisations is the activity of their individual members, leaders, staff and clients. When two organisations negotiate a relationship through a contract, it is individuals who handle the process. Managers will make initial approaches. Directors, perhaps, will handle the final negotiations and enter their signatures. A range of boundary spanning staff will implement the agreed tasks entrusted between the organisations – account managers, purchasing managers, project managers, frontline professionals and so on. Trust between two organisations may often grow out of informal social ties between particular managers; certainly, the inter-organisational relationship will not be sustained unless particular social ties are made to work and some individual trust is also cultivated between those individuals.

Strict methodological individualists, such as Hardin (1993), have to regard the description of trust in or by organisations as metaphorical rather than as a serious claim about the nature of trust relationships. Blois (1999) considers the business literature on trust weak because of its typical willingness to countenance such rhetoric. Yet, because organisations are collective entities, typically with legal personality and limited individual liability for directors, we cannot wholly reduce the behaviour of organisations to that of particular individuals. Nonetheless, the reasons for disregarding the personal dimension go deeper than this; when we trust an organisation because of its reputation, we typically know nothing of the individuals who are currently responsible for ensuring the quality of its performance. Managers negotiating a long-term strategic alliance may well not know whom in particular their organisation will be dealing with in the later stages of the arrangement to which they are committing the two organisations. The arrangements are entered with and by groups; moreover, these arrangements bind individuals, including those still to be recruited, and they define which individuals are to be bound and what counts as being bound. Still more fundamentally, these individuals are acting, deciding to trust to the degree that they do, under collective institutions that define the meaning of what they do. The fact that they are engaged in trusting across an organisational boundary is an institutional constraint which structures the procedures they follow, the certain kinds of decision procedures that must be gone though and the significance of the ritual acts (e.g. of signing contracts). The *accountabilities* which give meaning to organisations' trusting and being trusted are not ones that can meaningfully be described at the individual level (cf. Marsden, 1998).

As Currall and Inkpen (2000) argue, it is necessary to distinguish between the level of theoretical explanation, the level of measurement and the level of analysis. For many theoretical purposes, it is important to attend to the reality of organisational and inter-organisational institutions. However, with the exception of some documentary research and collection of performance statistics, examining inter-organisational relations in order to understand trust necessarily involves individual level measurement. The level of analysis will shift according to the principal purpose; when we want to understand the ways in which trust is initiated and sustained it may be important to conduct analysis of interpersonal relations, when we want to understand the long-run dynamics of inter-organisational relations methodological individualism is not sufficient.

In this chapter, the argument moves between levels of analysis because there are reasons for being interested both in the inter-organisational level, especially but not exclusively for understanding the genesis of formal relationships, and in the inter-personal level, especially but not exclusively for understanding the informal basis of relations between key boundary-spanning staff or brokers.

Theories of trust

Defining trust: distinguishing confidence and trust?

As Hoffman (2002) points out, despite the differences between theories there are some areas of agreement between the main writers about the nature of trust (Barber, 1983; Gambetta, 1988; Misztal, 1996; Sztompka, 1999). Hoffman's review suggests convergence on the propositions that:

- trust involves an attitude of willingness to place some of one's interest under the direct control of others;
- trusting relationships are behavioural manifestations of trust;

- there is variety in the intensity and scope of trust;
- trust involves forming beliefs which predict the future behaviour of others (albeit subject to error); and
- where there is complete certainty about such behaviour then there is no trust because there is no need for it.

In much the same vein, Blois (1999) suggests that there is agreement on the idea that, in trust, the principal places reliance on the agent in situations where the principal's interest are vulnerable to the actions of the trusted agent (Rotter, 1980; Baier, 1986). Swift (2001) develops Hosmer's (1995) argument to point to common acceptance of the principal's optimism about the agent's responsible behaviour, vulnerability to the agent, the condition of willing co-operation between principal and agent, the presence of significant costs and difficulties for the principal in monitoring the agent and enforcing direct control over their actions. Trust may be an act consequent upon deliberation or it may be taken-for-granted in all but the most extraordinary situations. In the present context, little need be said about taken-for-granted trust because it is of limited importance in understanding the determinants and consequences of co-operation between organisations.

However, on most views of trust, these features are not sufficient for something that can properly be called trust. The common features can be boiled down essentially to trust as reliance on an agent under conditions of risk. It is true that some studies of trust in inter-organisational settings do claim to use this definition (e.g. Currall and Inkpen, 2000). Nonetheless, we can rely on another person or organisation under conditions of risk without ever contacting them, let alone making any decisions or having any kind of institutionally specific relationship with them. After all, when we step outside our front door, we rely upon the firm that laid the path to the gate not to have built it so badly that it will give way underneath us; yet it would be stretching the meaning of the word 'trust' to speak of us as trusting the company that laid the path. 'Reliance' or 'confidence' would be more appropriate here, as we seem to lack any element of the choice which seems to be inherent in the idea of trust. By contrast, if we choose a builder to replace that path then a question of trust might arise.

However, drawing the line between trust and confidence is not a straightforward matter. There are broadly two traditions of theory about the determinants of more or less deliberate trust in the literature. Each offers a different definition of trust and, therefore, a different standard of what counts as trust and what as confidence, and thus contain divergent views about their specific causes and consequences. It is possible to synthesise these accounts, as will be done here, but no doubt purists in each tradition will consider that, in any such synthesis, something important is lost.

One tradition is essentially interest-based, while the other is at heart commitment-based. The *behavioural* tradition defines trust as the *judgment of confidence by one actor (the principal) that another actor (the agent) will, with very high probability, act in a way both predicted (expected) and desired by the principal on the basis that the actions expected from the agent are in the principal's interest; moreover, the agent is expected to act in the manner which is in the principal's interest not by chance coincidence of the interests of the two but because there are specific incentives for the agent arising from the ongoing relationship between the two which is expected by the agent to continue beyond the particular transaction, but the agent is assumed to be basically self-interested* (Luhmann, 1979; Lewis and Weigert, 1985; Zucker, 1986; Gambetta, 1988; Coleman, 1990; Hardin, 1993; Stinchcombe, 1990; Sztompka, 1999). Hardin (2002) describes this as the 'encapsulated interest' view because the agent's judgment of their interests encapsulates the principal's interests. The incentives arising from the relationship which serve to align the interests of the two may be of several kinds – which will be considered in detail later – but these include fear of sanctions, the offer of benefits in future, reputation effects or even some shared institutions between the two within defined communities based on ascribed characteristics. The importance of the behavioural or encapsulated interest view is that it 'reduces complexity' (in Luhmann's 1979 and 1988 terms) by limiting the incentives for opportunistic behaviour by the agent. In this sense, the tradition is consonant with transaction cost economic views which argue that the control of opportunism by agents is the central problem that all forms of economic organisation have to solve (Williamson, 1985).

In the second tradition, trust is defined not by the principal's judgment that there are sufficient *external* incentives to align the agent's interests with the principal's interests to ensure a high probability of their acting in the desired way. Rather, in the commitment tradition, trust is defined by the principal's judgment that the agent shows signs of sufficient *internal* alignment to the principal to ensure that they will act in a manner that conduces to the principal's interest. On this view, then, trust is *the judgment of the principal that the agent is sufficiently motivated by goodwill or recognition of a 'fiduciary duty' to the principal, rather than mainly by self-interest* (Barber, 1983; Ring and Van de ven, 1992; Sako, 1992); this commitment may arise through the existence of shared norms and values between principal and agent (Parsons, 1969; Ring and Van de ven, 1992) or simply through the principal's assessment of the characteristics of the particular motivation of the agent where the agent is found to be altruistically motivated anyway (Schurr and Osanne, 1985). By contrast with the 'calculative trust' of the encapsulated interest view, some commentators talk of the commitment view as positing either an 'affective', a 'normative' or a 'value based' conception of trust (Lane, 1998).

There are fundamental epistemological differences between these traditions, the first being based on behaviouralism and the second on more interpretive and hermeneutic outlooks in social science. Behaviouralists argue that intentions of the kind appealed to by the commitment tradition are unobservable. By contrast, interpretivists argue that the purely behavioural definition does not capture the distinctive nature of trusting relations and reduces them to mere degrees of confidence about gambles (Seligman, 1997; Uslaner, 2002); behaviouralism boils trust down to mere calculation. Adherents to the commitment school regard the absence of ruthlessly instrumental calculation about partners as the very essence of trust (Seligman, 1997). Conversely, from the rational choice perspective, the commitment approach postulates excessively demanding conditions. Indeed some advocates of the commitment view of trust are prepared to accept that their criterion leaves trust playing a very limited and special role while most actual co-ordination is achieved on the basis of calculative assessments of others (which might be called 'confidence'); Seligman (1997) is the most explicit proponent of this view. Certainly, if trust is defined to require such demanding standards as goodwill or internal acceptance of fiduciary duties *prior* to joint action, then it is clear that trust cannot be a necessary condition for such co-operation. For, as Axelrod's (1984) study showed in game theoretic terms, this co-operation can be achieved simply on the basis of calculation of pure self-interest and the balance of incentives and disincentives offered by the other. Co-operation under fear of sanctions is known as 'deterrence-based trust' (Lewicki and Bunker, 1996), and is, in effect, the limit case of calculative, encapsulated interest trust; for here, even the 'tit for tat' option celebrated by Axelrod (1984) is hardly available.

The two views also differ in their assumptions about motivation. Those who view individuals and organisations as driven by prudent self-interest tend to argue that the commitment view is excessively romantic. Those who argue for the possibility of irreducible altruism regard the encapsulated interest view as unacceptably reductionist. Moreover, each has a different view of the nature of power relationships between principals and agents (Hardy *et al.*, 1998). Behaviouralists (e.g. Dahl, 1957) take power to be the achievement of *instruments* (such as sanctions, incentives and institutional constraints) while interpretivists regard power as the achievement of the shaping of motivations and preferences (Clegg, 1989; March and Olsen, 1989; Lukes, 2005 [1974]). Trust is of interest for inter-organisational relations because of its contribution to the emergence or construction of institutions to stabilise co-ordination between actors; these two approaches therefore also differ in their understanding of such co-ordination. Behaviouralists regard co-ordination as a process of establishing institutions that constrain the range of available actions, taking interests as given, while many of those who cleave to the commitment approach tend to argue that co-ordination cannot be effective unless it is also involved in the shaping of preferences and defining of interests. As a result, therefore, each view tends to articulate the case for different kinds of institutions that will achieve coordination and promote trustworthiness (March and Olsen, 1989).

Notwithstanding the profound theoretical disagreements between these approaches, in recent years efforts have been made to develop syntheses of them by detaching the definitions of trust from their epistemological assumptions and treating them instead either as types or levels of trust or as points within a spectrum of forms of trust. This strategy presumably implies an acceptance of the more capacious epistemology of the interpretivist school, since hermeneutic methods allow for more than just behaviour to be researched.

In this vein, the conceptual frameworks adopted in two monographs can be noted. In a study comparing Japanese and Western types of contracting and joint venturing, Sako (1992), for example, distinguishes within contractual relations, competence trust and goodwill trust. The latter is a manifestation of trust taken from the stable of the commitment approach; Sako's goodwill trust is what Brenkert (1998) describes as extended trust. Contractual trust also involves an element of overt commitment because it implies the judgment that the agent will adhere to the principle of promise-keeping (this corresponds roughly to Brenkert's (1998) category of 'basic trust'). Competence trust – the judgment that the agent will perform their role competently – is described in Sako's work as essentially calculative. In a study on public trust in large organisations to handle personal data in ways that respect confidentiality and data protection principles, 6 *et al.* (1998) distinguish between three slightly different cases. They identify the pure case of calculative trust – which they describe as prudential or minimal trust – in which the principal treats the agent's statements of intent as credible statements of what they will likely try to do (whether or not the principal welcomes those intentions or has sought to elicit them), as well as contractual trust and goodwill trust. Whereas Sako treats the judgment of competence as both a distinct form of trust and the most important element in calculation, 6 *et al.* regard each type of trust as involving a primary judgment of intent and secondarily of competence. Lane and Bachmann (1998) distinguish the following types of trust: calculative; value or norm based; and that based on common cognition, roughly the same as the non-deliberate trust discussed briefly earlier.

These types are essentially concerned with what will here be called the 'task' entrusted; that is, with the question, 'what does the principal trust the agent to do or refrain from doing?' However, in moving beyond behaviourist approaches, it is important to examine also the reasons for which people place trust in others, and in the next stage, to explore the relationship between reasons for trust and the extent of the tasks entrusted. The next section examines developments in theory and empirical research on these matters.

Determinants of trust and trustworthiness

Studies can be divided into those concerned with the determinants of personal and (inter) organisational trust and trustworthiness and those concerned with their consequences.

In principle, assuming that people and organisations are not systematically irrational, the categories of reasons that lead them to perceived trustworthiness in agents – and so place their trust in them – ought to correspond to the categories of pressure upon agents for trustworthiness. That is, although of course people make plenty of mistakes about the true trustworthiness of particular agents, they are unlikely either to look for whole categories of characteristics or processes that typically have no significant effect upon trustworthiness or to miss out whole categories of reasons.

It follows from the nature of an agency relationship that, in order to explain when trust is more likely than not, we need to understand the range of available *reasons* for placing trust in a particular person (as opposed to reasons for needing to find someone to place trust in) and the kinds of *tasks* for which people might place trust and offer trustworthiness. Therefore, trust is quite distinct from esteem, in which no tasks are required, and from respect, where even clear and distinct reasons may be absent. It is a contingent matter whether someone will only trust the people that s/he holds in high esteem or respects, and *vice versa* and, if so, whether esteem comes first or trust comes first.

The most useful taxonomy of the basic types of reasons is found in Zucker (1986) (for her classification neatly subsumes those on offer in the subsequent literature) whilst the most serviceable general classification of the types of task are to be found in Barber (1983) and Sako (1992).

Zucker's (1986: 60) distinguishes between:

- *process-based* trust, 'where trust is tied to past or expected exchange as in reputation or gift-exchange' (for example, selecting an agent on the basis of what one knows about their track record in matters of the relevant sort);
- *characteristic-based* trust, 'where trust is tied to a person, depending on characteristics such as family background or ethnicity' (for example, selecting an agent on the grounds that they are a member of the same social circle as oneself); and
- *institutionally based* trust, 'where trust is tied to broad societal institutions, depending on individual or firm-specific attributes' (e.g. certification as an accountant) or on intermediary mechanisms (e.g. a solicitor's client account).

An example of institutionally based trust might be deciding to trade with an unknown partner in a foreign country because that state requires that such people in the relevant industry be qualified, their firms regulated, and because it has a developed system of contract and company law on the enforcement of which one can rely. Brenkert (1998) speaks of trust that is buttressed by appeal to legal institutions – such as contractual protection in the event of default – as 'guarded'.

It is sensible to split Zucker's first category into two. One the one hand, we might trust on the basis of the principal's own past *experience* of dealing with the person or organisations. On the other, we might trust on the basis that the person or organisation has a *reputation* (capturing the experience of others). Reputation based reasons might work in either (or both) of two ways. We might take evidence of that reputation as a kind of reference, trusting on the basis of the reported experience of others. Alternatively, we might infer that the person or organisation will value that reputation and behave in a trustworthy way, in order not to damage it; in this case, a reputation acts like a kind of hostage. Zucker's distinction within institutional factors – between 'person-specific' and 'intermediary' – is perhaps rather abstract. We might more helpfully speak of *generic* institutional factors, such as the availability of legal redress through contract law in the event of default for those things that apply to everyone, and of *specific* institutional factors such as warranties (or other 'hostages') that the agent may offer us more or less uniquely.

Although Zucker uses the term 'institutions' to refer to *formal* institutions, as Chapter 3 explained there is also a considerable range of *informal* institutions which make up the basic institutional forms of social organisation and which also shape the nature, role and meaning of experience, reputation and characteristics in processes of trust. As Zucker (1986) emphasises, many of the 'characteristics' of organisations are institutionally defined rather than being simple natural types. This means that some such characteristics might collapse into institutional factors. For example, if we prefer to deal with someone of the same ethnicity as ourselves simply because of their ethnicity, and we are Muslims, and what underpins our preference for buying food from a fellow Muslim is that we believe that fellow Muslims can be brought before the courts of the Islamic community or face informal ostracism in that community, then this has more to do with particular institutions than the person's characteristics. The less clear, direct and task-specific the nature of the accountability which links the identity of the agent to their incentive to be trustworthy, then the more likely that a truly characteristic-based reason is at stake. Shared characteristics are indeed often a proxy for institutional capacities for mutual surveillance and reputation sharing in highly multiplex and dense yet clearly bounded networks. The findings of many researchers that in strategic partnerships between Western and Russian firms it is critical that Russian nationals (rather than Western expatriates) are used in key roles no doubt indicates reputation and surveillance processes sustained by institutions in the Russian community, although it may also serve to indicate long-term commitment to the Russian market (e.g. Ayios, 2003).

Some types of reasons are not easy to classify. Sometimes people say 'I just trusted him/her' on the basis of a face-to-face meeting. Institutions seem largely irrelevant here and the principal may know little of the of agent's track record. Perhaps the immediate eyeball-to-eyeball decision should be interpreted as being based on some hard-to-define characteristic. In many cases of trust, of course, we have multiple reasons; it should not be imagined that typically people have reasons of only one type for each trust decision.

How, next, are we to classify the tasks – using the term in the fairly general sense of meaning the actions, inactions, commitments of agents that principals want agents to do, not do, or make, but which they cannot directly supervise – entrusted by individuals or organisations to others in a suitably general fashion? First, we need some characterisation of the most basic tasks entrusted. Elster (1989), drawing on the game theoretic tradition of the analysis of threats and offers (Schotter, 1981, 1986; Dasgupta, 1988; Sugden 1989; Dowding, 1991), defines as 'credibility' the limit case that the agent's threats or commitments to act can be believed by a principal, whether or not the action threatened or committed would be welcomed by that principal. We can call this *minimal* or *prudential* trust.

We now need a way of classifying the more demanding tasks. Barber (1983) distinguishes between:

- a general sense of reasonable expectation in the persistence of the natural and social orders;
- an expectation that other agents will perform specific roles with adequate technical competence; and
- an expectation that one's partners in some interaction will carry out their fiduciary obligations or responsibilities (that is, go beyond what may be specified in any agreement or duty – if necessary, even setting it aside – in order to act in the principal's best interest.

The first of these is, as we have suggested, more about hoping than about trusting. Much of Barber's study is concerned with the last two, which, as shorthand, he calls *technical* and *fiduciary* trust. As already noted, Sako (1992: 37–38) distinguishes between *contractual* trust, 'predicated on both partners upholding a universalistic ethical standard, namely that of keeping promises', *competence* trust, where the principal expects the agent to carry out their role competently in technical terms and *goodwill* trust, which is 'more diffuse' and 'refers to mutual expectations of open commitment to each other. Commitment may be defined as the willingness to do more than is formally expected ... there are no explicit promises which are expected to be fulfilled ... nor fixed professional standards to be reached ... Instead, someone who is worthy of "goodwill trust" is dependable and can be endowed with high discretion, as he can be trusted to take initiatives while refraining from unfair advantage taking.'

It seems to us that Barber's technical and fiduciary trust broadly correspond to Sako's competence and goodwill trust. Sako's distinction between contractual and competence trust is one drawn within those situations where the agent is trusted to co-operate, in the first case merely with sincerity or good faith and in the second with expertise. However, there is no distinction here in the weight of the task entrusted between contractual and competence trust in the way that distinguishes these two, prudential trust and goodwill trust. Moreover, technical competence or capability is an important question, whatever the scale of the task entrusted. In the present context, it is therefore more helpful to treat them together. However, we must also allow that the 'contract' may be entirely implicit or the task committed may be one that, if there is any remedy for it at all (and often there will not be), would be in tort rather than contract law. Therefore, perhaps it is better to speak of *duty* or *obligation trust* rather than of contractual trust.

Finally, we need a category for the highest end of the spectrum. For we do not trust our closest friends for anything in particular (and certainly not just 'for' conversation or 'for' willingness to keep secrets or provide us with emotional support or whatever); rather, we trust them *tout court*. We often say that we trust them 'absolutely'. Therefore, it is helpful to speak of *absolute* or *moral trust*. Where all the other levels of trust are transitive, moral trust is intransitive. Often it has no task. For this kind of trusting, it is, at the very least, unnatural to say, as Hardin (1993: 506–507) does, that:

> Trust is a three-part-relation: A trusts B to do X ... Only a small child, a lover, Abraham speaking to God or a rabid follower of a charismatic leader might be able to say 'I trust you' without implicit modifier. Even in their cases, we are apt to think they mistake both themselves and the objects of their trust.

Hardin seems to be suggesting that moral trust is irrational. Yet it is hard to see why small children should not, in his own example, grant their parents moral trust or that a rational person will restrict herself to nothing more than goodwill trust. However, in most inter-organisational contexts (other than, for example, spiritual organisations), this level of task entrusted is not very important.

The work of Zucker and Sako provides an account of the basic varieties of, respectively, reasons for trust and tasks entrusted. How are these related? We are especially interested in which kinds of reasons might normally be required to achieve particular levels of task entrusted. One way to explore this is to cross-tabulate reasons and tasks and then to examine what would be required to fill each cell (or to move between cells). Cross-tabulating these categories yield the following matrix (Table 5.1) (6, 1994, 6 *et al.*, 1998, 2002).

In many situations, if we trust at all, we will trust for a combination of reasons. Moreover, if we have reached goodwill trust, then implicitly we have already achieved contract trust. Likewise, one cannot place contractual trust without first placing minimal trust. Therefore, we should think of any particular trust relationship as being represented not by occupying one cell in the matrix but rather by covering an area of the matrix. Furthermore, change over time in trust relations cannot credibly be represented as simple

Table 5.1 The dimensions of trust: reasons and tasks

Tasks *Reasons*	*Minimal* *(prudence)*	*Duty*	*Goodwill*	*Absolute* *or moral*
Experience				
Reputation				
Characteristics				
Specific institutions				
Generic institutions				

moves around the matrix that involve vacating one cell and occupying another. Rather, developments that reinforce trust and trustworthiness typically look like ink spreading over blotting paper to the right (while shrinking of such an inked area to the left would represent falling trust perhaps as the consequences of some betrayal).

It is not necessarily the case that having forfeited our goodwill trust, the person or organisation will retreat all the way to the left hand border of the matrix or even back to prudential trust. They may still be trustworthy under contract, provided we retain reasons for trust that lead us to think that breaking a contract would:

- be so out of character that even the negative experience of failure to provide goodwill does not lead us to imagine that they would do so;
- damage a valued reputation;
- break some duty owed by virtue of particular characteristics; or
- run risks by way of some institution such as contract law or a prior specific warranty.

The matrix in Table 5.1 provides a framework upon which a number of alternative possible hypotheses can be defined and prepared for testing, because it enables us to ask such questions as 'What kinds of reasons or combinations of reasons are most likely to yield moral trust?' and, conversely, 'How far rightward will particular types or combinations of reasons enable a person to move?' For example, in 6 *et al.* (1998), quantitative survey evidence was used to estimate several statistical models of the relationships between variables in the different cells of this matrix (in only slightly reduced form) in the context of individuals' trust in organisations for a particular type of task. Although trust in other individuals as potential ties does call for different kinds of information from trust in organisations, many of the same factors come into play. This is especially true in relation to social ties of acquaintanceship and collegial ties in work setting, which are typically understood as more instrumental relationships, and are often pursued for reasons to do with securing advantage from within organisations, such as information about or preferment in jobs (e.g. Burt, 1992; Heimer, 1992; Granovetter 1995 [1974]).

The institutional ubiquity of trust

Trust and trustworthiness are important for co-ordination in *all* kinds of inter-organisational relations. It is sometimes argued that networks are uniquely co-ordinated on the basis of trust, whereas markets are co-ordinated by prices and hierarchies by command (e.g. Bradach and Eccles, 1989; Powell, 1990). It has been argued in Chapters 3 and 4 that this argument is misleading for several reasons; networks are not a single kind of thing but several and there are, among other sorts, hierarchical and market-like networks.

Moreover, it is not true that markets and hierarchical organisation achieve co-ordination without trust, unless one is prepared to adopt such a very high standard of what is to count as 'trust' that only a limited range of relationships, commitments and attitudes could possibly meet it. Consider markets first. If we have any choice at all about with whom or what organisation we contract (and sometimes we do not), then to enter into that contract requires placing at least some confidence in the particular organisation selected that they will perform their obligations. Moreover, if there is any option about the nature of the contract offered and negotiated, or about taking the contract at all, then it seems reasonable to suppose that we must have some confidence that the particular form of contract finally negotiated is one that is valid (that is, we must place some confidence in the background institutions of law that they would enable us to rely on the contract in the event of a dispute). If this kind of confidence is not trust, then the special definition of trust which excludes it requires a good deal of justification. Moreover, markets stabilise on the basis that actors expect to encounter each other again and therefore they have incentives to invest in their reputations for being reliable, honest, and so on; if this is not to be called trust, then, again, we need a very strong argument to exclude it from the definition (Ricketts, 2001).

While in the short run, each transaction within a hierarchy does not rely on voluntarily placed trust between principal and agent – after all, as Williamson (1985) argues, that is the point of hierarchy, for thereby it economises on certain transaction costs – it is not the case that, over the longer run, hierarchy can survive without the placing of a good deal of confidence both in its underlying institutions and, in particular, in its high status role-holders. At the level of the individual command or exchange within a hierarchical system, that system can only function if its members have confidence that a particular command is indeed authorised, comes from the role-holder that it purports to and that it is legitimate within the operating rules of the organisation. Securing this requires institutions for verification – for example, that the document is indeed a valid Papal bull or military decree – and settlement of queries, which in turn relies on the competence, honesty and reliability of those who conduct the checking. If this confidence is not to be called trust, then, once again, some special justification is needed to defend the definition of trust implied.

The Soviet Union was in many ways a hierarchical system, in which the power of the party–state nexus to issue command was grounded in a status order authorising senior party officials to dispose of economic and human resources by direction without requiring negotiation or true prices. Its collapse is generally explained by the corrosion of confidence in the capacities both of the system and the leadership. The symptoms of that lack of confidence became increasingly visible, including the growth of the informal economy and crime, the steadily increasing importance of bribery and corruption of officials and finally the haemorrhage of population to the West.

In clubs, clans and enclaves, it is certainly true that trust is important in holding these organisations together. Without the placing of trust by their members in their institutions and in each other's commitment not to free ride, they may dissolve even more quickly than hierarchies. Nevertheless, we have already shown in Chapter 3 that trust *alone* is not sufficient in enclave forms. For example, clubs do generate certain fragile kinds of leadership; what Weber called charismatic leadership is often, it was argued, a provisional solution to part of the problem of securing commitment, co-ordination and action in clubs. This kind of leadership may require the establishment among followers of a certain trust, but it cannot be conceptually reduced entirely to trust. The principle of the rough internal equality of members and the sharp boundary between members and non-members are not just defining structural features of clubs, clans and enclaves or of the transaction environment to which these organisational and inter-organisational forms are more or less intelligent solutions. Rather, these two features perform real work in enabling co-ordination; the internal equality helps to sustain commitment and the sharp boundary helps to define responsibility. So, just as 'pure' markets use prices, contracts and transaction-by-transaction negotiation and 'pure' hierarchies use commands, status differentiation and clear boundaries between members and others for their co-ordination and governance, so clubs use charisma, internal equality and sharp membership boundaries for the same functions.

In each of the three broad types of organisational forms, the placing of confidence by participants both in those they deal with on a transaction-by-transaction basis and, over time, in the underlying institutions, play a critical role. The nature of that role is modulated by the characteristics of the form of organisation; crucially, though, trust is present and important in each type but in none is it the sole or unique feature that produces co-ordination.[2]

Institutional forms of social organisation and styles of trust

Thus far, drawing on the standard theoretical literature, it is possible to derive a reasonably plausible general account of the roots of trust at the level of the *particular* decision to trust another person or organisation. This affords a conceptual framework supporting a variety of general hypotheses. However, as most commentators have recognised (e.g. Gambetta, 1988), institutional setting and context determines the meaning, purpose, likelihood and wider significance of trust. Without specifying the range of possible contexts, this level of explanation does not help very much, for it does not tell us which social mechanisms are more likely to be found in which contexts. For people in institutionalised organisations do not simply enter the decision to trust or to behave in a trustworthy manner as reasons for action. Nor are the institutions relevant to trust limited to the more or less formal institutions at stake in Table 5.1. A wide range of informal as well as formal institutions define what kinds of ties are available, thinkable, meaningful or feasible, and which kinds of people under which classifications and descriptions. This chapter shows how the neo-Durkheimian institutional theory can provide the required account of context.

Drawing on the theoretical models presented in Chapter 3, it is now possible to develop a richer account of the range of institutional forms of trust. That this range of situations in which the different social mechanisms interact can be plotted on the matrix in Table 5.1 might be expected. The argument will proceed by way of showing that people in different institutional settings will look for different reasons for trust and be ready to trust to different levels of task entrusted, as set out in general form in Table 5.1. The argument of the next part of this chapter is that key network structural characteristics (Chapter 3) explain much of the variance in the forms of trust (for a statement of this general view from a rational choice perspective, in marked contrast to the present one, see Huang *et al.*, 1998). In each case, examples are given from the literatures both on interpersonal and inter-organisational trust, because ties between individuals are often very important in shaping or sustaining links between organisations.

Trust in isolate settings

Let us look first at the institutional conditions that make for isolate forms. As Banfield and Banfield (1958) showed in the southern Italy of the 1940s and 1950s, the only ties between the peasants that exhibited particularly strong trust were those within relative closely related kin; hence, he described their trust strategies as ones of 'amoral familism'. Between peasants themselves and between peasants and the local shopkeepers trust was very limited. Indeed, if there was any goodwill trust, then did not extend in most cases much beyond the immediate kin and household members. Acquaintances and friends, to the extent that the Montegranesi practised friendship in any very rich sense, attracted much lower levels of trust. It might be imagined that the sanctions and accountabilities of organised religion might have provided institutional pressures and disciplines that would lead to trust; such hopes would have been disappointed in the Montegranesi. In the climate of suspicion and gossip within the town, even reputations could hardly be regarded as reliable sources of information and were, indeed, not much relied upon in practical decision-making about whom to trust with information, still less credit. The economic institutions that governed peasant life so tightly – and the political institutions of neglectful state authority and occasional organised crime – combined with the prevailing uncertain and marginal financial circumstances (the 'given fact' element in their social regulation) to make all but personal experience an unreliable basis for decision-making about trust and to ensure that much more than minimal or prudential trust – the credibility of actual promises and threats – was difficult to achieve.

International relationships between national defence procurement agencies are also essentially isolate in structure (Chapter 8). For each is heavily constrained by domestic law and military priorities as well as by the location of states in the international order, and also possesses reasons to want the weakest available integration with other states (even with their allies within military coalitions such as NATO). Separate countries distrust the international arms sales permitted to non-allied states by others even within alliances and each has reasons to want to preserve the capabilities of national firms. Strategic alliances and joint ventures across national boundaries are by no means unknown, but, as the chapter shows, they tend to be driven more by the commercial interests of the contractors than by the commitments of the procurement agencies. This makes for a system of distrust in defence procurement that is at least in part described by neo-realist theory of international relations (e.g. Waltz, 1979); while, to be sure, neo-realism does not capture all of the phenomena observed in the whole of international relations, the narrow field of defence procurement does exhibit many of these characteristics.

Figure 5.1 therefore describes the relationship between reasons and tasks that the isolates find available to them in their patterns of ties. Note that the

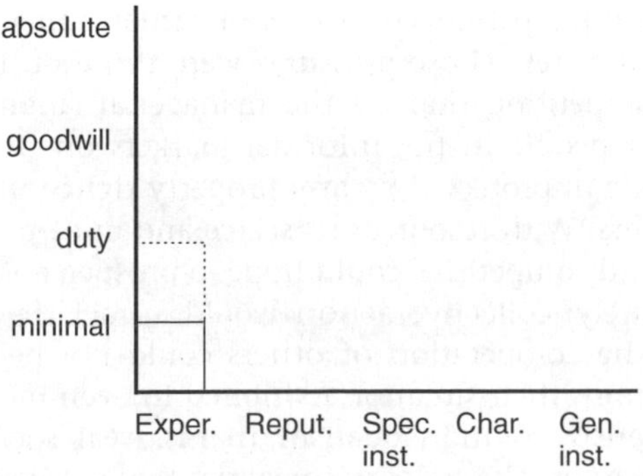

Figure 5.1 Trust for isolates.

order of the types of reasons, now arrayed along the horizontal axis, is slightly altered from that in Table 5.1. This is in order to provide a sequential ordering from those reasons which provide information that is most directly and specifically related to the task entrusted – namely one's own or the principal organisation's relevant experience or that of trusted others encoded in reputations – through to the least directly and specifically related which are the longstop provisions of generic institutions. The key change is that characteristics – for example, gender, ethnicity, place of origin, religious affiliation, country or region of headquarters or main shareholders – provide *less* direct and specific information about any given task than do specific institutions. The dotted line shows that in those cases where fiduciary duties can be strongly enforced in (fairly) readily evident ways (for example, because some aspects of task performance can be measured by principals), it may be possible for isolates to achieve this level of trust. In essence, this figure shows the Hobbesian character of trust in isolate settings.

We can now use the same method to characterise the relationship between reasons and tasks that can be expected in individualistic contexts.

Trust in individualistic networks

Consider next the patterns of instrumental social ties of Burt's (1992) advancement-seeking corporate managers in the United States as they 'network' their way through their contacts within the present firms and in other organisations where they might hope for a more senior post than their present ones. Here, reputation effects work in just the way that game theory (Schotter, 1981, 1986) predicts; reputation follows experience, and, if the institutions are underpinned properly, falsehoods about individuals are often found out (Burt and Knez, 1996).

The individualistic institutions of the North American labour market are by no means unique in the world. Studies of interpersonal ties among those surviving in the illegal and informal markets that characterised much of economic life during the last decades of socialism in Central and Eastern Europe suggest that the patterns of trust look rather similar, and in response to very similar pressures. Those pressures were those of, if anything, even more ruthless competition than in the managerial labour markets of the United States, for people in the informal markets on the margins of the socialist order were unprotected by any property rights or redress for violations of agreements. With resources so scarce and uncertain, only the most entrepreneurial and competitive could hope to prosper, and even then probably not indefinitely; collective action would attract the attention of the authorities and the co-operation of others could not be underpinned by institutions. In short, their situation exhibited in even more extreme form, the basic characteristics of individualism, that is, weak social regulation and weak social integration. The styles of social ties that are available under individualistic institutions, then, are more complex and contingent than those available under the similarly weak socially integrated conditions that govern isolates. For in these situations, people must make different decisions about investing trust and trustworthiness according to the institutional availability of different kinds of reasons for trust. Where there are formal institutions of either a specific or a general character that can provide warranties or longstop redress, as in the case of North America or most Western countries, individualism affords higher levels of trust, and thus more long-term action. For example, the inter-organisational relationships found among dedicated biotechnology firms (DBFs) in the late 1980s (Chapter 9) seem often to have been quite individualistic in this sense. At that stage in the development of the field, there were few constraints upon the choices of partner organisations for research, marketing, manufacturing. Individual researchers were able at that time relatively readily to create new DBFs or to work with existing ones. Over time, the evidence suggests, this situation changed, but it seems to have characterised the field for perhaps as long as a decade.

Under individualistic institutions, great emphasis has to be laid upon practical experience of others in order to determine whether they are trustworthy. For in the absence of strong institutions of external regulation or shared membership of a common community, there is little else to go on. Trust decisions therefore are made in the first instance experimentally and then either continued or discontinued according as the agent is found to be trustworthy or not. Individualistic institutions, then, create imperatives for people to act in ways not unlike those modelled by Axelrod's (1984) 'tit for tat' strategy in solving Prisoner's Dilemma problems; one co-operates with those who proved co-operative last time around and withdraws co-operation from those who withdrew their co-operation on the last occasion of contact.

In the literature of interfirm networks and strategic alliances, Gulati's (1995a) is one of the most important examination of just this thesis about the nature of trust in networks which are marked by relatively weak shared characteristics or regulatory institutions and by loose and sparse ties. According to the tradition of theory associated with Powell (1990), for example, we should expect such networks hardly to exhibit trust at all, at least not in any very strong manner. However, Gulati shows that this is incorrect. Rather, what we observe is a distinct signature of trust. Gulati studied data on strategic alliances over almost twenty years (1970–1989) in the fields of biopharmaceuticals, new materials and automobiles. These are all fields in which patterns of alliances are constantly shifting and in which firms make no great claim to be working on the basis of long-term loyalty. His central finding was that strategic alliances were less likely to be equity based – that is, to rely on strong contractual substitutes for hierarchical control – where the alliances was one between partners which had previous experience of working together in strategic alliances. Initially, before such mutual experience had been built up, he found, equity-based strategic alliances were much more common. This is exactly the kind of trust signature that the present neo-Durkheimian theory would expect from an essentially individualistically structured system. Moreover, to reinforce the point that there can be strong trust in individualistic market settings, some of Gulati's examples demonstrate – in the absence of equity shares – a measure of *goodwill* trust.

However, reliance upon experience and a very distinctive manner of using second-hand experience through reputations actually seem to go together (cf. 6 *et al.*, 1998, studying trust by individuals in large organisations to handle their personal data properly, found that reliance upon experience and upon reputation as a reason for placing trust clearly reinforced one another). Larson (1992) also examined qualitatively a series of networks of entrepreneurial firms in individualistic structures in such industries as high technology computing, catalogue clothing, telephone equipment, circuit breakers and support sales. She noted the instability of partnerships, the looseness of the ties between partner forms and the fact that by no means all firms seek partnerships and strategic alliances; these are, of course, the structural hallmarks of individualistic network structures. However, she discovered that reputation could provide an important basis for supporting quite high levels of trust. Firms took reputations about potential partners from a wide variety of sources and not only from their immediate peers or from existing social networks. These reputations served as the basis on which initial experimentation with trust would be made. Trust would evolve, where it did in fact evolve, thereafter on the basis of experience and could reach levels of goodwill trust, as measured in Larson's (1992: 95) study by the recognition by firms of their partner's sense of moral obligation to them.

In such contexts, reputation effects can be made to work well because information can be verified and therefore can be used as the basis for trust decisions. Experience can be relied upon much more because the uncertainty of conditions that make induction so unreliable in isolate conditions is partly removed. Both of these reasons can support goodwill trust, because people will have the incentive to behave in a trustworthy manner with a view to the long term and therefore others will use these reasons to consider trusting them. Contracts can be enforced, torts can be remedied, and so many kinds of reasons will work tolerably well for reaching duty trust. Because of the weak social regulation, individualism – like enclaved as we shall – enables and to some degree may mandate a search for personal 'authenticity' as a characteristic reason for trust. This provides a provisionally and potentially sharper barrier between friends and others – such as business and work contacts or acquaintances – than may be available in other institutional settings.

The result then looks something like Figure 5.2. Where individualistic institutions work for short-term contexts, then there is no particular reason to expect more than minimal trust (shown by the small box). The large box shows the role of contractual institutions in stabilising longer term commitments in such settings. In the absence of more collective institutions, the only effective means of securing trust and trustworthiness at the goodwill

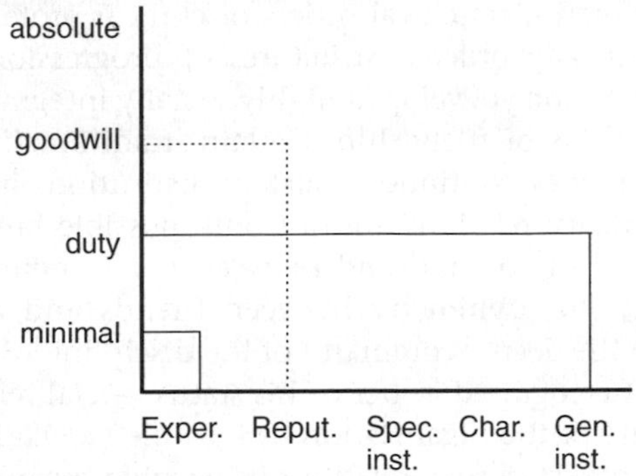

Figure 5.2 Trust under individualistic institutions.

level – as many years of game theoretic work using individualistic assumptions have shown – is to rely on reputation effects. The relative fragility of reputation effects in the absence of collective institutions is represented by the dotted line.

We now consider how things might differ when collective institutions are introduced.

Trust under hierarchical institutions

Contrary to the fashionable claims in sociology that much of the world has been through 'modernisation' – or even 'postmodernisation' – resulting in the irreversible disappearance of hierarchy in favour of generalised individualism in personal relationships (e.g. Giddens 1991; Misztal, 1996), or even that any hierarchical relationship by definition cannot be 'true' or genuine (Wilkinson, 2000), hierarchical forms of both acquaintance and friendship continue to be important. For example, patron–client relations continue to be important social bonds and even defining features of social structure in many societies (Eisenstadt and Roninger, 1984; Roninger, 1998). Certainly, there are individualistic forms of patronage; for example, in the rather economically volatile conditions of New Guinea, the relationships of 'big men' to 'rubbish men' exhibit patron–client forms but within a wholly individualistic context (cf. Thompson, 1979, using data from Meggitt, 1967 and Rappaport, 1967). Roninger's (1998) review of the literature, for example, concludes that many forms of patronage–clientelism in contemporary politics are in fact hybrid forms between individualistic brokerage systems and more hierarchical patrimonial systems. In economic conditions more stable than New Guinea offers, where institutions afford strong regulation to protect the position of certain roles, rather than individuals, hierarchical patterns of patronage and clienthood become perfectly sensible forms of social ties.

Hierarchical social ties are common in very large and bureaucratic organisations where strong role definitions prevail, such as hospitals which are dominated by defined hierarchical orders of clinical professions each with internally hierarchically ordered structures of progression and expertise. Religious orders have long developed highly socially integrated practices and institutionalised forms of friendship. Certain 'traditional' academic collegiate environments may continue to sustain institutions in which patterns of asymmetric tutelary relations are not only possible but expected, both between senior and junior staff and between departments and institutes. In true hierarchy, the asymmetry between friends and acquaintances is grounded both in the deeper command of the discipline which the superior possesses which is recognised in her or his status (social regulation), and in the collegial nature of the organisation as a whole (social integration) that gives the tutelary aspect of such relations its peculiar meaning and purpose.

Although in most contemporary Western governmental bureaucratic contexts, and in most business settings, this hierarchical element is much less sharply marked – and is often overwritten with the signatures of the other institutional forms – it hardly ever disappears completely. Indeed, to the extent that informal ties sustain the capabilities and disciplines of such organisations, at least as much as the formal transmission of collective memory through tuition and promotion through the ranks on merit and experience, it probably cannot completely disappear.

Hierarchical networks between organisations are by no means uncommon and they are marked by a distinctive signature to the basis of trust between the organisations within them. For example, there are some important and common kinds of relational contract in which there is a dominant organisation which is located in the centre of a highly centralised network and where either external state regulation creates sufficient barriers to entry to protect an incumbent or through internal and informal regulation operates by way of *de jure* or *de facto* standards (Brunsson *et al.*, 2000). Rugman and D'Cruz (2000b) describe these networks as dominated by a 'flagship firm'. That firm's dominant position, procurement rules and *de facto* standard-setting ability enable it effectively to impose regulation upon the network of suppliers, sometime strategic partners, junior competitors, and so on, and to define the boundaries both of its own 'bloc' network of allied firms as supplier, partners and customers, but also often the wider network of the industry through its *de facto* standard-setting capabilities.

In such settings, people are likely to look first for institutional reasons to place trust in another organisation. Those institutions may include both: (a) assets provided by the agent at risk under more or less clear contractual arrangements or guarantees as hostages in the event of default; and (b) acceptance of tight regulation through the voluntary binding of the agent perhaps through codes of conduct or legal schemes or surveillance by third parties through auditors or inspectors. In turn, these institutions can only be maintained at all in conditions of abbreviated competition. These, then, are the conditions of hierarchical networks.

Faulkner's (2000) study of eight strategic alliances includes some examples of hierarchical networks and, in these cases, institutional reasons seem to have been very important in enabling sufficient trust to allow the relaxation of more direct controls (which would again have been exercised through contractual mechanisms). For example, Faulkner considers one case in the field of European banking. This is an industry marked by very close regulation at both the national and supra-national level (by states and by the industry) where market concentration is high and firms must build trust with consumers and with external regulators through heavy investment in hostage assets and self-binding through compliance with voluntary codes. The Royal Bank of Scotland's (RBS) strategic alliance with Banco Santander (BS) was not cemented until equity stakes were taken, and each of the partners needed the fact that the other was a member of a number of European banking clubs and consortia (such as IBOS which handles money transfer between banks as institutional hostages) in order to make their decisions about each other. Faulkner reports that, by contrast with the kinds of informal trust that other studies find in highly entrepreneurial individualistic or in close-knit enclaved settings, in the RBS–BS strategic alliance the agreement document is given great importance as an institutional structure providing reasons for trust. Moreover, there have been developed some relationship-specific institutions (such as joint committees with surveillance powers), some joint senior appointments with powers in both banks and a formal system of performance measurement for the work of the alliance. Over time, the institutional basis has come to occupy a more background role as experience-based trust has grown, but the document, the committees and the joint appointees have not diminished in importance; that is to say, in hierarchical networks, the relationship between institutional and experience-based trust is not one in which the latter steadily replaces the former – rather, experience accretes around the institutions and bolsters them but the institutions continue to do much of the heavy lifting of interorganisational trust building.

In their comparison of supplier relations between US and Japanese companies, Sako and Helper (1998) (re)confirm the forms of long-term relational contracts that are now well known to characterise interfirm relations in Japanese business. However, their data were collected on the automotive industry, which in Japan – as now in most other countries – is marked strongly by exactly the kinds of flagship firm networks that Rugman and D'Cruz describe, in addition to the importance of state *dirigisme* especially in international trade, foreign direct investment and global strategy which have long been the central concerns of the Ministry of International Trade and Industry (MITI) in that country (Best, 1990).

The pressure to control transaction costs is by no means irrelevant in sustaining the particular pattern of trust in hierarchical networks. Although hierarchical networks do incur the transactions costs of much greater formality than is found in individualistic ones, they also economise on other categories of transaction costs that actors in individualistic settings must bear. For example, reliance upon standard procedures, shared decision-making and oversight structures has the merit of avoiding the need to create procedures afresh for each new problem that might call for a separate trust decision; for hierarchical solutions are designed for the long term by players who expect to deal with each other repeatedly. To the extent that the hierarchical formality works as intended (Stinchcombe, 2001), it automates the oversight process and pools the costs between the transactors rather than leaving the costs to be borne solely by the specific boundary spanning agents (such as account management divisions that initiate or handle the focal elements of the series of transactions).

In such contexts, then, goodwill trust can be secured, and, in certain special cases (such as that of the subaltern and the spiritually authoritative superior in the religious context) perhaps even absolute or moral trust can be attained. Goodwill trust is sustained in hierarchies on the basis of a wide range of types of reasons that the institutions support. Informal institutions can be important, such as those provided by membership of a community bound by patron–client bonds, by the spiritual or academic discipline or by corporate accountability. Characteristics, too, can be important where these are more or less reliable markers of membership of a bounded group that may be subject to shared collective institutions. Reputations are sustained not only through the flow of personal gossip, as under individualistic institutions, but also by reference to the verifiable information about trustworthiness and competence that is embodied in the role and status occupied by an individual (Burt and Knez, 1996). Specific institutions abound in true hierarchy, for the system of rule and role provides authorisations for the trustworthiness of individuals and sanctions for their untrustworthiness. Still more important, though, are the generic institutions of such hierarchies for they give definition to the conceptions of personal integrity and commitment to the collective which reach far beyond the job-related context into the personal life of the members of the institution (for a discussions of different practices of informational privacy under different institutional conditions, see 6, 1998).

Of course, hierarchy has its deformations, just as the other institutional forms do, and social science has become accustomed mainly to focus on the corrupt or self-disorganised forms of hierarchy. The deformations of patrimonalism and clientelism are well documented in the classics of social science (e.g. LaPalombara, 1964; Eisenstadt and LeMarchand, 1981). Roninger (1998) is careful to note, however, that hierarchy has advantages. For these reasons, there is, as Stinchcombe (2001) has recently argued, good reason also to focus on what Durkheim would have called the 'normal' form, for it is impossible to understand the deformations without understanding the normal form (which is where the self-disorganising dynamics of each of the institutional forms of social organisation begin). Figure 5.3, then, describes the trust signature of reasons and tasks in social ties under hierarchy.

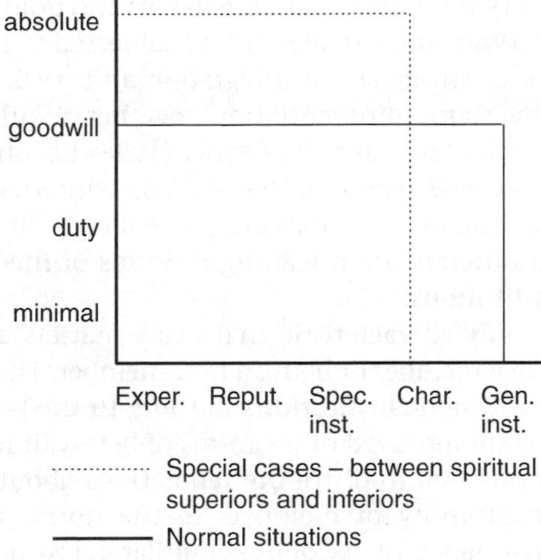

Figure 5.3 Trust under hierarchical institutions.

Trust in enclaves

Trust in enclaved contexts looks rather different again. In small, highly collective and internally egalitarian settings, the multi-lateral social ties sustained can be extremely supportive, emotionally deep and intense. For example, Marks (1998) re-examines the data from the Hawthorne studies in Chicago from the late 1920s and the 1930s in order to explore the dense ties of 'inclusive intimacy' among women co-workers in 'the test room' who shared a roughly equal employment status and who worked closely together. The friendship structure was very much that of a group rather than a set of dyads. Indeed, Marks notes (1998), the data suggest that – as the neo-Durkheimian theory has long predicted for enclaves (Rayner, 1982, 1988; Douglas, 1996) – when dyadic bonds became strong and apparent to the other members of the groups, jealousies were aroused that could have threatened schism for the group as a whole. The patterns of informal ties that were studied in poor working-class residential neighbourhoods by the generation of 'community studies' sociologists of the 1960s and 1970s (e.g. Young and Willmott, 1957; Hill, 1975; Pahl, 1975; Okely, 1983; see the review in Crow and Allan 1994) exhibit a structurally similar pattern, modulated by gender and by the differences that co-residence rather than co-working make. There are clear demarcations between members and non-members. The high density – and the medium or high strength, proximity, cliquehood and multi-lateral character – of social ties of this form came to be associated by sociology in that period with working-class practice by contrast with the more individualistic pattern of middle-class friendship (Bulmer, 1986; Allan, 1990). The content of what passed along the ties within these groups is, for the most part, a far cry from the sectarian religious and political organisations that Rayner (1982, 1988) and Douglas (1970) subjected to neo-Durkheimian analysis. Nonetheless, strong social integration and weak social regulation by discipline or by status differentiation together require very complex systems of rules to maintain equality. Rayner (1998) has shown empirically, for example, that enclaves require rather extensive internal regulation – for example, of democratic decision-making procedures – in order to prevent too much internal differentiation leading to forms of inequality that clash with their basic institutions.

In enclaves, the only characteristic that really matters as an indicator of trust is that of being a member or being a non-member. There is very limited reliance on external generic institutions; turning to the police or suing, for instance, are deeply disapproved of (as forms of betrayal) in many enclaves. The enclave functions well to distribute reputations about trustworthiness, as measured by conformity of members to the norms and rules of the enclave, as a consequence of its dense multilateral structure; within the enclave, goodwill trust is sustained. To those outside the enclave, however, the presumption of suspicion can really only be overcome by practical experience of having a proven reliable reputation with other members of the enclave or else offering quite specific warranties.

Like those living under individualistic institutions, then, those in enclaves are much preoccupied with authenticity and genuineness (the effect of weak social regulation), albeit measured this time by the relative commitment of individuals to the standards of the enclave rather than by individual characteristics of emotional performance. Again, like those living under individualistic institutions, there is a provisional barrier between friends – for all enclave members are potential friends (comrades, brothers and sisters in Christ, 'one of us') – while those outside the enclave are typically candidates for acquaintance, at best.

There are many examples of this type of trust in the literature on inter-organisational, corporate and business 'social capital' and 'embeddedness'. Coleman's often-cited (1988) article – introducing the concept of social capital – presented good examples of the kinds of trust used in enclaves. Coleman's definition of social capital that stressed the *closure* of networks, by which he meant both that the network has a clear boundary between members and non-members and that the network is dense in the sense that very high proportions of the total possible set of linkages between individuals or organisations in the membership set, are in fact realised in his case studies. One was the case of the very densely tied and tightly bounded community of wholesale diamond jewellers in New York. One of the ways in which the boundary was marked was, he noted, the role played by the New York Jews, whose networks were multiplex (i.e. ties between the same individuals were employed in many different functions – business, social, leisure, religious, etc.). In the terms of the present analysis, then, membership of the Jewish business community functioned as a shared characteristic type of reason for trust. For Coleman, a powerful indicator of the degree of the trust achieved among these diamond traders was the fact that they would quite routinely allow fellow merchants to take away bags of stones worth hundreds of thousands of dollars for inspection, without a contract, quite confident that they would be returned intact. Another of his examples was the network of traders in the Kahn El Khalili market of Cairo, where family and intermarriage connections functioned in the same way to mark boundaries between members and non-members and as a shared characteristic reason for trust. In both cases, the multiplexity of the ties, based on shared characteristics that could be socially construed as being ascribed also served a second function by providing a social structure along which information about reliability and trustworthiness and, indeed, personal endorsements and guarantees for others could pass. In the terms of the present analysis, then, there is in enclaves an intimate structural relationship between shared characteristics and the flow of reputations. The density and boundedness of the enclave structure is recognised and perpetuated by insiders by the use of shared characteristics and this, in turn, provides a social infrastructure for the control of reputations and the exercise of surveillance.

Since Coleman's work and Granovetter's (1985) article, many studies use definitions of 'embeddedness' that essentially describe the network structure of an enclave; namely, a system of ties of accountability which is characterised by high density and a rather clearly marked boundary between the densely tied group and others. For example, Rooks *et al.* (2000) define it as repeated transactions between a limited same set of partners under social institutions that allow for credible commitment; of course, such repeated interactions within a small group will soon reinforce the identity, boundary and density of an enclaved group.

Uzzi (1997) contrasts embeddedness very sharply with what is here called individualistic network structures, with their 'loose' and 'constantly shifting' sets of ties and strong 'market' orientation. For him, embeddedness means personal and relational systems in which contract documentation is of secondary importance (if used at all), 'thick' systems of tacit information cultivation and exchange, and satisficing rather than maximising on price (although Uzzi also wrongly ascribes trust only to strongly socially integrated network forms such as those characterised by 'embedded' ties). However, in operationalising the concept marked by this cluster of properties, Uzzi focuses specifically on fields of economic action in which very dense, bounded and multiplex ties dominate. His case study of the women's garment industry in New York city serves precisely this purpose. This is, as Uzzi describes, a rather inward looking market dominated by small- and medium-sized firms densely tied to each other and in which particular ethnic identities – especially New York Jewish and New York Chinese – enable the flow of reputations and sustain the possibility of mutual surveillance.

There are, Uzzi noted, some echoes of the role of the *tertius*, the broker diagnosed by Burt (1992) as critical to the operation of individualistic networks, but in the New York garment trade the *tertius* does not operate as a freebooting entrepreneur. Rather, he is an intermediary of multiplexity, introducing new members of recognised communities of shared characteristics into the business network of the trade and using their own reputation based on that membership to sponsor new entrants as reliable. Whereas in Larson's (1992) study of entrepreneurial settings reputation functions as an initiator of trust – and reputations are taken from a wide variety of sources and from outside the charmed circle of potentially multiplex ties – in Uzzi's and Coleman's enclave cases reputations are taken from a narrow range of sources within a set of bounded communities through multiplex ties and reputation is something that is sustained within the community. Furthermore, in Larson's entrepreneurial settings firms invest in their reputations as a *generalised* asset but they invest in being known to be trustworthy in *specific* tasks they may be contracted to carry out. In Uzzi's enclaves, firms invest in their reputations as an asset that is *specific* to their communities, but they do so in *generalised* ways that reflect their multiplex commitments to the communities in which their contractual business is embedded. In short, the relationship between the generalised and the specific in trust is exactly reversed between the strongly and the weakly socially integrated forms of networks.

Although both Coleman and Uzzi are principally concerned to identify the strengths of what are here called enclave forms, Uzzi at least is well aware that they have weaknesses. 'Over-embeddedness' is possible, leading either to stagnation due to excessive investment in single sources of information and ideas or else to feuding.

Once again, transaction costs are by no means irrelevant in enclaves, although the manner in which they are handled is quite distinct. The costs of establishing reputations for trustworthiness are pooled across the membership of the bounded communities in which the particular transactors are located. As in individualistic settings, the costs of formality in contracting are eliminated but at the price of having to bear the costs of sustaining the density of ties and the boundaries around the communities defined by shared characteristics and also of establishing reputations afresh for each new entrant (albeit these costs are not borne by the transactors in the focal contract but pooled). Figure 5.4 therefore describes the structure of trust between individuals who may be potential friends or acquaintances in enclaves. Goodwill trust can be achieved within the group slightly less reliably on the basis of shared characteristics (the dotted line) than by reputation effects, which can be buttressed by the collective institutions and the high levels of shared information within the collectivity. However, lower levels of trust are granted, and only on the basis of fiduciary duties, to those outside the enclave.

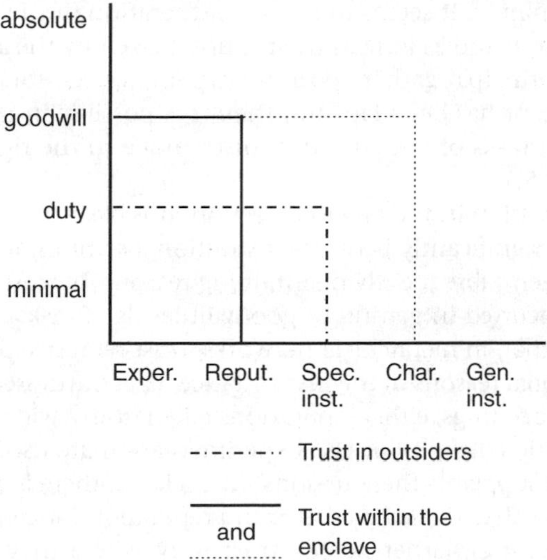

Figure 5.4 Trust under enclaved institutions.

The argument of this chapter is, then, that in order to understand the nature of social trust and its importance for public policy as it is designed to influence social structure, it is necessary to shift the level of analysis from the level of relational or network structure – at which Table 5.1 works – to the level of institutional structure. The four trust graphs (Figures 5.1–5.4) display the ways in which a kind of reduction of relational level factors for trust to institutional syndromes of trust can be performed.

The dynamics of inter-organisational trust

So far, this chapter has presented a static analysis of the neo-Durkheimian typological approach to understanding the determinants of and the extent to which trust can be achieved between organisations in different settings. It is now necessary to examine the more dynamic processes that both make for and then undermine that trust.

Dynamics of trust-reinforcement

In some older theoretical writings about trust there are blithe assertions that trust is self-reinforcing, that it is an asset unique in that it increases rather than decreases with use, that placing trust itself promotes trustworthiness and so, in general, the dynamics can be represented by a virtuous circle of trusting and trustworthy behaviour (Fox, 1976, *passim*; cf. Hirschman, 1985). Few empirical studies either of interpersonal trust or of inter-organisational trust have borne out any claim that the virtuous circle is a generally observed or necessary dynamic. It seems to be an exaggeration of the straightforward observation that, if and as long as trust is not broken by the agent and if and as long as the principal gathers positive experience reinforcing the perception that the agent has been faithful, then it is possible in many settings to begin to entrust tasks of a high order (or to move to the right in the terms offered in Table 5.1).

From the discussion in the previous section, it is clear that trust-reinforcing dynamics differ significantly between institutional settings, in respect of both initiating and then subsequently maintaining reasons for trust and in the costs and difficulty incurred in getting to goodwill levels of tasks entrusted. It has been suggested that, in hierarchical networks, trust-reinforcement proceeds by way of institutional reasons in the first instance, later buttressed by experience. In individualistic settings, either reputations taken from a wide range of sources about task-specific reliability or else experimentation are used to initiate, but experience then supplants these reasons. In enclaves, there is an intimate relationship between shared characteristics and reputation for generalised reliability. In isolate settings, either people trust only where they must or where experience suggests they can and, even then, only provisionally and rarely beyond the duty or contractual levels of tasks entrusted.

Dynamics of distrust and forgiveness

On the other hand, there are a great many writings which offer the bleakest possible view of the consequences of breaches of trust. Psychologist of risk perception Paul Slovic (1993), for example, writes that, once perceived to have been broken, trust is almost impossible to regain and people acting as principals typically move not to a position of neutrality or lack of trust but to a negative position of distrust or mistrust (for an argument that positive, neutral and negative measures of trust should not appear on the same scale, see Swift, 2001). For example, Sitkin and Roth (1993) suggest that betrayal will lead to escalating cycles of ever deeper distrust between former partners.

Equally, however, it does not seem to be true that, in all contexts, trust having been broken, people and organisations are wholly unforgiving, and unwilling to consider entering into any kind of trusting relationship with an agent that has betrayed their trust in the past. Clearly, failure to prove trustworthy in one field of activity may well not indicate inability to be trustworthy in all other fields; just because someone proved inadequate in their advice on careers it does not follow that their medical advice would be untrustworthy. But more than this, people and organisations make different decisions about forgiveness in different institutional settings. Consider, for example, the well-known differences between British and US business willingness to trust someone who has been declared bankrupt in the past or a business that has filed for protection from creditors under Chapter 11. American business is famously forgiving of bankruptcy and administrative protection and, among small businesses, a bankruptcy in the past is regarded by some as evidence of a commendable willingness to take risks. By contrast, in the United Kingdom, it is still true that a record is stained by bankruptcy and that a marked stigma clings to a formerly bankrupt individual; British companies that have gone into administration rarely survive in the same form, unlike American companies which often persist and are still trusted to some significant degree.

Some institutional settings seem specifically to provide mechanisms, however informal, for the rebuilding of trust. Indeed, since, by and large, societies do hold together and do not normally collapse into civil war, feuding and inability to conduct governance and trust, these institutional settings must in fact be rather common despite the many and obvious obstacles to trust (Shapiro, 1987). The formal rules of Chapter 11 and the informal, tacit institutions of much of business life in the United States constitute a set of institutions by which former bankrupts can be reintegrated into networks of trust after having once proven untrustworthy in the past. These institutions seem to represent a hybrid of hierarchical systems of governance in the body of the law, in the role of the rating and ranking agencies for investors and also in the role of institutional and venture capital investors, with more individualistic practices in day-to-day trading credit, lending and borrowing relationships.

By contrast, in enclaves and isolate settings, people find it much more costly to sustain institutions by which forgiveness and reintegration can be offered to those found untrustworthy. In religious sects, which are often enclaved in structure, for example, forgiveness and reintegration is highly ritualised and is often the cause of schism. In isolate systems – such as nineteenth-century Sicily or mid-twentieth century Corsica – ending feuds proved extremely difficult and costly. Some of the recent outpouring of social science research on distrust and the challenge of restoring trust in the context of environmental conflicts between resident communities and large companies siting risky installations in their neighbourhoods are really studies on the problems and difficulties of persuading communities that have become increasingly enclaved in their structure to be willing to trust larger corporations (see for example, the essays in Cvetkovich and Löfstedt, 1999). Much of that research has been focused on the efficacy in this task of the system of transactionally high cost but politically imperative ritual for conflict containment that have been developed for the purpose of achieving some level of trust in those enclaved communities, including consensus conferences, community visioning exercises, mediation, citizens juries and stakeholder workshops (Dukes, 1996).

The dynamics of distrust therefore exhibit some important affinities along the diagonals of the matrix used to represent the four basic institutional settings, where the possibilities for reintegration after betrayal of trust are less demanding on the positive diagonal (in individualistic and hierarchical networks) than they are on the negative diagonal (connecting isolate and

Table 5.2 Types of dynamics of trust by institutional setting

Social regulation ↑ **Isolate**	*Social integration* → **Hierarchy**
Trust-reinforcement: (limited) experience and some specific institutions *Trust-undermining*: opportunism and anticipated opportunism, difficulties in re-binding partners after trust has been lost *After trust has been broken*: may lose even prudential trust: very difficult to rebuild higher levels of task entrusted	*Trust-reinforcement*: initially specific institutions, then experience to supplement *Trust-undermining*: Systems of institutions become too transaction costly *After trust has been broken*: can be rebuilt beginning with contractual trust if institutions can be made effective, and if reparations are made for breach under institutional rules
Individualism *Trust-reinforcement*: initially reputation from wide sources on specific tasks or, then experiment relying on generalised institutions, then experience *Trust-undermining*: Incentives from gains from placing trust elsewhere lead to unstable patterns of trust *After trust has been broken*: can be rebuilt on the basis of experiment and experience: organisations and individuals can make fresh start, for example, after bankruptcy	**Enclave** *Trust-reinforcement*: Initially generalised reputation based on flows of information within specific narrow community defined around shared characteristics, then informal institution building *Trust-undermining*: Risks of declining innovation from inward-looking enclaved community, or schism and feud *After trust has been broken*: may lose even prudential trust: very difficult to rebuild higher levels of task entrusted

enclaved networks). Table 5.2 summarises the key differences in the main dynamic processes.

At the level of what we might call second-order dynamics, there can be change in the institutional forms. The simplest case is the collapse or overthrow of, say, hierarchy and its replacement with, say, more individualistic relations; more complex cases involve hybridisation and the development of settlements articulating something of two, three or all four of these types. In such hybrids, we should expect to observe corresponding combinations of each of these trust dynamics.

Conclusion

The relationship between trust and the forms of inter-organisational networks is, then, much more complex than some of the writings of the 1980s and early 1990s tended to suggest. Articles such as Powell's (1990) manifesto for networks and Bradach and Eccles' (1989) statement of theory suggested that trust was uniquely a property of networks rather than other forms. These have turned out to be misleading, unless trust and networks are defined in so narrow and idiosyncratic ways as to make the claims true by definition (and also uninteresting). Second, the claim that trust is a prior condition for successful networks, alliances, joint ventures or partnerships – that it is an independent variable, an unmoved mover that makes inter-organisational relations possible – also has also turned out to be, at the very least, also misleading. Rather, to understand the relationship between trust and the different forms that inter-organisational relationships can take, we need to examine the flows of causal influence in both directions; that is to say, we need to develop models in which trust and inter-organisational network forms are endogenously and sequentially generated, undermined and regenerated. The neo-Durkheimian institutional theory presented here provides a synthesis of the evidence in the literature, including an account of the main features of these bi-directional relationships in the main types of institutional settings. In each case, the network structure and the institutions of which that network structure is the distinctive empirical form shape and select the type of trust that is most likely to emerge. That form of trust in turn reinforces the network structure and the institutions, both formal and informal. However, that reinforcement process can go too far and become self-disorganising, causing breakdowns and moves to other institutional, network and trust forms. Alternatively, the reinforcement process can be undermined by external shocks and by conflict with forces articulating other institutions; for example, by the assertion of more entrepreneurial individualistic forces, by the recrudescence of more hierarchical regulation and oligarchical control, by the communal assertion of enclaves or by the simple leaching away of the exhausted and the disillusioned into isolate structures. Trust and network forms can be understood neither by linear Weberian histories – in which hierarchies decline, then markets rise and decline and finally networks arise – nor by equilibrium models in which any one type of institutional form can be assuming always to be homeostatically self-stabilising. Rather, we need dynamic disequilibrium models which allow space both for local processes of reinforcement and undermining of each of the four basic forms to be present simultaneously and in conflict, and for hybrids or settlements between two, three or all four, which too can only be provisionally stable (Thompson M, 1979, 1982, 1992, 1996).

This approach to understanding trust has some normative implications. At the very least, it suggests that it is important for managers in organisations to take some pains to develop rich appreciations of the specific contextual and institutional characteristics of the network environment – and the trust relations of this environment – and to make their decisions about the strategies for trust and trustworthiness in the light of this appreciation. For the strategies appropriate to the management of trust and trustworthiness clearly differ significantly between institutional settings. For policy makers, the importance of developing clear understandings of the trust environment in fields of public policy – such as the provision of health care – is, if anything, even greater. For, when governments try to reorganise a sector, they very often seek to change the forms of inter-organisational relationships in ways that put pressure on the established institutional supports for trust and trustworthiness, which means that it is crucial that they can identify and develop different and more appropriate forces enabling people to develop appropriate degrees of trust relatively quickly if reorganisation is not to lead to disorganisation.

Part II

6 Governing and Managing Across Networks: Tools and Strategies

Management within networks

Management within networks is a term used to mean a range of decision-making activities such as resource acquisition and allocation, production, distribution and exchange, co-ordination, positioning, planning and strategy development, collective sense-making, and so on. These activities impact, either intentionally or unintentionally, upon the size, structure and location of power within networks, whether they are collaborations between individual or organisational peers or connections of upstream suppliers and downstream customers.

Exercising management – or governance – across several organisations, rather than within a single one, might be thought to bring special challenges. In some part, it will be argued later, this is true, but, we will also suggest that many of the requisite techniques, concepts, strategies and capabilities for network governance and management are familiar from – and in part developed within – systems of management in single organisations.

In general, the goals of management are to arrange and co-ordinate resources, interests, commitments and sense-making to pursue the aspirations of a particular agency. This is undertaken within prevailing constraints, such as, for example, the legal and contractual limits on the manner by which aims can be pursued. Management is the activity of trying to shape organisational ability, individual willingness and available resources in order to sustain collective action in pursuit of the objectives of either a single organisation or a system of organisations (Eccles *et al.*, Nohria, 1992). Typically, it is undertaken from within the agency or network.

By contrast, governance is the steering of the overall network from an external standpoint; that is, from the position of an actor who is not themselves a member of the network being governed. This may involve the manipulation of financial resources, permissions to become members, regulation of activities, and so on (Bache, 2000). La Porte (1996) distinguishes those exercising external governance as 'network throwers' from 'network riders' (who possess high centrality inside the network) and also from 'network pullers' (who are semi-isolates outside the network seeking membership or at least more or closer ties).

The basic tools of management are the same when working between several organisations as they are for working within one. It is often said that the crucial difference between the two is that, in the inter-organisational context, a manager cannot exercise authority or legitimate power to command over an organisation in which she is not employed or where she does not hold a board-level non-executive position. However, even when working within a single organisation, there is only a limited number of activities in which managers engage that actually involve the straightforward issuing of commands backed by threats so strong as to amount to coercion (albeit frequently implicitly). Much of what managers do involves rather limited exercise of authority or combination of authority with other kinds of tools. Indeed, in many situations, resort to authority alone would merely prove counter-productive. Subjected more to authority than to persuasion or incentive, staff may lose motivation and some may leave; morale may fall, goodwill may be withdrawn, and managers may find that they must work much harder to secure crucial information. In hierarchies, the commitment by managers of an organisation to a strategy may rest in part upon implicit authority – and the understanding of others of the will to use it – but command is a weapon that often weakens effective authority through its explicit use. Implicit authority can be secured from a range of sources and need just be based on vertical integration; as we have seen in Chapter 3, there are contractual relationships, for instance, that can sustain it. The point is certainly not that authority is never necessary, rather that it is not always so and certainly rarely sufficient.

Most managerial time is spent in any organisation on defining problems, persuading people and being persuaded, responding to requests and complaints, negotiating finances, hiring people and entering other contracts, writing draft plans, arguing the merits of strategies, measuring achievements and non-achievements, monitoring, developing suggestions, brokering between people and organisations to reduce or at least contain conflict (and sometimes to increase it) and, probably, more than anything else, making inquiries and asking for information. These are also the main activities to which managers devote their time when they work across two or more organisations.

The scope for governance and management of networks: theories

Each of the main theories introduced in Chapter 2 suggests different accounts of the scope for governance of networks and for management action by organisations within networks; Table 6.1 summarises these.

Table 6.1 The implications of the major theories of inter-organisational networks for governance and management

Theories	Governance of networks can be exercised effectively	Management within networks can be exercised
Rational choice, transaction cost	By modulating transaction costs with regulation, by defining the resources available for pursuit by individuals and organisations	By controlling transaction costs, by choosing between opportunism with guile or longer term more co-operative enlightened self-interest
Organisation competence and learning	To a limited extent because of the limited capacity of those outside the networks of organisations in particular fields to be able accurately to predict the changing competence requirements of those fields	By defining key competencies and learning benefits to be sought and identifying which should be determining which should be through alliance or other ties
Personalistic	To a limited extent, because informal network forms will emerge to get around formal restrictions imposed by governance, and because there are limited means available for governance using informal means	By micro-manipulation of the available social structure to use existing ties, to reach new ties
New institutionalist	Limited: by the defining of institution for coercive isomorphic processed, by the development of standards for mimetic and normative processes	By following prevailing normative institution or not following them at the risk of sanctions or disadvantages, unless institutions permit defiance to be organised on such a scale as to enables institutional change
Ecological	By using regulatory power to define available resources	By making basic choices between specialist and generalist strategies, growth or stabilisation strategies, etc, on the basis of assessment of niche lifecycles and stage in the cycle of the community of organisations
Problems and technology contingency	To some extent, by regulatory control of available technologies	By seeking to optimise network form for contingency of technology, problem, task etc
Macro economic and technological determinist	In limited ways, because governance bodies can have limited power over wider trends in network forms	By standard economic competition for relative position and for absolute quantities of resource
Weberian	By the use of rational regulation	By the adoption of ever more standardised, rationalised processes and ever deeper commitment to instrumental rationality as a world view
Socio-technical (actor network theory)	Unclear	Using constrained agency
Neo-Durkheimian	With some scope, but most effective when institution-making and informal institution-building is undertaken working on informal institutions to secure settlements between the basic solidarities	By formal and informal action differently selected according to the prevailing forms of solidarity that define each of the basic network forms

Certain general features emerge from this table. Those theories that privilege interests – and take them to be more or less exogenous – tend to allow the greatest scope for the governance of networks. Theories which stress the role of informal institutions allow less scope, and least scope is granted by those theories which stress informal and individual-level network structures as capable of working around and undermining formal institutions. The same rough clustering of theories also divides views on the nature of, but not so much the scope for, management within networks. Interest driven theories focus on management around more or less readily measured variables, while institutional or structural theories focus on the (either explicit or, more often, implicit) role of management around less readily measured factors around social structure.

Power in networks

Managing within and governance of networks both require that the organisation or actor engaged in this management or governance can achieve a position from which to exercise power. Sustaining that power necessitates that it be legitimated which, in turn, involves some kind of consent to its exercise as constrained by the prevailing institutions that define the network. Such legitimate power – contained in and constrained under the influence of institutions – is, in effect, a schematic definition of authority. In those forms of legitimation in which power is vested in an individual occupying a role then that authority is sensibly parsed as a relationship between leader and followers.

The notion of power is not always well handled in the discussion of inter-organisational networks. For, conventionally, power is defined in respect of single organisations possessing systems of accountability articulated through the mechanisms of direct employment, in the case of individual staff, or of ownership, in the case of superior and subsidiary organisations, or relative voting power, in the case of partial ownership. Where it is discussed, it is sometimes suggested that, in these inter-organisational structures, power may be expressed and mobilised through other means. Since several types of networks have been distinguished, it is reasonable to allow the possibility that power may take different forms – or at least be constituted as differently weighted combinations of a number of basic forms of power – according to the type of network.

The classical literature in the social sciences is strikingly convergent in the ways in which the basic instruments of power are delineated. This is despite the well-known underlying theoretical problems in understanding how and when power is used and, in particular, in defining the appropriate counterfactuals against which to determine when power has been exercised (Lukes, 1974; Clegg, 1989). For example, Etzioni (1961) distinguished coercive (taking direct organisation control and steering of other organisations as both coercive), remunerative and normative power. French and Raven's seminal (1959) theory of organisational power similarly identified coercive power; reward power; legitimate power (based on beliefs, norms, traditions); expert power (another variety of persuasion based on technocratic information); and referent power (based on identification, which actually seems to be another kind of legitimate power).

In the later literature on the tools of government, these same forms of power came to be analysed through instruments rather than activities. Hood (1983) calls these basic tools of power, respectively, organisation (substitution), authority (steering), treasure (incentive, negotiation), nodality (information and legitimation). Likewise, de Bruijn and ten Heuvelhof (1998) distinguish regulatory, financial and communicative instruments. Recently, and more graphically, Bemelmans-Videc *et al.* (1998) speak simply of 'sticks, carrots and sermons' (see 6 *et al.*, 2002, for a more finely grained synthesis of the tools literature).

Scholars of strategic management work with a classification of styles which is not fundamentally different from these. For example, Mintzberg and Waters (1994) present a very complex taxonomy, but many of the forms they distinguish can in fact be shown to be hybrids of just four of their types: planned and deliberate strategy (executed using command and control, etc.); entrepreneurial strategy (executed using pricing and incentive); ideological strategy (executed though persuasion); and imposed strategy or pure emergency (executed through more or less opportunistic coping).

Summarising this convergence, it can be said that the basic instruments of power are *control* (direct authority, substituting internal organisation, mandation, prohibition, permission of other organisations); *inducement* (incentive, pricing, compensation, purchase, contracting, lending and granting fungible resources such as money); *suasion* (use of information, appeals to norms, values, arguments, ideas, identification, traditions, standards, expertise); and *coping* (opportunistic behaviour to secure survival in situations where the other instruments are unavailable or ineffective because others have greater capacity to exercise them than does the actor in question).

The exercise of each of these basic instruments of power will incur different kinds of costs in different organisational and institutional contexts. It is true that control is most readily associated with hierarchy because there the institutions are *explicitly* geared to its exercise. In settings where people or organisations broker their way individualistically to form the ties that are of greatest use to them and seek to exploit the temporary advantages of being the main route between any pair of others, they are most likely both to respond to and to offer inducements and incentives. Similarly, in community-like or enclaved forms, suasion is the principal means of ensuring cohesion, precisely because other tools are unavailable or have been deliberately eschewed. Coping is one of the most intelligent things to do in a context in which one has few options. This is because the alternative instruments are controlled by others so that the environment is structured heavily by what are, from the point of view of the actor, given facts and where the possibilities for collective action with peers are very limited; this is the situation of isolates. Thus, the four basic forms of organisations and of multi-organisational networks described in this book have close affinities with each of the basic instruments of power.

Nonetheless, control can be exercised, as Stinchcombe (1990) showed, in the absence of hierarchy, albeit that it requires quite complex design of contracts. Equally, within bureaucratically organised systems, it is possible to introduce internal market systems of pricing and to make them work without fundamentally removing all hierarchy, although this requires careful institutional design. Moreover, in many organisational settings, these four instruments are not used alone but in consort with at least some of the others because the instruments are interdependent; for example, many markets are given more or less stable structures. This means that power will be exercised in networks not only by the instrument with which the network form has its main affinity but also by using some differently weighted combination of all four instruments (Table 6.2).

Table 6.2 Relationships between inter-organisational patterns and the tools of power

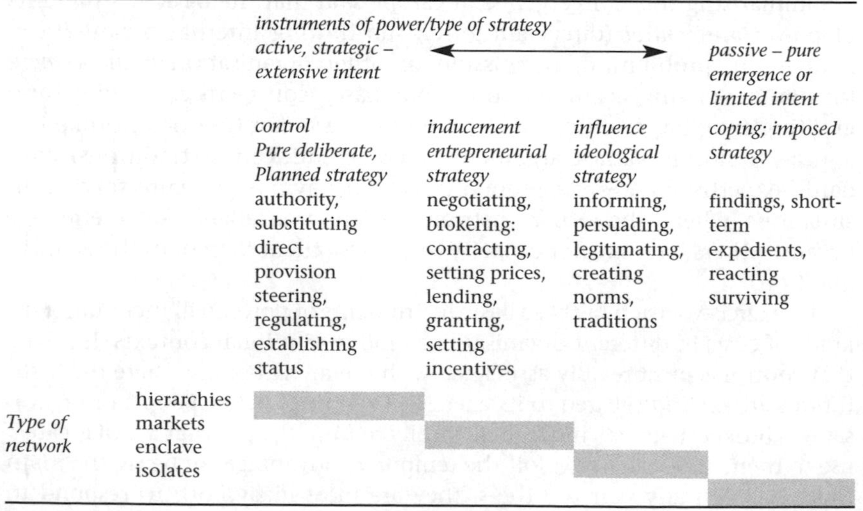

		instruments of power/type of strategy *active, strategic – extensive intent*	⟵	⟶	*passive – pure emergence or limited intent*
		control *Pure deliberate, Planned strategy*	*inducement* *entrepreneurial strategy*	*influence* *ideological strategy*	*coping; imposed strategy*
		authority, substituting direct provision steering, regulating, establishing status	negotiating, brokering: contracting, setting prices, lending, granting, setting incentives	informing, persuading, legitimating, creating norms, traditions	findings, short-term expedients, reacting surviving
Type of network	hierarchies				
	markets				
	enclave				
	isolates				

Note: Cells marked in grey are those that exhibits affinities.

The distinction between control and inducement is perhaps not always as sharp as the table might suggest. For very strong inducements may be irresistible, as the film gangster's stock phrase about making someone 'an offer [s]he couldn't resist' reminds us. Conversely, control is costly to enforce, and there will be some free-riding where incentives to avoid control are strong. As the expense of inspection, monitoring, and enforcement in regulation rise, those upon whom control is being exercised will be more likely to calculate the costs and benefits of compliance against those of non-compliance. This equation is influenced by the probabilities of being caught and punished for non-compliance and of the gains from such behaviour, in just the same way that organisations will calculate the value of inducements. At the purely instrumental level, then, control can be regarded as the strongest case of inducement.

Being principally instrumental in its effect, and being designed to elicit a practice of calculated rationality or even formal cost–benefit analysis among those targeted by power, inducement is subject to a law of diminishing returns. Suppose that a government wants to induce its citizens to replace their older polluting cars with newer, low emission vehicles. Suppose further that, to achieve this, the government seeks to use a combination of road tax, petrol tax, tax on the purchase of cars, mileage treatment in tax for company cars, tax treatment of car manufacturers and petrol retailers and retailers of alternative fuels, and others. It will find that the cost to the taxpayer and to individuals and companies will rise sharply in order to induce, say, the last 10 per cent of vehicle owners to buy a new low emission vehicle.

Nevertheless, the symbolic meanings of control and inducement are importantly different. A decision to use control indicates the much greater moral weight that is attached by policy makers to the targeted risks and opportunities than does a decision to use inducement. For example, when radical environmental groups object to decisions made to substitute taxes on polluters for older systems of coercive regulation what they fear is not only that the inducements will be less effective but also that they signal a relaxation of social and political concern. Although the sanctions involved in control are normally seen as the strongest case of a disincentive, when examined in the context of its symbolic meaning as the severest form of praise (mandation) or condemnation (prohibition), control can be seen not as the limit case of inducement but as the limit case of influence.

Distinguishing between the two levels at which the instruments of power can work, and showing that control can be read as the limit case of the other two active instruments, suggests that the relationship between the tools may typically look something like that set out in Figure 6.1. In both the contexts of governance of and management within networks, then, appeal is made to the same limited repertoire of basic tools.

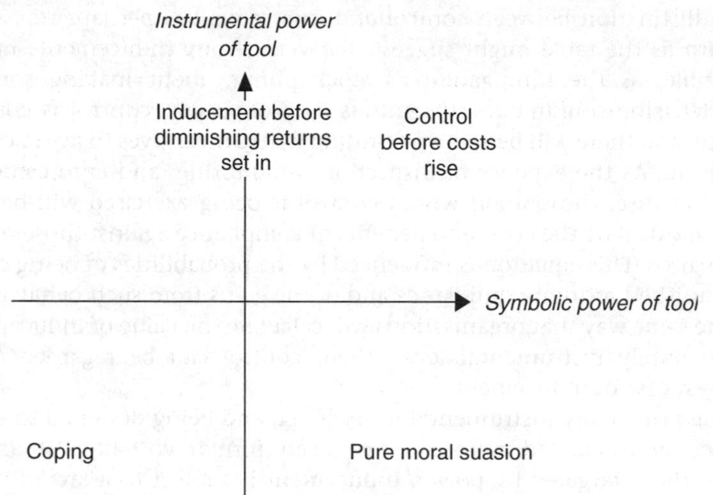

Figure 6.1 Instrumental and symbolic powers of tools of governance: relationships between tools.

Tools of management within networks

The tools available to managers and organisations with which to exert power and influence over networks are essentially the same general tools of power that were identified in Table 6.2. In order of decreasing strength – or coerciveness – upon those organisations and people to which or whom the tools are directed, the basic options are those of

- *commanding* an organisation or people, or creating substitute organisations that can be commanded – here, command includes mandation, prohibition, authoritative permission, and the background activities of putting in place the institutional conditions under which these specific powers can be exercised;
- providing *incentives* for organisations and people – here, incentives include purchasing, selling, negotiating and setting prices, negotiating and determining wages, and a range of non-monetary rewards, and include negotiating and settling the institutional agreements under which incentives of these kinds can be administered;
- using *information* of various kinds – here, information includes setting norms and standards, exercising persuasion, providing background information on the basis of the possession of which people are likely to behave in certain ways, establishing and sustaining traditions, granting status, using rituals, creating and spreading reputations; and
- *coping* – here, coping includes a variety of more or less short-term adaptations to circumstances that are taken as given.

In addition, there are various combinations of two, three or four of these options. We have argued each of these is easiest to use in networks which are already, respectively, hierarchical, individualistic, enclaved and isolate in form. However, the argument of the previous section has shown that achieving a salient position in the network structure can permit organisations and individual managers to use command, incentive and information even in networks that are hybrid in form but in which there is a secondary element in the mix.

Although it is commonly said that the tools of authority are unavailable to be used across the boundaries between organisations, Chapter 3 pointed out that this is not really true for it is quite common to use combinations of tools to enable the use of command. Stinchcombe (1990), for instance, showed that contracts can be written that allow one firm to exercise authority over another. Indeed, many long-term relational contracts allow for this; the many studies of seamless supply chain systems beginning in the 1970s with studies on Japanese firms have shown contractual relations within which large companies purchasing inputs from smaller companies acquire the rights to exercise command deep into the productive 'core' of the supplying firm (e.g. Westney, 2001). Joint ventures in the field of defence contracting are typically hierarchical in form and use contractual relations to allow prime contractors to exercise command over their sub-contractors in the specification of standards, interoperability, processes, quality control and the like (Kelley and Watkins, 1998).

Monopsonist organisations (and also oligopolistic cartels) can effectively force suppliers to work with them on certain terms for lack of any alternative; this has a huge impact on the shaping of the network. In these circumstances the only tool available to the suppliers seems to be that of coping. What the monopolist purchasing party does to structure the network can be read at one level as a limit case of incentive; there is always the option for the suppliers of exiting the market altogether. On the other hand it can be read as a liminal case of implicit command, since the option of exit is one of absolute last resort for most organisations. Conversely, monopolistic suppliers can also achieve huge power, as is shown by the continuing power of large local NHS Trust hospitals over their local Primary Care Trusts (PCTs), despite that the PCTs hold the purse-strings for the vast majority of the work that the hospitals carry out.

The straightforward use of incentives through purchasing and selling is most common in vertical ties, nonetheless it is not unknown in the context of horizontal networks. For example, many clubs charge membership fees and offer valuable goods and services in return for which members can use to set themselves apart from others and which therefore function as incentives. Doz and Hamel's (1998) examples of clan-like multilateral technological research and development networks involved the payment of fees and contribution of some intellectual property to the co-ordinating structure in return for access to a defined body of shared knowledge.

Institutional instruments

If the previous section has described the basic strategic tools with which networks can be managed, deploying these tools require managers and organisations to secure some degree of formal commitment between the organisations involved. At the extreme corner of all four types, this may be avoided for various reasons. In the loosest forms of individualistic network, actors may prefer to avoid formal commitments precisely because they intend to pick and leave particular ties with the lowest exit cost. Similarly, there are hierarchical networks in which the lead organisation prefers not to be tied down to any commitments, leaving those located in the periphery of the network structure to operate by coping mechanisms. Moreover, there are clan like networks in which formal documents are avoided because of the fear that the negotiation process required to agree them might undermine the fragile trust between the parties. Overall, though, most individualistic market systems require contracts, and many hierarchical networks and many clubs of organisations adopt formal constitutions.

A variety of theories is available in the management literature which offer to predict which of the specific types of empirical arrangement – strategic alliances, mergers, and others – might be chosen in particular circumstances. Broadly, these theories divide into what might be called 'objective contingency' theories, 'Machiavellian interest and contingency theories' and 'subjective bias' theories. The first two groups presume at least bounded rationality on the part of at least some of the participants in the network. Objective contingency theories predict that, under conditions of bounded rationality, people will choose the structure that best fits the needs of their environment and their interests as they understand them, given their anticipated estimates of the costs, risks, benefits and opportunities of each of the available forms. Transaction cost theories are of this type; Gulati and Singh (1998) offer a theory of the selection of structures which is an example. The second category is really a special case of the first, because it presumes that one or more members of the network are more rational or less boundedly so, more knowledgeable and more strategic. As a consequence, they can manipulate the perceptions of the others of the likely costs and benefits in order to secure agreement, perhaps even under conditions of deception, to the structure that best suits their private interests. The third variety makes much weaker assumptions about the rationality of the participants, focusing instead on the biases and blinkers that each brings to negotiations about the structure for the network and predicting that these will shape the selection made. Theories which view organisational culture as pre-eminent are of this type, as are theories of framing. For example, Doz and Hamel's (1998) argument about the initiation of co-operation focuses on how various ways of framing the problems for which network forms are presented as solutions, and various biases in expectations and understandings of the capabilities and commitments of others, can all skew the settlement of structural instrument chosen.

It was noted earlier that Stinchombe (1990) demonstrated that market based inter-organisational forms can readily replicate the core features of hierarchy to form hierarchical networks. In more recent work, Gulati and Singh (1998) take the argument to the next stage in a study of data on strategic alliances in biopharmaceuticals, new materials and automobile industries between 1970 and 1989. The study revealed that hierarchical controls were, in a significant number of cases, produced through contractual and other alliance mechanisms in order to produce forms of effective regulation within these strategic alliances, even within inter-organisational relationships where the initial decision to enter the alliance or partnership or group is wholly voluntary.

One form of power which is strongly associated with governance of networks, but which plays a more limited role in management within networks, is explicit regulation. Such regulation is the defining and setting of standards that network members are required to meet either using legitimately coercive means or using voluntarily adopted systems (Brunsson *et al.*, 2000), where the enforcement of those standards using some means of detection of violations and subsequent sanctions. In most forms of regulation, network members are subject to some kind of discipline by which they provide information to others which signals their role in the network and their status in relation to consumers. Sometimes organisations are subject to accreditation, sometimes simply to the assessment of market analysts and rating agencies. In either case, they must behave in ways that will impress those who receive information about the network if those information-receivers have quasi-regulatory or standard-monitoring powers and capabilities. The simplest form of regulation for highly socially integrated networks is the set of membership rules imposed by clubs. In less socially integrated networks, lacking internal means, regulation – in the strict sense of the term – in reality must be sourced externally.

In many types of networks, explicit contracts may be used. In vertically organised networks, typically, the procurement and sales relationships are organised through contacts. However, as is well known, the concept of a contract covers a wide variety of ties (Macaulay, 1963). These range from long-term relational contracts involving high trust and relatively limited explicitness to short-term spot contracts with low trust and extensive detailed explicit provisions (Macneil, 1974, 1980; Williamson, 1985).

Goals of management within networks

Our argument is that success in managing across networks consists of the same things that constitute success in managing a single organisation. What matters is that effective collective action is secured, that the right assembly of resources is achieved, that shared sense-making is developed among the people involved in the network and that commitment is sustained as long as is required.

A key level at which goals are sometimes formulated concerns the *structure* of the network. In general, people may have goals either to preserve or to transform the structure of a network. For example, someone finding that they are working with a network with an essentially individualist structure might decide that, if they can secure a certain kind of position from which to exercise leverage, they would like to work to preserve that individualistic structure. Alternatively, if they would like to turn the network into some kind of group with more of an identity, and therefore with a structural boundary, that may predicate either an enclaved or a hierarchical network. In the latter scenario, strategies might include creating a joint decision-making body on which all actors would be represented, or, in the case of efforts to create a more hierarchical order, they might try to use mergers and acquisitions. Conversely, facing an enclaved or a hierarchical network, it is quite possible that someone who believes that they can achieve sufficient leverage might seek to transform it into a more individualistic structure. This might involve, in the first instance, introducing more market-like contractual arrangements and payments that more accurately reflect true prices, thus allowing members to purchase services from outside the boundaries of the group as freely as from within and consequently introducing greater discretion and weaker scrutiny of action, and the like. However, the transformations sought need not be bilateral; in many cases, goals will be to create hybrid structures of two, three or all four of the basic network structures.

It is worth noting that each of these management strategies for bringing about structural change first involves attempts to bring about institutional changes. In other words, changing accountabilities; for example, weakening authority (merger and acquisition) for hierarchy; or collectivising decision-making for enclave; and less fettered discretion for nodes in the network for individualism. This reinforces the arguments within Chapter 5 that, in the long run, institutions shape structure in networks, rather than the other way around.

Of course, none of the basic goals of management require that weakly integrated networks be turned into strongly integrated groups. Individualistic networks can, like the others, sustain collective action under certain circumstances and subject to certain risk and weaknesses. A major challenge for network management is to make the judgment of whether the circumstances constrain the possibilities for transformation of a network to the point of effectively eliminating choice, and if not, whether the risks of any of the forms and the potential disruption of delivery outweigh any expected benefit of change.

However, it is not necessary for management across networks to be effective for those exercising it to have explicit goals about the network structure. In many cases, the conscious and deliberately adopted goals in dealing with other organisations will be framed in quite other terms, but their pursuit will still have consequences for the network structure. Apart from being framed *structurally*, then, goals may be framed:

- *instrumentally*: that is, in terms of resources to be secured from other organisations in the network (such as information, capital or revenues, specific inputs, knowledge or ideas, or people to be 'poached') or in terms of outputs (such as joint assessments, joint projects, joint appointments, joint oversight committees);
- *relationally*: that is, in terms of the relationship sought with a particular other (for example, seeking a long-term strategic alliance not necessarily just seen in terms of particular resources wanted for work to be undertaken in the immediate planning horizon); and/or
- *narratively*: that is, in terms of impact upon sense-making (for convergence upon or divergence from commonly recognised bonds, roots, ideas, worldviews, accounts of remembered history and anticipated futures) – organisations often seek to work with particular others because it is important to their sense of their own mission, trajectory, loyalty and identification that they are associated with certain organisations or, at least, certain kinds of organisations (for example, many organisations join trade associations, campaigning federations, chambers of commerce, professional colleges and institutes, etc.) on the basis that they need to demonstrate to themselves and to others with which peers they belong.

The pursuit of instrumental, relational and narrative goals will have the consequences of either reinforcing or transforming the structure of the network; conversely, structural change will have consequences for the flow of resources, the pattern of dyadic relations and the kinds of narrative sustained.

However, these distinct levels at which goals for network management can be formulated operate over different time horizons. The instrumental pursuit of resources can be quite short term. Relational goals can be for the short or long term, depending on the nature of the relationships sought. However, narrative goals tend to be relatively long term for they describe the fundamental character, purpose and mission of organisations and of networks. They are frequently enduring, at least as long as the organisational field persists. Structure, then, will change at different rates and with different degrees of dramatic transformation or remarkable stability, depending on whether it occurs in response to agency framed by goals in instrumental, relational or narrative terms.

Structure and the capacity for goal formation in managing within networks

Agency is, of course, constrained by the institutions that define the structure within which people seek to exercise management over networks. This immediately raises the following question: *who* has explicit, conscious goals for networks? In general, those with sufficient leverage within the initial network structure to be able to conceive of taking action to pursue their goals will be most likely to convert their preferences, aspirations, resentments, disappointments into goals of this kind. Those who have or feel that they have little or no leverage will hardly bother.

Management within a network might be undertaken to provide the basis for subsequent authority affecting the whole network in the situation in which an organisation or an individual seeks to secure a position of *centrality* (Wasserman and Faust, 1994). There are many centrality concepts in the mathematical graph theory of networks. However, a simple one is that an actor has greater centrality the more ties that the actor has to the other actors in the network. Where only a few actors have or, in the limit case, just one actor has, high centrality, the network as a whole exhibits high centralisation (Wasserman and Faust, 1994). An actor that can use techniques of management within a network to achieve high centrality might thereby be able to exercise techniques for management affecting the network as a whole. However, *management affecting the whole network* should still be distinguished from *governance of the network*, because, in management affecting the whole network, the process is still undertaken from a position of membership, whereas governance is exercised externally. Certainly, an actor with high centrality in a highly centralised network (see later) can be predicted to be able to exercise greater leverage over bodies able to carry out governance than actors in other situations might.

Using the understanding of network structure presented in Figures 3.1 and 4.1, we can identify relatively readily where organisations or individuals capable of exercising this type of managerial agency will be likely to be located.

We may begin with the weakly integrated and weakly regulated structure, and the strongly regulated, strong integrated one. For in these cases, it is relatively clear just which network positions afford the leverage required.

In an individualistic network, those who occupy a 'broker' position, spanning a 'structural hole' between two cliques (which may be enclaved, hierarchical or even further individualistic networks) will have the greatest leverage (Burt, 1992), for the easiest way for someone in either clique to reach the other clique is go through that broker. For, by the definition of the broker position in the structure, the cost to a clique member of creating a new direct tie will be greater than the cost of using the broker. It is this relative cost advantage that gives the *tertius* this leverage in the absence of any bounded accountability.

In a hierarchical network, those in the core of the star-shaped structure will be best placed to have the leverage to make it worthwhile to develop clear goals. It is their ability easily to reach much of the periphery in the core–periphery structure of this network form that gives them leverage over much of the system. The fact of the boundary in the accountability system provides them with this leverage.

Isolate networks, again by definition, afford very limited leverage for anyone to secure collective action among the scattered and weakly bonded organisations or individuals within the frame of consideration, which, of course, lacks any boundary of accountability or clear definition of 'membership'. Therefore, to the extent that anyone in the frame has goals for more collective action than is sustained by individual coping, they must seek to do things that will transform the network in some way.

The enclaved network structure presents peculiar challenges for management generally and, in particular, for the formulation of goals. Like hierarchical networks, and unlike individualistic or isolate networks, enclaved ones are groups. As such, they have a membership boundary and already possess some narrative about what binds members together. Unlike hierarchical networks, no single organisation or individual has any greater network centrality than any other, for all have high centrality. No sub group of authorised leaders, therefore, has any greater right to leverage than any other member organisation or individual in the network. Therefore, any putative leader must seek to emerge by demonstrating slightly greater commitment to the principles which define the group and its membership than other member organisations or individuals, but without the advantages of authorised asymmetric (greater) status, asymmetrically greater resources or asymmetrically greater centrality. This leads to the growth of charismatic leadership; the problem that the charismatic leader faces is to formulate any goals that might change, rather than simply conserve, the direction of the enclaved group (Douglas and Mars, 2003). This is the problem faced, for example, by many terrorist leaders of enclaved radical movements who try to negotiate terms with states or businesses that their network grew up to oppose. In such cases, these leaders cannot be sure that, on return to their network to propose a compromise, they will not be rejected. The reason is that, within an enclave, potential leaders have no authority with that group other than their marginally greater but flamboyantly demonstrated commitment (which is what charisma fundamentally consists in), to its existing principles which they are in the eyes of their followers apparently about to compromise. Therefore, it is very difficult to introduce goals for such enclaved networks without at least trying to change their structure towards some kind of hybrid with at least one of the other basic forms of network structure present.

Each of these basic forms has both strengths and weaknesses. Often the most appropriate strategy, if it can be achieved, is to try to compensate for the weaknesses of each by creating networks that are hybrids of all four of these types. There is a place for management to limit the fissile character of enclave and to discipline the waywardness of individualism. Equally, excessively hierarchical forms require tempering with the conscience and motivation of the enclave and the imagination of the individualist context and, without some element of articulation of the isolate form, there are real dangers of hyperactivism and exhaustion.

Positioning strategies

For the organisation or individual seeking to exercise management across a network, the first challenge is to understand their initial position within the network, the structure of the network they are located within and the scope afforded by the institutions that shape the network for *changing their own position* within it. In network management, the crucial point is that *salience is what gives leverage*. For, in individualistic and hierarchical networks, one can only gain leverage over a network by first changing one's position to one that is more salient, that is, to secure a *tertius* position to exploit a structural hole or to secure a central position, respectively. In enclaved and isolate networks, such *robustly* salient positions are not available. In these configurations, therefore, it is necessary either to work to preserve the form of the network or else to transform it. In the isolate network case, preservation means simply pursuing the survival of one's own organisation within the system and taking opportunistic advantage of one's contacts with others. By contrast, enclave affords the option of exit (isolates have, by definition, nothing to leave) or else of working within the network through a charismatic strategy to secure a position of *fragile* salience. Chapter 8 argues that defence procurement is an isolate network, in which each national procurement system seeks to secure its autonomy in an international environment where all face heavy constraints. Here, salience is the fragile achievement of temporary hegemony. At present, the United States has achieved some salience in defence procurement, but even the United States has been unable or unwilling to secure co-ordination even within NATO on defence purchasing, specifications or standards.

The empirical research on inter-organisational linkages within the biotechnology industry (Chapter 9) usefully identifies some of the ways in which salience is achieved. In some cases, in what are essentially hierarchical networks, as instanced by a number of the larger pharmaceutical companies, salience is in effect *inherited* by virtue of size, internal diversity of product and capacity for purchasing products and services and capacity for lending reputation by endorsing smaller organisations (Powell and Brantley, 1992; Owen-Smith *et al.*, 2002). In the early years of new dedicated biotechnology firms (DBF), some leading universities such as Stanford found themselves occupying salient roles. They were able to provide 'incubator' services for spin-off companies initially located on their own business parks, staffed by their own academic research staff, and supported by their knowledge transfer and business development agencies (Walsh *et al.*, 1995; Walshok *et al.*, 2002). In the defence field, salience has often been achieved through mergers and acquisitions and through the control of subcontracting by the large prime contractors (see Chapter 8).

In more individualistic networks, of which once again the US biotechnology industry also provides good examples, salience has to be achieved by steadily and entrepreneurially building ties to other clusters and cliques. For example, a start-up company is set up perhaps by a university-based researcher, which is then able to develop molecules, of the potential usefulness of which it can persuade a variety of backers including prestigious individual scientists, venture capital firms, pharmaceutical or agronomy giants, marketing specialists, and so on. In turn, with some luck and competent management both of research and development and of the business processes, this may attract more investment which should bring in new talent, enabling more molecules to be developed and so more patents to be obtained, and so sustaining growth. Such a company thus achieves a degree of network centrality (Smith-Doerr *et al.*, 1998). In the ideal-typical case of an individualistic networking strategy within an individualistic network, this would be done by minimising redundant multiple links to the same clique. However, the ideal-typical case may have become less common as the biotechnology industry matured through the late 1980s and early 1990s. For as the first-movers established network salience, they increased either the measure of social regulation or the measure of social integration within the network. This means that future new entrants congregate in clusters around the first-movers either in hierarchical or in enclaved form, increasing the density of the network structure of the industry as a whole (Kogut *et al.*, 1992; Walker *et al.*, 1997).

Networks with an enclave structure affording only fragile salience can sometimes be found in the public services. Sullivan and Skelcher (2002), for example, review the experience over more than two decades of local partnerships in the United Kingdom for the promotion of co-ordination in activity to combat crime and social disorder (see also Chapter 10). During the Conservative administrations led by Prime Ministers Thatcher and Major, the emphasis was on largely voluntary partnerships. They show that, in such conditions, some localities achieved much with dense groups of the very energetic and others much less in the absence of such committed and connected activists. The Conservative governments rejected various proposals for a statutory basis of duty for this work, perhaps on the basis of their distrust of local government and their view that this should not be a major priority for the police. Sullivan and Skelcher argue that this made the achievement of salience within local partnerships difficult for any single type of agency, leaving only fragile salience to be achieved where local activists could establish it on the basis of demonstrated organisational and personal concern.

Once an organisation has achieved some kind of salience in a network, the structure of the network thereby becomes more centralised; even if only slightly, as in the case of the already dense enclave type of networks. This serves two distinct functions. First, it represents an important achievement of network management in its own right, because a central node in a centralised network has more access to resources from others in the network than less centrally located nodes. Second, it provides a base from which to mount future operations, and from which to develop goals for management of the network through the manipulation of the resources that can now be reached through the ties achieved.

It is helpful to distinguish between two kinds of network management strategy that can be pursued from a position of some salience, often simultaneously. First, an organisation can pursue a *defensive* network management strategy. This involves focusing resources and energies on trying to preserve an existing network position, whether one of salience or peripherality, against perceived threats. It might include both bolstering existing ties and trying to block rival salient organisations from securing direct links, without going through one's own node, to other resources with which one has priority links. The second is the more positive or *offensive* strategy of seeking to improve one's network position, for example, by cultivating new ties to cliques or clusters. There does not appear to be much research on the conditions under which these strategies are more or less likely to be pursued or in which their goals are more or less likely to be achieved.

Each of these strategies for achieving salience represents a step away from the isolate form and in many cases, though not all, will involve the attenuation of enclave. For, it is the situation of the individualist broker and the hierarchical authority from which greatest influence can be secured. The challenge is to make sure that a simple two-way hybrid between individualism and hierarchy is avoided, for this will tend to reject unwelcome but important information that only the internal articulation within the network of enclave and isolate experience can provide. Without that information, the danger is of external shocks from people articulating those concerns much more forcefully.

Influencing network form

The extent to which managers can, by their own efforts, influence the form of the organisational network in which their own organisation is situated is constrained by the prevailing institutional forces. One of the most important constraints is the inherited pattern of inter-organisational relationships with which they must begin and the degree to which that is institutionalised, through informal practices and tacit rules and norms. One feature of that pattern will be the salience of their organisation in the network and the fragility or robustness of that salience vis-à-vis other organisations, as measured (for example) by network centrality and centralisation. Other constraints will include the preferences of forces external to the inter-organisational network, such as those dictated by public policy governance and those derived from the strategies of other organisations in the network. Positioning strategies to secure a measure of salience provide the greatest chance of agency through leverage over structure, but these positions too are often vulnerable to the strategies of others and to institutional constraints. Finally, events in the industry will reshape institutional constraints, enabling loosening or tightening of networks (Madhavan *et al.*, 1998). Some studies suggest that managers can relatively easily choose which inter-organisational structure is most appropriate for their purposes and simply work to put it in place (something like this seems to be implicit in the work of Chiesa and Manzini, 1998).

Some support can be found in the literature for the merits of networks exhibiting features of each of the three 'active' forms; that is, for individualistic, enclaved and hierarchical network forms. As we should expect, which form a given study commends will depend in part on the criteria being used in the evaluation. For example, if the criteria in use are those of the capacity for overseeing and steering of the network then it is not surprising that studies will conclude that hierarchical networks are superior. Provan and Milward's (1995) and Milward and Provan's (2001) work on networks of purchasing and providing in US mental health services is a good example of this. Focusing quite specifically on the effective delivery of services and the minimisation of transaction costs, they conclude, as does Williamson, that network structures with clear principal–agent relationships are superior.

By contrast, if the criteria stress *innovation* or dynamic efficiency, flexibility and the capacity to respond, then individualistic networks tend to be preferred. The key body of literature from this perspective is that which examines inter-organisational links from the perspective of the promoting of organisational *learning*. Summarising much of this work, Powell *et al.* (1996) finds that learning is best promoted by network forms that exhibit a good deal of fluidity of membership and freedom for each organisation to terminate particular ties and seek others, and also where each organisation can seek to secure positions of centrality in both horizontal links with peer organisations – that may be both competitors and collaborators on different projects – and vertically with organisations providing finance, manufacturing, research and development or marketing.

Third, if the criteria to be used for the appraisal are those of securing *legitimacy*, then it is not surprising that enclave or clan forms are found to be both preferable and typically actually preferred. This is because the internally egalitarian structure and the limited capacity of each organisation to secure proprietary control of resources provided by the others enable a certain type of trust in those situations where jointly produced goods and services would not otherwise be produced, and also where defensive strategy is more important than offensive. For example, in the commercial world, trade associations, some research and development networks and many lobby groups find this form to be superior. Doz and Hamel (1998) document the SEMATECH alliance in the United States in the 1980s and the Japanese Ministry of International Trade and Industry promotion of the Very Large

Scale Integration network in the 1970s. Both were established to pool expertise in response to perceived defensive threats to technological leadership and, in both cases, dense multilateral structures were required in which there were carefully designed agreements to ensure that no single firm dominated or was felt by others to be exploiting the intellectual property of the others. In public services, many of the local partnership structures documented by Sullivan and Skelcher (2002) take this clan-like form for essentially similar reasons; namely, that in its absence, it would be difficult to secure acceptance, legitimacy and trust between organisations that might otherwise feel unacceptably dominated.

Which type of criteria, or what weighting of these types in combination, is most likely to be adopted when managers consider their strategy for network management will be in large part a function of institutional factors. These are not, however, limited to constraints and forces making for inertia. Rather, it is the institutional configuration that will create the visibility of opportunities for network change. Those opportunities for change of form are most likely to be found in situations in which the inherited network structure is hybrid, for these provide more institutional capacities for change of direction than monological organisations and networks can.

Activities of management in networks

The peer-reviewed literature provides richer accounts of the specific activities of or mechanisms for managing within networks than it does of strategy. In part, this is the result of the fact that it is easier to detect the ways in which people seek and manipulate ties through observation or through surveys than it is to make reliable inferences from these data to what strategies might have been in place. In part, as Agranoff and McGuire (2001) state, it reflects the now institutionalised ambition of organisational sociologists and public management scholars in the field to find an equivalent for inter-organisational management of the POSDCORB (planning, organising, staffing, directing, co-ordinating, reporting and budgeting) sequence of activities identified by Gulick and Gulick (1937) in the classical literature on managing single organisations.

The majority of the studies on activities, however, are conducted on more or less clearly bounded groups, that is, in the terms used in this book, on hierarchically and enclave structured networks. Therefore, they are focused more heavily on the processes of group formation, operation and dissolution, rather than on the processes by which, for example, isolates use their restricted networks for short-term coping or individualists move more freely between ties.

Most of the accounts of activities organise them into sequences from initiation to termination while acknowledging that actual networks do not necessarily follow a set order of linear 'stages' but instead conduct some activities simultaneously or backtrack at various points (or skip stages or terminate and re-form more than once). For example, Lowndes and Skelcher (1998) are typical of both these approaches when they distinguish four stages with distinct activities:

1. *pre*-partnership *collaboration*, including developing trust and identifying common purposes;
2. partnership *creation*, including the definition of procedures and rules and of decision-making authority for the network (this, in the terms used in our argument, presumes that a measure of hierarchy is more or less expected in the course of network management as Lowndes and Skelcher understand it);
3. partnership programme *delivery*, including contracting, securing resources, jointly producing services or sequencing flows of service production and delivery activities between members of the network; and
4. partnership *termination or dissolution*, which may mean either a full stop or else the transfer of staff, resources and commitment to other agencies.

Agranoff and McGuire (2001) and McGuire (2002) attempt a synthesis of North American public management research on the activities of network management; they too distinguish four categories of activities, although they miss out termination, albeit insisting more heavily on the simultaneity of these activities. Again, their main interest is in bounded groups. Their categories are:

1. *activation*: identifying participants and their interests, tapping their skills, knowledge and resources, arranging an initial network structure, facilitating leadership roles albeit of a fluid kind at this 'stage'; they also include *deactivation*, meaning rearranging a structure found unsatisfactory, introducing new members;
2. *framing*: establishing the operating rules, influencing the prevailing norms and values, persuading people to change their perceptions and ideas, celebrating shared purpose and vision;
3. *mobilising*: inducing members and potential members to commit to the new undertaking, selling the idea, developing clear shared objectives and the commitment of the coalition to them;
4. *synthesising*: creating a favourable environment, blending participants' perceptions and skills into a pattern conducive to working well together, establishing information exchange, changing incentives to encourage co-operation, developing rules and roles for interaction, helping the network to become more self-organising.

Controlling for the more American focus on 'values and visions' and the British emphasis on 'setting rule', framing, mobilising and synthesising seem to correspond fairly clearly to some of the main stages summarised in Lowndes and Skelcher's 'creation' category.

In the Dutch tradition of public management research, Kickert *et al.* (1997) distinguish the following network management activities (they use the word 'strategies' although more in the sense of 'strategems' than in the sense of grand strategy):

- activation, or initiating interaction to solve problems;
- arranging, or making implicit or explicit agreement to participate;
- brokerage, or allocating problems and resources to each other;
- facilitation, or creating favourable environmental conditions;
- conflict mediation and arbitration; and
- restructuring or tinkering once created.

Examining the management of strategic alliances in the private sector, Doz and Hamel (1998) do not set out a single overarching classification but their argument is structured around a distinction between:

1. *initiation*, including recognising need for collaboration, identifying suitable partners, mobilising them, defining common ground, making initial formal mutual commitments;
2. *design*, including developing agreed structures for decision-making, clarifying contributions to and benefits from task integration, developing governance mechanisms, ensuring that control systems are compatible with learning; (for them, the basic design options are between 'co-optation', 'co-specialisation' and 'learning and internalisation', in order of deepening mutual involvement, or, in the terms used here, of increasing integration); and
3. *re-evaluation*, adjustment and learning over time.

While each of these lists represents a slightly different way of slicing up the activities, there is clear convergence between these descriptions and classifications, notwithstanding some underlying divergences of theoretical approach. The following seem to be the common elements:

(a) *Initiation*: Each begins with some kind of initiation process involving selection and recruitment;
(b) *Objective negotiation*: Each recognises a set of cognitive activities, in which aims, objectives, norms, values, worldviews, goals and objectives are worked out;
(c) *Design*: Each proceeds to identify one or more activities of preparation, negotiation, rule-making, structural design, conflict management;
(d) *Environment management*: Each recognises that some work needs to be done outside the confines of the group to secure external resources and legitimacy and acceptance from key stakeholders;

(e) *Joint production*: Almost all identify some features of collaboration in the process of producing the services or goods or knowledge that is the shared task;
(f) *Adjustment*: Most recognise a set of activities involved in making changes in the course of the life of the group;
(g) *Termination, transfer or fundamental change*: Finally, many recognise a set of activities around fundamental change which might lead to termination and dissolution, or to transfer of functions elsewhere, or to very large transmogrification and rebirth in a largely new guise, either with changed members or changed activities (changing both would of course amount to termination of the original network).

There are some differences between these classifications. Agranoff and McGuire stress the importance of the selection of network whereas Lowndes and Skelcher begin their classification at a later 'stage'; yet we know that selection is crucial to the strategic shaping of networks. To reinforce the point that these activities are not undertaken in strict sequence, it is worth noting the findings of the few longitudinal studies of network change over time which have stressed repeated re-selection as critical for network shaping (e.g. Lorenzoni and Lipparini, 1999).

Perhaps the most remarkable thing about these activities is just how *un*remarkable they are; these are precisely the same activities that would be found in any ideal-typical schema of activities for managing a single organisation. Most of what gets done on a day-to-day basis in managing across networks looks very much like what gets done on a day-to-day basis in managing within organisations. Boddy *et al.* (2000) analyse in ethnographic detail the day-to-day and week-to-week process of Sun MicroSystems managing the relationship with one of its suppliers; they report initial negotiations, the greater authority exercised by the more powerful purchaser over the specification of what is to be done together, the existence of regular sequences of meetings between people with key boundary spanning roles, the location of each other's personnel on each other's sites for ongoing liaison, a set of standard document forms for handling flows of transactions, reporting and control, and so on.

Nor should this close similarity between managing networks *of the type* studied – at least in this majority strand of the literature – and managing a single organisation be considered surprising as these are studies of the formation of bounded networks which are, in effect, *interorganisational organisations*. It is certainly true that many writers on managing networks claim that there are big differences between the activities involved in single organisation management and in network management (e.g. Agranoff and McGuire, 1998). In making this claim, they place great emphasis on the activities of persuasion, negotiating, understanding others, writing agreements, sequencing activities through several agencies and the absence of the tool of simple authoritative command. However, the claims of clear and fundamental differences between inter-organisational and single organisation management are not based on empirical research designed specifically to test just how important these activities are in each type of management work.

In contrast, there is considerable empirical evidence for our position. In practice, exclusive reliance on authoritative command in single organisation management has been known to be ineffective for many decades, and at least since the work of the human relations school in the 1950s (e.g. McGregor, 1960). Most texts on single organisation management now stress many of the same activities of empathy, persuasion, negotiation and agreement writing that writers on inter-organisational management give such weight to (see Peck, 2005). In particular, the movement in recent decades of management thought towards stressing the importance of organisational culture – and the role of management in influencing it (e.g. Schein, 1992) – place greatest emphasis in defining effective single organisation management on exactly these tools and activities.

The public management literature on the activities of management in unbounded, more individualistic, networks is much sparser. By comparison, studies on the private sector, which are often framed as examining 'portfolios of alliances', can be found. As we should expect from the discussion in the previous section on positioning, these studies stress many network structural issues. Doz and Hamel's (1998) chapter on managing portfolios emphasises the importance of minimising redundancy in multiple ties to the same cluster and of ensuring separation between alliances in order to optimise one's own control over the portfolio by 'divide and rule' (the classical *tertius* strategy). Perrow (1992) too stresses the importance of tertius strategies of separation for exploitation in his study on small firm networks. However, Doz and Hamel also note the tendency of at least some 'portfolios' to gradually mutate into more bounded and internally structured competitive blocs or business groups (and can be expected to go through the kinds of activities identified by the writers on 'stages').

Some of the activities listed for groups are of course also relevant for managing the particular *bilateral* ties that make up the portfolio of ties in an individualistic network (which is not itself a group). Some kinds of initiation, negotiation, design, environment management, joint production, adjustment and termination are required for each of these ties. However, what may be different from more strongly integrated networks that have (eventually) coalesced into groups at the level of the particular bilateral ties may be: first, that it may make more sense for the agency seeking to perpetuate its freedom of manoeuvre and the individualistic character of the network that it should fight shy of too many very long-term agreements (and this more instrumental attitude to ties in portfolios is stressed, for example, by Doz and Hamel (1998) as important in their private sector case studies although the point is valid independently of sector); and, second, environment management may become, if anything, even more important than in managing group-like networks and more resource and attention have to be devoted to the ongoing search for new potential partners and to securing acceptance from others for the particular links sought and used at any one time.

It is important, briefly, to consider the question of just how far it is necessary that the activities of network management should be transparent, open and palpable to all the members of the network. There is a very large literature which suggests that this is absolutely required for trust (e.g. Huxham, 1996; Coulson, 1998, Sydow, 1998a). The argument for this proposition is that where tools are deployed in less than open ways, this will eventually be discovered, trust will be lost and may prove very difficult to rebuild (e.g. Sitkin and Stickel, 1996). However, there is some evidence to suggest that having lost trust in each other on some particular dimensions, organisations may not necessarily flip into wholesale distrust; for example, 6 *et al*. (2002) found that some networks in the provision of public services were established with apparently quite modest aims but where the lead organisations deliberately misrepresented the ambition of their longer term goals. They sought to lock their partners into the arrangement by building up asset specificities and sunk costs, so that by the time they realised the true scale of their commitment, they would be reluctant to withdraw. This strategy did not necessarily fail. This suggests that there is some scope, albeit certainly not unlimited, for guile in the use of tools in managing within networks, at least provided that the goals pursued with this guile are within the penumbra of the officially stated goals and are not perceived to run immediately and deeply contrary to the partners' own deeper and long-term interests.

What, if anything, is different about managing across networks from managing within organisational boundaries?

This chapter has argued that there are some important similarities between inter- and intra-organisational management. More specifically, it has been suggested that the *activities* of management are essentially the same, that the basic categories of tools by which mangers secure information about events and conditions and by which they attempt to induce change or indeed continuity in the behaviour of others, are also essentially the same in each context. Finally, it has been suggested that these are by no means unimportant respects in which to find similarity; on the contrary, the selection and deployment of activities and instruments are at the heart of management. Nor, indeed, does this account exhaust the features of management that are common to intra- and inter-organisational contexts. Many of the key general categories of goals of management are also common, such as the pursuit of co-ordination within and through a division of labour, cultivating learning, securing accountabilities to some shared tasks and common projects, the pursuit of efficiency together with effectiveness and legitimacy, and so on.

If many goals, most activities and all the tools of power are common to both contexts, then many of the skills of management must also be common. However, this is not to deny that there are some differences between the two contexts which can be important. The main differences, fairly obviously, flow from the nature of the *scope for selection, structures, boundaries* and *accountabilities* which define the two contexts.

As Agranoff and McGuire (2001) point out, a simple and key difference is that organisations have different kinds of choices in the selection both of partner organisations and of the kinds of structure they want to govern the partnership than they have in the selection of linkages between internal departments. Although organisations can choose whom to hire in the finance department and how flat an organisation chart to have in that department, they have rather limited choice over whether to have a finance department at all and over the kinds of relationships of reporting and authorisation that the finance department will possess with other departments. By contrast, at least in many fields, organisations have some choice about whether to form external links, as to the best mix of integrating functions internally, vertically or horizontally and over selection of potential partners.

In Table 1.1, there is a taxonomy of the main types of structural instrument for the definition of formal linkages between two or more organisations. Clearly, the spectrum of inter-organisational structures identified there differs significantly (save at one extreme) from the spectrum of relationships that can typically be found between the range of functional divisions within a single organisation. The one extreme – at which a variety of inter-organisational relations converge within a single organisational structure – is, of course, the limit case of merger. The qualifier, 'typically', in the previous sentence may seem to be a weasel word; there may be exceptional periods when economic conditions mean that this is not strictly true and organisations can then survive as more or less single organisations despite having internal structures linking their respective parts in much the same way that inter-organisational structures link distinct organisations. In the 1960s and 1970s, for example, market conditions appear, at least in some industries in some developed countries, to have permitted the survival – for a time – of a number of huge conglomerates operating in many different industries, united mainly in the fact that a single headquarters organisation or holding company handled relationships with shareholders for them all and provided some overarching board level direction. Within the conglomerates, there were a range of bilateral and multilateral ties between companies or divisions for some joint work, but often these were rather loose alliances. Nevertheless, this seems to have been an exceptional period in business history and one that was ended relatively quickly as market conditions became more competitive.

The boundaries between distinct organisations are often said to be becoming 'fluid' or 'blurred' as a result of deeper mutual involvement though the greater use of strategic alliances, joint ventures and many of the other structures for inter-organisational co-ordination. However, as Kraakman (2001) has argued, it would be quite misguided to draw inferences from the evident trend in many fields towards close collaboration, exchange of personnel, stationing of staff on each other's sites, joint decision-making bodies between organisations at the *operational* level, to any necessary merging of underlying *strategy* or any much grander decay of the boundaries of *accountability*, especially in the context of the importance of organisational boundaries for defining *property rights* in organisations. Moreover, the facts that ties take so much effort to negotiate – and that so many ties between organisations are temporary and are terminated either in abandonment or else with a feeling of their having performed their function – suggests that boundaries are far from being blurred at the strategic level.

The basic accountabilities of distinct organisations, across which inter-organisational management has to be carried out, are indeed distinct from and more challenging for managers than are the boundaries between divisions or departments within the same organisation. However, the fact that the same activities and tools have to be deployed in both contexts suggests that the two kinds of boundaries still have to be breached, to the extent that they are breached in the course of collaboration, in many of the same ways. Indeed, at the *operational* level, the same kinds of obstacles to collaboration are found at both kinds of boundaries; different professional disciplines, competing priorities, divergent legal obligations, incompatible cultures, personal rivalries and so on are all cited in the studies of problematic co-ordination both within and between organisations.

If the main differences between managing within and between organisations are those of selection, structure, boundary and accountability, it is also clear from this discussion, that these differences, even when they are large, are matters of *degree*. For the choice of potential partners is never unlimited and, equally, there is always some choice about how to organise internally. The competing internal accountabilities of different organisations are legally buttressed by the powers of shareholders, boards, Secretaries of State, and so on, but the very facts that they are permeable at the operational level using the same tools and activities as those deployed for internal co-ordination, that the same kinds of obstacles to co-operation are reported at both kinds of boundaries and that vertical integration is always at least a theoretical alternative to external networking, these all go to show that in *operational* and even *strategic practice*, if not in legal and economic theory, boundaries between organisations are of the same kind of phenomenon as those within organisations. They differ in order of magnitude and severity rather than in nature.

The management challenge

The evidence gathered here from a wide range of literature is powerful support for our argument that there is, if not yet a full discipline of inter-organisational management, at least a body of knowledge and practice which exhibits some convergence in its core propositions, both between public and commercial services and between the processes of management and of governance.

In general, as we might expect, texts written partly for practitioner readerships (such as Doz and Hamel, 1998) tend to be most optimistic about the efficacy of the techniques of inter-organisational management, while those written by political scientists (such as Bevir and Rhodes, 2003) are most pessimistic (and indeed disdainful of what they sometimes call the 'managerialism' of those who argue for the possibility of intelligent work to co-ordinate between agencies; see 6 *et al.*, 2002 for a critique of political science fatalism about inter-organisational co-ordination). Most organisational studies research, whether undertaken by organisational sociologists or by management researchers, falls somewhere in between these poles. The mainstream position is one that recognises that there are significant challenges, real problems and obstacles to be overcome, skills deficits and unintended consequences of using each and all of the tools available, but nevertheless considers that there are some things that competent managers can do, know how to do and which will often have at least some of the desired results. More than that is surely unreasonable to ask of any discipline based in and around the social sciences.

Most attention has been devoted in the literature to the nature of the *external* linkages, and there remains much to be learned about the *internal* capacities and capabilities that have to be cultivated in organisations, in order to make the best use of whatever external links might be available. Although concepts such as boundary spanning and absorptive capacity have been defined, the state of both empirical research and modelling on the determinants, alternative forms, consequences and relative significance of these phenomena remains weak. Also poorly developed are the dynamic models of change in network structure, culture and form and of the conditions under which those dynamics might be amenable to action to influence them. The neo-Durkheimian approach developed by Thompson M (1982, 1992, 1996; Thompson M *et al.*, 1990) is promising but has yet to be worked up and explored empirically in detail.

Theories in organisational sociology and management studies broadly divide into two groups. One group of theories see both organisations and inter-organisational systems as *resources*. Accordingly they take an instrumental view of them, focusing on cybernetic understandings of organisational processes, and they look for managerial action to optimise on key variables. This tradition includes Weberian theories of rationalisation, principal–agent theories

(Jensen and Meckling, 1976), transaction cost theories (Coase, 1937; Williamson, 1985; Aoki *et al.*, 1990), bounded rationality theory (Simon, 1955); early behavioural theory (Cyert and March, 1963), contingency theories (Lawrence and Lorsch, 1967; Galbraith, 1973), organisational fit (Miles and Snow, 1984), technology fit theories (Perrow, 1999 [1984]), exchange theory (Emerson, 1972a,b), resource dependency theory (Pfeffer and Salancik, 1978), some network theories (Burt, 1992) – and their derivatives in organisational ecology (Hannan and Freeman, 1989) – and, in management studies, the 'resource-based view' (Conner, 1991) and business process reengineering programmes (Hammer and Champy, 1993). While human factors are by no means irrelevant, the basis of the relationship between organisational factors and performance is that processes for the effective management of the organisation to achieve performance should be *rule-bound* and the organisation is regarded as a set of better or worse tools for this. Organisational form and inter-organisational structure, then, become something to be optimised in the same way. This outlook privileges the roles either of those charged with negotiating outside the organisation to acquire resources to achieve growth to optimal size or else those empowered to monitor output and resources in the organisational process by which performance is produced. On these views, the task for inter-organisational management is a technical one of designing structures that will deliver appropriate allocation of resources, skills, capabilities and information for the smallest outlay of direct and transaction cost.

The other set of approaches emphasise factors to do with *meaning* as key to a collective capability and stress a shared learning conception of how performance is elicited. The tradition includes the human relations school, institutional theory (Meyer and Rowan, 1977; Selznick, 1980 [1949]; DiMaggio and Powell, 1983; Perrow, 1986; Stinchcombe, 2001), power-centred approaches (Pfeffer, 1981; Mintzberg, 1983), theories of the centrality of organisational culture (Silverman, 1970, 1984; Hofstede, 1991; Martin, 1992; Schein, 1993), organisational ambiguity theory (March and Olsen, 1976), models of the reflective practitioner (Schön, 1983), emergent strategy models (Mintzberg and Waters, 1994), single- and double-loop learning accounts (Argyris and Schön, 1978), and organisational sense-making (Weick, 1995, 2001). While these theories need not dismiss as irrelevant the resource and cybernetic aspects of organisation, they see the relationship between organisational or inter-organisational process and performance as mediated by managerial *sense-making* or even *narrative*; cybernetic aspects are of interest only in understanding the constraints upon the kinds of sense that can in practice be made. Organisational form – in these views – is a less readily changed variable than within resource-instrumental views. Although it is never so institutionalised as to be unchangeable, form is regarded as something with which key stakeholders have to feel comfortable if they are to be committed. This sets limits on the extent to which it either can or should be changed purely to fit task requirements. Within this theoretical cluster, shared historical narratives and collective organisational memory are important for sustaining commitment and motivation, sense-making and the sense of membership and for defining capabilities. Here, the challenge for organisational management is one of developing viable and intelligent sense of a set of conditions that are always to some degree opaque, but by which motivation to co-operate can be mobilised.

In the argument of this book, it has been implicit that we should not have to choose once and for all between these views. Both these two styles of management theorising capture important aspects of organisational and inter-organisational life. The central challenge for theory is to integrate the two in ways that show both the scope for and the limitations of instrumental and narrative practices and understandings. For only by doing so can it be hoped that we can identify sets of reasonable expectations of what can be achieved in inter-organisational management across a robust taxonomy of different kinds of empirical setting and also, finally, construct an account against which the blanket pessimism of some of the political scientists and the bland optimism of some of the practitioner-oriented writing can be judged.

7

Learning and Leading Across Networks: Styles and Sensibilities

This chapter addresses two sets of issues that are concerned with the processes and capabilities within organisations by which they can support the strategies of, first, management in, and second, external management of, networks that were discussed in Chapter 6. To operate effectively in networks, organisations must be able to recognise and to make intelligent use of information from other organisations, whether that information is task-specific, structured and concerned with specific operational matters or is more general intelligence about the conditions in their field. That is to say, organisational learning is key to achieving effective influence in networks. This chapter draws on studies of capacities for learning in organisations to enrich the theory already developed. Here, we are concerned principally with management in and of networks rather than their external governance.

So far, much of the discussion has focused on the more or less instrumental matter of management. Viewed through this lens, management is essentially about power; it is concerned with the capacity to choose and use particular tools instrumentally to induce change in the behaviour of others in order to pursue specific goals. However, a neo-Durkheimian account also stresses the non-instrumental factors on which the capabilities for instrumental action ultimately rest. This brings us to the consideration of the other internal capability of management, or, perhaps more accurately, leadership. Leadership is about authority rather than power, meaning the style of legitimation of the right to manage and the capabilities required for its exercise. Whereas management is essentially instrumental, leadership need not be. Indeed, very often is not; the cultivation of loyalty, the appeal to the emotions, the binding in of people through ceremonial and the stylisation of those roles which grant at least the appearance if not necessarily the reality of decision-making, all have a relationship with organisational strategy that is, at best, indirect. Yet without some kind of authority – and not only at the 'top' (and the reader will by now suspect that there will be several kinds) – it is difficult for organisations or networks to sustain the cohesion required to engage in strategic action. Whereas organisational learning is the challenge of adroitly selecting instrumental information in ways that serve the specific goals of the organisation, leadership involves the giving out of symbolic information, often through organisational ritual. In the second half of this chapter, therefore, the initial account of learning is balanced by consideration of the forms of authority and leadership which make management and learning possible. Indeed, the connection between learning and leadership is often more intimate than this, for, as we discuss in the next section, frequently the individuals who are key to organisational learning across networks are those whose roles locate them at the boundaries between organisations and who can use this position of brokerage to exercise leadership for learning.

Internal capabilities for external linkages

Organisations require specific internal arrangements, roles and capabilities if they are to make the most of the networks in which they find themselves, let alone seek to transform them. Some of these capabilities for forming and sustaining relationships are important, but hardly specific, to the management of ties. For example, in their study of Korean high technology start-ups, Lee *et al.* (2001) define the internal capabilities required for the acquisition of resources externally as consisting principally in entrepreneurial orientation, technological competence and initial financial investment made during development; these are, of course, quite generic capabilities.

It is convenient to divide the more specific internal capabilities into four areas. The first two of these systems are specified at the level of individual people, their personal networks with other individuals, and the use that they can make of these. There is a body of literature examining the roles of individual staff members in organisations which sustain their occupants in the work of managing external relations of various kinds. These roles are often called 'boundary spanning' roles (other terms for their occupants include 'reticulists', and even 'boundroids').

The second set concerns the capacities that organisations require in order to *receive* inputs from other organisations. Where the priority resource to be taken into the organisation is knowledge, information or ideas, then, in Cohen and Levinthal's (1990) terms, this represents their 'absorptive capacity'; capacities for receiving, for instance, flows of payments is a well understood matter for finance departments, and does not raise such interesting issues for the present purpose, but it is, in essence, an absorptive capacity for inputs other than knowledge. The correlative set of capacities for *providing* knowledge, information and ideas to other organisations in different network structures is much less studied and less well understood; however, it might be called 'disseminative capacity'.

We begin by discussing the roles of individual boundary spanners in interorganisational relations.

Leadership and boundary spanning roles

A vast prescriptive leadership stresses that leaders matter in networks, as 'champions', 'catalysts', persuaders and loci of authority (Gray, 1996; Luke, 1997; Huxham and Vangen, 2000). Studies on leadership over many decades have examined the importance in leadership of cultivating, shaping and organising personal social networks of individuals within the same organisation (Bass, 1990 [1974]), but rather fewer have explored the nature, skills, dynamics and consequences of leadership in and across inter-organisational networks. However, the general findings of Bass' review of that literature are no doubt relevant to inter-organisational contexts – that effective leaders need to achieve network centrality, defined areas of influence and span structural 'holes' (in Burt's 1992 sense). The large literature on supply chain networks is mainly concerned with contract specification, and thus management rather than with leadership, although in stressing the importance of leadership in strategic planning, co-ordination and mutual exchange, this work reinforces findings from the wider inter-organisational network literature (e.g. Day *et al.*, 2001). A wide variety of normative writings call for the development of a discipline of 'external leadership', including a guide for NHS managers (Stewart, 1996 [1989]) and some more recent writings on leadership in the NHS (e.g. Goodwin, 1998; Conner, 2001). There are many studies which find that leadership makes a difference to the success with which inter-organisational networks can operate (e.g. Volkoff *et al.*, 1999 show that the successful development of interorganisational data systems is importantly dependent on product champions working across organisational boundaries; by contrast, Sydow, 1998b finds that centrally located leaders in successful hub-and-spoke networks for franchising have limited importance because of their limited span of control). Nonetheless, few have defined very exactly just what kinds of leadership are available and what difference they make and how. For example, in their study of local partnerships in US public administration involved in the joint adoption and use of geographical information systems (GIS) based technologies Brown MM *et al.* (1998) find that their measures for the presence of active leadership was a statistically significant – and positive – factor in all of their assessments of outcomes, but were unable to say anything more finely grained.

Bardach's (1998) analysis of his case studies led him to suggest that 'effective' leadership was important for network success, both in his interviewees' estimation and in his own research evaluation. He distinguishes between facilitative – more neutral, consensus-building – approaches and advocacy approaches which are more partisan (e.g. which are readier to leave people out of coalitions). Bardach is not able to demonstrate the different conditions within networks for the efficacy of using each type of his identified approaches to leadership. However, it seems plausible that advocacy styles would be more likely to be effective in individualistic or hierarchical networks and facilitative styles more likely to be legitimate in enclave type networks.

However, one fruitful way to think about leadership – once it is recognised that it is to be found at every level in organisations and networks and not just at the level of top management – is to look at the structural position of leaders in their personal networks, that is, to consider their role in organisational networks from the viewpoint of the interaction between their personal networks and the inter-organisational structure. This suggests that we should look at leaders in the present context as 'boundary spanners'.

The origins of this concept are to be found in Thompson's and Lawrence and Lorsch's work in the 1960s. Thompson JD (1967) presented a model of the organisation as consisting in a core of throughput activities, the boundaries of which are buffered by certain functions which protect the integrity of the core, but also spanned by certain categories of role-holders charged with bringing in certain resources and inputs (or them taking out). These roles may thus be involved in both shielding the core from external threats and in bridging to external opportunities. Thompson distinguished between cases in which the boundary spanning function worked to highly prescribed rules on transactions with external organisations and those where the boundary spanners have discretion. Reflecting the relatively rigid mass production techniques which dominated large organisations in the period in which he was writing, Thompson argued that great discretion for boundary spanners could create internal problems, for the rest of a large organisation could not, it was then widely believed, be expected to be highly flexible. In his model, therefore, managerial efforts to exercise control over boundary spanners were of great importance for viability of the organisation. To the extent that changing technologies of both manufacturing and service delivery have enabled greater flexibility in recent decades, the balance between bridging and shielding of organisational cores – and therefore between organisations operating alone or with others in networks of any kind – is now driven more by considerations of competitive advantage and knowledge and by the imperative to minimise transaction and other costs, rather than by technological imperatives for protecting the technical core.

Thompson went on to distinguish between three strategies of boundary bridging: contracting or negotiation for inputs from outside; co-opting or absorbing organisational elements from outside; and creating joint ventures or temporary combinations. These distinctions are not always clear cut. Contracting covers a wide variety of actual network forms, with organisations often very interlinked (Chapter 8). Equally, co-optation does not only comprise mergers and acquisitions but also board-level interlocks (Scott WR, 1992). Likewise, joint ventures can range from very loose to very tight arrangements.

In the later development of Thompson's ideas in resource dependence theory (Pfeffer and Salancik, 1978) and then in population ecology theories of organisational fields (Aldrich, 1979), boundary spanning roles and activities came to be seen as functions that were critical not only both to the structure and competence of each organisation but also to the structure of the whole organisational field, for they are seen as the individuals in whom the inter-organisational network is represented and by whom it is changed. Insofar as there is scope for agency to change these structures, it came to be seen as lying, at least at an empirical level, more with boundary spanning staff than, for example, with senior executives or strategists. In later resource dependence and population ecology accounts, much greater flexibility in core organisational capacities came to be recognised as possible and desirable, making the problem of core managerial control over of boundary spanners less salient than in Thompson's model. In Thompson's work, boundary spanning was defined functionally and is done as much by groups as by individuals (see Ancona and Caldwell 1992 for a recent study researching boundary spanning groups).

There is a strand of strategic management research that has examined the importance of boundary spanning units or agencies that are located at the periphery of large organisations and shown that their local decisions are often critical in shaping the strategy of the whole (e.g. Regnér, 2000). Certain types of role are often defined within organisations as dedicated to boundary spanning, such as account management (Birkinshaw *et al.*, 2000) or procurement management. Then there are specialists in boundary spanning who are not attached by direct organisational accountability (such as employment by a single client) to a member of the network across which they supply connecting services and who are not just members of the network like the others because they are involved in, for example, upstream vertical supply to the rest of the network of a crucial resource or, in the pure case, in supplying nothing but access to social ties. Thompson GF (2003) points out that studies on certain sub-types of venture capital firm, business angels and business introduction services seem to be of this type.

In much of the more recent literature, however, boundary spanners are defined as individuals rather than units, whose social networks – whether informally arranged and conducted or specifically sanctioned in their authorised roles – are important to the management of inter-organisational relations. Those who take a personalistic view of inter-organisational networks hypothesise that organisational linkages are embedded in personal social networks (Granovetter, 1985), while institutionalists tend to predict the reverse direction of causation.

Examples from commercial organisations would include account managers who are responsible for managing downstream vertical ties with customers and purchasing and procurement managers charged with handling upstream vertical ties along the supply chain (Katz and Kahn, 1966). There are also boundary spanners responsible for horizontal network maintenance, because they are charged with liaising with particular inter-organisational groups, representing the organisation externally, or forming coalitions (Aldrich and Herker, 1977). In organisations providing services to the public where there are ongoing relationships rather than simply a series of transactions with particular clients (general medical practitioners, case social workers, probation officers, etc.), frontline staff may be considered as spanning these boundaries (although these staff are not of interest here).

A boundary spanning individual works most effectively when she or he occupies the fulcrum point in a 'bowtie' or 'butterfly' structure network; that is, when s/he occupies a *tertius* position between two clusters (Conway, 1997). For the boundary spanner, such a position is highly valued. Empirically, however, the value of such people to the members of the network as a whole depends on whether she or he facilitates the flow of information and resources and transactions or acts as a bottleneck (Cross and Prusak, 2002).

Much of the research on boundary spanning has focused on the requisite skills, the actual or believed characteristics and the experiences of the people who occupy these roles, rather than, for example, the organisational structures and the managerial practices that might sustain them. Some of the research examines people with inter-departmental roles within organisations rather than inter-agency roles; it is not clear from the literature whether the nature and pressures of spanning internal and external boundaries differ in important ways and, if so, how. Very little of the research on stress, for example, is comparative, so it is not really possible to determine whether, in general or in particular types or cases, boundary spanning work is more or less stressful than other kinds of work (such as being a chief executive, being a harried front line junior service provider or, indeed, being unemployed, all of which are also known to be stressful).

The studies on requisite skills tend not to be based on the actually measured attributes of particular individuals but on the requirements of particular posts or types of posts, often examined deductively and, at least in part, independently of the post-holders. To the extent that network management is conducted by identifiable boundary spanners, then it is possible to determine at least some of the ideal-typical skill requirements. This was the approach taken by Friend *et al.* (1974), who used the term 'reticulist' to describe the skills of forming ties on behalf of organisations, sustaining those ties through inter-personal relationships and working contacts to gain information, cultivate appreciations of problems and possible solutions, understand the perceptions and values of others, undertake negotiation and become sensitive to other organisational cultures (cf. Hosking and Morley, 1991). Other approaches stress entrepreneurial skills, creativity, lateral thinking and capacities to generate trust in organisational commitment through trust in themselves as individuals; see Williams P (2002) for a review of some of this literature on skill requirements.

Another body of work has examined the hypothesis that these boundary spanners face peculiar stress arising from role ambiguity – and even role conflict – because of the pressures placed upon them both by their own organisation and the others with which they develop linkages (Robertson,

1995; O'Toole, 1998). Unfortunately, this research is neither extensive nor satisfactory. It can be hypothesised that, in Merton and Barber's (1976) sociological terms, boundary spanners would often exhibit high structural ambivalence in their accountabilities because of the potential conflicts and tensions in their roles, having pressures both from their employing organisation and from the organisations with which they develop links. This should be expected to produce certain challenges (Pratt and Doucet, 2000) which may well require distinct kinds of emotional labour (Hochschild, 1983); however, there is little comparative research to examine whether these psychological processes are qualitatively different or different in consequences from other ambivalent situations.

It is important to note that nothing in the boundary spanning literature shows that there is anything particularly distinctive either about the activities or about the skill sets of boundary spanners working between organisations when compared, for example, with colleagues working between departments within an organisation; essentially, the same processes of initiation, negotiation, diplomacy, problem-solving and strategic development – and the same tact, ability to move between accountabilities, energy to motivate others and so on – are required in both settings. Indeed, much of the literature moves seamlessly from the inter- to the intra-organisational context.

Absorptive and disseminative capacity

Organisations learn from each other across a wide variety of vertical and horizontal ties. They may enter into interorganisational relations principally for the purpose of explicit or tacit learning, or such learning may be a by-product of seeking credit, legitimacy, prestige, outlets, outsourcing or other things. An organisation needs some quite specific capabilities in fact, in order to know where to devote its limited resources for creating ties to other organisations; and, second, to be able to make use of the information that it finds.

In a very widely cited article, Cohen and Levinthal (1990) introduced the concept of 'absorptive capacity'. This refers to an organisation's ability to recognise the value of new information, assimilate it and apply it to their organisational purposes. It requires much more than the presence of people or units charged with keeping up to date with the latest developments in the field or even the presence of an in-house research and development function because these alone would hardly secure the capacity to make good use of what is learned. Cohen and Levinthal argued that it must include features of the organisational culture, such as its style and utilisation of shared memory and the extent to which there are shared vocabularies, tacit understandings and explicit disciplines. Further, it needs to incorporate the instrumental systems by which knowledge is transferred from those in the organisation who might first acquire it to those who must make use of it; this may involve transfers across some considerable geographical, grade and departmental distance. They hypothesised, on the basis of other literature on knowledge management, that in order to support effective communication the general form of an optimal absorptive capacity would have to consist in a series of internal units possessing partially overlapping interests underpinned by non-overlapping distinct bodies of knowledge. As a consequence, therefore, specialisation should be limited. Absorptive capacity makes outsourcing of some functions possible whilst it cannot itself wholly be outsourced. Absorptive capacity is, they propose, amenable to more or less deliberate investment and is, at least potentially, cumulative over time. Pennings and Harianto (1992a,b) confirmed that cumulative investment and experience in networking between firms with overlapping skill sets within an industry matters greatly in shaping long-term absorptive capacity for acquiring skills. Organisations with strong absorptive capacities are predicted by Cohen and Levinthal to be more pro-active in working their networks to secure new and useable knowledge; conversely organisations with weak absorptive capacity are expected to be more reactive.

However, as Cohen and Levinthal see it, this capacity tends to be specific to a particular domain. Lane and Lubatkin (1998) argue that absorptive capacity is even more specific than this; that it varies with each tie to other organisations in the focal organisation's network. They find that levels of learning are higher from ties to organisations with a high degree of similarity in basic knowledge and lower management formalisation.

It is not always clear just which of these features of an organisation's absorptive capacity are found there by virtue of Cohen and Levinthal's definition and which are empirically and contingently associated with it. However, some features are clearly contingent – and important – in network management. For example, Scott J (2003) finds that entering into research partnerships does expand absorptive capacity. More recently, some research has suggested a typical trajectory over time for small firms, from making use of ties to creating research institutes, suggesting that they begin with fields with 'low information gaps' and, as their absorptive capacity grows, they are able to tap 'high information gap' areas, stretching their absorptive capacity much further. A study on strategic alliances among biotechnology firms found that absorptive capacity explained much of the variation in the relationship between characteristics of the alliances and the performance of the member firms (George *et al.*, 2001).

Unfortunately, many of the studies on absorptive capacity measure it in precisely the way that Cohen and Levinthal said was inadequate – namely, the presence of an in-house R&D group (e.g. Veugelers, 1997) or by other indirect proxy measures. Rather few studies provide much rich information about the internal processes that support absorptive capacity. Vickers and Cordey-Hayes (1999) suggest that organisations that take in learning about cleaner production technologies benefit from an organisational culture that encourages a pluralistic and participative approach; this suggests an internally enclaved form. However, it is not clear how far this finding can be generalised. For example, Cockburn and Henderson's (1998) study of pharmaceutical research and development suggests that incentives for individuals engaging in learning and research are very important, which might suggest a more individualistic form of internal organisation. Although Lane and Lubatkin's (1998) measure of low management formalisation might be an indicator that strong internal hierarchy predicts poor absorptive capacity, even this cannot be assumed to be generally applicable because there are, for example, health care and military organisations with strongly hierarchical systems that have shown considerable aptitudes for absorbing new *explicit* knowledge over many decades; although they sometimes find it more difficult to absorb innovative tacit knowledge which requires subtle changes in practice (see Fountain, 2001, on organisational learning associated with technological change in the US military).

March (1999 [1991]) distinguishes between two basic styles of organisational learning – namely, exploration of and for new knowledge, frameworks, approaches, skills and techniques, as well as exploitation, or the deepening application of, disciplines, knowledge and capabilities already possessed. Whilst every organisation undertakes some of each type of learning, March argues that the combinations of these two that organisations can typically achieve are usually weighted markedly towards one or the other. March's conceptual framework should be of help in understanding the nature of an organisation's absorptive capacity. Organisations with styles and practices of learning that emphasise exploration would, it was argued in Chapter 3, more likely be located in individualistic networks of organisations because these network structures provide greater opportunities for – and more fluidity of access – to resources across the system of ties than can the more bounded network forms. Conversely, it was argued, exploitation would be predicted to be the dominant strand in more hierarchical and enclaved networks. To date, there has been limited empirical testing of this hypothesis.

The logical corollary of this thesis – that organisations need certain capabilities in order to receive information and knowledge across ties from other organisations and to make use of it in organisational learning – must be that particular capabilities are also required to organise information and present it in a format that other organisations with which they are tied can make use of (in what might be called organisational teaching). This calls for a concept of 'disseminative capacity'. Presumably, like absorptive capacity, this too would typically be specific to a domain or even to particular ties and would be grounded in the possession of at least some overlapping bodies of knowledge between the originators of the knowledge in the organisational core and the boundary spanners at the periphery who are charged with its dissemination to other organisations in the network. Unfortunately, there appears to be very little empirical research directly on the measurement, content and institutional origins of disseminative capacity. In one such, Sabel (2001, cited in Thompson GF, 2003) argues that communication skills required for effective dissemination across networks include the development of 'pidgin conversations' using vocabularies that combine the languages (and recognise the underlying organisational cultures) of both the disseminator and absorber organisations.

Learning and competence

Competence and learning based approaches to understanding inter-organisational relationships differ sharply from traditional neo-classical economic models. In the latter, the focus is on allocative and productive efficiency; in the former, the main interest is in adaptive efficiency (Colombo, 1998). In contrast, the literature on learning organisations has not converged upon well-developed and settled typologies for the types of network that are produced as a result of learning- and competence-driven interactions. However, a number of key variables have been identified.

Since the work of Brown JS and Duguid (1991) and Wenger (1998), one important concept has been the community of practice, referring to a network of individuals which implicitly or explicitly organises shared learning and dissemination. However, most studies using this idea have concerned networks within single organisations – with exception of some of the studies on NHS collaboratives (Bate and Robert, 2002) – or have simply used it as a metaphor or description. However, since communities of practice are treated as dependent and not independent variables, the key drivers of the structure, extent, density and role of the 'communities' in question tends to be explained by the nature of the information and knowledge being learned or by institutional variables (Tsoukas, 2002), including the structure of regional economic districts (Brown JS and Duguid, 2002). At most, the rhetorical use by practitioners of the notion among themselves has been shown to be important, but mostly as a motivational tool in settings which were ready for such exhortation (Swan *et al.*, 2002).

Exploration and exploitation as defined by March (1991) as each lead to seeking different kinds of ties. Exploration is the experimental search for new competencies or knowledge and involves blue skies research, the pursuit of highly innovative things to do and novel ways of doing them and being prepared to risk problems of implementation in order to secure competitive advantage. By contrast, exploitation is the application of existing competence and knowledge to secure comparative advantage from using such knowledge more fruitfully and expertly. Any individual organisation or linked set of organisation will need some balance of these. Periodic hyperbole in the management literature may suggest that competitive advantage has wholly replaced comparative advantage during high technology booms (e.g. Porter ME, 1998). In practice, however, exploitation of at least some existing skills continues to be vital in any organisational field, even where remaining at the leading edge of technological development is also vital.

Over-emphasis on either of these activities therefore risks different kinds of vulnerabilities.

If exploration and exploitation are distinct learning styles, it is also likely that they will require distinct approaches to external networking. Networking for exploration is likely to put a premium on reaching organisations with different skills sets, in different locations in the industry or in different industries, whereas networking for exploitation is more likely to call for vertical links up and down the supply chain, at least in many instances.

In respect of content, the competence and learning tradition in the understanding of inter-organisational links has given great weight to the distinction between explicit and tacit knowledge (e.g. Tsoukas, 2002). Explicit knowledge is that which is written or otherwise encoded and that can thus be stored, retrieved, and readily shared. Explicit knowledge takes its place as part of a more or less integrated body of knowledge around which a network of expertise – or even a profession or a discipline – can emerge and which is the focus of systematic gathering, ordering and attempting verification. By contrast, tacit knowledge is 'know-how', is almost necessarily unwritten, is difficult for anyone to retrieve or use save the person who possesses it; as a consequence, it can only be shared by in-service training and acquisition of expertise (and not by classroom teaching). It is usually structured in fairly haphazard and unsystematic ways and only verified in contexts other than the ones in which it is used. The classic example of tacit knowledge is the skill of riding a bicycle which no one ever acquires by reading texts, for example, on the role of the inner ear and the relationship between motion and balance (Polanyi, 1962).

In general, science-based organisations – or science-based divisions within organisations – tend to value and cultivate explicit knowledge highly, as do those organisations or parts of organisations – such as finance departments and accounting firms – that are geared to the processing of structured, formal and factual information in more or less prescribed ways. Again, organisations in which everyone is strongly dependent on everyone else, perhaps for safety-critical activity, and where learning from mistakes is vital, also tend to value and even enforce the disciplines of turning tacit knowledge into explicit knowledge as far and fast as they can. The armed forces, for example, conduct extensive 'lessons learned' exercises after every operation and manage succession carefully by ensuring that key competencies are codified and transmitted (Stinchcombe, 2001). In many safety-critical engineering organisations, the (re)writing of procedures following each case of informal learning is a vital discipline that can save lives. The discipline involved has to be associated with a certain kind of organisational structure and specific modes of accountability, or else people might shirk the obligation to codify and pass on their knowledge through these processes. By contrast, tacit knowledge is more important in those organisations which are craft-based or in which a great deal of discretion is left to the individual professional about what to work on and how to work. Similarly, tacit knowledge is important in organisations where the division of labour is structured to limit the dependence on people upon others or where there is a great deal of internal competition of promotion or control of resources. The building and decorating trades, academic research, some clinical specialties, social work (other than in child protection or mental health), management consultancy houses, barristers' chambers and stock brokering firms tend to be of this type. These types of organisation will, in consequence, not only pursue links with others for different purposes, but these linkages will have different institutional characters. Broadly, and first, we can expect the accountabilities required in organisations that emphasise learning of explicit knowledge to be more socially integrated and those which emphasise tacit knowledge to be less so. Second, those which emphasise the conversion of new tacit learning into new explicit knowledge as new procedures are also likely to have to develop more social regulation, for this is an activity that requires the continuous institutional pressure to conform to the discipline of knowledge management.

A third variable stressed in the competence literature on organisations is the expected durability of what is learned. This is a function both of the rate of change in the task environment and of the commitments of the particular organisation. In very fast-changing technological environments, where much explicit knowledge is very quickly out of date, and only a core set of explicit understanding of both underlying theories and practical know-how is enduring, there is little point in trying to learn by capturing and storing internally a large body of explicit knowledge. Rather, it is important to ensure that key personnel can access the most up-to-date explicit knowledge which is developed and held externally when and as they need it to solve the particular problems on which the organisation is working. This is true at the moment in, for example, genomics, but less true in general surgery or in much of the more routine work on general medical practice. By contrast, in fields where the basic knowledge is reasonably stable or else is growing incrementally and steadily (in any given period), it may make more sense to try to store and manage a body of explicit knowledge for the long term. In much of vernacular architecture, for example, the understanding of the core problems of stresses upon materials and load-bearing do not change very rapidly and can be sustained for the medium term. This suggests that the style of learning – and therefore of inter-organisational linkages – will be strongly linked with the time horizon which dominates the organisation's strategic activity (see Peck and 6, 2006, ch. 3).

The neo-Durkheimian approach to taxonomy was originally developed from within an institutionalist tradition that emphasised constraints and costs as drivers in organisations rather than benefits. However, in recent years, other scholars have attempted to show how it illuminates problems of organisational learning and have emphasised the institutional basis of information processing in organisations (e.g. Thompson, M and Wildavsky, 1986) and of organisational memory and forgetting (e.g. Rayner, 1982; Douglas, 1986; Peck end 6, 2006). Table 7.1 shows how, at the level of taxonomy, its approach would capture the drivers of organisational learning and competence that have been identified in this section as shaping the various network forms. Underlying this, in neo-Durkheimian theory, is a functional model of explanation in which the styles of learning both express

Table 7.1 How different network forms are associated with styles of organisational learning

Social regulation ↑ ; → *Social integration*

Isolate	**Hierarchy**
Balance of exploration and exploitation: Neither is more important: one has to be opportunistic in using either, depending on what one actually can do in the situation *Control of learning*: Little hope of securing control of learning *Tacit and explicit knowledge*: Little point in trying to influence balance of tacit and explicit, but on balance where temporary control of tacit knowledge can be achieved, this may help with short-term survival *Time and learning*: Focus on learning for the immediate future, for beyond that, all that has been learned will be out of date	*Balance of exploration and exploitation*: Over the long term, exploitation is more important: most new ideas are fads and are rebadged versions of enduring wisdoms: exploration should be managed over the long term in well-planned and progressive research and development programmes *Control of learning*: Maximise internal control of core competencies, seek to build strong relational terms into any external ties entered into *Tacit and explicit knowledge*: Focus on ensuring that as much learning is possible in explicit form in order to ensure transfer over time *Time and learning*: Seek to institutionalise learning for the long-term future: the future will be built on the basis of the past
Individualism	**Enclave**
Balance of exploration and exploitation: Ongoing exploration is more important, because conditions change quickly, others may secure control of knowledge, and no knowledge can be exploited indefinitely *Control of learning*: Maximise proprietary control of core competencies and knowledge; outsource non-core competencies on spot or relational terms as required *Tacit and explicit knowledge*: Ration efforts to turn tacit into explicit knowledge to that which is essential *Time and learning*: Seek to learn and forget competencies as task, environment and event contingencies require	*Balance of exploration and exploitation:* Ongoing exploitation is more important, because it is important to focus on the principles that bind the group or organisation: exploration is only important in the early stages to develop core skills with which to pursue those principles *Control of learning*: Maximise internal control within an organisation or within a densely tied, mutually accountable and bounded group-type network over all competencies *Tacit and explicit knowledge*: Focus on ensuring as much learning as possible is made explicit because of the difficulties of trusting those using tacit knowledge *Time and learning*: Seek to institutionalise only until the principal purpose of the group is achieved

subserve the underlying institutions which also shape the selection of network form (Douglas, 1986).

Authority and leadership

In order to understand scope for governance over and management of networks, it is important to consider the kinds of authority and leadership that may be exercised in different kinds of networks. The tradition in social science that has devoted most attention to forms of authority is that descended from Weber. Indeed, this tradition is still the most fertile source of thinking about authority and leadership and the one which is drawn upon most frequently in the social science literature, although less so in the purely managerialist literature. For in his monumental *Economy and Society* (1978), Weber sets out to analyse the varieties of social organisation by the distinct forms of power and authority that he diagnosed in each. It is not necessary to accept his very elaborate, and at times highly speculative, model of developmental history to accept that his taxonomy of forms of authority is useful (Schluchter, 1989). The model is helpful in thinking about inter-organisational contexts because it is concerned with broad social, economic and political leadership (although Weber was not greatly interested in management within organisations).

Weber's approach to understanding authority is complex; nonetheless, several strands can be picked out here. He begins by asking how each form of authority is legitimated, which leads him to explore the style of argumentation to which it appeals. Second, he always explores the manner by which each kind of authority achieves control or discipline – which he defines to mean the habituation of consent under given institutions – in whatever form of social organisation it sustains. These two modes of authority are brought together in his concept of legitimate order, which consists in the institutional form that is sustained by the form of argumentation (including beliefs and ideas) and the style and extent of discipline. Next, he classifies forms by the extent to which power and authority is individualised in a leader – to the extent at least of a figurehead with some autonomous decision-making power – or is collectively held in some group. Although Weber seems to have thought of his models of leadership and authority as operating within organisations, each can be discerned at work in inter-organisational contexts.

Weber distinguished several forms of 'rationality'. In many ways this is the weakest element in his approach, although it is still widely used in social science to explore the nature of authority. Weber distinguishes between instrumentally rational, value-rational and affectively rational standards. Instrumental rationality focuses on the selection of ends that conform to material interests, and the selection of the most effective means for their pursuit; by contrast, value-rationality selects both goals and means in relations with others for their symbolic and intrinsic characteristics and their overall consonance with prevailing commitments; 'affective' rationality is that which selects actions as appropriate for the emotional tenor of relationships in which an individual finds herself or himself, or by extension, an organisation finds itself tied to others. In Weber's theory, there is a general trend in world history away from affective rationality, and also from value-rationality, towards the institutionalisation of ever more instrumental rationality. More useful are his distinctions in the form of discipline between rule-bound (explicit law), expertise-defined (professional) and voluntary (democratic) types. Clearly most inter-organisational systems involve some element of each of these.

Finally, he distinguishes several forms of authority, which he argues to exhaust the available social repertoire. The best known forms are the merchant adventurer, the patriarch, the patrimonial leader, the charismatic leader, and the bureaucratic manager. Each is distinguished, he suggests, by the style of rationality exhibited. For Weber, the charismatic leader scores most highly on affective rationality, the patriarch on the 'traditional' form of affective and value rationality (by emphasising the repetition of past action on the basis of received authority), while the bureaucratic manager scores most highly on instrumental rationality, evoking both rule-bound and expertise-defined systems of discipline. The others appear to be intermediate cases.

The patriarch is the individual leader whose rule is sustained by some greater explicit and institutionalised norms than the pure charismatic leader. The patriarch's control is essentially sustained by the individual's ability to secure control of resources and to sustain continuity over time. The patriarch therefore seeks to cultivate some enduring institutions rather than solely secure resources for personal use as the merchant adventurer does. Although dynastic means were the historically used strategy for investing in and sustaining continuity over future time, this is presumably not essential to Weber's definition of the patriarchal form of leadership.

The patrimonial form is additionally defined, in a slightly *ad hoc* manner, as more tightly attached to geographical territory than the others. Patrimonial forms consist in the accretion to this of modest bureaucratic rule and classification of followers and greater division of labour between the accountabilities of different groups within the patrimonial leadership's jurisdiction.

For Weber, the process of institutionalisation is one of increasing rationality and routinisation, terminating in instrumentally rational bureaucratic forms of authority being steadily extended over the whole of the social system. Bureaucratic leadership, the acme of instrumental rationality, is therefore the terminus of his evolutionary scheme (and something not particularly celebrated, since it may represent the 'iron cage' of rationality).

Although Weber was most interested in historical periodisation and evolution in ways that (we would argue) should not be defended, it is not difficult to discern cases in contemporary organisations of each of these types. Equally, although Weber's interest in leadership was limited only to

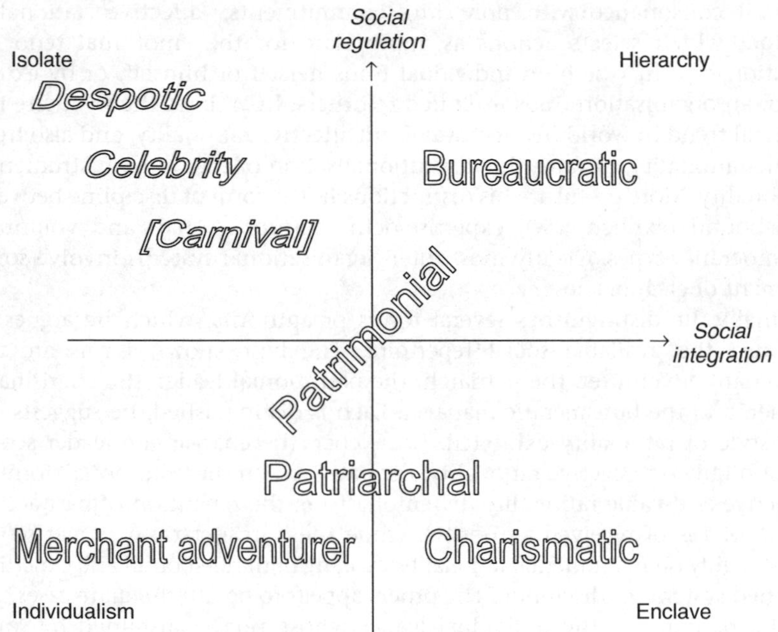

Figure 7.1 Forms of authority and leadership: Weberian forms mapped onto neo-Durkheimian taxonomy.

the supreme leaders of social structures, there is every reason to believe that much the same repertoire is available at each level of organisations and of inter-organisational networks as at the very top.

In fact, these basic forms can be mapped relatively readily onto the neo-Durkheimian taxonomy that has been used as an organising device in this book (cf. the simpler version offered in Douglas and Isherwood, 1979). Figure 7.1 shows that the patriarchal and patrimonial forms are indeed intermediate or hybrid.

Weber sometimes writes as though charismatic leadership is a strong form. However, in fact, this is not the case, and Weber's argument about the routinisation of charisma implicitly recognises that it is not a strategy that is sustainable for very long. However, when we consider the problems of holding together a strongly socially integrated albeit a weakly socially regulated network, it becomes clear that charismatic leadership is the obvious solution; for weak regulation rules out bureaucratic means while strong integration interdicts individualist solutions. Charisma – and the claim to additional degrees of insight and commitment – makes most sense when the network consists in a densely tied group with internally egalitarian arrangements but exclusive relations with outsiders.

Mapping these forms onto the neo-Durkheimian framework enables us to see what is missing and why. This is manifested clearly when consideration is given to the nature of authority in each of these institutional settings. In any network, authority must come from the basic forces that hold the network together, for there is no other source; whatever the personal characteristics of any potential leader, without the appropriate institutional basis these traits cannot be recognised let alone be expressed effectively. In hierarchical networks, for example, authority for the individual must come from status and status must derive ultimately from rule and role, for this is the nature of the fundamental accountabilities that define and hold the network (or, for that matter, single hierarchical organisation) together. In networks with highly individualist institutions, authority can only come from the degree to which ability to control and to access resources is centralised by the entrepreneurial individual. This individual must signal to others an ability to distribute those resources or show that others must work through her or him to obtain them. On the negative diagonal, however, authority is often a little more fragile. In enclaved networks, the 'common cause' is what holds the network together. Hence, common values, ideas, norms, information and commitment underpin relationships. Therefore, only the ability to personify, express and mobilise around those features among others who – under these institutions – have no greater or lesser formal status or access to resource can enable any potential leader to secure the somewhat fragile authority afforded by the context. Authority, understood as the *legitimate* right to exercise leadership, is most problematic in isolate settings. Limited possibilities for collective action are present due to weak accountabilities between those within the network and the extent to which control of the instruments of power lies elsewhere. This means that authority must be exercised externally and with very limited legitimacy at all ('despotism') (see Coyle, 1994) or that a prominent individual may wield 'authority' over a brief duration ('celebrity') or else the 'authority' is wholly ironic in character (the 'carnival queen'). In short, in isolate settings, authority, in so far as there is any, either comes from without or else from luck or occasion. The hybrid forms of authority – patrimonialism and patriarchalism – arise with similar logic from institutional contexts which exhibit combinations of these solidarities.

These forms can be seen as the origins of the more fashionable contemporary distinctions in the forms of leadership used in the management literature. Charismatic leadership styles continue to be the focus of study (e.g. Bryman, 1992), although still too often mistaken for a personality trait rather than understood correctly as an institutionally shaped style adopted in response to a particular organisational problem. Contemporary concepts of 'transformational' leadership (Burns, 1978) most neatly map onto the styles shown in Table 7.2. These are possible in the more socially integrated quadrants, for it is in these institutional settings that there is the greatest scope for leadership

Table 7.2 Ritual forms associated with each basic form of authority

Social regulation ↑

Isolate	**Hierarchy**
Exemplars of ritual style: satirical stand-up comedy *Emotions elicited in ritual, when successful in its own institutional terms*: irony, ridicule, stoic will to endure *Emotions elicited when less successful*: bitterness, sense of arbitrariness, opacity and banality	*Exemplars of ritual style*: procession *Emotions elicited in ritual, when successful in its own institutional terms*: respectful deference for status, amour-propre for own role, commitment, sense of security *Emotions elicited when less successful*: Demoralisation, confusion and bemusement at opacity and complexity of institutions, sense of banality
Individualism	**Enclave**
Exemplars of ritual style: trade fair, street market *Emotions elicited in ritual, when successful in its own institutional terms*: aspiration, excitement, controlled envy for competitive rivalry *Emotions elicited when less successful*: insecurity, dejection at own defeat, frustration at what seems futile and self-defeating rivalry	*Exemplars of ritual style*: religious revivalist meeting, militant picketing strikers meeting *Emotions elicited in ritual, when successful in its own institutional terms*: passionate commitment, collective effervescence, passionate rejection of outsiders and those seen as insiders who have betrayed the institution *Emotions elicited when less successful*: schism

→ *Social integration*

Source: Peck *et al.*, 2004: 107.

agency to influence the definition of the task, the structure of accountabilities, the ties between individuals or organisations and, above all, the preferences. By contrast, in the less integrated contexts, it is harder to shape the preferences of those who are or might become followers, and therefore they must be taken as given. Theories of transactional leadership, popular some years ago but now rather in disfavour, have greatest application in contexts structured heavily by individualism. Only here will the individual-level calculation of the value of offers in negotiation, upon which this style depends, be effective; however, without a measure of hierarchy, the wider institutional environment is unlikely to be stable enough for even this to work. Therefore, we should expect to find transactional leadership in two-way hybrids, in which individualism is the dominant element and hierarchy the subordinate. In weakly integrated but highly regulated contexts, it will be difficult to distinguish leadership as adaptive response from leadership as the authorisation of technical response, or simple management (Heifetz, 1994), and therefore in these settings task-orientation in leadership is more likely.

It was noted above that these forms of leadership can be found at almost any level in organisations. Much of the literature on individual roles in inter-organisational networking is concerned with boundary spanning roles (Thompson JD, 1967). In studies on vertically tied networks, some key boundary spanners in private sector organisations are procurement and purchasing managers for upstream linkages and account managers and sales staff for downstream linkages. Where there are contract-like arrangements in the public sector for internal markets or for contracting-out, roughly corresponding functions will exist. In addition, project managers who work in client-facing roles are increasingly important boundary spanning staff in many organisations. The Weberian approach to understanding leadership enables us to understand not only chief executives or chairs of boards but also to comprehend the ways in which these boundary spanning staff in more subaltern roles in organisations might be able to operate.

What remains critical to each of these styles of leadership is the capacity to mobilise the symbols and rituals of authority – that is, of course, authority appropriate to the particular individual's location in and between organisations – both to sustain people's commitment to the type of network and to sustain the capacities for learning and management. Associated with each of these leadership and authority styles are distinct styles of ritualisation, even in the context of meeting management. For example, reviewing the studies on boards, Peck *et al.* (2004) find that most boards are not in fact used principally for instrumental purposes of strategic decision-making at all, despite the elaborate efforts made in many organisations and partnerships to present their work as being just that. They argue that each of the basic forms of institution is associated with a distinct ritual style, producing distinct patterns of emotion when successful and when unsuccessful, and which can be seen in the styles of meeting management used at board level for the production of authority in partnership structures to govern networks. They offer as a case study a partnership board which readily fell into a hierarchical ritual order. The meeting format was that of a procession, in which each of the representatives paraded their status and perspectives in sequence. This proved difficult to sustain, as particular groups of health and social care stakeholders' practices and aspirations could not be contained within the ritual order, and some key groups appeared to move into isolate positions, adopting ritual styles alternately stoic and ironic in relation to the partnership board's style. Faced with this, a dual approach was adopted, that provided for a partly separate enclave structure within the ritual order of governance in the partnership (which exhibited a ritual style more akin to the revivalist meeting). The tensions nonetheless remained at the point where observations ceased. What was at stake in that case were rival ritual forms of symbolic communication arising from the efforts of different groups to exercise distinct styles of leadership and authority within and across the network in question. Table 7.2 summarises the key differences in ritual style.

It is interesting to note that one of the problems with a purely Weberian approach to leadership, especially in the context of inter-organisational relations, is its disdain for the importance of what he termed 'affective rationality'. For it is by the production of a variety of different emotions within organisations that leaders secure commitment to the actions they want and how – unintendedly – they provoke actions they would rather not see (Fineman, 2000).

Styles of networking for brokers and leaders

In this chapter, we have argued that individuals play important roles in managing networks. The tacit knowledge upon which any network can draw lies in the control of individuals and – whether those individuals are leaders or led – it is difficult to ensure that they will share that knowledge to enhance learning between organisations. Networks with different institutional forms attempt to solve that problem in the different ways that their institutions either leave open or positively cultivate. Whatever the strategy, there is no route to learning in networks that does not go through such emotions as fear, commitment, greed or pride, and leaders and brokers play a key role in sustaining these emotions through the ritual performances for which they have peculiar responsibilities in organisational life. This means that the micro-foundations of a theory of learning in organisational networks cannot be individualistic; it must be grounded in the institutions of social integration and regulation, types of ritual and types of leadership afforded by those institutions. For instance, instrumental rationality of an individualistic kind cannot be sustained without affective rationality which depends on appropriate ritual forms in every inter-organisational context such as meetings, negotiations, press conferences and celebrations of achievements. The basic styles of learning – tacit and explicit, exploration and exploitation – are ones that make more sense in some types of institutions shaping networks than in others.

This chapter concludes the presentation of the theory. The neo-Durkheimian account argued for here represents a significant enrichment of conventional approaches as well as being a synthesis of their most valuable features. This part of the book has explored some of the key intermediate variables through which underlying institutional mechanisms shape inter-organisational relations, including transaction costs, information conditions, forms of power and governance, strategies of management and processes of change, styles of learning, forms of trust. The result is a genuinely holistic account, but one which also has micro-foundations (even if they are not methodologically individualistic).

The theory as a whole has not been explored empirically by the present authors. However, it is possible to use the wealth of empirical studies already published on inter-organisational networks to examine how well it performs. The next four chapters do just that. Each reviews in detail the main findings in the literature on a distinct industry. We examine two industries in which supply is predominantly from the private sector – defence matériel contracting and biotechnology – and two in which the public sector is, in many countries, heavily represented (combating crime and disorder and health care). Moreover, defence and health care are often fields in which the public sector is the main purchaser, whereas in biotechnology demand mainly comes from commercial companies. Despite these differences, each of these sectors is known to be an area of collaborative working. In the final chapter of the book which follows these case studies, we compare and contrast the findings to examine how well they bear out the theory presented in the first half of the book.

Part III

8
Networks in Defence Procurement and Supply

Introduction

This chapter examines networks in two distinct but closely related areas: arms procurement and arms supply. Markowski and Hall (1998) identify six dimensions of arms procurement: user requirements (what to buy?); division of labour (make or buy?); contracting (what type of contract?); source selection and competition (how much competition?); organisational (who should have the authority and responsibility for making procurement decisions?); and international collaboration (what should be the drivers of international procurement?). This final dimension – the extent of international collaboration between sovereign governments that underpins the other five dimensions – is the focus of discussion of procurement in this chapter. As the specifiers and paymasters for most new weapons systems, thus acting in effect as monopsony purchasers in contractual arrangements that can take up to twenty years to complete and with keen economic interests in the protection of domestic suppliers, the behaviour of governments is central to shaping the supply side of the defence industry.

Gansler (1995) presents a three-dimensional matrix (see Figure 8.1) which highlights three important aspects of this supply industry. First, it can be divided into a relatively small number of prime contractors – in 1991 only 25 companies received 46 per cent of the value of all US Department of Defense (DoD) prime contact awards and the seven largest defence-dependent companies accounted for nearly 25 per cent of all prime contracts – and the potentially very large numbers of subcontractors and parts suppliers with which they work. This range of interlinked suppliers needs to create and sustain collaborative arrangements in a competitive market place over extended periods of time whilst being subject to considerable numbers of interventions by procurement agencies. Furthermore, these supply chains typically cluster in relatively small geographical locations. Second, these contractors can be in either public or private ownership. Third, there are a number of distinct technologies that armaments require, many of which can be developed and manufactured in conjunction with potential civil uses (termed 'dual-use' technology). Although the purchaser has significant influence over the precise specification for particular weapons systems, the development of arms technology is frequently driven by the research of providers and the linked aspirations of the military. These three characteristics have significant implications for the nature of the networks that arise in the defence supply industry; in short, patterns of defence procurement and supply have created a market which is far removed from the classical economic model.

The procurement and supply of defence systems in and between Europe and the United States was the subject of extensive comment and some empirical study in the period 1960–2000 considered in this chapter. The review of this literature has been limited by geography (i.e. studies relating to the members of NATO and France) and the nature of the equipment (i.e. defence specific equipment such as fighter planes and not the acquisition or supply of civil hardware and software for military use). It transpired that the key words for this review – such as network, partnership, collaborative venture – rarely appear in the indexes of the major works from any of the four decades that this review has covered. However, careful sifting of the literature reveals both prescriptive and descriptive accounts of the relationships between procurers, between suppliers and between procurers and suppliers that allow us to explore the nature of networks in this field in terms of the framework developed in Chapter 4.

Most of the literature covered by this review originates in what is referred to as the post-Cold War era (that is, after 1989), but before the onset of the so-called war against terrorism (that is, after 2001). It exhibits common assumptions, therefore, about the necessity for the downsizing of the provider capacity in the arms industry which drive much of the discussion of alliances, collaborative ventures and mergers. Markusen and Costigan (1999a) articulate

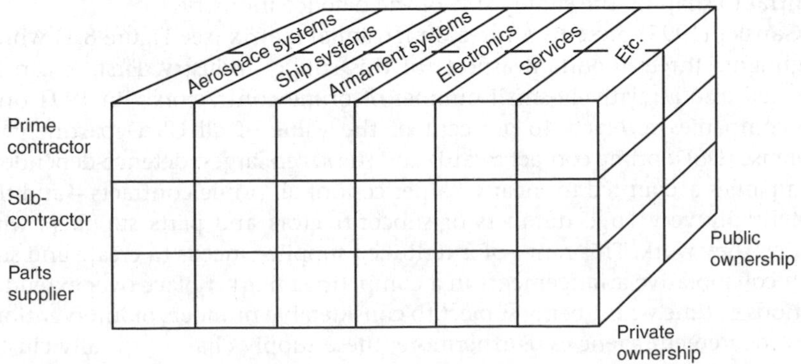

Figure 8.1 The structure of the defence industry.
Source: Gansler, 1995: 21.

these assumptions when they observe: 'as the century draws to a close, the United States and its allies are enjoying a period of markedly diminished threat and relative stability in international relations' (p. 6).

The literature on networks in arms procurement and supply has three broad foci: the networks between countries for the procurement of arms; the aspirations and activity of governments in the encouragement of networks between providers for supply; and the development of networks between these providers based on mutual interest. Of course, these foci overlap, but they are sufficiently distinct to be dealt with separately; they form the framework for the analysis of the literature carried out next. The first and the third can be characterised as dealing with the internal management of networks whereas the middle one could be conceived as relating to the governance of networks. Much of the literature in the next section area focuses on Europe and tends to be more prescriptive than that examined in the subsequent two sections. Finally, it is important to note that none of the literature reviewed here conceptualises the various forms of collaboration within the theoretical framework that informs this book; inevitably, therefore, the purposes of the review have formed the lens through which this literature is seen.

Networks between countries for the procurement of arms

In terms of collaboration between European governments, Creasey and May (1988) suggest that the advocates of European collaboration in defence procurement put forward a combination of political and economic factors to support their prescriptions. They identify five distinct economic drivers: rationalisation on a European level is inevitable as each domestic market is too small and incompatible national weapons systems are problematic in joint action; the costs of R&D are becoming prohibitive; the globalisation of the technological developments, especially around the fusion of information and communication technology; the contracting overseas market for arms and; the discrepancy between the amount spent by European countries on R&D in comparison with the United States. The assumptions evident here derive predominantly from ideas linked to rational choice and transaction costs; they almost bemoan the interference of political factors in the procurement process as illegitimate.

However, the story of European collaboration in arms procurement is broadly, in terms of the Neo-Durkheimian framework underpinning this book, is one of these adherents of economic approaches to networks attempting to persuade governments with strong isolate tendencies in this sphere of activity to come together into an enclave. As Figure 4.1 puts it, European governments may share a general sentiment about the benefits of collective defence procurement, but little genuine commitment to it.

The origins of European collaborative defence procurement lie in the creation of NATO in the 1940s. The presence of the United States within NATO has been described as both a positive and negative influence on such collaboration. Putting the case for the former, a paper in the International Defense Review (1991) draws attention to the Nunn amendment under which the US committed significant resources to NATO collaborative defence projects from 1986 onwards. On the other hand, Draper (1990) argues that, in the United Kingdom in the 1940s and 1950s, 'Foreign Office officials were more interested in the United States than in Europe ... there is little evidence that the Treasury saw advantages in European co-operation before ... 1960' (pp. 14–15). Even at that early stage, Draper identifies the reasons why standardisation of defence equipment across Europe was seen as implausible, reasons which echo down the years: 'the existence of trade secrets, patent rights, military traditions, the cost of scrapping existing equipment and the desirability of a self-supporting defence industry' (p. 14).

There have been a number of other factors that have impeded NATO becoming the engine-room for the promotion of European collaboration in defence procurement. First, France has not been a full member since the mid-1960s. Second, and despite the Nunn amendment, much US industry behaviour has been seen as competitive with Europe rather than collaborative (Pages, 1999). Third, there has been much academic and political debate about the extent to which the European partners pull their financial weight when compared to their American allies (Olson and Zeckhauser 1966, Gonzalez and Mehay, 1991).

The drive for collaboration has been led since 1976 by the Independent European Programme Group (IPEG), which has met at ministerial level since 1984 and embarked on a series of Cooperative Technology Projects (CTPs). Despite welcoming these initiatives, Heisbourg (1988) doubts that they would overcome the obstacles to joint procurement: 'the difficulties in making requirements and acquisition schedules coincide; the built-in costs and delays generated by collaborative ventures; the basic problem of clear-cut management leadership – all of these will limit the scope of common programmes in the coming years' (p. 77). Draper (1990) shares the view that the more the number of partners in a defence procurement project grows, the greater the prospects for disagreement, delay and increased costs. He also argues that, for someone pursuing a career in the defence procurement field, the consequences of being involved in a collaborative procurement project are not '*rosy*' (p. 96); being a boundary spanner in these circumstances is presumably not a comfortable or valued role.

Hartley and Martin (1993) challenge the assumption of writers such as Heisbourg (1988) and Draper (1990) that international collaborations in defence procurement are costly. They identify three categories of performance indicators for procurement – cost savings, output and development times – and then compare data for collaborative and national projects to produce military aircraft. They conclude that 'the evidence suggests that collaboration leads to cost savings and greater scales of output, with only limited support for the view that joint projects take longer to develop' (p. 210). Although they acknowledge that these indicators are only part of the cost–benefit analysis, this is an important finding which provides succour to the champions of collaborative procurement which 'can be presented as a cost-saving solution in an era of limited defence budgets whilst at the same time preserving a nation's industrial capacity' (p. 210). Markowski and Hall (1998) concur with this conclusion, singling out bilateral collaborations as working best, or 'in a multilateral context where one country provides strong market and technological leadership and other countries are "junior equity holders" ' (p. 30).

Walker and Willett (1993), discussing the IEPG Action Plan, highlight the notion of '*juste retour*' (fair return) in the access that European collaborators would have to the markets of others. This notion of balance implies, as they point out, 'this would not be a market in which the survival of the fittest would lead to a rapid re-division of labour based on competitive advantage' (p. 147). Rather, 'firms would adjust by forming alliances and rearranging their R&D and production to take advantage of the new European environment' (p. 147) and they point to emerging evidence of such rearrangements starting to occur across companies in Britain, France and Germany. However, despite the intentions of purchasers and the IEPG Action Plan, they argue that 'the adjustment to changing conditions in defence markets is totally unco-ordinated. Governments are largely reacting to events, and seem unable or unwilling to elucidate the kind of defence industry they would like to maintain in the longer term' (p. 153).

Since 1978, the European Parliament has been producing reports on the waste of resources represented by non-co-ordinated procurement, often aspiring to 'a single, structured European Community market in defense equipment' (Sandler and Hartley, 1995: 226). In its 1978 proposal for a European Armaments Procurement Agency, the Parliament could be characterised as calling for a hierarchical approach to replace the failed attempts to create an enclave. It did not happen. In 1988, the Parliament returned to the topic, focusing this time on supply, and promoting the benefits of a European defence industry capable of competing with the United States (see Sandler and Hartley, 1995: 229).

In keeping with much of the economic literature, Sandler and Hartley (1995) are keen to define clear policy options which governments should choose between and seem to lament the reality that, for instance, 'work is often allocated on the basis of political, equity, and bargaining criteria and not on the basis of efficiency, comparative advantage, and competition' (p. 235). Given the prevalence of their economic assumptions, it is no surprise, therefore, that they conclude that 'ultimately, a nation's involvement in collaboration will be determined by a comparison of the marginal transaction costs and transaction benefits from a joint program' (p. 236). *Should*, perhaps, but *will*? Heisbourg (1988) reports that 'more than a quarter of a century after the initiation of the first major cooperative ventures, joint procurement represents only a limited fraction of European weapons programmes' (p. 60).

In 1996, the Quadrilateral (United Kingdom, France, Germany and Italy) Armaments Agency was formed to increase the efficiency of collaborative procurement. Hartley (1998) fears that this new agency will face the same 'massive opposition from interest group of contractors, unions, towns, and regions likely to lose from such efficiency improvements' (p. 59) as previous arrangements set up to promote collaboration. In 1998, these four countries formed the Organisation for Joint Armament Cooperation, which aimed to facilitate the restructuring of the European defence industry by: 'lowering the barriers to the exchange of sensitive information and technology and ... [fostering] the harmonisation of military requirements' (Kapstein, 2002: 149). Four years after its formation, Kapstein is unsure whether this initiative will finally deliver a single defence market which mirrors the single European market in goods and services.

Those collaborations that have been attempted have scarcely been persuasive; examples of the very public failure of joint projects (e.g. the European Fighter Aircraft – EFA) appear regularly in the literature (e.g. Creasey and May, 1988; Heisbourg, 1988). The International Defense Review (1991) argues that the EFA proves the truth of the maxim that 'collaborative projects ... [produce] multi-role weapons that reflect a compromise between various national missions and hence are ill-suited to any single task' (p. 959, parentheses added). Creasey (1988) suggests that between 1960 and 1985 there were around 270 collaborative European projects, half of which were 'unsuccessful or abandoned in the early stages' (p. 91). Draper (1990), drawing on a case study of helicopter production in the 1980s, isolates two main reasons for lack of progress on collaboration: 'a failure to harmonise operational requirements and a lack of political will at ministerial level to insist on such harmonisation' (p. 84).

Inevitably, the long list of economic and political benefits of maintaining an isolate position in relation to defence procurement, and the apparent litany of failures when collaboration has been attempted, provide the context for the longevity of this position. From this perspective, there seems to be little evidence of a trend in the network forms adopted for this task. Overall, this short history suggests that no amount of structural innovation derived from purely economically rational theory is going to overcome the political barriers that obstruct collaboration in procurement from becoming the routine approach of the European allies (either between each other or between themselves and the Americans) when commissioning new weapons systems. It seems clear that in considering links between governments as procurers there is evidence for the validity of neo-institutionalist perspectives, where the extent of the interaction is limited by preexisting political and social constraints. The impact of a number of international attempts to promote partnership between national governments through external influence (from within NATO and the European parliament) has been muted. The predominant structural form of the relationship between these governments in relation to defence procurement continues to conform to an isolate pattern with low-density ties around specific projects (e.g. EFA), despite the development of the arguably enclave (NATO) and hierarchical (European parliament) approaches elsewhere in the relationships between these nation states. Part of the explanation for these low-density ties may lie in the nature of what is passed along them, that is, for instance, technical intelligence, which requires levels of trust which are difficult to maintain given the competitive advantage (for example, in international arms sales) that may be sacrificed by sharing (see Chapter 5).

The aspirations and activities of governments in the encouragement of networks between providers

A good summary of the concerns of this part of the post Cold War literature are provided by Markusen and Costigan (1999a) who pose a number of key questions: 'Should nations continue to keep existing production lines "hot", at considerable cost, ensuring their availability in the future? ... Should the Pentagon and its advanced weapons-making allies speed the dismantling of factories and facilities no longer needed, and, if so, are mergers among large contractors the best way to achieve this? ... Should dual-use firms and production facilities be encouraged or discouraged?' (pp. 3–4).

Implicit in these questions is the assumed legitimacy and plausibility of a national government using its power as a monopsony purchaser to directly influence the behaviour of the companies involved in supply. Markusen and Costigan (1999a) identify the levers that the Pentagon possesses: 'its role in antitrust approval, procurement awards and privatisation decisions' (p. 6). As they put it, 'few analysts would disagree with the proposition that the size, composition, and output of the defence industry should be driven by American security strategy and not vice versa' (p. 15).

Pages (1999) provides more details of some of these approaches. General antitrust enforcement in the United States under President Clinton in the early 1990s was largely hostile to mergers and acquisitions; the notable exception was defence where no major merger was blocked after 1992. In 1993, the government adopted a policy of subsidies to support consolidation in the sector (so-called 'pay-offs for lay-offs'). Oden (1998) estimated that if the mega-mergers proposed in 1996 and 1997 went through then three consolidated companies would be in receipt of one-third of total defence contracts in the United States. Pages (1999) outlines the potentially negative consequences for government of the triumph of consolidation over diversification: increased cost; decreased technological innovation; and the need for more government regulation over the market. Oden (1999) posits that 'following the current path risks reconstituting a defense industry that is even more isolated, sluggish, and exceedingly expensive to maintain' (p. 76).

As a consequence of such concerns, procurement strategy also emphasised the use of commercial components as opposed to ones just produced for military purposes and thus encouraged the use of innovative commercial technology as well as investment in dual-use R&D. Susman and O'Keefe (1998) report on the Technology Reinvestment Programme, where proposals from suppliers that used technology already being deployed in commercial settings were viewed favourably during procurement. Oden (1999) describes how the Clinton administration attempted to encourage defence contractors to team up with others and diversify out of arms supply through competitively allocated grants. This was a limited success because it had few attractions for politicians seeking to target resources on their home patch and generated lots of disgruntled losers, in particular some of the largest contractors which had pursued the alternative strategy of consolidated specialisation and saw this policy as subsidising the growth of competitors. Leitzel (1992) views such teaming 'as a useful device for spreading out the contract awards in an era of reduced demand for new weapon systems' (p. 50). Markusen and Costigan (1999b) are similarly positive, noting overall how government programmes have made more impact at a regional than a national level and supported firms willing to make the cultural adjustments, management commitment and use of outside expertise that diversification requires.

The focus of the Clinton administration's measures was thus on encouraging both consolidation and diversification amongst arms contractors. However, it is important to explore in more detail the nature of the pre-existing relationships between suppliers in which the Clinton government was trying to intervene in order to understand their impact.

The government approach that was adopted until 1989 involved, Oden (1999) argues, negotiated prices, dense specifications and contract regulation that ensured firms predictable income; this represented a very elaborate form of relational contracting. Some analysts (e.g. Anton and Yao, 1990) describe a four stage procurement cycle: initial design; development; production and reprocurement. Traditionally, competition is active in the design stage, and then the contract winners reap the high rewards of production whist the other companies prepare for the next design phase (and/or to compete for reprocurement). This approach had a number of implications. Kelley and Watkins (1998) suggest that productivity in defence companies is poor by comparison with that shown by civilian enterprises, reflecting low investment in technology as a consequence of cost-plus contracts alongside a lack of ongoing competition. Alic *et al.* (1992) attribute this to the historical context where 'in earlier years the American penchant for inventiveness and American domination of the upstream process [e.g. R&D] allowed U.S. firms to neglect the downstream process [e.g. production]' (p. 19, parentheses added). Martin *et al.* (1996) also find evidence in the United Kingdom to support the suggestion of poor productivity in defence suppliers which are heavily dependent on government contracts. In essence, therefore, the excellence of the innovations in R&D departments of defence companies is not replicated in the production activities of those same companies.

Oden (1999) points out that in this production phase the major defence companies rely extensively on subcontractors. Kelley and Watkins (1998) explored the relationships between prime contractors and sub-contractors in more detail in a study undertaken in 1991. They reveal 'that the dependence on subcontractors ranges from 60 per cent to more than 70 per cent of prime contractor's costs' (p. 255). This means that the prime contractors have a very significant number of relationships with other organisations; Kelley and Watkins cite one such company with around 3000 direct suppliers most of which had no direct contracts with procurement agencies.

One of the challenges to the orthodoxy in the arms supply literature (e.g. Gansler, 1992) that is represented by the Kelley and Watkins study is the finding that integration of commercial and military production was already well advanced, in particular amongst the subcontractors of the prime contractors. They estimate that in 1990, of the companies that reported shipping defence related products, well over half originated in companies that did most of their production for non-defence customers. In these circumstances, they argue, any government diversification programme – such as that pursued by the Clinton administration – which focused on prime contractors was missing the point that the majority of companies in arms production were already heavily diversified; in fact it was only those prime contractors that had pursued the route of consolidation.

Furthermore, Alic *et al.* (1992) argue that the increasingly international profile and focus of the prime contractors put these companies beyond the reach of government influence on their commercial affairs. Oden (1999) contends that 'the most powerful DoD actions by far were directed at supporting and subsidizing merger and consolidation in the defense industry' (p. 80), precisely because they were in line with the commercial realities of the industry. Mergers of major defence companies accelerated throughout the mid-1990s, on these accounts supported by, but not originating in, government subsidy. Oden (1999) and Korb (1996) both cite Lockheed Martin alone as receiving $1 billion from the Pentagon to complete its various mergers through allowable additional costs on current contracts. Oden (1999) concludes that 'there are, therefore, strong reasons to believe that maintaining production and development capability was more important than cost savings in permitting the permissive government stance towards mergers' (p. 85). Put another way, President Clinton's priority may initially have been cost saving and job protection; however, the Pentagon apparently viewed retention of specialist capacity as the overriding aim. In pursuing these parallel but distinct aims, both President Clinton and the Pentagon probably found ready allies amongst the Senators of those states in which the prime contractors were located.

The Pentagon's priority was, some writers suggest, perhaps not surprising. Leitzel (1992) suspects that the DoD in the United States has been the victim of 'regulatory capture' by the defence industry, and is complicit with the maintenance of a cartel of suppliers. In support of this suggestion, he points to the stable market share over time of the major defence contractors, with, for instance, major aerospace contracts appearing 'to be awarded to the firm that has a newly vacated production line, regardless of the merits of the proposal' (p. 49). Furthermore, he argues that, 'the potential for future employment [of DoD staff] in the defense industry may create some identification with the contractors, a situation that the contractors no doubt hope to encourage' (p. 51, parentheses added). Leitzel is one of the few writers in the literature, along with Alic (1998), to draw attention to the regular interchange of personnel between the commissioners, suppliers and users of defence products, although there seems to be no published study of the extent and impact of this phenomenon.

Nonetheless, Oden (1999) points out that the top 25 prime defence contractors in the United States shed over 600,000 workers – almost 25 per cent of their total workforce – between 1989 and 1994. Hartley (1998) reports a 50 per cent fall in the United Kingdom during the period 1980–95, with half of that reduction occurring in the last five years of that period. Small and medium-size specialist defence companies were also badly hit in the United States, with employment in one sample falling 37 per cent during the period 1989–93. Oden (1999) acknowledges that in the United States the impact on small dual-use subcontractors was much less pronounced with sales values (including defence sales) and employment levels changing very little between 1989 and 1993, partially due to their existing diversification.

Thus, although some of the larger companies did diversify successfully after 1989, there is little evidence of the Clinton administration's competitive investment strategy having much connection with these successes, raising the question of the extent to which governments – or, indeed, other external agencies – can drive the creation or development of effective alliances or collaborative ventures through financial incentives. Indeed, Pages (1999) suggests that 'despite the efforts of both industry and government to promote greater internationalisation and commercialisation in the defense sector, technological and political trends actually are moving in the opposite direction' (p. 208). Further, Oden (1999) contends that 'the list of diversification failures is almost certainly much longer than successes' (p. 90), confirming that this was a high-risk activity for companies that had little previous experience of commercial production. Finally, in relation to diversification, Peck and Scherer (1962) serve to remind us that government support for such initiatives is scarcely new, and from which Gansler (1995) takes the lesson: 'one conclusion gleaned from past defense conversions is that government initiatives on their own are less likely to be successful than strong industry initiatives with some government support' (p. 80).

Pages (1999) suggests that government approaches to the new defence conglomerates will have to rely on increased regulation of production and enhanced robustness of contracts relevant to the needs of the industry rather than pursuing policy based on conceptions of a traditional free market. Alic (1998) agrees that all the evidence from studies of the defence industry 'suggest that stimulating competition in the absence of a functioning market is ineffective' (p. 343). This is particularly the case, he argues, where defence budgets, defence capacity and defence competition are shrinking. He goes on to pose the 'ultimate dilemma in acquisition policy: lacking the discipline of a marketplace, how to manage a process involving such huge sums and huge stakes?' (p. 348). One answer seems straightforward: 'DoD should focus on active management of major programs (as opposed to auditing and oversight), recognizing the unique character of the contractor relationship and seeking to develop the kind of in-house skills and expertise needed to achieve better outcomes' (p. 343).

However, career military personnel do not see acquisition as an attractive stop on the career path, as the road to the top is through operational commands. Markowski and Hall (1998) describe the job posting cycle of military personnel leading to 'baton changes' and 'kinds of myopia specific to military procurement agencies' (p. 30). Civilian managers stay longer, but are less trusted by the services. Even they, given the rivalries between the services and the fact that more weapons systems are in design than can be produced, are prone to disguise problems in their programmes rather than reveal and deal with them. Interestingly, creating a cadre of arms commissioners who can effectively and independently steer both individual projects and the industry as a whole is, Alic (1998) implies, unlikely. Nonetheless, it is one of the strategies for change regularly – and understandably – suggested by commentators (e.g. Gansler, 1992). Surprisingly, the inevitably transitory nature of governments and ministers within governments are rarely discussed as factors in the literature.

Overall, therefore, it appears that despite the attempts by the government in the United States to change the focus of and relationships between defence suppliers, the major impact of their interventions has been to support the mergers of prime contractors which fitted the strategic aspirations of the companies themselves. Failure to deliver on other objectives seems to have been a consequence of the differences of perspective between government departments and between policy-makers and politicians, alongside a misunderstanding of the subcontractor industry in defence which undermined the policy of diversification amongst prime contractors. Furthermore, this spate of mergers has made it more likely that procurement will in future be based on specification and regulation rather than competition. In these circumstances, civilian commissioners may struggle to assert their authority caught as they are between the experts in the armed forces and the experts in the prime contractors. It is important not to overstate this case. As Kelley and Watkins (1995) contend, it would be perverse not to recognise that 'the government (as buyer) exercises considerable control over sellers' *internal* operations through its direct involvement in the development of new weapons and its auditing of supplier's costs' (p. 526, emphasis added). The form of the resultant internal operations will inevitably influence, albeit indirectly, the nature of the collaborations that the prime contractors pursue.

Nonetheless, based on the evidence from these studies in the United States, it seems plausible to argue that the impact of public policy aspirations for, and the activities of commissioners on, the design and behaviour of networks are destined to be significantly influenced by the nature of the market within which these networks operate; in respect of arms markets they will apparently be very limited. This empirical finding is further evidence that the simple distinction between markets and networks that informs much writing in this area is misconceived. It appears that networks in arms supply will be largely shaped by the market interests and behaviours of the prime contractors and their suppliers. It is to consideration of this topic that we turn in the next section.

The development of networks between providers based on mutual interest

As argued in the previous section, the aspirations and activities of government have to be set in the context of two industry factors: the nature of the existing relationships between providers; and their own ambitions for the future given the pressures that they face, of which the impact of government initiatives will be only one, and perhaps not the major one.

As noted earlier, in the 1990s the most marked trend in the industry was merger, with the dominant firms thus becoming larger and more international in scope, reflecting developments in manufacturing more generally (Korb, 1992). By 1997, three companies had revenues over £10 billion per annum, representing around 50 per cent of the supply in the Western axis. Susman and O'Keefe (1998) report the major reasons senior executives of these companies gave for these acquisitions: to diversify within the defence industry; to bring elements of their supply chain into ownership through vertical integration (i.e. using acquisition to make more elements of their networks internal to the company); and to enter foreign markets. However, also as discussed earlier, much of the revenue attributed to prime contractors was then passed onto subcontractors. The detail of this connection between prime contractor and subcontractor needs to be unpacked to understand the types of liabilities entered into between organisations over extended periods of time.

These relationships have obviously been affected by the decline in the industry. Pages (1999) estimates that cuts in the number of subcontractors on weapons programmes ranged from 50 per cent to 80 per cent and although Oden (1999) is more optimistic about the fate of small and integrated firms, Gansler (1995) thinks that both limitations on the number of suppliers and the entrance of foreign suppliers are both impacting upon traditional patterns of subcontracting. Nonetheless, the description by Kelley and Watkins (1998) of the nature of these relationships in 1991 remains the most detailed reported in the literature and thus warrants careful study.

Once again, Kelley and Watkins (1998) challenge received wisdom in the field. They found more 'collaborative networks' (p. 271) in manufacturing companies with defence contracts than in those without. On 19 out of 43 measures of collaboration the former had 'stronger or more prevalent collaborative external links than the latter' (p. 271). Figures 8.2 and 8.3 summarise their findings, with the first focusing on the collaborative networks of defence prime contractors and the second on those of defence subcontractors. These figures include only those nineteen measures where external connections were stronger, and the arrows indicate the direction of the connection. The authors' analysis of this material is reproduced in edited form in Box 8.1.

Hagedoorn (1995) finds from his data that the defence industry does not follow the cyclical pattern of network creation and dissolution of other industries. It transpires that, when measured by network density, in the late 1980s 'at least 20% of the theoretically possible inter-firm links between groups of leading firms ... are actually found' (pp. 212–213) and that defence companies also show a high degree of stability in these networks over time (e.g. in large bidding consortia) although there are also discernable geographical patterns to these networks (e.g. US, European, Japanese). Common to the networks, however, is the influence of prime contractors: 'nodal companies increasingly weave webs with a large number of partners through a wide variety of inter-organizational modes of cooperation such as joint ventures, joint R&D pacts, and technology sharing agreements. The "open" character of these networks, with some degree of stability, indicates the dynamic nature of character of partnering behaviour of many leading companies that use these alliances as part of a wider competitive strategy' (p. 226).

These data present a picture of ties between collaborators in the defence supply networks that could be consistent with the individualistic form (with individual bundles of ties mediated through the nodes of their separate relationships with the prime contractor) but are actually more suggestive of the enclave form. This interpretation is strengthened by the geographical proximity of the companies found by Bishop (1996) in his study of the Devonport Dockyard. Examining the spatial location of supply linkages, he demonstrates that almost 50 per cent of the value of expenditure by the agency running the dockyard took place in the south west region, with over a third of that expenditure and 19 per cent of suppliers concentrated in Devon, with over three-quarters of that 19 per cent located in Plymouth. Also focusing on the south west of England, Williams' (2000) study suggests

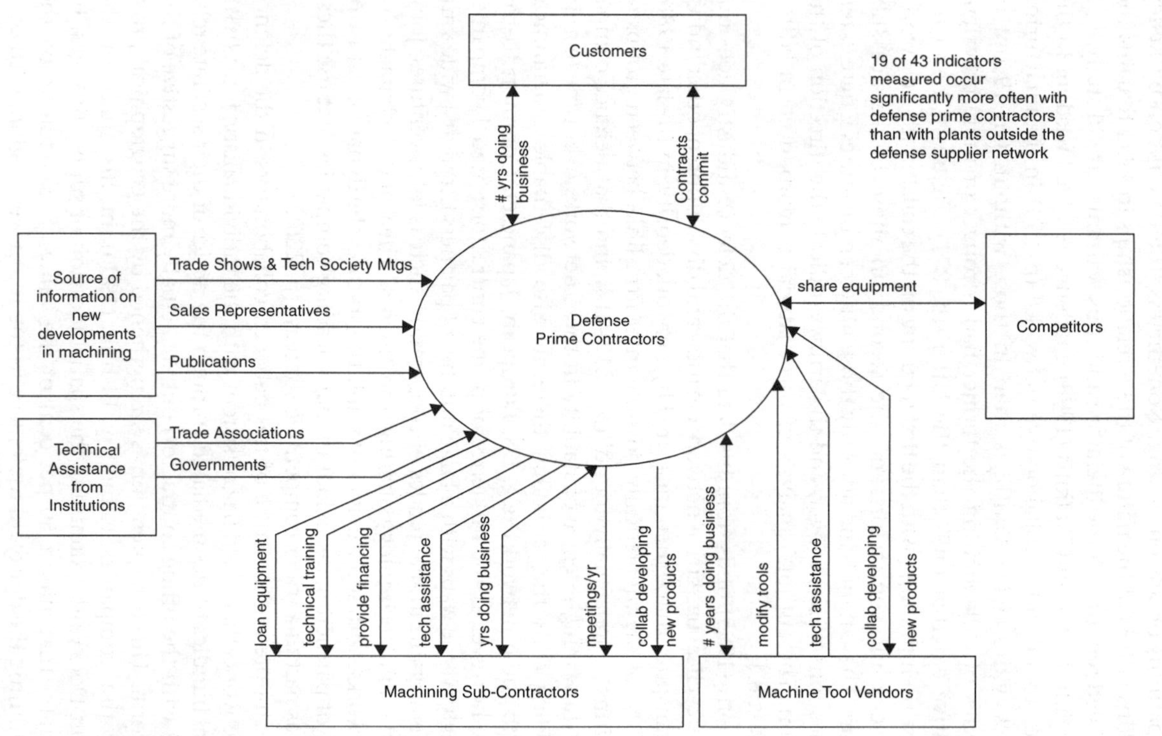

Figure 8.2 Collaborative networks of defence prime contractors.
Source: Reproduced from Kelley and Watkins, 1998 (p. 272, figure 17.6).

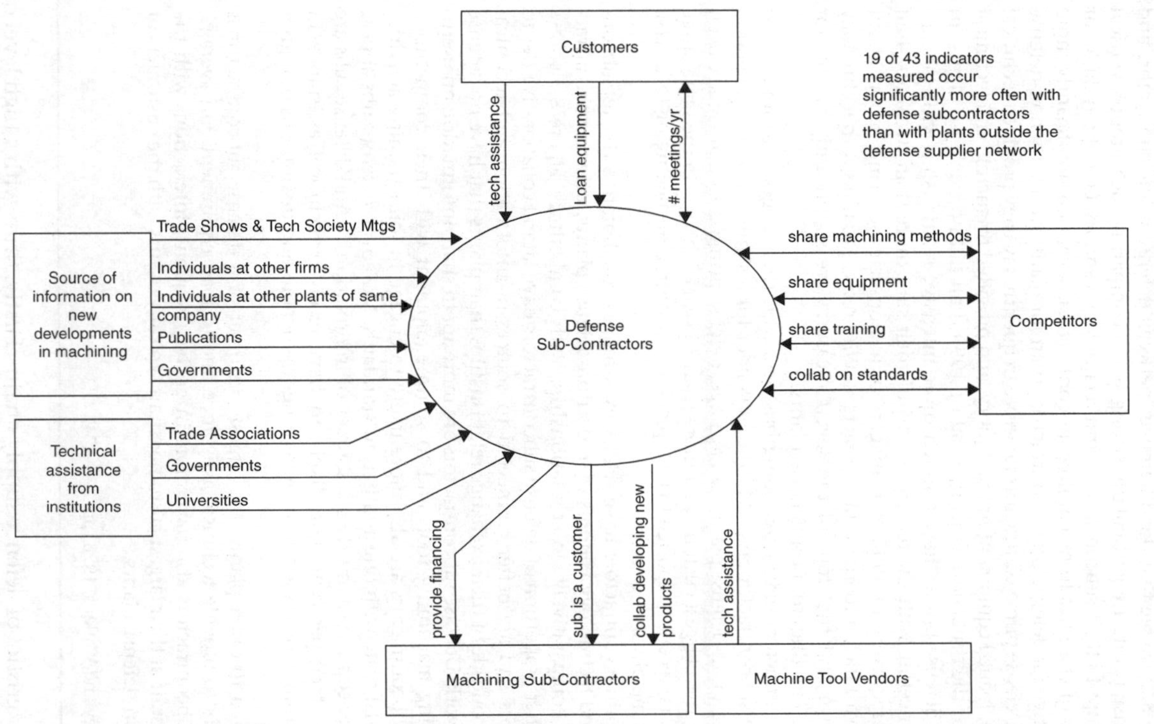

Figure 8.3 Collaborative networks of defence subcontractors.

Source: Reproduced from Kelley and Watkins, 1998 (p. 272, figure 17.7).

Box 8.1 An exploration of collaborative supply networks in the defence industry

(In Figure 8.2) we see that the differences between defense prime contractors and non-defense plants are particularly strong when comparing each group's vertical relationships to their subcontractors and technology vendors. Out of ten different indicators of close ties to machining subcontractors, seven are significantly more collaborative for defense prime contractors than for plants in strictly non-defense markets. Defense prime contractors far more frequently say they provided technical assistance, loaned equipment or machinery, and provided financing, and technical training to their subcontractors in 1989 or 1990 than did non-defense plants. In addition, defense primes have a much more intensive relationship with subcontractors, meeting with the technical staff of their subs more than two-and-a-half times as frequently in 1990 as managers from non-defense plants report about contacts with their important subcontractors. With respect to links with technology vendors, we find that four of the seven measures are significantly greater for defense primes than for non-defense plants.

Prime contractors have been doing business with their largest customer, most important subcontractor and technology vendor for a significantly longer period of time than non-defense plants. On average, defense prime contractors have been supplying their largest customer for more than 16 years, which is in the same range (15–20 years) recently reported to be typical of subcontractors belonging to *keiretsu* in Japan's metalworking sector.

While prime contractors have relatively stronger collaborative ties to subcontractors and technology vendors than do non-defense plants, defense subcontractors have comparatively closer relationships with competitors. Figure 8.3 shows that a higher proportion of defense subcontractors have lateral collaborative ties to competitors and are better connected to sources of information and technical assistance outside of their exchange relationships than plants that have no defense contract work. Defense subcontractors are more apt to share information on methods of using machining tools and to share equipment with their competitors. Defense subcontractors are also more likely to engage in joint training activities and to collaborate with one another on standards. Moreover, defense subs appear to be better connected to external sources of information ... And defense subs are also at least 60 per cent more likely to have received technical assistance in 1989–90 from trade associations, government programs and institutions of higher education.

Compared to other plants, the largest customer of a defense subcontractor is more likely to provide technical assistance and to loan equipment. On average, defense subcontractors also have more intensive (frequent) interactions with the technical staff of their largest customer than typically occurs with the customers of strictly non-defense plants.

Source: Kelley and Watkins, 1998 (pp. 272–274).

two characteristics of defence supply chain: 'Firstly, firms with a high level of defence turnover (defence companies) are likely to purchase more of their inputs locally than companies with a low level of defence turnover (civil companies) ... Secondly, the study further supports the conclusion of localisation in the sample as firms with predominantly local competitors are more likely to purchase a higher proportion of their inputs locally' (p. 325). He also concludes, in keeping with Crump's (1993) study in the United States, that 'defence expenditure has formed a de facto regional policy through the generalisation of localised linkages' (p. 325).

The literature examined earlier maps the extent of the networks in supply. However, apart from the arrows in the figures of Kelley and Watkins (1998) – which suggest considerable reciprocity between prime contractors and subcontractors – there is little information in these studies about the way in which these networks are governed. Fortunately, there is one study, undertaken by Dussauge and Garrette (1993), that provides data on this issue.

Dussauge and Garrette (1993) define a strategic alliance as a 'collaborative agreement between two or more firms competing in the same industry, which contribute assets and resources to a common endeavour, while maintaining their individuality and independence' (p. 45) and report on their study of such alliances in aerospace and defence between 1950 and 1990 where 70 per cent of the 70 alliances studied involved defence or 'dual use' production. Rather than focus on specific aspects of the individual alliances, they attempt to study variables and develop a typology which 'describe[s] the way in which tasks are carried out within the alliance and the governance structure established to organize the relations between the partner firms' (p. 47, parentheses added). From analysis of fourteen potential variables, the authors characterise the alliances into three distinct types: semi-structured projects; business-based joint ventures and unstructured co-production projects. In the first category, only specific tasks (typically marketing) are carried out jointly; all other tasks are distributed amongst the partner firms (arguably an individualist network form). Business-based joint ventures are ones where a separate joint venture is established to control an aspect of the partners' business, usually without time-limit (suggestive of the hierarchical network form). In the last category, no task is carried out jointly and no distinct legal entity is created (perhaps an example of an isolate network form). They note that projects can move from the last category to the first (that is, from isolate form to individualist), but that other transformations do not seem to occur.

Dussuage and Garrette (1993) also find evidence for the transaction cost theory of partnerships becoming more integrated, arguing that there is a correlation between the increasing number of partners and the likelihood of a separate joint venture being created attributable to the wish of partners to avoid transaction costs. They note that: 'the role and scope of the joint ventures set up at different periods tends to increase over time [which] may indicate that co-operation is evolving towards forms closer to traditional industry concentration' (p. 61). They suggest a preliminary hypothesis that links the commercial success of the alliance with its form that is, most mature unstructured projects can be viewed as commercially less successful than semi-structured projects and speculate that 'the main discriminating factor between these two classes being precisely the existence of a specific marketing and sales organization in one and not in the other, it is tempting to attribute this success to that very structure' (p. 61). They reveal that there is an apparent trend over the period studied away from the unstructured alliance and towards the more structured alliance. Overall, this study suggests that: 'the main discriminating factors ... are the organization of tasks within the alliances and the legal form given to the partnerships' (p. 59).

Stimulated by a small number of case studies from Europe, Creasey (1988) is also interested in the factors that influence changes within networks. She puts forward a model for a co-operation agreement (Figure 8.4) and the 'change forces' that might lead to its reconfiguration. She suggests that 'successful cooperation agreements serve their purpose well without disrupting the strategic well-being of the partner firms ... the key to forging mutually satisfactory cooperation agreements is a realistic assessment of the strengths (and weaknesses) of the firms in the proposed venture' (p. 94). Anticipating the findings of Dussuage and Garrette (1993), however, she also argues that 'cooperation agreements may be transitory organisations that firms embrace to obtain an advantage more quickly, but the most stable ones are those where the agreement is a joint venture and has its own economic resources' (p. 94). Although firmly rooted in the tradition of organisational economics, the model devised by Creasey (1988) has the virtue of emphasising that alliances are dynamic rather than static, and are constantly responding to a range of economic, political and organisational factors, albeit that there is also the suggestion that the more hierarchical forms are likely to be the most stable (and thus most successful in economic terms). There are echoes here of the trend in networks in health and social care and crime, disorder and drugs, where innovative individualist or enclave networks are viewed as effective by government and thus become the focus of policy initiatives that move them towards more hierarchical forms.

There also seems to be support for the ideas derived from organisation competency and learning theories in these studies, where some prime contractors seek through networks to enhance their core competencies, be these exploratory (in search of new knowledge) or exploitative (capitalising on current knowledge), although in both the knowledge in question is predominantly explicit rather than tacit. However, there are also suggestions in the literature that Weberian perspectives hold some explanatory power in analysing joint ventures, focusing as they do on the importance of clarity of hierarchy and accountability. As suggested in the introduction to the theory of networks in Chapter 2, thorough exploration of networks may encompass a number of theoretical schools in order to reflect their variety, although this review indicates that three or four may have more explanatory power than the others. This is a point to which we will return in the conclusion.

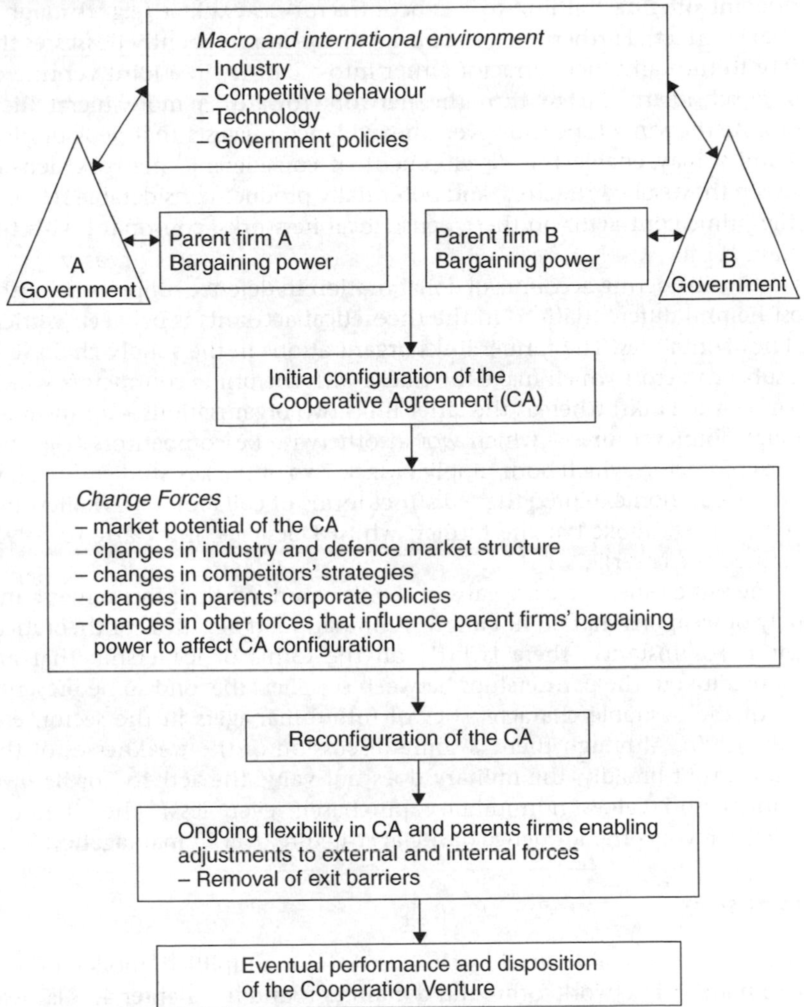

Figure 8.4 A model for a co-operative venture in the defence industry.
Source: Reproduced from Creasey and May, 1988 (p. 95).

On the supply side, the dominant influence on partnership seems to be the consolidated defence-specific prime contractors and the nature of their relationships with often geographically proximate subcontractors with which they work for significant periods of time. To some extent these networks are co-ordinated through the nodal position of the predominant member – and could thus be characterised as individualist – even though this co-ordination may at times be as much implicit (e.g. through the prime contractor offering training to a subcontractor) as explicit (e.g. through a formal contract). Furthermore, the prime contractor frequently possesses the ability to turn any subcontractor either into a partner in a joint venture or into a subsidiary (i.e. to turn the network towards a more hierarchical form). At the same time, however, the evidence suggests that geographical proximity may enable the development of considerable network density between these subcontractors, and potentially produce considerable reliance of the prime contractor on these dense local networks, consonant with the enclave form.

When considering accounts of collaboration in defence supply, one of the most helpful differentiations in the theoretical accounts is between vertical and horizontal ties. The former links organisations in the supply chain (e.g. the subcontractors which make the tracks with the prime contractors which assemble the tanks) whereas the latter links two organisations – for instance through joint ventures – which would otherwise be competitors (e.g. two prime contractors which both supply tanks). Two of the key studies discussed in the last section explored these distinct forms of collaboration (Kelley and Watkins, 1998, looked at the former, whilst Dussuage and Garrette, 1993, examined the latter).

At the same time, there are gaps in the literature on the procurement and supply of weapons that do not allow illumination of key areas of theoretical interest. For instance, there is little on the forms of leadership that are demonstrated in the partnerships between suppliers (beyond some prescriptions of the desirable characteristics of future managers in the sector, e.g. Draper 1990). Although there is some discussion of the weaknesses of the procurers (put broadly, the military does not value the activity for its own personnel and values non-military purchasers even less), the literature implicitly favours the influence of social structure over human agency.

Conclusion

Linking the discussion in this chapter to the simplified model of the determinants of network forms and dynamics found in Chapter 4, it is clear from the defence literature that the prevailing institutional factors ('the weight of the past') feature significantly in the networks of both procurers and suppliers, and in particular this is where the actions of the former – for example, through regulation – has the most impact on the latter. There is evidence for three of the factors identified in that model being influential on supplier networks as 'forces of the present' – that is, the current trends in the organisational field (e.g. the trend towards prime contractor consolidation), the balance of transaction costs (e.g. the advantages of joint ventures) and the information, learning and knowledge requirements (e.g. the extent of the networks across R&D, subcontractors and competitors). Furthermore, the 'shadow of the future' (e.g. cuts in defence spending) is revealed as a major driver in the present (e.g. prime contractor consolidation). The procurer networks are more influenced by the task environment in interaction with the 'weight of the past', for example, where specific aspects of the technical and output problems suggested collaboration to some countries and not to others (for instance, on the EFA). Finally, the basic form of organisational relations differs between the networks of procurers (enclave–isolate) and suppliers (individualist–enclave–hierarchical) and thus the nature of feedback that each system prompts and hears.

If the overall story – of the prevalence of three or four theoretical schools (that is, economic, neo-institutionalist, organisation competency and learning theories) in the defence literature – is accurate, it has consequences for expectations of the impact of either external governance or internal management of networks. With the exception of the regulatory authority that is available in rational choice/transaction cost accounts, there is limited apparent leverage in defence procurement and supply to be exercised by external governance of networks. Rather, the balance of power lies in the internal management of these networks themselves, significantly mediated by the predominant forms that these networks adopt and the impact of any influences towards their transformation.

9
Networks in Commercial Biotechnology

The biotechnology industries

Biotechnology is one industry in which there have been a number of instructive quantitative studies on the nature, structure and function of several different kinds of interorganisational ties. Strictly speaking, biotechnology is not a single industry. Rather it is a set of techniques which are applied to the transformation of a number of industries, such as agronomy, pharmaceuticals, chemicals, veterinary science and even waste disposal (Powell and Brantley, 1992; Powell *et al.*, 1996). The core technologies are those of sequencing and synthesising DNA and cell fusion. The cost of many of the basic pieces of apparatus required has fallen significantly in the quarter of a century since these technologies were first developed. In the 1970s and 1980s, when biotechnology first began to be commercialised on a large scale, it represented a major discontinuity in the technological paradigms upon which pharmaceuticals, agronomy and several other industries were working. The emergence of dedicated biotechnology firms (DBFs) in those years therefore threatened the position of the incumbents in the industries where products could be developed with commercial application. Those incumbents responded in various ways to limit that threat and, in some cases, they were relatively successful, although the resulting mature industry structure neither, as many predicted in the 1980s, eliminated the DBF sector nor transformed that sector in an industry with traditional interorganisational relationships (Kenney, 1986).

The industry is closely tied to a range of wider scientific and technological development communities. Professional scientists are crucially important to the way in which the biotechnology industry is organised; the management of relations between the organisations and these individuals (who possess mission-critical competencies, who compete with each other but who also possess important collective power) is central to the understanding of how the field has developed. Moreover, commercial biotechnology is relatively capital-intensive, because state-of-the-art technologies, apparatus and informatics systems are needed. This factor is important in shaping imperatives to seek alliances (Gersony, 1996). The nature of the discovery and regulatory product approval processes mean that biotech firms needs to plan many years ahead and must expect to wait long periods before they can return a profit on their initial investment. Biotechnology firms require real estate and, as we shall see, they need to ensure that they locate their research and development functions in particular places (which may be expensive per square metre).

DBFs are of particular interest for several reasons. First, the field appeared during the late 1980s and 1990s to exhibit a pattern of highly networked collaborative relations which was read in two contrasting ways in those decades, according to the main prevailing views taken in the scholarly and practitioner literature. Either these arrangements were seen as peculiar and exceptional in the commercial world, interesting but expected to be transient and eliminated as the industry matured or else they were seen as a harbinger of future trends in many other industries. The first view was based on the argument, that in the early stages of an industry life-cycle such as biotechnology, there is great market uncertainty because the intellectual property rights régime has not fully adapted to the kinds of knowledge for which patent applications are being made, making it difficult for firms to be secure in their capacity to collect profits on their inventions. In response, they will seek collaborative links with others both to create infrastructure and to access the influence of established firms which already have influence with patent authorities. However, as the technology matures, financial pressures lead to mergers and acquisitions and the property rights régime adapts, the nature of any remaining collaborative ties will become more classically oligopolistic, while others will become conventionally competitive or else based on vertical supply chain purchasing (Gemser *et al.*, 1996). The opposite view is based on the idea that a more fundamental change is under way in the nature of inter-organisational relationships, especially and initially in high technology sectors, reflecting changing market conditions to greater competition in response to which collaboration in order to assemble new competitive structures is almost functionally necessary (Powell, 2001) and changing public sector conditions towards greater outcome-orientation mandating collaboration (Alter and Hage, 1993). As a science-intensive 'sunrise' industry, and growing at a time when geographical clustering was being becoming important in a wide range of industries, the DBF sector was of interest because it might indicate alternative models of economic organisation to that of outright competition.

A scholarly literature has grown up specifically on biotechnology networks in the United States and a smaller body of work has done on other countries. Much of the work is published in sociological, rather than management or business, journals and uses a large scale database with excellent coverage of the US industry – which is maintained by the industry directory, BioScan – to explore hypotheses developed in sociological theory of networks using a variety of statistical tests. In particular, important work has been carried out by US teams led by Walter Powell, Bruce Kogut and Lynn Zucker, and, in Europe, by teams led by Luigi Orsenigo. Broadly, the studies on networking in the biotechnology industry can be divided into those which examine the ties between biotechnology companies and university-based scientists and those which examine either ties between DBFs and other DBFs or between DBFs and other kinds of firms such as venture capital firms, pharmaceutical companies and so on.

None of the studies reviewed here was originally designed to test the neo-Durkheimian theory presented in this book. Therefore, appropriate caution should be given to our interpretation of their findings. However, we showed in Part I that the neo-Durkheimian concepts of solidarities and dynamics can be translated readily into the kinds of concepts and measures used by network sociometric researchers. These translations can serve as operationalisation of the neo-Durkheimian framework onto the sociometric literature, enabling it to be used to explore the theory. Here are some examples. The presence of enduring patterns in which large organisations maintain high centrality in moderately dense networks can be used as a reasonable proxy for hierarchy. Fluid patterns of frequent creation and termination of short-term ties of limited multiplexity are good indicators of individualism. Dense, strongly cliqued formations exhibiting homophily on a reasonably wide variety of characteristics indicate enclave forms. Absolute paucity of ties or limited numbers of ties to heterophilous others, with little centrality, would indicate an isolate situation.

Types of ties in biotechnology

Much of the research examines vertical ties by which a focal organisation secures vital inputs – such as access to tacit knowledge or explicit knowledge in the form of rights to use intellectual property held by others, finance, endorsements or less formal associations that add to reputation – or ties by which the organisation reaches potential customers, which are generally other businesses in the pharmaceutical, agronomic, venture capital, specialist marketing and other industries. In general, horizontal ties seem to be strongly associated with patenting, unlike vertical ones (George *et al.*, 2001).

However, some collaborative ties created to access inputs along the supply chain are with other firms that may, at other times or on other projects, be competitors; that is, a multiplex tie can be both vertical and horizontal. Consortia are typically not ones in which each player brings the same skills and simply add capacity but are more often built to bring together distinct but complementary skills in which there is a division of labour.

Many of the studies present classifications of ties by function or purpose. For example, Audretsch and Stephan (1996) distinguish between the following three roles that university scientists may play in their ties with DBFs:

- They may facilitate knowledge transfer. In this case, they are likely to be active partners with executive roles in the DBF and, in many cases in the early years of the industry, university scientists were funders of DBFs, creating them specifically to commercialise inventions that they had made and perhaps patented while in their university employment.
- They may signal the quality of the research undertaken in the DBF to the capital markets and to others. In this capacity, they may not in every case need to take very active executive roles, although that is of course one way to achieve this.
- They may be involved in charting the direction of the research and the company strategy. This is a role that again could be played either from the very core of the organisation or as in non-executive capacity.

Powell and Brantley (1992) present the following first classification of the types of formal and explicit ties between DBFs and other DBFs or other organisations including venture capital firms, banks, large pharmaceutical companies, public sector research organisations and so on (Barley *et al.*, 1992):

- receiving research grants;
- in-licensing technologies (including patented molecules or proteins) under formal agreements for access rights to the intellectual property;
- marketing agreements; and
- joint development agreements.

This has been refined in various ways in other studies. For example, research grants hardly exhaust the range of financial relationships. Arora and Gambardella (1990) examine degrees of capital control, distinguishing between:

- minority shareholding participation in ownership; and
- acquisition by other firms.

At a more finely grained level, inter-organisational relations can be distinguished which are involved specifically in supporting research and development, including (Powell *et al.*, 1996):

- agreements for basic research;
- agreements for product development; and
- agreements for development of applications from products which are ready for commercialisation.

More recent work has emphasised ties for financing of R&D, perhaps because the important drivers of industry development have shifted in this direction (Powell *et al.*, 2005). For example, Lerner *et al.* (2003) show that when stock markets are tight, small biotech firms turned heavily to large corporations for R&D finance.

There is no particular reason to expect either vertical or horizontal ties – or ties used to access any of these types of resource – typically to take any one of the neo-Durkheimian types; supply chains may be vertical but need not be hierarchical and consortia may be individualistic in being created and terminated opportunistically and without loyalty.

Many inter-organisational ties are carried by individuals, even if the individual level cannot provide a sufficient explanation of the form taken by such links. The types of links which support different functions for ties in biotechnology can be distinguished as follows:

- board-level links, include interlocks (overlapping board memberships for influential individuals), but also including less formal links;
- professional-level links, including informal ties between scientists in the same sub-discipline, and more formally sanctioned links in the course of collaboration in research and development; and
- other staff-level links, including between marketing staff, account managers, project managers for joint projects and strategic alliances.

There are also full joint ventures in biotechnology; that is, wholly owned subsidiaries as separate organisations.

Although most of the studies of inter-organisational networks within the biotechnology industry do not examine this in any great detail, it may be significant that these collaborative arrangements have flourished in a period in which the US competition policy régime has shifted significantly away from the '*per se* rule' – which held all collaborative arrangements between companies that might be thought ideally to be competitors to be *per se* suspect – to one more tolerant of collaboration, especially in pre-competitive and research and development activities. Indeed, one of the few studies of the effect of strategic biotechnology alliances among incumbents upon rates of new founding or market entrants suggests that at least some kinds of network relations between Canadian biotechnology firms did indeed depress market entry and therefore one measure of competition (Calabrese *et al.*, 2000).

Informal and formal ties appear to be symbiotic in the biotechnology field, much as one would expect. Informal links are, more or less by definition, more weakly socially regulated, and therefore indicate the presence either of individualistic or enclaved elements in the mix. Initial links between individual scientists and firms seem to be informal but are made formal if they are found to be valuable; for example, through involvement in founding, association in research and development or in governance roles

(Audretsch and Stephan, 1996; Zucker *et al.*, 1996, 1998). Liebeskind *et al.* (1996), for example, find that informal links are critical to the ways in which new biotechnology firms access scientific knowledge, and that successful biotechnology firms are organised precisely to facilitate the kind of informal tie-building and maintenance around the university-based and commercially based scientific communities.

Geographical clustering of ties

Biotechnology is, like many other industries or quasi-industries, a field of organisations which is very markedly clustered by geography. In the United States, most firms are located in the San Francisco bay area, the San Diego area and the Boston Back bay area. Similarly, the Cambridge area, and nearby towns such as Huntingdon, provide homes for a significant cluster of the British biotechnology industry; other clusters may be emerging around major university centres in Israel (Kaufman *et al.*, 2003).

In some respects, the commercial industry thus replicates the structure of the university-based life sciences, which are both increasingly densely networked and clustered within regions (Katz, 1994; Hicks and Katz, 1996). In biotechnology, both physical facilities and institutional support for academics to form or join start-ups and locate them geographically close to their universities have been important to the development of the industry (Prevezer, 2001).

Much of the wider literature in economic geography, economic sociology and urban sociology has been preoccupied with the nature of industrial districts and the dynamics by which clustering of industries takes place (Piore and Sabel, 1984; Castells, 1989; Sassen, 1991, 1997) and with the structure of networks in industrial districts (Lorenz, 1988; Streeck, 1992). A central finding in some of the wider literature on biotechnology has been that its take-off has in large part been facilitated by the role of some key universities in encouraging their leading scientists to patent whatever they created that would be patentable and to create spin-off companies (or otherwise engage in 'knowledge transfer'). Because of these interests, a number of the studies on biotechnology have been concerned with the question of just how local are the links between companies and individuals and between companies themselves.

Research on the city-region of San Diego suggests that keys to the take-off of the biotechnology industry in the region were large universities committed to knowledge transfer, a local culture of entrepreneurial businesses, social ties between key individuals and a built-up stock of intellectual capital in the area (Walsh *et al.*, 1995; Walshok *et al.*, 2002).

In their preliminary study, Zucker *et al.* (1996) concluded that most links between individual scientific collaborators were relatively local, both between firms and universities and between scientists employed in DBFs. This pattern appears to be common internationally: McKelvey *et al.* (2003)

report, analysing data on the Swedish sector, that geographical co-location of partners is more salient in firm–university ties than in firm–firm. Zucker and Darby (1997) showed that using networks into academic science to buy in new biotechnological skills proved crucial to some large incumbent traditional pharmaceutical firms. However, Audretsch and Stephan's (1996) study – using a richer data set – identified a more complex picture, with significant differences between the regional clusters of the industry in the United States and between companies. They found that the different roles played by scientists explained a significant part of the variance. Knowledge transfer, for example, appears to be associated with more local links. They explain this on the grounds that many knowledge transfer links originate in the founding of companies by 'star' scientists, perhaps even initially on university science parks and that, even when this is not the case, a great of deal of the knowledge transferred is tacit in character (being about craft techniques of research and research management) and so its transfer calls for intensive face-to-face contact. By contrast, where scientists serve the function of providing endorsements of the quality of the research being conducted, or where they are helping to chart the company direction, it is less necessary that their involvement in face-to-face communication be protracted and, therefore, many more such ties extend much more widely across the country. Nevertheless, they found, even controlling for this, that there appear to be differences in the practices of developing ties between the DBFs in different regions; broadly, the Californian biotechnology sector appears to be more willing to bear the costs of sustaining long-distance ties with scientists from around the United States in a way that the Massachusetts companies seem not to be. It is not possible to know from this fact alone whether this marks a difference in the network form of scientist–DBF relations, but it would be of interest for future research to examine whether this might be associated with greater individualism in the Californian pattern and more enclaved styles in Massachusetts biotechnology firms during this period.

It is worth noting that the tightness of the linkage between the scientific and the technological networks is a matter of some dispute. Powell *et al.* (1996) imply that the two networks are quite tightly coupled, and rely on inter-organisational links to establish this. However, studies using bibliometric analysis of citations suggest that the two networks are importantly distinct (e.g. Murray, 2002).

Owen-Smith *et al.* (2002) were able to compare the inter-organisational networks of life sciences across the university, governmental, non-profit and commercial sectors generally, within which DBFs play a relatively small but probably typical part. They find that in the United States there are overlapping interregional networks, while the European networks are marked by regional specialisation and limited inter-regional ties (where there are fewer links with the commercial sector and where large cross-national alliances are dominated by the large pharmaceutical companies). In this respect, then, the European pattern appears to be closer to the hub-and-satellite forms of network arrangement dominated by a 'flagship firm' analysed by Rugman and D'Cruz (2000a,b); here the flagship provides strategic direction for both its upstream suppliers and its downstream customer firms and significantly influences a cluster of smaller sometime-collaborator-sometime-competitor firms through strategic alliances. This can readily be understood as a form with tendencies towards hierarchical ordering of networks.

Network forms

Powell and Brantley (1992) examined the types of ties and linkages used and showed that many of the ties between DBFs took the form of long-term relational contracts. This indicated that they would presumably be seen by managers in these companies as strategic rather than opportunistic, and also of great value. This suggests that these will be more strongly than weakly socially integrated.

In a later study, Powell *et al.* (1996) examined research and development alliances, rather than, as their earlier paper had, looking at ties with venture capital or public research grant makers. Four hypotheses were found to be supported by their data:

- First, the greater the number of ties at an earlier time, the more diverse was the portfolio of subsequent ties. All other things being equal, such diversity suggests (but does not of course establish) weaker social integration.
- Second, they showed that the greater the number, the diversity and the length of experience with research and development collaboration ties, the greater centrality in the network of biotechnology firms was the position of a given firm. The presence of some firms with high centrality of this type suggests some degree, however modest in the earlier period they examined, of hierarchy within the mix.
- Third, the greater the firm's network centrality and its experience in managing ties, the more rapid was its growth.
- Finally, network centrality in an earlier period predicted the number of research and development alliances in later periods, so competing the feedback loop.

These hypotheses were supported, even controlling for the age of the firms; importantly, size was an outcome – not a predictor – of network position.

That there are hierarchical network patterns that fall short of actual vertical integration, but in which major pharmaceutical firms play the role of 'flagships' (Rugman and D'Cruz, 2000a,b) is confirmed by Traill and Duffield's (2002) review of the strategies of several major European agro-food life sciences companies (although they note that even the combination of flagship type networks and actual consolidation neither outweighs the rate of new entrants nor other types of network forms). Downstream ties between DBFs and the large corporate sector have produced, as we should expect, marked clustering in the character of the networks within the DBF sector around the major strategic alliance groups in pharmaceuticals and agro-chemical products. This has been studied by, among others, Delapierre and Mytelka (1998) who identify six major clusters of pharmaceutical and biotechnology firms.

As they are more closely regulated by ownership and are long-term, integrated entities, we should expect joint ventures to be more hierarchical in character. Hierarchical organisation seeks to contain risk and, as socially integrated, to focus on shared values. This is confirmed for biotechnology joint ventures by Richards and DeCarolis' (2003) study which found that cultural compatibility and low country risk were more important predictors of any pair being able to form a joint venture than were prior experience or similarity of business.

Reputation effects can, in different contexts, work to support any network form save perhaps the isolate. Nevertheless, where information with which to make up a reputation is scarce and costly, and where the authority of individual brokers is relied upon to grant an imprimatur on a reputation, this would be a prima facie indicator of an individualistic strand of organisation. In biotechnology, Stuart *et al.* (1999) show that the use of ties to secure reputation by associating oneself with more prestigious others is common in links with organisations. By contrast, where a rule-governed institution is used as a source of authority with which to underpin regulation, this would be prima facie evidence for a hierarchical element in the system because formal institutions tend to make their judgments on the calibre of organisations on the basis of their capacity for behaviour that would be assessed in rule-bound ways and subject to strong classification. Shan *et al.* (1994) argue that public funding for DBFs serves as a reputation variable for large pharmaceutical companies. However, hierarchical networks may simply be worked around in enclaved or individualistic fashion by those who find them less useful, or bypassed where the hierarchical institutions adopt too narrow a classificatory focus for their largesse. For example, in their study of EU sponsored research networks in biotechnology by comparison with material sciences, Peters *et al.* (1998) found that the EU focus on agronomic research not only missed much of the European biotechnology industry but produced network patterns that differed more sharply from market-based network patterns than in their comparator field.

The literature also suggests that many biotechnology companies are, at different points in their life cycle, located in networks of different types. Oliver (2001) found evidence that the use in organisation learning to which alliances are put varies with the stage in the organisational life cycle; early alliances serve learning by exploration – or the search for new ideas – while later on alliances are undertaken to support learning by exploitation, that is making better use of ideas already acquired (following March's 1991 distinction between exploration, the search for and first uses of ideas which are new to the organisation, and exploitation, or the steadily deeper use and incremental development of ideas already understood by the organisation). Rothaermel (2001) finds that incumbents tend to develop ties of strategic alliance for exploitation through leveraging complementary assets and skills more often than for exploration, such as building new technological competences. Moreover, particular ties change their micro-institutional character over time in response to changing experience, conditions and so on. Reuer and Zollo (2000) found that more broadly scoped alliances in the biotechnology field tended to change their governance structure more often than narrowly defined ones and that expansion of alliance roles required new monitoring mechanisms. This suggests increasing hierarchy in at least some cases, but since others were terminated or became looser it is clear that conditions and experiences can militate in a number of directions.

Network change over time

The behaviour of organisations in creating, maintaining and ending ties should result in changes to the form of the structure of the networks that characterise the field as a whole.

Studies by Kogut *et al.* (1992) and Walker *et al.* (1997) stressed the importance of path dependency and of first-mover advantages. The greater the number of new ties, it was found, the greater the number of those links which are with firms similarly situated in the network structure of the industry; this might suggest a measure of enclaving developing. Having developed these networks, firms are then constrained in later periods in the ways in which they can form new agreements. However, first movers are often more sought after than seeking.

These findings were confirmed by a similarly large scale quantitative study by Orsenigo *et al.* (1997): with industry growth, network size increased but the basic structure remained the same, especially in respect of the core–periphery profile. Orsenigo *et al.* also find that new entrants seek to collaborate more with established ones, which stands in some tension with Kogut's team suggestion that there is extensive collaboration between similar firms.

If the general tendency is for all organisations to form more and more ties with others in the field, this should increase the density of the network structure and eventually – if ties within the industry are denser than ties to firms in other industries (venture capital firms, marketing agencies, etc) – this might lead to greater social integration. The finding from Kogut and his team's early work was that any such tendency to ever greater density is constrained by the ways in which initial decisions are made to form ties; many possible ties rule out others.

The findings that firms tend to form ties with others similarly situated, and that early decisions to form ties constrain later ones, suggest that network change might be limited and that the expected form of the industry-wide network will be a series of enclaves. By contrast, it might be the case that entrepreneurial companies might be prepared, as competitive pressures increase over time, to abandon these enclave structures and focus instead on building ties between enclaves in order to secure greater betweenness centrality for themselves (the findings of the team led by Powell are only that centrality in general matters but not necessarily only that centrality which is derived from betweenness situated astride cliques, so the two sets of findings are compatible). In their later work, Kogut's team (Shan *et al.*, 1994) argue that, in fact, the tendency toward enclavisation and conservatism in network structure is a more powerful force that any tendency towards individualistic networking. Describing the enclavisation strategy as a 'social capital' hypothesis and the individualistic strategy as a 'structural hole spanning' one (following Burt, 1992), the results of the estimation of the model were unambiguously that path dependency effects are powerful.

However, the picture of conservatism should not be overstated, for path dependency reflects a positive feedback dynamic which itself brings about change, and – if pursued sufficiently far, the neo-Durkheimian theory predicts – a change that can undermine the cohesion of the network form which gives rise to that dynamic. Even if change over time does not show up in the form of change in the general form of the network structure at the industry level, there are significant changes in the lifetime of particular strategic alliances. Reuer *et al.* (2002) studied the changes in the forms of governance used to oversee strategic alliances such as contracts, oversight committees and monitoring mechanisms. In their study of both alliances between DBFs and between DBFs and pharmaceutical companies, 40 per cent exhibited changes in these governance systems after the formation of the alliance. Changes were least likely when the division of labour was already very clear or where the alliance had a very narrow scope. Previous experience of collaboration also seems to facilitate post-formation changes in governance.

Industry life-cycle would be expected, on some theories at least, to be associated with network change. Based on two case studies, Weisenfeld *et al.* (2001), for example, argue that a structure like the EU sponsored Biotechnology Industry Platform – a non-profit subscription based organisation with research and development clusters (a club structure with partially enclaved structure of member ownership and partially hierarchical ordering from EU support and regulation) – is more appropriate to the phase of industry development in which the focus shifts from original research and development to collaborative efforts to bring products to market, whereas, in earlier phases, less institutionalised and smaller, more intensively collaborating structures are more appropriate.

In many ways, though, the trend toward enclavisation has probably not been the dominant one among DBFs, although certainly the trend toward greater density in cliques and clusters has been marked; both enclave and hierarchical forms exhibit these features but they differ in the degree of authority and regulation featured. For the biotechnology industry has begun to move towards networks organised around 'flagship firms' (Rugman and D'Cruz, 2000a,b) which have significant control over the DBFs who work with them. Over the same period, some industry-wide institutions have begun to emerge that cultivate accountabilities beyond the single firm towards common ethical and management standards. In sum, then, although certainly there remains a sub-sector of DBFs which continue to operate individualistically, the general trend has been towards greater hierarchy and some enclavisation.

In their most recent and extensive modelling work, Powell *et al.* (2005) have examined in more detail the process of change in the US DBF sector from 1988 to 1999 using the BioScan database. They attempt to measure the evidence for four dynamic processes over the decade in the network patterns. These are: cumulative advantage (or, in neo-Durkheimian terms, an increasingly polarising individualistic pattern of positive feedback); homophily (ties to those with a significant number of similar characteristics, indicating enclaving); imitation of prevailing trends in networking among others (which could reinforce any neo-Durkheimian type); and multiconnectivity (development of multiple links to each partner, both direct and indirect, which could support either individualistic or enclaved forms since limited number of routes to a single node are more characteristic of the strongly regulated network forms). In general, they find limited evidence for cumulative advantage dynamics and for homophily. They identify more support for diversity-seeking and for imitation of others, initially rather than later. These are also data to indicate developing multiconnectivity, at least up to a point of perceived diminishing returns (cf. Deeds and Hill, 1996; Powell *et al.*, 1999; Owen-Smith and Powell, 2003). Overall, they confirm earlier findings that incumbents do seek out new entrants, in many cases for their innovative intellectual property.

Powell and his colleagues argue that these results should be interpreted as showing the effects of the shift from an earlier period dominated by the imperative for commercialisation of discoveries and inventions made in academic contexts to a later one when financing and commercial investment in research and development reshaped the industry. This transition reduced the dominance of some of the initially important large international pharmaceutical companies which sought 'flagship' centrality in networks which they could locally dominate. It also reflected the attraction of new entrants which developed new cohesive clusterings around new flagships. The field is marked, they find, by diversity of ties and multiconnectivity.

In neo-Durkheimian terms, a number of cohesive hierarchical clusters appear to be surrounded by more fluid and individualistically networked structures. The whole field exhibits, at a higher level of analysis, a reasonably strong sense of common membership – and hence of boundaries – because of the continuing importance of collegiality and mutual dependence in the scientific endeavour, despite the need for proprietary knowledge, which imparts a density that would give the industry as a whole in the United States a more enclaved character than that of many other industries (even though particular zones within the industry network are varied in their local network form). Finally, a number of peripheral firms can be discerned in isolate positions (contrast the finding from McKelvey *et al.* (2003) that the Swedish sector exhibits such a sparse pattern of ties that there are more relative isolates). In short, over time, a rough and ready institutional variety of forms appear to be exhibited. Although positive feedback dynamics may develop in any of the forms, these are often offset either by their own effects – for example, growing numbers of ties, even if undertaken instrumentally and individualistically, can lead to increased density which can bring about greater social integration – or by negative feedback from others, as when major global corporations seek to establish a measure of leverage over an otherwise threatening cluster of innovative companies.

In short, on the evidence of Powell's own research, his (1990) thesis that market and hierarchical relations are being generally superseded by network forms that are distinct from both of these can now be rejected. On the contrary, his own recent work can be read as showing exactly the variety and multi-directional dynamism and interplay of positive and negative feedback that the neo-Durkheimian theory predicts.

Conclusion

The neo-Durkheimian theory proposes that network forms are the effects of underlying institutional forces best measured on the dimensions of social regulation and integration. In the biotechnology industry, the role of institutional shaping is clear. The combination of collegial practices of scientific publishing and an individualistic 'star' system profoundly shaped the ways in which DBFs were formed, accessed expertise and secured reputations. On the other hand, the institutional character of the large pharmaceutical, agronomic and other client industry conglomerates has profoundly shaped the network structure by providing central foci for 'flagship' style clustering, especially reinforced by being able to offer financing during periods when venture capital firms would not or could not. The public sector has contributed both to the enclave and to hierarchical elements in the pattern of ties through research funding and support for non-profit clubs and industry fora. This institutional shaping has worked through the moulding of information conditions in respect of accessing both hard information about scientific innovation and soft information about reputations through influencing the transaction costs of alternative network pattern choices, especially in respect of technology in-licensing and the relative costs of access to different sources of R&D funding. There are very few studies of inter-organisational networks in biotechnology that enable us to examine the institutional endogeneity of preferences, but to the extent that some kinds of behaviour reported in the literature are sufficiently unambiguous in character that they admit of only a limited number of possible preferences in explanation, it may be possible to risk some inferences. For example, the industry's reliance on the social structure of reputation management from the non-profit university sector seems likely to be best explained by the institutional shaping of preferences for particular ways of accrediting potential suppliers of expertise.

This is an industry with very long lead times between initial investment in R&D and result, with high uncertainty about the profitability of particular investment choices, subject to risks of regulatory difficulties and – in the later years of the period examined – a shift from high public expectations to problems of public distrust. It is an industry, moreover, where some investors are looking for rapid commercialisation and profits from sales while many entrepreneurs are more concerned to develop R&D capacity. In these circumstances, it is likely to be one that exhibits performance ambiguity and at least moderate goal incongruence, in Ouchi's (1980) terms. It is therefore hardly surprising that some of the network forms that result lie toward the right hand side of Table 4.4. However, the neo-Durkheimian theory leads us to expect that any field will exhibit, in some measure, each of the four forms, rather than an unending domination of any of them. The recent research by Powell *et al.* clearly shows that this is indeed the case.

The combination of multiple institutional pressures explains this. For the combination of co-operation and competition between the imperatives for and against keeping scientific information and other information about firm competencies proprietary and between public funders and university-based science professions on the one hand, and commercial and financial interests on the other, produces an unstable disequilbrium system. The resulting network pattern is indeed highly path dependent, as the work by Kogut and by Powell has shown, but positive feedback does not and cannot simply produce more of the same because it can undermine its own forms – illustrated by the fact that the tendency of incumbents to hoover up new entrants proved unsustainable – or it can provoke negative feedback elsewhere in the system, as when regulatory bodies and public funders have used their powers to try to influence the industry.

The strengths and weaknesses of the network patterns of the industry are distributed as one would expect. Rothaermel's (2001) finding that the flagship dominated clusters are focused by the major corporate bodies on exploitation, but are dependent on the prior creative exploration work of the more entrepreneurial DBFs or the more heavily socially integrated university-based teams is a case in point. The flagship structure has provided

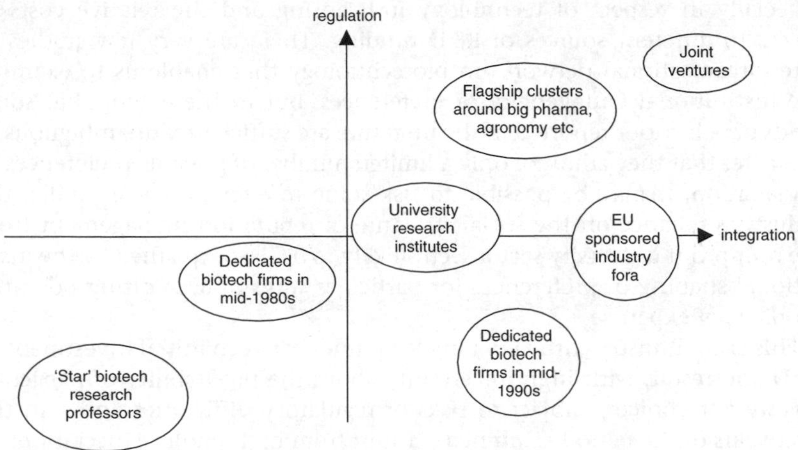

Figure 9.1 Network forms in commercial biotechnology.

security for at least some in the more difficult years, but at the price of restricted scope for innovation.

Figure 9.1 summarises some of the basic variety that is suggested in the literature reviewed, with examples of broad types of development in three of the four quadrants. The absence of an entry in the isolate quadrant should be read with care. Clearly, there are relative isolates at any one time. However, if the whole body of work on the benefits of collaborative ties in this industry is accepted (Arora and Gambardella, 1990; Powell and Brantley, 1992; Audretsch and Stephan, 1996; Powell *et al.*, 1996, 1999; Oliver, 2001), then those isolates will do relatively badly and will seek patterns of ties more like at least one of the other quadrants, or some hybrid, or else will be anticipated to exit from the industry.

10
Combating Crime, Disorder and Drugs

Introduction

This chapter considers the development of networks designed to combat crime, disorder and drug misuse within the United Kingdom since the 1980s. These networks are largely designated *partnerships* within the literature. The period covered by this review reveals three distinct approaches to partnership development in this sector which are themselves informed by broader public policy trends in governance: early network initiatives typified by non-financial voluntary partnerships between enclaves; the overlay of formalised, contract-based relationships between purchasers and providers within internal markets; and, finally, the development of hierarchical hybrids in the form of statutory partnerships in which networks between agencies were mandated rather than encouraged and a suite of joint partnership structures (network forms) for monitoring, predicting, analysing and preventing crime and disorder were developed. The balance of material considered in this review concerns the formation of hierarchical hybrids, whose reported strengths and weaknesses are considered in the light of the neo-Durkheimian framework.

While the review presented here is limited geographically to the United Kingdom and historically to studies conducted between 1980 and 2004, multi-agency partnerships in this sector have been extensively described and (to a lesser extent) empirically explored during this period – the search terms 'network', 'partnership' and 'collaboration' revealing a wealth of material including commentary as well as descriptive and analytical papers. It is important to note that while none of the material discussed below directly employed the neo-Durkheimian framework explored in the current text, the descriptive detail of management in and governance of networks in this sector lends itself to examination of hypotheses related to the neo-Durkheimian model such as the strategies used by those seeking to manage networks and the role of positive and negative feedback dynamics in shaping network change.

Policy context

The concept of community safety emerged during the 1980s in the light of rising public fear of crime, heightened awareness of its impact on victims and a political imperative for cost containment. The earlier welfarist approach, in which penal concerns were traditionally expressed in a language of rehabilitation, was supplanted by a new penology expressed in terms of crime *management* (Garland, 1997; James and Raine, 1998). Consistent with this broader trend, partnership approaches to crime management during the early 1990s reflected a conceptual refocusing away from *structural causes* of crime toward crime management *per se*, with a consequent increase in emphasis upon situational crime reduction strategies within geographical communities (Garland, 1996; Kemshall and Ross, 2000).

The policy was informed by an influential review of 231 widely differing prison rehabilitation schemes conduced between 1945 and 1967 which concluded that such schemes had little impact on recidivism rates (Martinson, 1974; Lipton *et al.*, 1975). While the authors intended to promote alternatives to prison, their findings were enthusiastically adopted by the political right to justify a reduction in educational and psychological reform programmes and increases in sentences, under the slogan 'nothing works' – except, by inference, prison. Martinson and colleagues' negative conclusions were challenged on the grounds that the methodological quality of the original studies was so poor that firm conclusions concerning their efficacy could not be drawn. Further, the broad generalisations of the conclusions overlooked many instances of individual success (Gendreau and Ross, 1979; Gendreau *et al.*, 1996). Later literature reviews using filters for methodological quality provide promising evidence of the effectiveness of social intervention programmes in assisting behaviour change in people who offend (McGuire, 1995; Andrews and Bontanna, 1998; Andrews *et al.*, 2001). This reanalysis posed a simple yet crucially important question – what works?

The UK Labour government's approach to crime reduction partnerships from the late 1990s onwards marks a sharp discontinuity with the 'nothing works' approach and a return to social models of crime prevention. In order to engage with the 'what works?' agenda, the Home Office commissioned a review of available evidence on ways of dealing with offending behaviour (Curtin *et al.*, 2001; Goldblatt and Lewis, 1998). The report's authors concluded that crime reduction would be best served by a combination of long-term investment in children and families, together with immediate, situational crime preventive measures in identified 'hot spots', and the adoption of 'problem-oriented policing' (POP). Based on the work of Goldstein (1990), POP starts from the assumption that policing should target underlying problems within a community. In order to do this, locally based officers require information on related incidents and the support of senior officers in developing imaginative solutions to specific local problems (Leigh *et al*., 1996).

Consistent with 'third way' politics, New Labour's political vision rests on stated values of equal worth, opportunity for all, responsibility and community (Blair, 1998), and the practical politics derived from this value base places partnerships between the state and civil society alongside the need for individual empowerment and market-based opportunities. The value of partnerships within this paradigm is that they offer the potential for increased participation by citizens in public life, encouraging a sense of shared values and responsibilities between state and citizen. In the context of criminal justice, the concept of partnership thus includes the promotion of both private and non-profit contributions to crime prevention and treatment, together with an emphasis on the responsibilities of citizens to prevent crime. This shift of emphasis reformulates the 'crime problem' as one requiring the management of cross-system goals, necessitating collaborative action across multiple agencies, professional groups and active citizens.

Common across multiple social policy areas, 'partnership' is thus an umbrella term covering a multitude of networks between public, private and voluntary agencies and between agencies and service users. As a form of collaborative relationship, partnerships place the emphasis on process, consisting of common aims and a means of achieving the desired outcomes:

> Partnerships should be treated as specific forms of co-operation based on shared agreement on action to be taken and/or shared objectives and a commitment to achieve those objectives. This leads to a separate process and/or organisation in which responsibility for decision-making and action is shared on an agreed basis. (Clarke and Stewart, 1997: 4)

The rhetoric of partnership promises to put communities at the heart of regeneration. Yet, community involvement and partnership are difficult to achieve (Taylor, 2000a), and the language of partnership masks a series of tensions between accountability and flexibility, participation and representation, and consensus and diversity (Taylor, 2000b). Thus, the very necessity for accountability for public money may frustrate the risk taking that communities might wish to see. Community leaders are frequently criticised for being unrepresentative, and there is a risk of reliance on a small pool of silo activists. Where constituencies are large and issues complex, consensus will be difficult to reach, and participants will require information and support in order to contribute. Similarly, there are tensions between the need to identify differences and avoid a populist majoritarianism, while identifying common interests and avoiding fragmentation.

Sullivan and Skelcher (2002) conceptualise three broad periods of partnership development within the crime and disorder context: early initiatives; strategic development; and statutory partnerships. While they do not use neo-Durkheimian terminology, their taxonomy is extremely useful for current purposes as it explicitly identifies three distinct phases in the governance of networks within the sector against which the neo-Durkheimian framework may be explored. Thus 'early initiatives' are typified by largely non-financial voluntary partnerships between police and local authority enclaves and voluntary activists; the 'strategic development' phase refers to the overlay of formalised, contract-based relationships between purchasers and providers in internal markets; and 'statutory partnerships' refer to an additional mandated layer of hierarchical partnerships (network forms) for monitoring, predicting, analysing and preventing crime and disorder. Each provides an opportunity to explore the neo-Durkheimian framework.

1980s and early 1990s – the early years

Early partnership activity by the Home Office in the 1980s concentrated on 'situational' crime prevention, including Neighbourhood Watch partnerships between local residents and police, in which residents monitored potential criminal activity. There was a particular emphasis on environmental improvements and surveillance in order to address social and situational aspects of community safety, often initiated by local authorities in response to particular issues of public concern and facilitated by the Home Office Crime Prevention Unit (established in 1983). Relationships between local authorities and police were often tense, reflecting an underlying conflict between the two concerning perceptions of whose domain this was, and who should lead. Emerging networks were thus typically a hybrid of individualistic and enclave forms, to the extent that they were constituted by developing relationships between well-defined and separate police/local authority enclaves.

Tilley (1993) identifies an 'emergent' effect upon the outcomes of situational initiatives as an initial emphasis on situational crime prevention broadened to include social aspects such as racial harassment and domestic violence (Hague and Malos, 1998), which is attributed to the articulation of concerns by well-organised voluntary sector partners. In neo-Durkheimian terms, this suggests that during this period some voluntary sector activists were able to occupy *tertius* positions between police and local authority enclaves and act as 'brokers', gaining leverage over the content of initiatives.

Early to mid-1990s – strategic development

The rise of New Public Management (NPM) influenced the development of partnerships away from informal, non-financial arrangements towards contract-based purchaser–provider partnerships. Heavily influenced by public-choice theory (Niskanen, 1994), at the heart of NPM lie a set of beliefs about the potential for improved economy and efficiency in service provision by limiting the role of state agencies and encouraging multiple service delivery agencies exposed to market forces. New right political thought argued for a core of state activity, covering policy-making and regulation of a mix of privatised, contracted-out and residual direct service provision; a 'hollowed-out' state (Sullivan and Skelcher, 2002). The internal logic is that increased user responsiveness would follow from the creation of markets in which service users were able to express choices over services.

Cross (1997) reviews the complexities of the term *partnership* in the context of probation services at this time, noting the multiplicity of forms ranging from a unitary purpose project limited to two partners to multi-agency undertakings with multiple goals. Drawing on Locke (1990), Cross notes different levels of formalised activity, from loose liaison relationships to corporate integration on policy-making, service planning and resource allocation. She suggests a classification system based on the extent of formalisation and integration, re-expressed by Crawford (1998) as ranging from multi-agency work without significantly affecting the work that the agencies do, to inter-agency partnerships in which working practices and service delivery patterns are radically transformed. Gibbs (1998) gives an overview of a range of formal and informal relationships between the probation service and voluntary organisations, additionally highlighting models of good practice.

Notwithstanding the heterogeneity evident within the sector at this time, political and legislative changes in the early 1990s led to a sharp increase in formalised, contract-based relationships between probation services and the voluntary sector (Home Office, 1999, 1992). Linked to new managerialist and quasi-market approaches to public sector management (Hood, 1991; James and Raine, 1998; Clarke *et al.*, 2000), this development resulted in the organisation of probation service-voluntary sector partnerships on a purchaser/provider model, concentrating activity on the provision of structured programmes of offender supervision. While many of the accounts of such initiatives for substance misusing offenders are anecdotal, some empirical research is available on the characteristics of successful partnerships (Rumgay and Cowan, 1998). Two issues were found to be important in this regard: championship by the probation agency; and partnership as enhancement. The former required a 'link' between probation officers and partner substance abuse workers. The latter required the perception that substance abuse workers would enhance probation officer's direct work with clients. In the absence of such perceptions, Rumgay and Cowan (1998) report instances of 'sabotage' by probation officers. This suggests the need for *rapprochement* between professional enclaves in order for partnerships to flourish. More recently, the 'what works' agenda has emphasised the use of individualistic Cognitive Behavioural Therapy (CBT) approaches with offenders; this has made it more difficult for probation services to work in partnership with other agencies that pursue less individualised approaches.

The increasing use of contract-based purchaser–provider arrangements rather than informal and non-financial partnership arrangements affected not only the way that probation services conducted their business with the voluntary sector, but also the *role* of the voluntary sector. Changes in this sector included the need to bid for work contracts, funding tied to specified service provision rather than overall voluntary agency goals and increasingly becoming part of the statutory process. These changes were variously viewed as aiding voluntary agencies to focus on a more specialist service for service users or compromising their aim to supply services only to voluntary clients (Gibbs, 2001). Voluntary agencies increasingly became sub-contractors; thus the National Association for the Care and Resettlement of Offenders (NACRO) grew as a recipient of urban programme monies to provide tightly specified services. Other voluntary groups fell victim to the changes:

> Some probation mangers felt that the market niche of these groups was too small to make contract viable, and were therefore not willing to 'risk' funding such groups because the clients might not emerge. What this suggests is a discriminatory approach which effectively, because it was based on a business approach to prioritise supply and demand, meant that the needs of minority group clients, in some cases, went unaddressed. (Gibbs, 2001: 20)

For Crawford (1998), NPM exacerbated inter-agency tension as internal agency priorities took precedence over collaborative aims. The conjunction of hollowing-out, with its consequent fragmentation in service delivery, and a political imperative to combat 'wicked issues' (such as community safety), cutting across the boundaries of a fragmented organisational landscape, led to the creation of multiple inter-agency partnerships. The context of high organisational fragmentation required resources to facilitate negotiation and delivery of public programmes (Skelcher, 2000). In response to such increased transaction costs, integrative mechanisms were seen as imperative to align policy across organisational boundaries.

While rejected and shelved immediately on publication in 1991, the Morgan Report identified a number of difficulties with emergent partnerships and later provided the key inspiration for much of the New Labour multi-agency social crime prevention schemes post-1997. The main thrust of the report was that the concept of crime prevention is limiting in scope and generally police-driven, with other agencies having a marginal stake. In contrast, the report promoted community safety to progress beyond a situational definition of crime to a broader, social definition of crime prevention, consistent with earlier (pre-1979) social models.

In neo-Durkheimian terms, while some localities were able to achieve much with dense groups of committed activists, in the absence of such commitment little was achieved. In enclaved networks, no single organisation has greater centrality than any other, so that any would-be leader must demonstrate greater commitment to the principles defining the group without recourse to status, resources or centrality. In the absence of a statutory duty for the work, salience for any single agency was thus difficult to achieve; a fragile salience became established only on the basis of personal and organisational commitment by local activists. Seemingly acknowledging this difficulty, the report recommended that local authorities be given a *statutory* duty to co-ordinate crime prevention strategies within their locality – invoking a hierarchical hybrid network form in order to avoid the difficulty over salience due to enclaves. Yet, the Home Office rejected the suggestion of an increase in local authority influence in favour of a continued voluntarism, consistent with the view that enhancing statutory responsibility would undermine a 'problem-solving' focus (Liddle and Gelsthorpe, 1994).

Liddle and Gelsthorpe (1994) chronicle the formal and informal structures, modes of leadership, involvement of external agencies and relationships to local and central government at this time. Their study was designed to investigate and assess multi-agency approaches to crime prevention based on eight areas, with a less detailed survey of 22 additional localities. While their account is descriptive of formal structures rather than evaluative, a number of issues of general concern may be distilled. Most importantly, while favouring voluntary rather than statutory arrangements, the authors do appeal to the need for support from the most senior officers of the relevant agencies and, additionally, raise concern over difficulties of co-ordination in the absence of a full-time co-ordinator. While these do not address the issue of salience in enclaved networks considered earlier, the development of formal arrangements with support from senior officers and full-time co-ordination suggests recognition of a need for increasingly hierarchical modes of collaboration, an impetus given an additional boost post-1997 with the creation of statutory partnerships.

Late 1990s: statutory partnerships

The Crime and Disorder Act (1998) replaced the voluntarism characterising earlier community safety partnerships with a statutory duty for local authorities, as recommended in the Morgan Report (1991). Under the Act, local authorities and police authorities in England and Wales are required to work together, to jointly lead a strategic Crime and Disorder Reduction Partnership (CDRP) comprising all relevant stakeholders in the public, voluntary, private and community sectors. Consequently 376 statutory crime and disorder partnerships were established in England and Wales (Phillips *et al.*, 2002).

The establishment of partnerships as the key delivery vehicles for policy outcomes marks a significant shift:

> The 1998 Crime and Disorder Act illustrates 'third way' politics by introducing measures to ensure agencies co-operate at both strategic and

> operational levels; that crime prevention strategies are developed from information provided by many kinds of agencies including community and informal groups; by emphasising the need to support and reinforce the responsibilities of families in bringing up their children; and by adopting an inclusive approach to reinforce the importance of all citizens having a say. (Gibbs, 2001: 23)

Such partnerships are envisaged as broad, diverse and inclusive, offering the prospect of increased opportunities for agencies and citizens to work together. Yet, while the proposals strengthen local responsibility for community safety, new funding programmes and the establishment of the Home Office as monitor of local Crime and Disorder Partnerships strengthen the hand of central government in influencing their priorities. Three principal difficulties with this arrangement may be discerned: lack of conceptual clarity over community safety; the statutory nature of partnerships; and an underlying managerialist agenda.

The concepts of community safety (and disorder) that underpin the statutory partnerships were not clearly defined (Crawford, 1998), opening the possibility of disagreement between partner agencies on the scope of activities. Indeed, Crawford (1998) identifies fundamental conflicts over ideology, purpose and interests leading to major implementation difficulties, due to the various perspectives of the enclaves involved. While hierarchical elements in mandated partnerships provide clear mechanisms for establishing salience, there is still potential for challenge as enclaves assert themselves against such deployment.

Second, by default, the statutory nature of such partnerships prioritises the role of the lead agencies – local authorities and police – leaving secondary roles for probation and health and tertiary roles for other (typically voluntary sector) partners. Such a situation requires concerted proactive behaviour on the part of statutory agencies if tokenism is to be avoided, especially with regard to service user involvement. Indeed, it may be more realistic for lead agencies to identify those specific areas of work where user contributions would be most valuable, such as service delivery, and pursue rigorous engagement only there.

Third, New Labour's policy stance retains and extends the dual emphasis on decentralisation and performance management contained within NPM; commentators have satirised these continuities by coining the term 'Modern Public Management' (Newman, 2000). In the context of crime and disorder partnerships, there is much emphasis on the importance of crime audits, strategic priorities, action plans and evaluations against the plans. Such technologies constitute a significant increase in regulatory oversight associated with guidance and monitoring; that is, a strong system of performance improvement with an underlying emphasis on increased accountability to government drawing on a set of central targets (McLaughlin *et al.*, 2001).

While still hybrid, retaining enclave and individualist elements, the resultant networks are strongly hierarchical. Crime and disorder partnerships reflect a strongly managerialist agenda, albeit one couched in the language of the partnership ideal of sharing, co-operation and equity. The difficulty is that such an outcome-oriented approach may be in tension with a longer term vision of the wider benefits of crime and disorder strategies. Crucially, central targets set without reference to local plans undermine the problem-oriented approach. *Calling Time on Crime* (HMIC, 2000) identified clear tensions between the local determination of priorities as envisioned by the 1998 Act and the perceived imposition of central priorities in burglary, vehicle and violent crime. In the original audits, 87 per cent of CDRPs identified domestic violence as their top priority, yet this was not included in the April 2000 central targets. Similarly, the Audit Commission (2001) reported:

> There is, inevitably, a tension between national crime reduction targets and local issues of community safety. Partnerships that follow the national focus alone will fail to take account of local issues and will not serve local people well. (Audit Commission, 2001: 3)

This tension was also identified in a report on the funding and implementation of the £30M Targeted Policing Initiative (TPI) designed to support problem-oriented policing. The central drive was perceived as eroding the foundations of the local partnership approach and the report highlighted the need to balance centralised performance indicators against identification and solution of crime and disorder problems at local level (Bullock *et al.*, 2002). In the absence of time and training to gather the right data, analyse it properly and devise targeted solutions, many of the bids for TPI money were judged inadequate.

Crime and Disorder Reduction Partnerships

Sections 5 and 6 of the 1998 Crime and Disorder Act (CDA) place an obligation in local authorities and the police, in partnership with other agencies, to complete a specific cycle of activities every three years. The four stages involve audit of local crime and disorder problems; local consultation on the basis of the audit; determination of priorities and formulation of a strategy; and implementation and monitoring of the strategy.

The Home Office undertook an evaluation of the CDRPs, consisting of a series of 12 case studies under the 'Pathfinder' initiative (Bratby, 1999; Fulcher, 2000; Home Office, 1999), designed to provide developmental lessons for wide dissemination. They also commissioned an independent evaluation consisting of documentary review, participant observation and semi-structured interviews with stakeholders in three partnerships with widely different socio-economic and demographic profiles (Phillips *et al.*, 2002).

Both studies focused on audits, consultation and strategy formation during the first three years of partnership activity following the CDA, including an overview of structures and terms of reference.

The two evaluations identified a broad range of structures and terms of reference within the sites, consistent with a lack of detailed structural guidance for CDRPs within the Act. While variations in structure within and between unitary and two-tier structures made it difficult to identify a 'best-practice' model, it was clear that strategic bodies required good links with practitioners in order to disseminate crime reduction approaches (Liddle and Gelsthorpe, 1994; Crawford, 1998; Phillips *et al.*, 2002).

The existence of coterminous boundaries across agencies aided local accountability. Unitary authorities had an obvious advantage, although the existence of multiple area police commanders in large cities was a complicating factor. Liddle and Gelsthorpe's (1994) earlier study of multi-agency partnerships in two-tier authorities identified a number of factors that may impede the involvement of district and county council representatives in partnership work. These include political antagonisms, perceptions that county councils were far removed from local issues and that central funds were rarely forthcoming. The difficulties of managing two-tier structures are also noted by the pathfinder report, which identifies county structures as the most challenging to administer given the multiple agencies, groups and responsibilities. Complex boundaries pose further problems for engagement of health care trusts and education authorities, some of which face multiple requests for involvement.

While most Pathfinder sites delegated management from the local authority chief executive and area police commanders to community safety officers, the extent of proactive executive involvement varied greatly. Senior involvement was considered a valuable asset as such staff have more discretion and are also more credible within their own organisations and thus more likely to be able to 'sell' a compromise back at their own organisations. Officers reported that leverage with agencies was enhanced when the top tiers of management within their organisations were visibly involved (Home Office, 2000; Audit Commission, 2002). The role of community safety officers in managing the network is thus critical, requiring multi-dimensional capabilities incorporating skills around public relations, political influence, project development and general management. The need for support and training in the development of these skills has been noted and support made available via the partnership support programme involving the Home Office, Local Government Association and National Police Training (Phillips *et al.*, 2002).

There is support for Gilling's (1993) observation of cultural dissonance between partners, in the sense that, through observation, it is clear that agencies may be characterised by very different understandings on the part of their staff and that attempts to resolve differences hierarchically stimulates negative feedback from enclaves:

> Police and local authority cultures have to address the issue of language within the partnerships, but on a national basis there are wide variations and understandings of precisely what the terms actually mean. This becomes more critical when the partnerships begin jointly to commission, disseminate and publish documents. It is fair to say that the two cultures have made great strides to understand each other's respective roles and functions but there is still some way to go before they sit comfortably within each other's domain. (Home Office, 2002: 9)

Or more starkly:

> Police and local authority structures and cultures are not naturally compatible with one another. It is accepted that this will need further time to develop. (Home Office, 2002: 10)

The audit process is designed to capture a realistic picture of the patterns of crime and disorder within a community in order to develop a consultation document and to aid strategy formulation. The analysis should be holistic and the resultant picture recognisable to members of the community. In developing their audits, partnerships faced a number of data limitations including missing or incomplete, inaccessible and inaccurate data and a lack of co-terminosity between agency boundaries. Despite provision for exchange under Section 115 of the act (and the existence of information exchange protocols), difficulties arose:

> [A] heath representative commented that some A&E hospital departments would bc ablc to providc, for audit purposcs, information about thc number of people with knife wounds, but that they would be reluctant to provide details such as patients' postcodes: 'We can't say which postal districts they live in unless the numbers are so huge in each postal district that you can reasonably preserve anonymity.' (Phillips *et al.*, 2002: 23)

The auditing process outlined in Home Office Guidance was intended to encourage inter-agency data sharing and a holistic analysis of local problems. Yet, the experience of the case studies reported by Phillips *et al.* (2002) was of inadequate time and resources to dedicate internal staff to the process and a consequent reliance on external consultants, leading to reduced ownership of results by partner agencies.

The issue of linkage between CDRPs, Drug Action Teams (DATs) and youth offending Teams (YOTs) was raised; all subject to different timetables and accountability structures yet interrelated. Such difficulties are beginning to be addressed through the Local Strategic Partnership (LSP) framework, and closer co-ordination between YOTs, DATs and CDRPs. Despite the centrality of strategic planning to the model, given the time pressures imposed by the timetable the partners were not able to undertake detailed analysis of problems identified as priorities; rather, decisions were made on the basis of past experience (Phillips *et al.*, 2002). Thus, despite a range of situational and social crime prevention approaches, there was little evidence of a thorough problem-centred approach. The lack of financial support for core partnership activity affected the quality of auditing, consultation and strategy; a demanding bidding process was an additional obstacle. Phillips *et al.* (2002) are hopeful that funding through the Partnership Support Programme and training provision will mean CDRPs feel better supported in future.

The notion of statutory lead agencies implies hierarchical relationships between partners and there is some evidence that this can cause resentment by representatives of smaller voluntary and community organisations (Phillips *et al.*, 2002). This raises the prospect of their withdrawal (Gilling, 2000) with a consequent diminution of local voices. However, Phillips *et al.* (2002) found no evidence of the exclusion of less powerful groups from key decision-making through informal networking (Crawford, 1994; Phillips and Sampson, 1998), suggesting that the partnerships were adopting an inclusive approach.

Youth Offending Teams

Introduced under the 1998 Crime and Disorder Act, the policy background to the establishment of YOTs originates with New Labour while still in opposition and forms part of their much-quoted commitment to be 'tough on crime and tough on the causes of crime'. Replacing the former social service youth justice teams – and created under the 1998 Crime and Disorder Act – YOTs reflect a changing ethos towards greater inter-agency accountability for youth crime management by broadening the number of agencies involved in the supervision of young offenders. YOTs are required to include a police officer, probation officer, a social worker, and representatives from health and education services. While these latter two agencies have traditionally not been involved in the post-sentence supervision of young offenders, their involvement reflects a desire to tackle issues which can place young people at risk of becoming involved in crime, such as truancy and school exclusion, substance misuse and mental health problems.

The term 'partnership' may conceal conflicts arising from the power inequalities between local statutory agencies. While previous research pointed to the dominance of the police in many inter-agency partnerships (Blagg *et al.*, 1988; Kosh and Williams, 1995), Williams (1999) reports a more complex picture with regard to YOTs. While police had considerable experience of pre-trial work with young offenders, probation officers and social workers had a monopoly of expertise in post-sentence supervision of young offenders and preparation of court reports. While the police had sophisticated information systems, youth justice team's client records are considered more up-to-date and accurate in some areas. Further, some areas of expertise are contested by multiple agencies; for example, group work with young offenders and their families on issues such as parenting and anger management may be claimed as the remit of health, probation or social services. Williams (1999) reports 'turf wars' over the appropriateness of different agencies developing these areas of work, which is as one might expect in such enclave networks.

Drug Action Teams

In 1986 the DoH required every district (health authority) to set up a multi-agency drug advisory committee comprising health, social services, education, police and voluntary groups. An external evaluation commissioned by the DoH based on fieldwork from eight areas reported wide variations in effectiveness in strategy and resource allocation (Roger Howard Associates, 1994). In conclusion, the report recommended placing accountability for success in collaboration with the chief executives of the then district health authorities.

Launched in 1995 within the *Tackling Drugs Together* White Paper, DATs were charged with a strategic planning role with representation from multiple agencies. Drug Reference Groups (DRGs) – consisting of expert practitioners – were charged with advising the DATs and helping with implementation. While advice to DATs echoed the Howard report's insistence of a chief executive level membership for multi-agency partnerships – in order to allocate resources without recourse to major consultation within agencies – many DATs members were below this level of seniority with consequent loss of decision-making authority (Mounteney, 1996).

A review of progress based on documentary evidence, postal questionnaires to DAT chairs and members and DRG chairs and six case studies (Cabinet Office, 1997) identified a number of outstanding difficulties, including lack of coterminous boundaries. While the decision to allow local flexibility in determining boundaries was considered helpful, the tension between the desire for efficient functioning and accountability to central government and the alternative desire for local accountability and responsiveness to local needs and communities was still identified as an issue (Cabinet Office, 1997).

Building on the earlier experience, The White Paper *Tackling Drugs to Build a Better Britain* (1998) outlined a ten-year strategy for tackling drugs. This charged DATs with facilitation of inter-agency commissioning strategies and co-ordination of provision of treatments for drug misuse. In order to achieve greater co-ordination, DATs boundaries became coterminous with local authorities – at either unitary or county level – under the Crime and Disorder Act (1998). Government policy on drug treatment envisaged all planning and budgetary decisions in relation to drug treatment services being undertaken jointly through DATs; and, in order to underpin this activity, 97 per cent (141/145) of DATs had established joint commissioning groups by April 2002 (NTA, 2002). Partner agencies include local authorities, PCTs, police and probation services. Furthermore, DAT guidance explicitly requires the active engagement of elected members in order to guard against democratic deficit.

Local Strategic Partnerships

The duty to have many different partnerships with overlapping functions and involving huge transaction costs has been termed 'fragmented holism' (6 *et al.*, 1999, 2002). In order to join up the various initiatives – and reduce the number of plans local authorities are obliged to produce – LSPs were launched in March 2001. They are intended to bring together public, private, voluntary and community sectors under a single, over-arching local co-ordination framework within which more specific partnerships such as YOTs, DATs and CDRPs operate. Unlike CDRPs, their establishment is not mandatory. However, their formation is a condition of eligibility for Neighbourhood Renewal Fund monies and all local authorities are expected to develop LSPs as part of the process of fulfilling a statutory duty to develop a community strategy. While local authorities are identified as being 'well-placed' to lead LSPs, there is no compulsion in this regard. The Local Government Association (LGA) supports closer working between YOTs, DATs and CDRPs under the LSP umbrella as a means of establishing co-ordinated local anti-crime strategies (LGA, 2001). While almost all LSPs include police, health and local authority representation, further membership is very varied and may include employment services, chambers of commerce, transport agencies, community and voluntary sector representatives (DoT, 2003). Local authority representation is typically through both elected members and officers. LSPs are structurally diverse, although typically comprise a board, thematic sub-partnerships, an officer support group and a wider consultative forum. The most common partnership links are with Crime and Disorder Community Partnerships, Local Learning Partnerships, Health Improvement Partnerships and Single Reservation Budget (SRB) Partnerships (DoT, 2003).

A baseline quantitative questionnaire evaluation of LSPs reported in February 2003 that, of 367 local authority areas, all but 40 had developed LSPs, and only one had no plans for their future development (DoT, 2003). Several issues and dilemmas for the emergent LSPs were highlighted: these included stakeholder engagement; resources and capacity; effective working; developing the agenda; and external issues. As might be expected, funding joint action poses difficulties of external constraint and political acceptability.

Community engagement was also considered a problem, posing difficult tensions between inclusively and manageability in membership, particularly when engaging with the wider community is broadly defined to include both geographical communities and communities of interest. A related issue concerns the interface between LSP and local democracy, particularly the role of elected members in LSPs and the balance of power between members and officers; difficulties include balancing the leadership role of elected members with the desire for an inclusive local politics facilitated by partnership working and avoiding council domination. A specific issue is the tension between the medium- to long-term aims of the LSP and the mostly short-term needs of elected members.

LSPs reported the need to ensure effective working relationships either through rationalising existing partnership arrangements or supporting co-ordination without taking over successful groupings. The need for connectivity with adjacent LSPs raises difficulties which are further compounded in two-tier districts involving county and district divisions of responsibility. The main difficulty is focusing on a limited number of agreed priorities as well as resolving conflicting priorities within a complex agenda; partner agencies often have difficulty giving ground to support joint aims (DoT, 2003).

Furthermore, while LSPs are themselves non-statutory, the sectoral performance indicators of individual partners can conflict with effective partnership working; central government departments still (at least partly) hold individual organisations separately accountable which can create tensions within the LSP. Finally, tensions between national and community-determined priorities and targets may remain, notwithstanding the Public Service Agreement system which provides opportunities for negotiation over targets.

Management within crime and disorder networks

The literature identifies as management challenges in this field: the problems of inter- and intra-agency conflict (which can clearly be seen to flow from the enclaved structure of some networks); the role of reticulists; managing in conditions of high political salience; and handling accountability issues.

Gilling (1993, 1994, 1996) is primarily interested in the ideological and historical roots of discourses on crime prevention and how they become realised in institutional practice. While the logic of collaboration is irresistible, Gilling offers a deconstruction and contextualisation of the meaning of crime prevention and the ways that the signifier has been deployed as a rhetorical device by the major agencies. Focusing particular attention on the police and probation as illustrative examples, he traces the historical origins of each agency and shows the effects on their respective contemporary conceptual frameworks and practices. The dominant police discourse places emphasis on crime control via proactive and reactive deterrence. In contrast, the dominant theme in probation services is of reform and treatment (Gilling, 1993). While good public relations work, collaboration will tend to be dominated by the police discourse given the wider politics of law and order. This will tend to favour situational crime prevention approaches, given the pressure for audit and the ease with which their effects may be monitored. While his attempt to pigeonhole agencies in terms of dominant conceptual frameworks appears crude, he does draw attention to the tensions between situational and social crime prevention faced by collaborating agencies.

Crawford (1994, 1995) and Crawford and Jones (1995) critically engage with multi-agency collaboration in crime and disorder, drawing on data from a two-year research project in the Southeast of England exploring eight proactive community projects. Their emphasis is on the complex, reflexive and negotiated character of multi-agency practice, and on a critical engagement with meanings of community. In contrast to the benevolent versus conspiratorial approach to representing existing perspectives typified by Gilling *et al.* (1995) argue that consensus and conflict are inherent in multi-agency work and point to the creativity of multi-agency workers in negotiating the structural conflicts and oppositions that exist; in neo-Durkheimian terms, they stress the importance of suasion in managing across enclaves.

However, the impact of political salience in this sector is also worth considering. Since 1997, there has been much policy activity on the need for joined-up working in crime and disorder partnerships across multiple agencies as exemplified by new statutory responsibilities under the 1998 Act. Yet, the sharp-end of the crime and disorder political agenda is rarely if ever concerned with inter-agency collaboration. Of much greater salience are the widely publicised crime figures for violent offences, car theft and burglary; the pressure on police forces is to clean-up crime, not join-up with other agencies. While a problem-oriented, inter-agency approach may be exactly what is required to tackle issues, the political need to be seen to be doing something quickly may become irresistible. This is evinced by the use of centrally set priorities and targets for crime reduction which are unrelated to the priorities identified by CDRPs in their local audits. Under such circumstances, the development of joined-up working across networks is likely to be seen by many as of secondary importance. The paradox is that joined-up inter-agency collaboration is exactly what is required to improve service quality in the medium term. Overall, the experience of CDRPs is that performance targets set without reference to locally defined needs will undermine 'problem-solving' approaches that seek to provide innovative solutions to locally identified problems (Bullock *et al.*, 2002).

If governance is defined as the steering or regulation of networks by external agencies, a number of tensions between collaboration and governance processes may be identified which are of particular relevance to statutory partnerships (Sullivan and Skelcher, 2000). The first relates to the joint role of formal partnerships such as DATs and CDRPs as both *delivery mechanism* and *governance process*. Such partnerships are a key means by which central policy is delivered, mandated as local agents for central aspirations and audited against targets. Their use as delivery mechanisms sits uneasily with notions of good governance in the public domain, which encompasses notions such as transparency, standards of conduct, public debate, local autonomy and self-determination. Thus, the fit between uniform delivery of 'what works' and local democracy is problematic. This is clearly seen in the effects of central target setting on the problem-oriented policing initiative. While partnerships were encouraged to undertake local audits to inform specific, multi-agency, problem-oriented responses to local priorities, they were simultaneously being judged on their ability to reduce specific categories of crime chosen without reference to local concerns. Tensions between enclave and hierarchy are evident over the mix of local priorities, police service objectives and national priorities (Audit Commission, 2001), and lack of evidence of a problem-oriented approach to priority setting (Phillips *et al.*, 2002).

The second governance tension is between partnership as *political process* and as *managerial technique*. While a strong ideological emphasis on public involvement provides opportunities for political engagement, the members of partnership boards predominantly consist of managers (which suggests that their primary role is that of a managerial device for inter-agency service delivery). The Audit Commission (2002) identified the need for ongoing dialogue with local people, perhaps particularly important in the context of persisting public concern over crime. They recommended a number of strategies for improved public engagement, including consultation with hard to reach communities of interest (e.g. people vulnerable to homophobia or domestic violence) co-ordinated between partnership agencies.

A third tension in governance relates to the release of capacity and the exertion of control. The creation of an LSP composed of representatives of diverse groups does not necessarily ensure an accurate reflection of the diversity of interests within metropolitan areas. Interests will be both filtered in and filtered out, and the net result is a powerful alliance of key institutions and individuals behind a particular vision for the locality under the banner of the common good. The concern is that the particular blend will not be to the benefit of all. The Audit Commission (2002) identified large variations in inter-agency involvement between partnerships, and while health, social services, probation and education services delivered significant benefits when fully involved, often they were not full participants.

The final tension is that between collaboration as *structural entity* and *dynamic process*. While formal structures are manifestations of a commitment to collaborative activity, collaborations are fundamentally predicated on dynamic processes through which individuals and organisations negotiate mutual interests (Huxham and Vangen, 2000). Issues of flexibility and personal loyalty thus arise within the context of collaborative activity. The ability of community safety partnerships to dynamically engage with the partnership agenda was questioned by the Audit Commission (2002), which identified patchy involvement at strategic level by some key agencies, poor use of problem-solving techniques and poor information sharing between partner agencies. Key areas for improvement were identified as ownership of community safety linked to willingness to change behaviour, sustained focus on local priorities and capacity to deliver community safety as part of basic services.

Conclusion

While the shaping of networks in this sector was profoundly influenced by the development of 'New Public Management' forms of governance in public policy, the role of institutional shaping in line with neo-Durkheimian theory is also apparent. Early individualist/enclave hybrid networks provided scope for activists to occupy *tertius* positions and influence the content of initiatives towards greater emphasis on social aspects such as racial harassment and domestic violence. Voluntary networks with fragile salience were highly dependent on the ability of local activists to establish leadership on the basis of personal commitment and, consequently, achievements were highly variable. The later development of statutory partnerships may be seen partly as a response to such difficulties; however the assertion of hierarchy resulted in both the undermining of local problem-oriented approaches due to the political salience of alternative issues and negative feedback from enclaves without hierarchical position.

11
Networks in Health Care

Health care networks are international phenomena that can be found within all types of health care system from publicly funded systems in Europe, Canada and Australasia to the private business models of the United States. Moreover, networks in health care include a wide spectrum of agencies including purchasers, providers, professionals, consumers and policy-makers. The range of agencies involved in health care networks reflects the often fragmented nature of health care delivery, particularly for vulnerable client groups (such as the frail elderly) and for complex chronic illnesses that are now the most prevalent health problems in terms of both cost and impact in developed countries. The rise of clinical and hospital networks has been a system-response to this new paradigm of care. As Wagner (1998) describes, the current challenge for health systems is the development of a chronic care model, the features of which include the integration of primary and secondary care; the co-ordination of health and social care; and the development of team-based services where the skills of nurses and doctors are used to their best advantage.

In many countries, therefore, a growing interest has developed in hospital and/or clinical networks that concentrates on the creation of new linkages between primary, secondary and tertiary care. Indeed, in countries with traditionally hierarchical systems of health care (such as the NHS in the United Kingdom) the idea of 'network organizations' is increasingly being drawn into mainstream policy. In Scotland, for example, such mainstreaming began in the late 1990s through the construction of 'managed clinical networks' across both specialities (such as neurology) and diseases (such as diabetes and cancer) (Woods, 2001).

The emphasis on clinical networks as a way of sustaining access to a range of care is of particular importance in the debate. Hospitals throughout Europe and other parts of the world have begun to shed functions to multidisciplinary community-based health services and such hospitals have begun to specialise as a result (McKee and Healy, 2002). In addition to the impact of the emerging chronic disease paradigm of care, the process has accelerated due to informational and technological advances regulations on the working hours of doctors and the encouragement of provider plurality through the use of public, private and overseas providers. Consequently, the notion of a single hospital providing all facilities necessary for a local population has become no longer tenable (Baker and Lorimer, 2000) and the formation of hospital and clinical networks has gained favour as an alternative method. Hence, it has been common for networks of two or more hospitals to develop (in both public and private systems) as strategic alliances for mutual survival in competitive and/or resource-limited environments (Weil, 2001). Moreover, national health care policies have recognized the need to innovate in network-based approaches to care delivery. In the United Kingdom, for example, the influential Calman and Hine (1995) report broke new ground when it suggested how cancer services should be delivered through networks of professionals in order to reduce delays in diagnosis and treatment. In theory, the approach should sustain access to care to patients of those local services threatened by closure whilst ensuring patients receive a standard investigation.

The literature on health networks reviewed by Goodwin (2004) shows that they have principally been developed for a series of key tasks as follows:

- To provide or purchase services that are more appropriate for patients;
- To reduce costs to health and social care procurement agencies (such as governments, PCTs, local authorities, and private or public insurance agents);
- To reduce costs between providers of care;
- To share scarce capacity, usually specialist human resources and to enable 'critical mass' (most often between hospitals but also through joint commissioning between procurement agencies); and
- To share knowledge, to develop ideas and to pilot innovation.

However, what is also clear from the literature is that belief in the value of networks as an effective model of health care delivery remains based on a series of expected advantages rather than known outcomes. Hence, reviews have shown that there is little empirical evidence on the value and effectiveness of network models, particularly for client-based groups such as older people (Polivka, 1999), whilst the evidence for effective clinical networks is limited to a few specialties, such as cystic fibrosis (Foucaud *et al.*, 2002). Indeed, the literature on networks in health care is generally characterised by a wealth of opinion leaders engaging in normative discussions of the process of network development (Calvin, 1998; Collins, 2000; Kunkler, 2000; Baker, 2001; Cropper *et al.*, 2002; Edwards, 2002; Frater and Gill, 2002; Thomas, 2003). Case descriptions on networks in the early stages of development are also common (Sardell, 1996; Mundt, 1997; Moir *et al.*, 2001; Tait and Baxter, 2002). Furthermore, attention is also drawn in the literature to the benefits of facilitating network development through the use of clinical information systems (Teich, 1998; Tanriverdi and Venkataraman, 1999; Snyder-Halpern and Chervany *et al.*, 2000).

Since the majority of the literature tends not to be based on research and evaluation studies, the lack of evidence has led to a strategic debate on their effectiveness. For example, whilst the NHS Confederation (2002) was able to describe the *potential* advantages of clinical networks (that they make more efficient use of staff; reduce professional and organisational boundaries; help share good practice; improve access; and put the patient at the centre of care) they were unable to provide firm evidence that such favourable outcomes would result. Questions such as who should be in charge of clinical networks and the degree of formal financial and administrative infrastructure needed to achieve clinical integration have thus not been answered due to a lack of in-depth empirical investigation (Leutz, 1999). Moreover, whilst many reviews of health networks have attempted to examine factors that hinder or support their development (e.g. Leggat, 2000; Shortell *et al.*, 2000), no overarching theoretical model of health care networks, including different network forms and their associated management and governance needs, has ever been developed and employed in this field (Sheaff, 2000). However, following the wider systematic review of studies on interorganisation networks on which this book is based (6 *et al.*, 2004), and the neo-Durkheimian theoretical framework developed here (see Chapter 1), it is now possible to answer some of these questions in the context of health care networks.

Types of networks found in health care

Analysing the literature on health care networks is problematic since the term 'network' has been used synonymously with a wide range of approaches under the general banner of 'integrated care' or 'partnership working'. Hence, there is a very broad church of writings in the field of health care networks but little in the way of synthesis. Nevertheless, a common thread in the literature is the identification of a 'continuum' of network forms based on the level of formality in the ties between the agencies and individuals within them. For example, within the integrated care literature, Leutz (1999) provides a three-level typology of 'linkage', 'co-ordination' and 'full integration' based on the degree to which the integration of institutions involves the creation of a 'loose' network of health care agencies or something more structured and hierarchical.

Other taxonomies of health care networks are similar in their concept and design. For example, the work of Bazzoli *et al.* (1999, 2000, 2001) and Dubbs *et al.* (2004) created network typologies in the US context as a tool for policy-makers, practitioners and researchers to examine the relative performance of health care organisations. In order to develop their taxonomy, the latter team examined the level of differentiation, integration, and centralisation of hospital service-mix, physician arrangements and insurance product developments in order to classify the activities of health networks. What was uncovered in their research was a wide spectrum of network configurations between hospitals and/or insurers (see Box 11.1) and a highly dynamic environment in which the level of vertical integration of services, and/or degree of financial and managerial mergers, shifted and realigned dramatically over time (Bazzoli *et al.*, 2001; Shortell *et al.*, 2000).

Further, in comparing a number of different network 'clusters'; they were able to show a significant shift from 1994, where the majority of health networks were categorised as 'moderately centralised', to 1998 where the dominant form of inter-relationship had become 'independent' and 'decentralised' (Dubbs *et al.*, 2004). As the authors argue, this significant

Box 11.1 Dubbs *et al.*'s (2004) taxonomy of health networks in the United States, 1994–1998

Network cluster 1: independent hospital networks
(1994 = 55 cases; 1998 = 131 cases)
Characterised by a lack of vertical relationships, these networks involve little centralisation of hospital services, and have a relatively narrow differentiation of hospital services, physician arrangements and insurance product development. They tend to comprise hospitals with small bed sizes located in close proximity to each other, with only a few hospitals in the network.

Network cluster 2: decentralised networks
(1994 = 4; 1998 = 38)
Characterised by decentralised hospital, physician and insurance activity, these networks have a significant degree of differentiation of hospital services, physician arrangements and insurance products. They are large networks comprising many hospitals over a wide geographical area and most with large bed sizes.

Network cluster 3: centralised hospital networks
*(1998 = 22)**
Characterised by highly centralised hospital services and a very narrow differentiation of service, physician arrangements and insurance product activity. They tend to be a small group of hospitals working within an affiliation structure and tend to be geographically close to each other.

Network cluster 4: centralised physician/insurance networks
*(1998 = 25)**
In contrast to cluster 3, these networks are characterised by extensive network-level activity between physicians and insurers. Hospital services are decentralised, but insurance products are only moderately differentiated and physician arrangements even less so.
* In 1994, the typology used the terms 'moderately centralised' (of which there were 105 cases) and 'centralised' (29 cases). There has thus been a great reduction in network centralisation over the four years of the research.
Source: Dubbs et al., 2004.

(and highly responsive) shift in the nature of networking in the United States appeared to signal a retrenchment from the more integrated vertical systems of health care delivery in order to allow greater independence and autonomy for organisations to respond quickly to local market changes. This taxonomy differs slightly from that of Leutz (1999) in that it is rooted in the degree of centralisation and/or decentralisation of key functions rather than in the level of service integration. Nonetheless, using the neo-Durkheimian analysis developed in Part I, both typologies are primarily concerned with describing structures and the degree of social regulation between institutions.

In synthesising the considerable material on health networks, Goodwin (2004) identified a conceptual 'continuum' of network forms in health care (see Figure 11.1). The further to the right of the continuum a network appeared to sit, the more this network has begun to define structures and mechanisms for the individuals and organisations within it to operate in an integrated manner. Hence, the continuum is a conceptual measure of the level of 'managed' integration manifest in terms of the level of management centrality, resource control and organisational complexity.

An important observation about this continuum of network forms in health care is that networks have the ability to change over time as they respond to local needs. This challenges a common assumption in the health care network literature that the managed network (the most hierarchical) is the most 'effective' form of care network to which fledgling networks should aspire. According to Hebert *et al.* (2003), for example, the fully hierarchical and managed network is argued to offer the most potential to develop comprehensive programmes that address the needs of medically and socially complex patient groups. The authors examined integrated service delivery programmes in North America, such as the California On Lok project (see Yordi and Waldman, 1985) and the Programmes for All Inclusive Care for the Elderly in Canada (see Branch *et al.*, 1995, Pinelli Beauline Associates Ltd, 1998). They argued that combining responsibilities, resources and financing from multiple systems under one organisational roof enabled the creation of

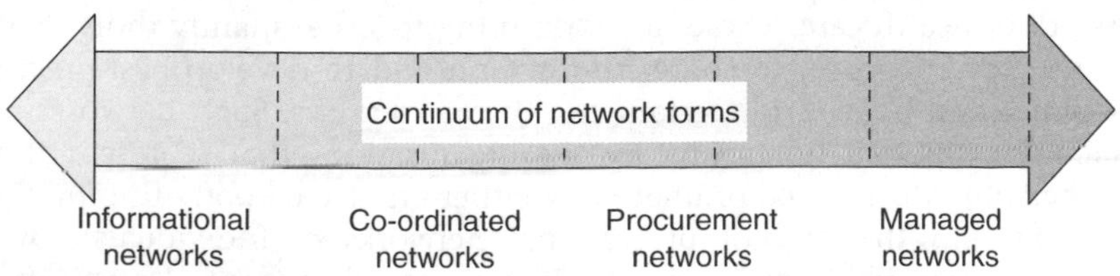

Figure 11.1 A conceptual continuum of network forms in health care.
Source: Adapted from Goodwin (2004).

a 'unified' service network with greater legitimation in the use of the range of co-ordination techniques such as disease management or integrated care pathways. Similarly, Kodner and Kyriacou's (2000) review of the integrated care literature suggested that the greater the move to a 'hierarchical' network, the better the level of integration and attainment of these goals for integration.

However, as Leutz (1999) suggests, such fully integrated models may only be appropriate for a small subset of chronically ill patients that have unstable and functional conditions and who frequently interact with health and social care systems. In other words, the fully integrated and hierarchical network may be appropriate only where all the agencies within the network are required to provide ongoing collaboration between professionals to provide the care. As the neo-Durkheimian network theory established in Chapter 1 would suggest, the hierarchical network may be an overly structural and overly managed solution if the potential gains to all network members are not fully realised or are offset by increasingly limited freedoms to innovate. Moreover, networks that start as clinical or professional associations (like enclaves) may not wish (and even work against) any suggested shift towards more managed hierarchical networks. The shifting characteristics of health network clusters in the United States uncovered by Dubbs *et al.* (2004) is clear evidence that the continuum of network forms in health care provided here should be regarded as bi-directional and should not be considered as an aspiration scale running merely one way.

The characteristics of the different types of network in health care

The following section provides a synthesis of the characteristics of each type of health care network that were summarised in Figure 11.1, bringing forward particular examples from the literature to illustrate the generalisations made. This section is then followed by an interpretation of these health care networks using the neo-Durkheimian framework.

Learning and informational networks in health care

Learning and informational networks are the most common form of network in health care. These networks bring together mainly individuals, but also organisations, to share information and to develop best-practice guidelines and policies for certain health care services. Such networks are generally supported financially by the organisations that represent their membership. Most are co-ordinated by either an elected body to represent the group (in the case of professional networks of individuals); by a Government agency that often subsidises events; or a 'neutral' institution providing support and facilitation to the network, such as a university. Typical examples include national and international associations and societies such as the National Pathways Association in the United Kingdom, the Canadian Health Services Research Foundation, the Dutch Institute for Healthcare Improvement, and the Centre for Case Management in Boston, USA.

The purpose of learning networks is to share best practice and often to align policies and strategies between institutions, but not necessarily to engender new integrated delivery structures. In the UK NHS, for example, there has been much debate about optimal methods for transferring research evidence to practitioners as a method of developing so called 'evidence-based' care (West *et al.*, 1999; Dopson *et al.*, 2001; Ferlie *et al.*, 2001; Bate and Robert, 2002). A common conclusion to such studies is that providing evidence does not necessarily (or, indeed, very often) lead to uptake of best practice unless a process of 'soft networking' is undertaken that combines the dissemination of knowledge with a personalised approach to make the findings relevant and meaningful through informal social interaction (Russell *et al.*, 2004).

One of the key developments within informational networks is that they now frequently employ sophisticated information technologies as a means of communicating learning and innovation (Fulk and DeSanctis, 1998). Hence, IT applications such as networked computing, e-mail, discussion databases, and video conferencing enable organisations and individuals to tap into otherwise dormant expertise of geographically dispersed, intellectually specialised professionals, and to perhaps co-ordinate reciprocal interdependencies (Kuldeep and van Dissel, 1996). Tanriverdi and Venkataraman's (1999) examination of professional networks in the health care industry in Boston, for example, emphasised how the use of telemedicine enabled consulting physicians access to a network of world-class medical expertise. Moreover, the study found that the use of telemedicine had enabled a reduction in the duplication of services, aided the development of common treatment protocols and better co-ordinated and streamlined care across different hospital facilities. By implication, the use of telemedicine thus gave competitive hospital organisations the opportunity to help their professionals expand their expertise (and hence retain the hospital's competitive edge). Indeed, exposure to intellectual challenges, learning material and contact with physicians with high professional reputations were positively related to the use of the professional networks assessed in the study.

Other forms of learning network have developed along more entrepreneurial (individualistic) lines as individuals or agencies, such as universities, develop businesses which enable the facilitation of knowledge exchange between professionals and/or institutions in networks with a specific theme. Such networks are often developed to address current perceived needs in health services but where individual hospitals or physician practices have little experience or knowledge on which to move forward. A good example reported in the literature is the Belgian–Dutch Clinical Pathways Network that was established by the Centre for Health Services and Nursing Research at Leuven University, Belgium (Sermeus *et al.*, 2001). The need for this network arose following changes to Belgian health policy which linked hospital budgets to national average lengths of stay alongside pre-existing goals for developing better quality and patient-focused care. Since the development of integrated care pathways (ICPs) was perceived as a successful approach to care management in countries such as the United States, United Kingdom and Australia (Zander and McGill, 1994; Portus, 1995; Johnson, 1997), the University-facilitated network promoted collaborative practice between hospitals on the development, evaluation and sharing of ICP procedures to the point where it was regarded as the 'essential tool' in the ICP developmental process.

The Belgian–Dutch network grew from an initial membership of three large acute hospitals in 1999, to seventeen hospitals by 2001 covering over 11,000 beds. By the end of this period, the network had operationalised over 100 ICPs (Sermeus *et al.*, 2001). Evaluation of the network showed the importance of it being 'benefit rich' in terms of the relevance of its mission to the participating hospitals; of being 'collaborative' and 'developmental' in ICP development rather than having ICP solutions imposed from 'outside'; and of being well structured and responsive in terms of network management and facilitation. Within the hospitals themselves, clinician awareness and understanding of the ICP approach, its benefits and implications, was an essential educational component in gaining the wider backing for the care management tool. Hence, professional acceptance was required for its successful implementation aligned to a process of education to help challenge established practice cultures. This final issue points to a common weakness in all types of informational networks; they can only go so far in helping organisations to change working practices. Nonetheless, whilst an effective informational network cannot guarantee success, it may provide a solid base on which to build.

Co-ordinated health care networks

Co-ordinated health care networks seek to develop new forms of integration between professionals and/or institutions through the suggested application of a new mode of operation, often based on a care pathway or joint assessment process. An important attribute of the co-ordinated network is that financial and clinical responsibilities of the parties involved remain separated and that the network is not subject to any binding contract. The appeal of the co-ordinated network is often centred on the belief that the creation of links between agencies within a network can both reduce costs and improve quality (Robinson and Casalino, 1996). However, their effectiveness in these terms is yet to be proven since the literature provides relatively little in terms of formal evaluation or review of network effectiveness, and is generally limited to case study analysis of process (Provan and Milward, 2001).

Co-ordinated hospital and clinical networks are a feature in many countries. Examples include managed clinical networks in Scotland, clinical networks for cancer, coronary heart disease and diabetes in England, medical programmes and 'Chains of Care' in Sweden, hospital 'clusters' in Hong Kong and Singapore and clinical streams and 'condition' models in Australia. At one level, such networks are versions of a 'hub and spoke' approach in which care providers co-ordinate the types of 'core' care activities undertaken by each 'spoke' whilst centralising specialist care to 'hubs' (Ham *et al.*, 1998). At a more managed (hierarchical) level, co-ordinated networks begin to manage the clinical activities of professionals more directly.

Hospital networks. Hospital networks are created for a range of reasons, such as:

- pressure to deal with the demands of increasing specialisation;
- a desire to ensure equality of access and consistency of treatments and outcomes;
- an aspiration to shift care to primary and community-based settings; and
- a wish to share risks and costs between providers under financial pressures.

This last point seems especially important where costs of provision are high and traditional hospital care is not financially viable. In the United States, for example, Weil's (2001) review of hospital networks reports show that network strategies predominantly reflect economic realities and the need to strategically differentiate activities in a competitive environment for mutual survival. In publicly funded systems, the driving forces for acute hospital reconfiguration referred to at the beginning of the chapter have led to similar networks developing in Northern Ireland and the West Highlands of Scotland, where small hospitals could only survive as part of a holistic primary and secondary care network using clear protocols (Clark, 2003; HSMC, 2003). Hospital networks, therefore, have primarily been adopted to address efficiency of service delivery. Ugolini and Nobilo (2003), for example, showed how a 'hub and spoke' network of hospitals treating cardiovascular diseases in the Italian region of Emilia Romagna was able to develop more appropriate transfers of cardiac patients from peripheral to central units based on a threshold protocol of case complexity.

Clinical networks. Clinical networks are based on professionals rather than institutions and have often been promoted by governments as a way of producing more patient-focused care across primary and secondary care institutions as professional staff work to agreed protocols for a specific group of patients (Frater and Gill, 2002). The clinical network, therefore, might be termed a 'virtual organisation' since the participants often develop shared clinical guidelines, audit tools and fund joint posts.

Clinical networks can be highlighted in a number of case examples, including the Government-led pilot programme in the Netherlands for the creation of networks in geriatric care (Nies *et al.*, 2003) and the emergent policy for managed clinical networks in Scotland (NHS Management Executive, 1999). Each has been an attempt to promote vertical integration of secondary and tertiary care services. For example, the Scottish policy for managed clinical networks was developed following a period of intense pressure on hospitals that had led to professional and political concerns that a rising tide of emergency medical patients were not receiving the care they needed (Kendrick, 1996). According to Woods (2001), this had been accentuated by the pursuit of greater efficiency in the operation of acute hospitals that had led to a decline in available hospital beds. Moreover, reduced hours of working for junior doctors and growing specialisation of clinical practice meant that it had become difficult to maintain services of an acceptable standard, most seriously in small hospitals in remote rural areas. Managed clinical networks were proposed as an evolutionary concept with the objective of securing access to locally delivered, quality-assured care through the management of hitherto separate clinical services. Amongst others, such networks encompass cancer, coronary heart disease, diabetes, renal transplantation, and palliative care (Woods, 2001). The evidence suggests that most managed clinical networks have been successful in gaining multi-professional agreement in terms of service priorities and have enabled the development of mechanisms to drive forward new forms of service delivery such as the creation of protocols and patient pathways, increased specialisation at local level, audit and implementation of quality standards and work plans for service redesign (Livingston and Woods, 2003). However, the actual degree of service change has remained limited as isolate and territorial behaviour (enclaved but within each hospital) by clinicians have reduced loyalty to the networks.

Since managed clinical networks in Scotland have been both centrally mandated and pro-actively managed they are very much at the hierarchical end of the network continuum. Indeed, the organisational process appears to be far more controlled and prescriptive, thus easily distinguished from professional clinical networks that act as enclave groups and which need a management style based on negotiation (Ferlie and Pettigrew, 1996). That fact that managed clinical networks are centrally mandated may be a problem given the compelling evidence from many studies of health and social care partnerships that suggest such top-down measures lead to local opposition and sub-optimal outcomes (Hudson, 2002). This suggests that effective management of, and within, clinical networks may rely on the contribution of local peer-respected champions, a factor that may bring into question both the long-term sustainability and efficacy of the networks themselves.

In the case of the Netherlands the Government-led pilot programme for the creation of networks in geriatric care, it was the fragmented and complex nature of secondary care for older people which caused the Dutch government in 1995 to state in a White Paper that networks in geriatrics should be established in all 27 health care regions in the country (Nies *et al.*, 2003). According to the White Paper, geriatric wards had to be integrated into a network with other hospitals, nursing homes, residential homes, home care organisations, general practitioners and community mental health care organisations in order to organise optimum care pathways. The proportion of incorrect referrals had to be reduced, and communication and mutual adjustment of services improved. Four pilot networks in specialised care for older people were initiated by the national government.

These pilots ran from 1996 to 1999 and were externally evaluated (Gerritsen *et al.*, 2001). According to Nies *et al.* (2003), although it was quite easy for network members to reach consensus on mission, objectives and key local priorities, when it came to the implementation of new structures, projects or innovative services, decisions would be postponed or only taken forward following significant delay. Two main barriers were apparent: first, networks that started with a very broad definition of their target group found it difficult to exercise effective decision-making; and second, that professional members had often different priorities which did not sit easily together. Compatibility of interests appeared to determine network productivity and social ties were generally weak due to the tension between autonomy and dependency. When experimental funding ended, it was perhaps not surprising that only a few structures and activities survived that were directly related to the network (Nies *et al.*, 2003).

This Dutch experiment represent one of the few detailed evaluations of clinical networks to have been undertaken, revealing how centrally defined objectives were hard to implement where no single organisation 'owned' the network. The fact that the research revealed sub-networks similar to Mintzberg's (1983) 'adhocracies', where ties were stronger and collaboration more operational, provides a key lesson to network functionality; that is imposed or mandated forms of network in health care which develop strong regulation do not sit well with clinicians and medical professionals whole ties are primarily enclaved. This is a conclusion that mirrors the early experience with managed clinical networks in Scotland.

Such observations have lead some observers to conclude that networks should become 'formalised' by contract to ensure effective integration (Andersson and Karlberg, 2000). According to Nies *et al.* (2003), 'it seems to be wise to define this as a core principle of care networks in order to improve decision-making and to come to actual provision of integrated forms of care' a view shared by Woods (2001) and Gröne and Garcia-Barbero (2002). However, as will be explained in the next section, developing networks based on contracts appears not to have had any greater advantage in terms of care integration. Indeed, it would seem that a call for a move towards contracts and markets as a way of facilitating networks is counter-intuitive to the development of collaboration between providers.

Procurement networks in health care

The system-wide integration of clinical care between hospitals through contractually-based networks of procurement has been a major trend in the United States where 'integrated healthcare networks' attempt to provide all elements of the care continuum from health insurance, outpatient and inpatient services to long-term care maintenance. Among the presumed benefits are better quality of care, enhanced accessibility, strengthened customer relationships, more effective operations, and reduced unit costs (see Coddington *et al.*, 1994; Conrad and Shortell, 1996). Moreover, it is assumed that such integrated healthcare delivery systems will demonstrate to consumers advantages of comprehensive benefits over competitors (Wan *et al.*, 2001).

The development of integrated healthcare networks in the United States has fundamentally different motives to the clinical network model. Managers of such networks still design services to maximize effectiveness, efficiency and quality (Luke and Begun, 1988; Scott W, 1993) but the strategic impetus comes from a range of organisational strategies as follows (Lin and Wan, 1999):

- enlarging the network size (corporate strategy);
- venturing into non-hospital provision (business strategy);
- integrating information systems and financial arrangements for co-operative purchases (functional strategy); and
- integrating clinical inputs through case management (functional strategy).

However, the literature and research on contractual networks suggests that only a 'moderate' level of integration can be achieved, particularly in the area of organisational culture manifest in low physician-system integration. Moreover, the attempt to enhance benefits to patients by providing a 'continuum of care' has been effort potentially not compensated by the additional costs involved in integrating services. This can be seen in the case of the Henry Ford Integrated Healthcare System (Box 11.2) that was rated third in a list of America's most integrated healthcare networks in 1999 yet which was losing money and having to make staff cuts (Bellandi, 1999).

Research into networks in the United States by Bazzoli *et al.* (1999, 2000) emphasises this point by showing how the broader the scope of activity within a procurement-based network, the harder it was to centralise management arrangements (and make a profit). They found that hospitals in single ownership models, such as the managed care system of Kaiser Permanente, had both a better financial performance and better health outcomes than those based on contractual networks. Moreover, in provider networks, the more centralised hospital networks appeared to perform better than looser affiliations. However, there was also evidence to suggest that centralised networks were often 'over bureaucratic' and inhibited innovation leading to the conclusion that moderately centralised systems performed best.

Box 11.2 Henry Ford integrated Healthcare System

The Henry Ford Integrated Healthcare Network integrates health care coverage through external contractual partnerships. The managed care plan that it offers provides an integrated set of hospice programmes and an ambulatory care network at more than 70 sites. It has a centralized design that includes:

- centralised decision-making between provider organisations;
- care integration packages;
- integrated information technology; and
- integrated purchasing.

The system was ranked as the third most integrated system in the United States in 1999, yet it is in considerable financial difficulties, showing a net 'loss' of $43.8m in 1998 compared to a net gain of $38m in 1997. The Henry Ford System cut its workforce by 425 employees in 1999. The Henry Ford System demonstrates a 'best effort' in the United States of providing an integrated system of care committed to 'a continuum of care' co-ordinated through case management and disease management programmes. However, the structural and operational characteristics of the system appear to be not economically efficient or profitable.

The evidence from the United States may suggest that a mixed model of direct ownership for 'core' services with a network of independent and competing hospital affiliates can work best. However, it is important to remember that the term 'network' in the United States is as much about the insurer's ability to enable choice and coverage within a plan as about developing shared care or common standards. Analyses of hospital networks in the United States, in which shared service arrangements exist between them, reveals a process that is as much associated with price-fixing arrangements as with generating efficiencies or sharing risk (Liebenhuft, 1996).

In publicly provided health systems, it has been argued that networks should become 'formalised' by contract to ensure more effective integration of professional and clinical activities (Andersson and Karlberg, 2000; Woods, 2001; Gröne and Garcia-Barbero, 2002; Nies *et al.*, 2003). This is sometimes known as care pathway commissioning and has been under active consideration in some UK PCTs and has been piloted by some county councils in Sweden through a 'Chains of Care' initiative (Ahgren, 2001, 2003). The theoretical advantage is that payment in the system is made for 'collective' health care efforts. Providers, therefore, would be incentivised to work within a provider 'network' to reduce duplication and share services and risk. Health care agreements, therefore, could become comprehensive yet operate across a range of independent agencies. Such a model is similar to the core principles of a Kaiser Permanente-type managed care system. Moves in Sweden to develop such purchaser–provider network models have been influenced by IKEA and its integration of sub-contractors into the value chain (Ahgren, 2003).

Chains of Care, developed in Sweden in the late 1990s, are seen as an important counterbalance to the ever-increasing fragmentation of Swedish health care (Ahgren, 2001). Like managed clinical networks in Scotland, they are seen as a cornerstone for future health care delivery and have been supported by almost every Swedish county council. National studies of the Chain of Care approach shows that they remain primarily based on chronic illnesses such as diabetes, dementia and rheumatism rather than examining general health care or wider health and social care needs (Ahgren, 2003). The main purpose of the approach to date has been to promote evidence-based medicine and clinical guidelines. Emphasis has also been given to the redistribution of medical workers between providers in the health care system. The number of Chains of Care developed has varied by county council in Sweden, though the largest county council (1.5 million inhabitants and 40,000 employed health care staff) has developed more than fifty Chains of Care (Ahgren, 2003).

Despite the support that most professionals within these Chains of Care have shown to overall goals and plans, development work within the network has, in reality, been a low priority in most areas. Indeed, no significant changes to clinical services have resulted. Key obstacles to network development have included the existing departmentalisation of responsibilities between medical professions and resistance from some managers due to fears of changes to their working routines (Sjöberg, 1999). Health care managers have found cross-agency and cross-boundary working problematic, particularly where network goals challenge the existing power structures yet provide weak incentives for compliance or uptake. Overall, managing the balance between corporate governance and local autonomy remains the biggest challenge faced (Ahgren, 2003).

Managed care networks

In much of the literature on health care networks, there appears to be an explicit assumption (or common hypothesis) that the creation of a fully integrated network is an end point to be reached in order to establish more durable and long-term relationships between organisations. The greater the move to a 'hierarchical' network, it is argued, the better the level of integration and thus attainment of the goals for integration. The fully integrated model is akin to 'network' organisations such as Kaiser Permanente (Robinson and Steiner, 1998; Kodner, 1999) and has a series of key characteristics:

- a population defined by enrolment;
- contractual responsibility for a defined package of comprehensive health and social care services;
- financing on the basis of pooling multiple funding streams, with or without fixed annual or monthly payments, independent of service volume (capitation) but including financial responsibility for all care costs;

- a 'closed' network (a selected group of contracted and/or salaried providers);
- emphasis on primary care and non-institutional (extramural) services;
- use of micro-management techniques to ensure appropriate quality of care and to control costs (utilisation review, disease management); and
- multi-disciplinary professional teams working across the network with joint clinical responsibility for outcomes.

Examples of the fully integrated, or managed, network include three Social Health Maintenance Organisations – federally funded demonstration projects that combine both acute and long-term care into a single care-managed delivery system (Leutz *et al.*, 1985; Robinson and Steiner, 1998). Such programmes have generally targeted elderly Medicare patients on the predication that integration will deliver more appropriate care and lower costs. The Social HMO models were subject to a three-year evaluation (1986–89) and the results were complex and to some extent contradictory (Kane *et al.*, 1997; Zimmerman *et al.*, 1998). The overall findings, however, suggested that the Social HMO network model fell short of expectations. Whilst the approach demonstrated the feasibility of combining responsibilities for finance and delivery of health and social care within a single organisational network, care management strategies *within* the network failed to produce clinical integration, better cost-effectiveness or significant changes to working practices. The Social HMOs have since attempted to employ protocols and integrated care pathways to improve integrated management mechanisms (Kodner and Kyriacou, 2000).

Similar managed care networks for older people's care have been established around the world and include:

- the Comprehensive Home Option of Integrated Care for the Elderly (CHOICE) in Edmonton, Canada (Pinelli Beauline Associated Ltd, 1998);
- the Program of All Inclusive Care for the Elderly (PACE) projects in the United States (Branch *et al.*, 1995; Eng *et al.*, 1997; Kodner and Kyriacou, 2000);
- a randomised controlled trial of integrated social and medical care and case management in Northern Italy (Bernabei *et al.*, 1998);
- an integrated service delivery network for the frail elderly in Montreal (Bergman *et al.*, 1997); and
- PRISMA, a model for integrated service delivery for frail older people in Canada (Hébert *et al.*, 2003).

Definitive evidence on the effectiveness and efficiency of these network models is lacking but the claimed beneficial impacts includes: reductions in number and duration of short-term hospitalisations; falls in the number of admissions to long-term institutions; decreased costs of services; and less functional decline in older people living in the community. However, success in and roll-out of these models have been hampered by the unwillingness of clinicians to work within managed models. Moreover, it is suggested that such models appear to work best only with small subsets of patients that have unstable and functional conditions and who frequently interact with health and social care systems; even here they do not necessarily perform any better than hierarchies or 'looser' networks unless there is effective management *within* the network.

Health care networks within the neo-Durkheimian taxonomy

This examination of networks in health care has revealed a mixture of individualistic, enclave and hierarchical types, with most usually being a hybrid across the general dimensions, and also subject to dynamic changes (Figure 11.2). *Informational* networks, for example, are often driven by their members without being externally mandated and are therefore relatively weakly regulated. However, whilst some appear to work primarily as

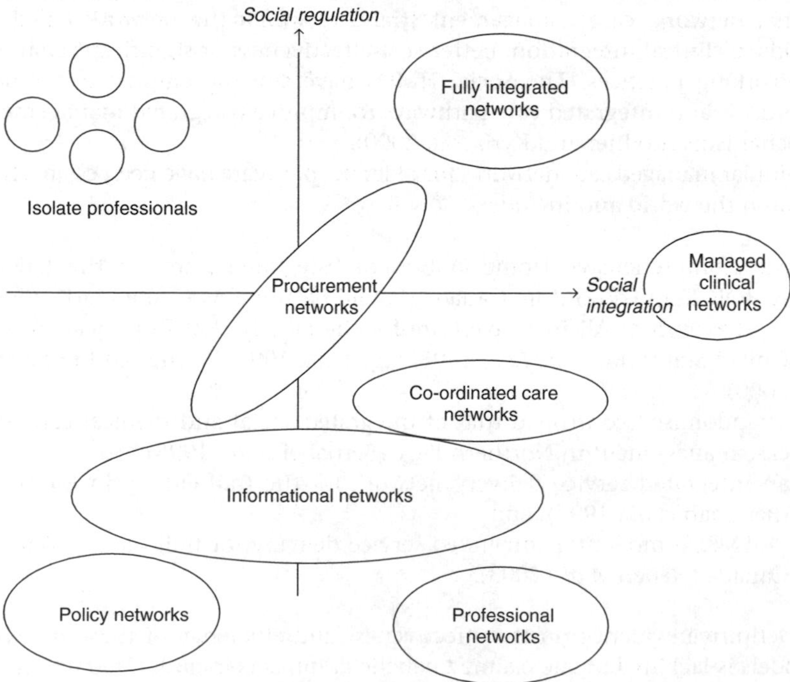

Figure 11.2 A typology of network forms in health care.

'enclave' forms of professional associations, others require some form of 'neutral' co-ordination by an 'individualistic' broker and/or small bureaucratic core to facilitate joint learning. For example, in the Belgian–Dutch Clinical Pathway example, internal regulation was sustained through the proactive co-ordination of the network by a university department that 'sold' the network to hospitals and their clinicians (Sermeus *et al.*, 2001). In Tanriverdi and Venkataraman's (1999) study of telemedicine and video-conferencing amongst Boston health care professionals, the commitment of members was primarily based on 'enclave-like' peer-based networks of colleagues.

The various forms of *co-ordinated* and *managed* networks, however, tend to contain a greater administrative 'core' and are thus primarily 'individualistic' and/or 'hierarchical' in nature. Within this category of networks lie a range of hybrid models that might place, for example, a simple hub and spoke network with little regulatory and social ties in the 'individualistic' category through to managed clinical networks that appear to be far more 'hierarchical' in design and often centrally mandated. Bate and Robert (2002) argue that cancer care networks in the English NHS have become, despite ministerial rhetoric to the contrary, essentially hierarchical network structures which have weakened their abilities to support the kinds of enclaved 'communities in practice' that are required to develop innovations and lead change. The fact that hierarchical networks in health care are characterised by professional enclaves *within* them is a major issue since it is clear that hierarchical models, despite being 'assumed' by many writers to be superior for integration, are potentially over-bureaucratic to the detriment of professional involvement.

Procurement networks follow the same dimensions as co-ordinated care networks, and are essentially a hybrid of hierarchical and individualistic forms. They are individualistic in the sense that they tend to be innovative and flexible in character, with membership being fluid as health insurance companies and/or providers exchange one strategic alliance for another over time. However, they are clearly also hierarchical in nature since the tight design of contracts and the use of financial incentives encourage tight vertical integration of care pathways.

Strengths and weaknesses of the different health care networks

As the neo-Durkheimian theory of networks might predict, none of these health care network 'types' appear to provide the 'best' solution. The less regulated 'enclave' type networks appear more appropriate where voluntary participation and high commitment from individual professionals and/or organisations are required, but such approaches are naturally difficult to 'manage' towards some form of new and specific approach to care delivery. Where controlled integration of a well-defined set of services is necessary, perhaps through the use of managed care pathways, then hierarchical networks might be more appropriate. Yet the evidence suggests such networks have generally been poor in gaining commitment from professionals since they restrict their freedom to practice. Hence, whilst Kodner and Kyriacou (2000) suggest that the existence of a single, accountable, organisational centre allows for the optimum impact on health care network integration, it is also clear that such centralisation of accountability and power within a hierarchical network is not of itself sufficient to ensure network efficiency. If the solution might then be to incentivise professional involvement in networks through contractual mechanisms, then individualistic approaches might appear a possible solution since they support the retention of creativity and motivation via incentives. However, the evidence from the health care literature suggests such mechanisms remain sub-optimal, especially as the number of partners within such networks expands.

The evidence on health care networks points to support for the neo-Durkheimian theory of the use of 'hybrid' network models in which the relative performance and internal dilemmas of each network type are to some degree 'traded off' and adapted over time. Hence, whilst the literature suggests that competing interests can co-exist in a network as long as core interests of all parties are catered for, managerial 'gaming' (for example, by large hospitals) to secure greater network centrality and control needs to be avoided as much as the potential tendency of individual clinicians to move to a more isolated and/or enclave form following their experiences of over-regulation (6 and Peck, 2004).

Managing and leading networks in health care: lessons from the evidence

Reflecting the general theory of networks developed in Chapter 1, exercising leadership and management across health care organisations and/or individual professionals brings special challenges because a manager can rarely exercise direct authority. Nevertheless, it is clear that network management in health care requires the attainment of a *tertius* position from which to wield power to effect change. Typically, this would need managers to control contracts, resources and/or knowledge (in the case of individualistic networks) and/or have direct powers of co-ordination and direction in more managed or hierarchical networks. In practice, however, the highly centralised managerial approach is rarely workable since health care networks generally comprise within them enclave-like sub-networks of professionals wishing to retain personal autonomy and clinical freedoms. Finding a central position through which to wield management power in health care networks is thus problematic, as they are often characterised by structural, cultural and professional inertia. The ability to negotiate tasks in an inclusive fashion across potentially competing professions is therefore important to engendering commitment and to stabilising network membership.

Such relationship-building tasks have often been regarded as a special feature of certain sorts of networks, yet the experience in health care networks suggests that the managerial tools required to help integrate care are broadly similar, regardless of type. Hence, all health care networks require strategies that enable cohesion, such as the clear definition of roles, goals and functions; the use of information technology to improve communication and to share intelligence; and the important role of boundary-spanners in co-ordinating inter-organisational relationships. In health care networks, the role of the network manager as a 'boundary spanner' is clearly crucial for proactive tie-building and educational roles. Hence, the ability to invest in specific network management and managers is central to their success. Such conclusions tend to support the overall thesis developed in this book that the tools of managing networks are not ostensibly different from those required to managing organisations.

One of the clearest messages emerging from the evidence on health care networks is the need to manage the balance between managerial and professional leadership. Tight regulation through imposed hierarchical networks, for example, risks disharmony and demotivation amongst members (as seen in the cases of managed clinical networks reviewed above). Consequently, a key lesson is the ability to actively engage charismatic professionals in network leadership, since their presence will better appeal to their peers. Sheaff *et al.* (2004), for example, found that professional self-regulation was a far stronger influence on the capability of English PCTs to develop clinical governance arrangements than top-down managerial compliance. However, if networks remain loosely regulated there is a greater risk of 'professional capture'. For example, managerial 'gaming' by large hospitals to secure their own network centrality has been a key feature of corporate strategies in the United States and Australia, whilst a simulation of cancer networks in England revealed the likelihood that they may create a 'provider cabal' forcing funders to conform to the wishes of the acute hospitals' version of network requirements (Office for Public Management, 2002).

There is thus a significant degree of managerial skill required in crafting effective health care networks since they need to be robust enough to endure, legitimate enough to become accepted, yet flexible enough to tackle the inherent weakness of each network type. Cultivating hybrid forms that allow some element of all three active types of network may be the only solution. For example, any kind of managed clinical network potentially needs to be combined with the use of professional incentives on an ongoing basis, incentives that might include both financial (contractual) rewards but also some degree of professional influence and authority over the network design itself. Providing the right incentives to network members, such that they agree to a collective system of regulation and governance, may be the solution to closing the apparent 'governance gap' in health care networks between managers and professional organisations and individuals.

Part IV

12 Comparisons and Conclusions

A theory of inter-organisational networks – one that purports to explain which collaborations form, when and why and with what kind of effects upon performance – should, like any satisfactory theory, strike a reasonable trade-off between the demands of parsimony, causality, generality and accuracy (Przeworski and Teune, 1970; Heckathorn, 1984). The trade-offs between these demands have to be driven by the nature of the problem to be addressed. Typically, the more general the problem, the more appropriate it is to place a premium upon generality, even at the expense of detailed accuracy (in the sense of being able to explain the detail of particular phenomena). The problem of understanding inter-organisational relations has been shown in the preceding chapters to be very general and thus to require a broad theoretical solution. A central weakness of most of the standard theories in this area – those that can distinguish only hierarchies and markets, such as Williamson's (1985), or hierarchies, markets and 'networks' – is precisely that they are insufficiently general. Moreover, because the present theory syntheses insights from these earlier theories, it seeks greater generality; a modest loss of control over details of particular cases may be an acceptable price to pay for such generality in a theory of a phenomenon that is both widespread and varied.

The relationship between causality and the three other virtues of good theories outlined above is more complex. A theory ought to be able to capture the main lines of causality, where that causality is complex, either because there are very important intermediate variables or because some of the causal processes are endogenous and involve feedback effects (or, indeed, both). In these circumstances, then, if generality is to be sustained, then parsimony may have to be sacrificed, unless the causal model can be at least partially reduced in some way to a simple underlying model.

Each of the standard theories – transaction cost, resource-based, personalistic and others – lacks generality, as we have argued in earlier chapters. To be fair, some do achieve parsimony, albeit at what might be said to be too high a price in terms of loss of accuracy, even in their own particular domains.

Yet others – such as the actor-network tradition – lack clear causality whilst those in the Weberian tradition lack clear typology which suggests that they can be confident of neither generality nor accuracy.

The theory we have offered is general, as we have tried to show both in the theoretical chapters and in particular in the empirical case study chapters, in that it can address phenomena in the public and the private sectors, at the micro and at the macro level, and in fields that exhibit very different cost and information conditions. The underlying causal model of the theory is clear, we believe, for it is based on a relationship between fundamental explanatory institutional variables and intermediate variables of transaction cost and information conditions, working through the two basic forces of positive and negative feedback in four distinct institutional syndromes.

Although Table 4.7 is certainly complicated, parsimony is achieved at the underlying level through the four institutional forms generated by the intersection of the two fundamental dimensions of social regulation and social integration. A criticism of the present theory could be that its very typological approach of recognising multiple institutional forms of organisation and therefore slightly distinct applications of the underlying feedback processes constitutes a loss of parsimony. Yet it is hard to feel the barb on this hook because a theory that aspires to generality will, by definition, require an explanation of diversity; if this can be achieved with the underpinning parsimony of just two dimensions of institutionalisation and deinstitutionalisation then this must surely be a virtue not a weakness.

It is sometimes argued that a fifth important virtue of a theory is determinacy (King *et al.* 1994); that is, the capacity of a theory to yield more or less unique predictions about the values of the dependent variables once the values of the explanatory factors are known. Certainly, theories such as conventional transaction cost theory and some types of rational choice theory exhibit this virtue (Hay, 2004). However, determinacy can be achieved at the price of causality if the causal process that produces such unique predictions is too mechanistic. Where there are reasons to believe that causality is objectively indeterminate because – for example – the magnitude or the direction of the feedback effects cannot be predicted in advance, then determinacy can appropriately be sacrificed for causality. Our argument is that this is indeed the case in the processes by which network forms are institutionalised and deinstitutionalised, and that the case studies have shown this process at work. The account given of 'surprises' (see Figure 4.5) is an important part of the theory. In biotechnology, for example, the initially rather individualistic structure of networks that seemed to be well captured by personalistic theories gave way, by the very mechanism of ever more individualistic brokering, to greater density that eventually yielded enclaving and hierarchisation. Hierarchy was also brought in more strongly by negative feedback, in this case by the efforts of the big pharmaceutical and agronomy firms to retain market share and control.

In summary, then, the present theory seems to make a reasonable trade-off between the fundamental virtues of theory which inevitably stand in some tension with each other.

Comparing the case studies

The four case studies presented in the previous four chapters provide an illustration of the power of the theory, even within the limitations of a study conducted by reanalysing published literature from studies undertaken originally for other purposes. Together, they show the full range of the static and the dynamic features of the theory at work in predicting and explaining network forms.

We can begin by considering the two dependent variables of network form and performance by examining differences between the four fields of organisations under consideration. Figure 12.1 displays the key differences, in each case showing the hybridity of the networks between the divergent institutional forms using ellipses spanning the relevant quadrants. This

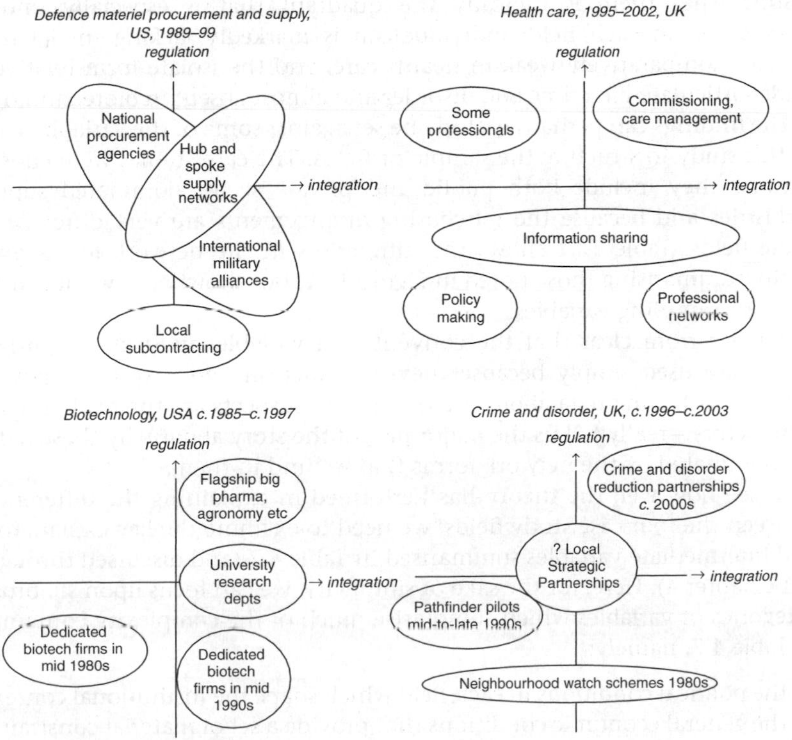

Figure 12.1 Institutional forms of networks in the four case study fields.

Table 12.1 Differences in institutional forms by sector and by purchasing arrangement

	Public sector provision	**Private sector provision**
Procurement monopsony	*Health care* Hierarchical purchasing from hierarchical suppliers; individualism largely at the periphery	*Defence materiel* Isolate purchasing from hierarchical and enclaved suppliers; individualism at the periphery only
Procurement from multiple purchasers	*Crime and disorder* Hierarchical purchasing from hierarchical, enclaved, but decreasingly individualistic suppliers	*Biotechnology* Hierarchical purchasing from enclaved and still some individualistic suppliers

figure summarises the main findings of the case study chapters about the forms of the various kinds of networks in these fields. It is clear that what distinguishes them is typically the quadrant that is especially under-represented in each field; individualism is markedly lacking in defence, enclave comparatively weak in health care, and the isolate form relatively under-articulated in crime and disorder and almost absent in biotechnology.

The findings can perhaps usefully be set against some of the variables used in this study to structure the sample of fields. The case studies were chosen because they include both public and private sector dominated supply industries and because the purchasing arrangements are very different in these fields. Table 12.1 shows the differences in the network forms once again, summarising those noted in Figure 12.1, but showing how they differ by these sampling variables.

It is far from clear that the conventional variables used in sampling – which are used simply because they are practical and easy to deploy in advance of having data about the things one suspects are the really important factors – really tell us the major part of the story about why these fields are dominated by the network forms that we find in them.

To see how well the theory has performed in explaining the differences between the four case study fields, we need to examine the key explanatory and intermediate variables summarised in Table 4.7 (and discussed throughout Chapter 4). Here, for the sake of simplicity, we can focus upon six broad categories of variables which summarise much of the complexity contained in Table 4.7, namely:

- the political conditions in each field which shape the institutional context;
- the general economic conditions that provide a set of material constraints (and which may also in some cases become institutionalised) governing the task environment;

- the transaction cost conditions;
- the information conditions;
- the prior organisational culture that dominates each field; and
- the role played by individuals.

Table 12.2 summarises the key differences between the fields that have been discussed in the case studies using these six key variables.

Unlike the economistic theories (such as transaction cost approaches) or internally oriented theories (such as the resource based views and the personalistic accounts), neo-Durkheimian institutional theory recognises the importance of political factors in shaping network forms. In defence procurement, political factors play a foreground role and the networks show the signs of active – and even case-by-case – shaping by government, while in biotechnology the political factors took the form of the background institutions that created the field in which the industry could develop. However, the relative absence of specific governmental interventions to shape particular networks certainly does not mean that, in biotechnology for instance, the political factors were unimportant; indeed, it could be argued that the relaxed stance of the antitrust authorities towards the emerging practices of collaboration in the industry was absolutely critical to its peculiar path of development. It is perhaps hardly surprising, but by no means trivial, that the hands-off approach taken in biotechnology allowed a more robust variety of less socially regulated forms to flourish.

We can turn next to the second sort of variable highlighted in Table 12.2, transaction cost conditions. This represents a key intermediate variable, shaped by underlying institutions of both political and economic conditions. In the defence procurement case, the high transaction costs facing governments in working together to procure material are in large part politically shaped. By contrast, it would be difficult to argue that political considerations alone are responsible for raising the costs of responding to tenders in ways that tend to reinforce the flagship and flotilla structure of the defence supply industry, for the complexity, duration and technical structure of the tasks probably require either very high levels of trust in suppliers or else extremely detailed specifications. However, on both the procurement and the supply side, the high transaction costs show a tendency to push the form of the networks into the highly socially regulated quadrant. The same phenomenon can be observed in the field of crime and disorder, where the problematic inter-agency relations created concerns about voluntary co-ordination that were thought to call for statutory duties, the effect of the solution used has again been to increase the hierarchical element in the mix of network forms. By contrast, the biotechnology field exhibits falling transaction costs, because of both the relaxation of the application of antitrust law to networks in the industry and the standardisation of the terms of technology in-licensing; correspondingly, as we should expect,

Table 12.2 Forces shaping networks – four industries compared

	Political commitments	Economic conditions	Transaction cost conditions	Information conditions – explicit information used in production	Information conditions – tacit, informal or ill-structured information e.g. about environment	Prior-to-network organisational culture of constituent organisations	Leadership, role of boundary spanners, individual brokers	Dominant network form(s)	Performance success by technical (not political) criteria
Defence procurement 1990s	Managing downsizing of Industry for 'peace dividend'; Preservation of national autonomy; EU states apparently free-riding on United States	General economic boom	High costs of separate procurement	Costly procurement specifications, some aspects of which have the status of state secrets	State secret information about other states strategies States access to commercially confidential information about suppliers	Secretive, mutually distrustful	Limited role for individual diplomats, military attachés etc	Isolate	Poor
Defence supply 1990s	Preservation of national R&D and production capacity Avoidance of concentrations of job losses	Falling state demand in west, rising in rest of world	High costs of bidding	Restricted information, full property rights in information	Difficult, ephemeral information about emerging markets in non-Western countries; Within group resources of trustworthiness with some proprietary information	Traditionally engineering dominated subcontracting sector; increasingly finance-driven prime contractor sector	No evidence of major role in negotiating networks, but likely to be significant in subcontract or to prime ties	Hierarchy/ enclave	Low productivity; serves interests of prime contractors

Biotechnology US, 1980s–1990s	Some regional policy initiatives Relaxation of US anti-trust policy	Falling capital costs of R&D equipment	Standardisation of technology in-licensing contract forms	Restricted Information, full property rights in information	Reputations of individual scientists	Science-led, collegiate, collaborative on published Work. Individualistic in research management	Key role of individual scientists and some venture capital incubators in periods when VCs are active	Individualistic becoming hierarchical and enclaved	Reasonably good, ford, an industry with long lead times from investment to profit
Crime and disorder, UK, 1990s–2000s	Ensuring national coverage; geographically bounded crime	None especially relevant	Professional, partly legally based concerns about sharing restricted and client confidential information	Some client confidential information	Still poorly structured and linked intelligence; opacity of crime statistics	Strongly mutually enclaved police and local authority sectors	Importance of individual local activists esp. in linking statutory with voluntary and community services	Enclaved becoming hierarchical	Mixed
Health care information sharing late 1990s–2000s	Better sharing best practice	UK: increasing state regulation of NHS	Entrenched local professionally defended practices	Restricted information, no property rights	Slow development of evidence base for best practice	Professionally dominated	Some evidence of critical role for dedicated network brokers	Individualistic enclaved	Modest
Health co-ordinated care late 1990s–2000s	Improved flow of patients through care pathways UK: Avoid hospital closures esp. rural Scotland, smaller English towns UK, some EU states: concerns about quality of care	UK: increasing state spending on NHS US: importance diversification on and search for specialisation niches	Specification and negotiation of care pathways, HRGs etc	Restricted information, some client confidential information	Limited mutual knowledge of other providers' exact patient pathways	Professionally dominate		Hierarchical /enclaved	

Continued

Table 12.2 Continued

	Political commitments	**Economic conditions**	**Transaction cost conditions**	**Information conditions – explicit information used in production**	**Information conditions – tacit, informal or ill-structured information e.g. about environment**	**Prior-to-network organisational culture of constituent organisations**	**Leadership, role of boundary spanners, individual brokers**	**Dominant network form(s)**	**Performance success by technical (not political) criteria**
Health care procurement late 1990s–2000s	US, some EU states: cost control	US: imperative to grow market share and diversify in mature market by vertical integration into supply	Difficulties in estimating returns in markets where professional control of production makes return hard to control	Restricted proprietary cost information, some client confidential information		US: Increasingly finance-driven health insurance, vs still professional dominated supply side		Individualistic becoming hierarchical	Limited improvements in productivity or cost control
Health managed care, late 1990s–2000s	US, some EU states: cost control Scotland: to preserve some services England: After 2004, market-driven approach			Restricted information, some client confidential information		US: Increasingly finance-driven health insurance, vs still professional dominated supply side		Hierarchical	Poor to modest

this leaves greater scope for the weakly socially regulated forms of individualism and enclave.

Nevertheless, transaction cost considerations alone are not sufficient to determine the network forms. Not only do differences in transaction cost conditions fail to distinguish between the columns of the basic matrix, there are clear differences within the high transaction cost group of cases. When we turn to the information conditions, it becomes possible to see why this might be. For the need to work with confidential information about clients tends to express itself in an imperative to define the circle of agencies that might be entitled to receive that information and the terms on which they might receive and use it. There are limits to the extent that this can be done hierarchically, although data protection regulation and the adoption of protocols are an important part of the story (and, indeed, fields such as health care which make heavy use of confidential and sensitive patient information have a more marked tendency to this form than do the others). Confidentiality is not the only respect in which access to information can be restricted. Where information of certain types can be kept proprietary, there are good reasons why individuals or organisations will seek to control access to that information in order to capture for themselves the rents to be earned from its exploitation which would – in the absence of stronger social regulation and social integration – allow space for more individualistic network forms. The in-licensing of proprietary knowledge in the biotechnology field is a good example of the ways in which, in that absence, individualistic structures can flourish, at least until their own individualistic processes of networking gradually undermine them by producing greater density and thus enhanced social integration.

In each of these fields, informal or ill-structured information and tacit knowledge are important in shaping the scope for particular institutional forms of networks to emerge. An ideally informationally equipped organisation would possess excellent intelligence about other organisations in its field and their capabilities and strategies, about the clients or target groups, and about the leading edge of techniques and practices. In the absence of such excellent information, an organisation will have to look for proxies for these assets. In biotechnology, the reputations of individual scientists associated with dedicated biotechnology firms serve as such a proxy. In some fields, where there is sufficient prior social integration provided, for example, by the professional networks that dominate the field, some of the required types of information can be rendered public so that the costs of wresting it from proprietary sources are significantly reduced. This is the case, albeit patchily, in field of medicine and other health care related industries, where bodies of evidence about best practice are being developed and made readily available to all in the industry at lower costs through professional and quasi-governmental structures (e.g. the arms-length National Institute for Healthcare and Clinical Excellence (NIHCE) in the United Kingdom). Those professional structures tend to make information available principally to those organisations which can show accreditation of the professionals within them or some other organisational status that show the same function; in effect, they must show that they fall within the boundaries of social integration of the organisational field. This tends to reinforce, of course, either hierarchical or enclaved forms, with the relative weighting between them generally being settled by other factors.

These factors are clearly linked to, and likely to co-vary to some extent with, the prior culture of the industry or organisational field. Professionalisation, whether led by research science or applied medical practice, or dominated by policing, brings a measure of social integration through the system of individual accreditation and reputation management. In the presence of other factors, professionalisation can also reinforce social regulation too. Indeed, each of the fields examined shows tendencies over the period of the studies considered for hierarchical elements in the mix to be reinforced.

The literature reviewed in the last four chapters suggests that the role of individuals is, typically, a dependent rather than an independent variable. Broadly, Table 12.2 shows, as the argument in Chapter 7 predicted, that the style of leadership reflects the institutionally created scope for such leadership. That is to say, whereas transaction cost and information conditions are important independent variables that can alter the nature of the institutional form and the quality of performance, leadership and brokerage styles are fairly well predicted by these other factors (so that, to a large extent, these styles depend upon the configuration created by the independent influences). Thus, for example, in the highly socially regulated field of defence, the roles played by individuals have attracted rather limited attention from scholars trying to explain the character of the networks. On the other hand, most of the writings about the biotechnology industry have focused on the role played by 'star' scientists in spinning off companies around the molecules they discover, in exploiting their own and others' reputations and in brokering deals up and down the supply chain.

The theory set out in Chapter 4 stresses the central importance of feedback effects and path dependence. One cannot explain the forms that inter-organisational networks take without looking at the prior institutional character of the field, including the earlier institutional forms of the networks within it. The theory stresses two causal mechanisms and the case studies bear these out well. First, the prior weighting of institutional forms among, for example, particular groups in an organisational field is often important; professionalisation of a field in an enclaved manner tends to reinforce itself through positive feedback in ways that might reinforce enclaving in the networks of such organisations. Second, the distinct institutional forms have the potential to unleash processes of negative feedback in ways that can sometimes undermine the initial institutional form of the network; this is clearest in the case of biotechnology, where the very processes of instrumental individualistic networking worked over time within a relatively defined and bounded industry to produce greater density within and also between the distinct geographical clusters in ways that began to articulate enclaved elements in the mix. In the case of crime and disorder, the negative feedback came from outside the field when central government found itself frustrated by the unpredictable quality of local organisation and attempted to introduce greater social regulation through statutory duties.

Networks in different fields appear to show very different qualities of performance. As Table 12.2 makes clear, there is no particular correlation between the efforts made to introduce greater social regulation and social integration in each of the fields and improved performance in every aspect of the work undertaken. As we should expect, the institutional form of the networks is by no means sufficient to explain *absolute* patterns of performance. In biotechnology, the collapse in interest by venture capital finance in the early 1990s – and again in the wake of the end of the dot com boom in the early 2000s – hugely affected performance. Similarly, the slump in Western governmental demand for defence material in the 1990s represented a major downturn in the industry. In good times, impressive performance is relatively easy for any institutional form.

However, the case studies do suggest that differences in *relative* performance have a good deal to do with the institutional form of the networks. In defence, the core–periphery structure of the field's networks seems to have enabled many of the core capacities of the industry to be retained through the years of drought in the 1990s (partially by the involvement of subcontractors in non-defence production). The rather flexible and individualistic structure of the biotechnology networks in the late 1980s and early 1990s seems to have served well the goals of good performance in innovation and R&D, even though it may not have served so well in supporting the scaling up required when demand from big pharmaceutical and agronomy firms began to revive. In health care, the most strongly hierarchical networks in the United States appear not to have performed particularly well, as measured by productive efficiency. By and large, and controlling for industry conditions, hierarchical institutional forms appear to have done for these organisations what the theory of types of failure set out in Chapter 4 predicts that they would; they provide stability, rules, some security of demand for labour or services from subcontractors, but also the tendency to overregulation and less rapid response to changing conditions. Obviously, these latter characteristics can limit performance. Conversely, individualistic solutions in biotechnology may be rather effective in motivating ambitious and entrepreneurial scientists and entrepreneurs, but are less effective in scaling up.

A defence against criticisms

This book has offered a theory of inter-organisational relations. The argument avoids celebrating networks, in the manner of much writing of the

1990s, because it suggests that the fundamental forces shaping networks are the same as those shaping all social organisation (both internally as well as externally). Moreover, we have emphasised the ways in which institutional types of network will fail, as well as the ways in which they can be expected to enhance performance.

Of course, a modest review of literature on four industries spanning a relatively short period of time is not sufficient to establish the theory. Much empirical work remains to be done to show the generality of its application, to explore the periods over which the feedback effects can be observed and to develop the account of hybridity. In particular, there will be a need for more empirical work to explore the theory of trust set out in Chapter 5. However, we believe that our empirical studies – limited as they are – suffice to show both the inherent plausibility and potential power of a theory that also has good credentials on the grounds of its integration with the mainstream of thought in social science and by the standards of kinds of trade-offs between theoretical virtues that it is reasonable to apply to a theory of this range.

One of the virtues of the theory, we have suggested, is its capacity for synthesis. It makes good sense of the particular insights captured by the more limited theories in the domain, such as those of transaction cost theory, of the 'new' institutionalism in organisational sociology and of the theories of dynamic change through feedback effects; it also helps us to understand some of their limitations.

Methodologically, the theory calls for the integration of quantitative sociometric studies of network structure with more qualitative research into causal mechanisms; interestingly, this is the approach to evaluation around which the leading edge of social science methodological thought is now converging (see e.g. Ragin, 2000; Mahoney, 2001).

Of course, the neo-Durkheimian theory has been criticised. The main criticisms that have been offered are summarised here; inevitably, because the theory has only recently been applied to inter-organisational networks, most of these criticisms are of applications in other academic areas, mainly in the study of risk perception. However, if these criticisms were valid there, they would have to be valid anywhere. They are:

- that the typology is too static to enable the explanation of change (Bellaby, 1989);
- that the theory is 'viciously' circular (Boholm, 1996) because it invokes prior institutional conditions in order to explain subsequent institutional forms;
- that the distinct forms do not occur in their pure manifestations (Sjöberg, 1997);
- that it is wrong in principle to use distal variables to explain phenomena (Sjöberg, 2003);

- that the pluralism of the four way typology is too great for an integrated theory (Alexander and Smith, 1996);
- that the pluralism of the four way typology is too limited to capture the full richness of the empirically observable variety (Renn, 1992);
- that its mode of explanation is deterministic (Nelkin, 1982; Renn, 1992); and
- that its mode of explanation is insufficiently deterministic (Boholm, 1996).

This is quite a litany of complaints, and not all of them are mutually compatible. Hopefully, enough has already been said in earlier chapters to show that these criticisms are misplaced. We will thus respond only briefly here to the main lines of attack.

The theory of social change is supplied by the account of feedback mechanisms. Feedback mechanisms are indeed circular, but by no means viciously so. A vicious circularity has to presume the very thing that it seeks to explain. The neo-Durkheimian theory does not seek to explain why human beings live under institutions, or to tell a just-so story about some supposed emergence of institutions from a primordial institution-free setting, but merely to show how institutions work. The theory, correctly understood, requires hybridity and not pure forms. Sjöberg's objection to any variables other than those which track the empirical phenomena to be explained would not only involve the abandonment of most social science – and most practical decision making aimed at influencing forces that cannot be observed directly – but also risks either a truly vicious circularity or else banality in explanation; a trade-off in favour of accuracy at the expense of parsimony, generality and causality of the kind that Sjöberg calls for is clearly a particularly unhelpful one. The objection that four basic kinds is too many for a social theory seems rather odd, especially from authors who also criticise other theories that work with hardly many fewer for being too simple. More importantly, nothing in Alexander and Smith's argument shows that any of the four can actually be eliminated. The charge of weak integration of the four into a common causal theory can clearly be rejected for the same basic feedback mechanisms are at work in each form. That there is huge empirical variety in network forms is hardly something that anyone denies. Nevertheless, if we are to do any better than 'thick description' of cases and a weary assertion of the uniqueness of each particular – or else accept the interpretations of each describer of such thick sets as authoritative (Geertz, 1973) – then some trade-off in favour of parsimony and generality has to be made, albeit at the expense of elaborate accuracy. The challenge for Renn is for him to show how his argument can be prevented from collapsing into the absurdity of Sjöberg's. The charge of determinism is puzzling when laid against a theory that predicts mobility over time in response to feedback processes (Rayner, 1992). More likely, it is really a protest that the theory privileges structure over agency. But what would satisfy the critic who demands more scope for agency? Perhaps they are looking for a theory that allows agents – such as organisations – to make inexplicable, idiosyncratic decisions and arrive at network forms that make little sense within the conditions they operate? If such a theory were acceptable, then it would need to do a great deal of explaining to show how such a social ordering might be viable over the longer term. In any case, the theory does in fact probably offer – although there is regrettably no space to show this here – a richer account of what kinds of agency are possible and what agency would mean in different institutional settings (Douglas and Ney, 1998) than do its competitors. For example, most rational choice theories in fact leave little real scope for agency (Hay, 2004) and many psychological theories seem to portray individuals as the playthings of randomly clustering psychological drives or factors.

Networks after the goldrush – a little of each, not too much of any

The theory, if it is accepted, is not only of interest to social scientists. Practising managers and professionals are entitled to ask whether such a theory of inter-organisational relations helps them to understand better what it is that they are doing, and whether it might help them to arrange their strategies more astutely or intelligently.

Like any institutional theory, the neo-Durkheimian account argues that managers do not and cannot have a completely free hand to choose and change the institutional setting under which they work, neither within their own organisation nor within their field. 'Change management' – and the common aspiration to 'manage cultural change' – is not an easy thing to do. They are not activities in which taking a particular action will reliably have a given effect. But the theory certainly does not suggest that managers are powerless. In Chapter 7, a theory of leadership was presented which shows the scope for individuals to secure different types of influence in each institutional setting, and the ritual basis that makes this possible. Consider Table 12.2 again. Individual leaders and brokers have a significant role to play in each of the fields that we have studied and their networking practices have, in the aggregate and over time, clearly played a part in reshaping the processes of institutionalisation and deinstitutionalisation that are at work in these industries.

The account given in Chapter 6 of the nature of power within networks is a central strand of the potential for the practical application of the theory. It provides an understanding of the scope for and limitations of each of the principal tools available by which managers can seek to influence the situation of their organisation within their field. At the most basic level, it offers an account of which instruments are most likely to emerge as normal and typical in each institutional setting. Beyond this, the theory provides an account of the limitations of each type of instrument, and the peculiar failures to which it might be prone.

Because each of the institutional forms of networks is vulnerable to particular weaknesses – and the risks of poor performance, disorganisation and failure – it is not sensible to draw a simple prescriptive conclusion that, where managers can exert leverage, they should unambiguously try to promote any particular institutional form. Some writers argue that at the very least one should always seek to avoid the isolate form; this is one way that we the read the arguments of those who urge organisations to cultivate their collective (and their individual managers' and professionals) 'social capital' (e.g. Burt, 1992; Lesser, 2000; Baker, 2001). Yet, the defence procurement study shows that even this does not always recognise the overriding institutional imperatives that people face. Isolate structures may not be the most technically effective in getting things done, but they are often adopted as ways of surviving in difficult circumstances; where mutual suspicion and tight circumscription cannot be avoided, they are often the only intelligent solutions.

A 'horses for courses' approach has something to commend it. At least it offers a first level recommendation that can often be a sensible use of a theory as a diagnostic tool for identifying the really important features of one's circumstances, in order the better to adapt to them. Yet the theory also shows the limitations of this maxim. For the theory shows how adapting to one's circumstances can, and typically will, bring about changes in the field over time. It may reinforce the existing institutional tendencies that can generate further positive feedback which will actually undermine the very institutional form that one is trying to sustain. The point of an effective 'horses for courses' approach is to identify the risks as well as the opportunities that one's situation presents, and the theory suggests that those risks of positive feedback are best addressed if one has resources that span more than one institutional form.

It is for this reason that many writers using the theory in other settings have converged on a principle of 'requisite variety' (cf. Ashby, 1947, 1956); namely, that whilst in the short term it might make sense to adapt the prevailing institutional conditions (cultivate one's place in the hierarchical networks in a hierarchical industry, etc), that the most intelligent long-term strategy is to develop a sufficiently mixed set of network patterns and institutional styles that one can respond to whichever set of dynamics break out. This is often described as a 'clumsy' strategy because it sacrifices optimisation on any one goal – or, in this case, any one institutional form – in favour of adequacy on many (Schapiro, 1988; Wildavsky, 1993; Thompson, 1997 a, b, c; Hendriks, 2004; Verweij and Thompson, 2006). Clearly, only organisations that expect to exist in the long- term need long- term strategies; those created as temporary structures, in which investors, managers and employees all understand the provisionality of the others' commitment, hardly have to worry about viability over the longer term. However, the theory predicts that such short-term and instrumental organisations will emerge most frequently in relatively weakly socially integrated contexts.

Achieving requisite variety and clumsiness is not easy. It enjoins no excess of any one form, at least over the long run, and an adequate representation of each. In this sense, it is at one level perhaps banal and uncontroversial. Now that there are ferocious advocates on the one hand for greater deregulation of networks and on the other for tougher regulation, on the one hand for more freewheeling and instrumental 'networking' and on the other for tightly bonded 'communities of practice', at another level it is a prescription that offends most of the writers about networks for it warns against the excesses of each. To date, we have few valid and reliable measures of what counts as an adequate articulation of each of the institutional forms in any network (or even in a single organisation). At present, the maxim of requisite variety can be only a rule of thumb. Yet even an astute but vague rule of thumb can be of more practical use than an exact and measurable instrument, the use of which can bring great risks.

Notes

4 An integrated theory of networks

1. There is no theoretical guarantee of success that settlements will be achieved or even theoretical presumption in favour of their stability, once achieved; still less is it presumed that settlements are progressive, each building on the last, in some Whig conception of institutional history. It is for this reason that the present theory is cybernetic and dynamic but not evolutionary in the sense used by Schotter (1981) and Mantavinos (2001).
2. Baumgartner and Jones (2002) define negative feedback very narrowly and somewhat oddly, restricting it to those cases where its produces system homeostasis, due to near-exact counterbalancing (cf. Dunsire, 1990, on collaboration). However, this is a special case of the more general phenomenon of negative feedback, meaning resistance, or countervailing force, even backlash, which may overwhelm, produce gridlock, or fail to counterbalance fully as well as balance exactly. The oddness of Baumgartner's and Jones' usage arises from the fact that all cases other than an outcome of homeostasis are deemed by them to be the effect of positive feedback. Here, the term is used to cover the full range of possibilities. Applying the present understanding of the concept to the cases studied by Baumgartner and Jones would lead to some of their examples being reclassified from their (2002) interpretation.
3. Durkheim (1984 [1893], 140ff, 200ff), criticising the utilitarians, the rational choice theorists of his day, commented that if people were driven only by interests, they would be capable only of 'transient relations and passing associations' (Steven Lukes retranslation: Lukes, 1973, 145); interests, Durkheim argues, are sources of conflict, and only in conditions of special institutional shaping can they be sources of settlement. In the neo-Durkheimian formulation, only under individualistic institutions before they have been subject to severe positive feedback, can we speak of interests driving co-ordinative action, and then only elliptically, the prior institutional work being taken for granted. It is in this sense that the theory presented here departs from rational choice as conventionally understood. To be sure, there are many variants of rational choice institutionalism (e.g. Ostrom, 1998; Mantzavinos, 2001). However, none of these models has fully acknowledged the fundamental and radical significance of the endogenous production of expectations and preferences. Certainly, the present theory regards most people as making intelligent decisions under conditions of deep institutional conditioning, and not irrational ones (If one grants their premises, then depressed, paranoid or obsessive-compulsive people are far from being irrational and are in fact highly rational. Indeed, they are probably too narrowly rational to be reasonable, since our standards of reasonableness require more pluralism and therefore incoherence than their illnesses sadly afford them). However, by allowing for the possibility and even probability of incoherence in the thought styles endogenously produced of each individual as they move between institutional settings (Rayner, 1992), the present theory deviates sharply from the methodological individualist assumption of a single self with a more or less coherent utility function that is stable over time and contexts (Douglas and Ney, 1998): it is possible, as Table 4.1 shows, for the

form of personhood to be narrowly logically consistent but not coherent in all the senses identified in the Table 4.1. To be sure, if rational choice theorists would allow as full a specification of the institutional conditions for choice as the present theory allows, and would concede that what is done under those conditions is not necessarily maximisation but often more like satisficing – at low levels of acceptance in isolate conditions, at very high levels in enclaved ones, etc – then a rather compatibility between the two approaches might be achieved, but at a price probably too high in the distinctiveness of methodologically individualist rational choice theory for its advocates to be prepared to accept.

4. Feedforward – deliberate anticipatory control action – is also possible, but can best be understood in the present theory as a subcategory of positive or negative feedback, in that special case where institutional pressures require or at least afford reflective action, and also so constrain action and conditions that there is some possibility that the intended consequences of anticipatory control action will be more significant than the unintended ones. This requires quite high levels of organisation, and hence of prior negative feedback with a roughly homeostatic outcome as institutional background.

5 Trust between organisations

1. There is a strand of literature which disagrees sharply with this view that trust is best analysed as task-specific. A recent important statement of the contrary view is given by Uslaner (2002). Uslaner argues that a really important factor in explaining outcomes at the macro-social level is what he calls generalised moralistic trust, by which he means an optimistic stance towards strangers that one might be expected to meet in the course of one's life that in general, when any particular task in question, more often than not, they will prove trustworthy. Nothing in this paper stands in contradiction with this empirical claim. However, Uslaner contrasts generalised moralistic trust with what he calls strategic trust, which he defines as a style of more cautious, experience-based sequences of particular assessments of particular individuals, without any general presumption in advance. The core of the disagreement here is in fact semantic: it turns on the question of whether what Uslaner's survey data and his concept are really measuring trust, *stricto sensu*, at all. As we read his account of generalised moralistic trust, it is not in fact an agency relationship, but an individual (and perhaps, if aggregated in the right way through a common culture, an organisational) psychological characteristic, indicating a provisionally greater degree of preparedness to enter into such relationships. Indeed, it might be better called 'esteem of strangers' than trust. Uslaner is of course building upon the celebrated work of Putnam (2000: 134–147): exactly the same point can be made about Putnam's decision to describe the survey data on which he relies as a measure of 'social trust', without necessarily implying anything one way or the other about the merits of his more controversial empirical claims. To the extent that Putnam's social trust and Uslaner's generalised moralistic trust are measures of that elusive notion of 'social capital' as optimistic esteem for unknown others rather than specific agency relationships and actual ties, then, individual social capital is clearly very different from the inter-organisational social capital which is the focus of studies such as those collected in Lesser (2000), where the focus is on actual ties between individual managers and organisations. It is these ties and agency relations which alone are directly relevant for this chapter, although there may of course be some indirect causal influence from background social esteem.

2. In the same vein as Bradach and Eccles (1989) but without invoking trust to the same degree, Powell (1990) suggests that reciprocity is the unique feature of governance in networks, by contrast with haggling in markets and administrative fiat with supervision in hierarchy. However, for many of the same reasons as those set out in relation to the claim about trust, this will not quite stand either. There is asymmetric reciprocity in hierarchy (see e.g. Dumont (1980 [1966]), and there is certainly reciprocity in markets, either of the specialist form of what the lawyers call offer and consideration or the generalised form where buyers and sellers expect to be repeat-players (Gouldner, 1960).

References

6 P (1998) [1994], *Trust, Social Theory and Public Policy*, London Demos: and Department of Social Sciences, University of Bath.

—— (1998) *The future of privacy, volume 1: private life and public policy*, London: Demos.

—— (2003a) 'What is there to feel? A Neo-Durkheimian theory of the emotions', *European Journal of Psychotherapy Counselling and Health*, 5, 3: 263–90.

—— (2003b) 'Institutional viability: a neo-Durkheimian theory', *Innovation: the European Journal of Social Science Research*, 16, 4: 395–415.

—— (2003c) 'The governance of technology: concepts, trends, theory, normative principles and research agenda, "white paper" for the ESRC Science in Society programme workshop', *Democratic governance of technological change in an era of globalisation*, FLAD, Lisbon, 23–26.02.03.

6 P, Lasky K and Fletcher A (1998) *The Future of Privacy: Volume 1 – Public Trust in the Use of Private Information*, London: Demos.

6 P, Leat D, Seltzer K and Stoker G (1999) *Governing in the Round*, London: Demos.

—— (2002) *Towards Holistic Government: the New Reform Agenda*, Basingstoke: Palgrave.

6 P and Peck E (2004) 'New Labour's modernisation in the public sector: a neo-Durkheimian approach and the case of mental health services', *Public Administration*, 82, 1: 83–108.

Agranoff RA and McGuire M (1998) 'Multinetwork management: collaboration and the hollow state in local economic policy', *Journal of Public Administration Research and Theory*, 8, 1: 67–91.

—— (2001) 'Big questions in public network management research', *Journal of Public Administration Research and Theory*, 11, 3: 295–326.

Ahern R (1993) 'Implications of strategic alliances for small R & D intensive firms', *Environment and Planning A*, 25: 1511–1526.

Ahgren B (2001) 'Chains of care: a counterbalance to fragmented health care', *Journal of Integrated Care Pathways*, 5: 126–132.

—— (2003) 'Chain of Care development in Sweden: results of a national study', paper presented to the WHO/IJIC International Conference on New Research and Developments in Integrated Care, Barcelona, 21–22 February, www.ijic.org.

Akerlof GA (1970) 'The market for "lemons": qualitative uncertainty and the market mechanism', *Quarterly Journal of Economics*, 84: 488–500.

Aldrich HE (1979) *Organisations and Environments*, Englewood Cliffs, NJ: Prentice-Hall.

Aldrich HE and Herker D (1977) 'Boundary spanning roles and organisation structure', *Academy of Management Review*, 2: 217–230.

Alexander JC and Smith P (1996) 'Social science and salvation: risk society as mythical discourse', *Zeitschrift für soziologie*, 25, 4: 251–262.

Alic J (1998) 'The perennial problems of defense acquisition', in Susman G and O'Keefe S, eds, *The Defense Industry in the Post-Cold War Era*, New York: Pergamon, 333–355.

Alic J, Branscomb L, Brooks H, Carter A and Epstein G (1992) *Beyond Spinoff: Military and Commercial Technologies in a Changing World*, Boston, MA: Harvard Business School Press.

Allan G (1990) 'Class variation in friendship patterns', *British Journal of Sociology*, 41: 389–392.

Alter C and Hage J (1993) *Organisations Working Together*, Newbury Park, CA: Sage.

Ancona DG and Caldwell DF (1992) 'Bridging the boundary: external activity and the performance of teams', *Administrative Science Quarterly*, 37: 634–665.

Anderson E (1990) 'Two firms, one frontier: on assessing joint venture performance', *Sloan Management Review*, 31, 2: 19–31.

Andersson G, Karlberg I (2000) 'Integrated care for the elderly: the background and effects of reform of Swedish care for the elderly', *International Journal of Integrated Care*, 1: 1, 21–35 November 2000, www.ijic.org

Andrews DA (2001) 'Effective practice – future directions', in Andrews DA, Hollins C, Raynor P, Trotter C and Armstrong B, eds., *Sustaining Effectiveness in Working with Offenders*, Dnas Powys: The Cognitive Centre Foundation.

Andrews DA and Bontanna J (1998) *The Psychology of Criminal Conduct.* Cincinnati: Andrews Publishing.

Anheier HK, ed. (1999) *When Things go Wrong: Organisational Failures and Breakdowns*, London: Sage.

Anton J and Yao D (1990) 'Measuring the effectiveness of competition in defense procurement: a survey of the empirical literature', *Journal of Policy Analysis and Management*, 9, 1: 60–79.

Aoki M, Gustafsson B and Williamson OE, eds (1990) *The Firm as a Nexus of Treaties*, London: Sage.

Arendt H (1963) *Eichmann in Jerusalem*, Harmondsworth: Penguin.

Argyris C and Schön DA (1978) *Organisational Learning*, Reading, MA: Addison-Wesley.

Arora A and Gambardella A (1990) 'Complementarity and external linkages: the strategies of large firms in biotechnology', *Journal of Industrial Economics*, 38, 4: 361–379.

Arrow KJ (1974) *The Limits of Organisation*, New York: W.W. Norton.

Arthur WB (1994) *Increasing Returns and Path Dependence in the Economy*, Ann Arbor, MI: University of Michigan Press.

Ashby WR (1947) 'Principles of the self-organising dynamic system', *Journal of General Psychology*, 37, 125–128.

Ashby WR (1956) *An Introduction to Cybernetics*, London: Chapman and Hall.

Audit Commission (2001) *Community Safety Partnerships*. London: Audit Commission.

—— (2002) *Integrated Services for Older People. Building a Whole System Approach in England*. London: Audit Commission.

Audretsch DB and Stephan PE (1996) 'Company-scientist locational links: the case of biotechnology', *American Economic Review*, 86, 3: 641–652.

Axelrod R (1984) *The Evolution of Cooperation*, New York: Basic Books.

Ayios A (2003) 'Competence and trust guardians as key elements of building trust in east–west joint ventures in Russia', *Business Ethics: a European Review*, 12, 2: 190–202.

Bache I (2000) 'Government within governance: network steering in Yorkshire and the Humber', *Public Administration*, 78, 3: 575–592.

Baier AC (1986) 'Trust and antitrust', *Ethics*, 96: 231–260.

Baker C (2001) 'Managed clinical networks: a start', *Health Bulletin (Edinburgh)*, 59, 6: 417–419.

Baker C and Lorimer A (2000) 'Cardiology: the development of a managed clinical network; *British Medical Journal*, 321, 7269: 1152–1153.

Baker WE (2000) *Achieving Success Through Social Capital: Tapping Hidden Resources in your Personal and Business Networks*, California: Jossey-Bass, San Fransisco.

Banfield EC with Banfield LF (1958) *The Moral Basis of a Backward Society*, New York: Free Press.

Barber B (1983) *The Logic and Limits of Trust*, New Jersey: Rutgers University Press.

Bardach E (1998) *Getting Agencies to Work Together: the Practice and Theory of Managerial Craftsmanship*, Washington DC: Brookings Institution.

—— (2001) Developmental Dynamics: Interagency Collaboration as an Emergent Phenomenon, *Journal of Public Administration Research and Theory*, 11, 2: 149–164.

Bass BM (1990) [1974], *Bass and Stodgill's Handbook of Leadership: Theory, Research and Managerial Applications*, 3rd edn, New York: Free Press.

Bate SP and Robert G (2002) 'Knowledge management and communities of practice in the private sector: lessons for modernising the National Health Service in England and Wales', *Public Administration*, 80 4: 643–663.

Baumgartner FR and Jones BD, eds (2001) *Policy Dynamics*, Chicago: University of Chicago Press.

Bazzoli G, Chan B, Shortell S and D'Aunno T (2000) 'The financial performance of hospitals belonging to health networks and systems', *Inquiry*, 37, 3: 234–252.

Bazzoli G, Shortell S, Ciliberto P, Kralovec P and Dubbs N (2001) 'Tracking the changing provider landscape: implications for health policy and practice', *Health Affairs*, 20, 6: 188–196.

Bazzoli G, Shortell S, Dubbs N *et al.* (1999) 'A taxonomy of health networks and systems: bringing order out of chaos', *Health Services Research*, 33, 6: 1683–1718.

Beer S (1966) *Decision and Control: the Meaning of Operational Research and Management Cybernetics*, Chichester: John Wiley and sons.

Bellaby P (1989) 'To risk or not to risk? Use and limitations of Mary Douglas on risk-acceptability for understanding health and safety at work and road accidents', *Sociological Review*, 38: 465–483.

Bemelmans-Videc M-L, Rist RC and Vedung E, eds (1998) *Carrots, Sticks and Sermons: Policy Instruments and their Evaluation*, New Brunswick, NJ: Transaction Books.

Bergman H, Beland F, Lebel P, Leibovich E, Contandriopoulos A, Brunelle Y, Kaufman T, Tousignant P, Rodriguez R and Scott G (1997) 'Hospital and integrated service delivery network for the frail elderly', *Ruptures, Revue transdisciplinaire en sante*, 4, 2: 311–321.

Bernabei R, Landi R, Gambassi G, Sgadari A, Zuccala G, Mor V, Rubenstein L and Carbonin P (1998) Randomised trial of impact of model of integrated care and case management for older people living in the community, *British Medical Journal*, 316: 1348–1351.

Best M (1990) *The New Competition: Institutions of Industrial Restructuring*, Cambridge: Polity Press.

Bevir M and Rhodes RAW (2003) *Interpreting British Governance*, London: Routledge.

Biggart NW (1991) Explaining Asian economic organisation: toward a Weberian institutional perspective, *Theory and Society*, 20, 2: 199–232.

Bijker WE and Law J, eds (1992) *Shaping Technology/Building Society: Studies in Sociotechnical Change*, Cambridge, MA: Massachusetts Institute of Technology Press.

Birkinshaw J and Hagström P, eds (2000) *The Flexible Firm: Capability Management in Network Organisations*, Oxford: Oxford University Press.

Birkinshaw J, Toulan O and Arnold D (2000) 'Global account management: linking external demands and internal abilities', in Birkinshaw J and Hagström P, eds, *The Flexible Firm: Capability Management in Network Organisations*, Oxford: Oxford University Press, 43–60.

Bishop P (1996) 'Buyer–supplier linkages in the defence industry: the case of Devonport Dockyard', *Area*, 28,1: 78–88.

Blogg H, Peasson G, Sampson A, Smith D and Stubbs P (1988) 'Inter-agency Co-ordination: rhetoric and reality', in Hope T and Shaw M, eds, *Communities and Crime Reduction*, London: Home Office.

Blair T (1998) *The Third Way*, London: Fabian Society.

Bleeke J and Ernst D (1991) 'The way to win cross-border alliances', *Harvard Business Review*, 69, 6: 127–135.

Blois K (1999) 'Trust in business to business relationships: an evaluation of its status', *Journal of Management Studies*, 36, 2: 197–215.

Boddy D, MacBeth D and Wagner B (2000) 'Implementing cooperative strategy: a model from the private sector', in Faulkner DO and De Rond M, eds, *Cooperative Strategy: Economic, Business and Organisational Issues*, Oxford: Oxford University Press, 193–210.

Boholm Å (1996) 'The cultural theory of risk: an anthropological critique', *Ethnos*, 61: 64–84.

Boschma RA and Lambooy JG (2001) 'Knowledge, market structure and economic coordination: dynamics of industrial districts', *Growth and Change*, 33: 291–311.

Bouchikhi H, de Rond M and Leroux V (1998) Alliances as social facts: a constructivist theory of interorganisational collaboration, Working paper DR 98037, École Superieur des Sciences Économiques et Commerciales, Paris.

Bourdieu P (1986) [1983], 'The forms of capital', in Richardson JG, ed. *Handbook of Theory and Research for the Sociology of Education*, Westport, CT: Greenwood Press, 241–258.

Bradach JL and Eccles RG (1989) 'Price, authority and trust: from ideal types to plural forms', *Annual Review of Sociology*, 15, 1: 97–118.

Branch L, Coulam R and Zimmerman Y (1995) 'The PACE evaluation: initial findings', *Gerontologist*, 35, 3: 349–359.

Bratby L (1999) 'State of the union', *Police Review*, 27: 22–24.

Brenkert G (1998) 'Trust morality and international business', in Lane C and Bachman R, eds, *Just Within and Between Organisations: Conceptual Issues and Empirical Applications*, Oxford: Oxford University Press, 273–297.

Brinton MC and Nee V, eds (1998) *The New Institutionalism in Sociology*, Stanford, CA: Stanford University Press.

Brown JS and Duguid P (1991) 'Organisational learning and communities of practice: toward a unifying view of working, learning and innovation', *Organisation Science*, 2, 1: 40–57.

Brown JS and Duguid P (2002) 'Local knowledge: innovation in the networked age', *Management Learning*, 33, 4: 427–437.

Brown MM, O'Toole LJ jnr and Brudney JL (1998) 'Implementing information technology in government: an empirical assessment of the role of local partnerships', *Journal of Public Administration Research and Theory*, 8, 4: 499–525.

Brunsson N, Jacobsson B and associates (2000) *A World of Standards*, Oxford: Oxford University Press.

Bryman A (1992) *Charisma and Leadership in Organisations*, London: Sage.

Bullock K, Farrell G and Tilley N (2002) *Funding and Implementing Crime Reduction Initiatives*, London: Home Office.

Bulmer M (1986) *Neighbours: the Work of Philip Abrams*, Cambridge: Cambridge University Press.

Burlat P, Besombes B and Deslandres V (2003) 'Constructing a typology of networks of firms', *Production Planning and Control*, 14, 5: 399–409.

Burns JM (1978) *Leadership*, New York: Harper and Row.

Burt RS (1992) *Structural Holes: the Social Structure of Competition*, Chicago, IL/ Cambridge, MA: University of Chicago Press/Harvard University Press.

—— (1997) 'The contingent value of social capital', *Administrative Science Quarterly*, 42: 339–365.

Burt RS and Knez M (1996) 'Trust and third party gossip', in Kramer RM and Tyler TR, eds, *Trust in Organisations: Frontiers of Theory and Research*, London: Sage, 68–89.
Cabinet Office (1997) *Tackling Drugs Locally*, London: HMSO.
Calabrese T, Baum JAC and Silverman BS (2000) 'Canadian biotechnology start-ups, 1991–1997: the role of incumbents' patents and strategic alliances in controlling competition', *Social Science Research*, 29: 503–534.
Callon M and Law J (1989) 'On the construction of socio-technical network: content and context revisited', *Knowledge and Society: Studies in the Sociology of Science Past and Present*, 8: 57–83.
Calman K and Hine A (1995) *A Policy Framework for Commissioning Cancer Services*, London: Department of Health.
Calvin J (1998) 'Clinical trial networks: a unique opportunity for critical care', *Critical Care Medicine*, 26, 4: 625–626.
Carney M (1998) 'The competitiveness of networked production: the role of trust and asset specificity', *Journal of Management Studies*, 35, 4: 457–479.
Castells M (1989) *The Informational City: Information Technology, Economic Restructuring and the Urban-Regional Process*, Oxford: Blackwell.
—— (1996) *The Information Age: Economy, Society and Culture, Volume 1: the Rise of the Network Society*, Oxford: Blackwell.
Chai S-K and Wildavsky A (1994) 'Culture, rationality and violence', in Coyle DJ and Ellis RJ, eds, *Politics, Policy and Culture*, Boulder, CO: Westview Press, 159–174.
Challis L, Fuller S, Henwood M, Klein R, Plowden W, Webb A, Whittingham P and Wistow G (1988) *Joint Approaches to Social Policy: Rationality and Practice*, Cambridge University Press: Cambridge.
Chiesa V and Manzini R (1998) 'Organising for technological collaborations: a managerial perspective', *R & D Management*, 28, 3: 199–212.
Chu D and Waxman M (1998) 'Shaping the structure of the American defense industry', in Susman G and O'Keefe S, eds, *The Defense Industry in the Post-Cold War Era*, New York: Pergamon, 35–44.
Clark J (2003) 'Perhaps small is beautiful after all?', *HSMC Newsletter*, 9, 2: 3–5.
Clarke J, Gewirtz S and McLaughlin E (eds) (2000) *New Managerialism, New Welfare?* London: Sage.
Clarke M and Stewart JS (1997) *Partnership and the Management of Co-operation*, Birmingham: Institute of Local Government Studies, University of Birmingham.
Clegg SR (1989) *Frameworks of Power*, London: Sage.
Coase RH (1937) 'The nature of the firm', *Economica*, NS 4: 386–405.
Cockburn IM and Henderson RM (1998) 'Absorptive capacity, co-authoring behaviour, and the organisation of research in drug discovery', *Journal of Industrial Economics*, 46, 2: 157–182.
Coddington D, Moore K, Fischer E (1994) 'Costs and benefits of integrated healthcare systems', *Healthcare Financial Management*, 48, 3: 20–29.
Cohen WM and Levinthal DA (1990) 'Absorptive capacity: a new perspective on learning and innovation', *Administrative Science Quarterly*, 35, 1: 128–152.
Coleman JS (1988) 'Social capital in the creation of human capital', *American Journal of Sociology*, 94 Supplement, S95–S120.
—— (1990) '*Foundations of Social Theory*, Cambridge, MA: Belknap Press of the Harvard University Press.
Collins K (2000) 'Managed clinical networks: time to act', *Nursing Management*, 6, 9: 13–15.
Colombo MG (1998) 'Some introductory reflections', in Colombo MG, ed., *The Changing Boundaries of the Firm: Explaining Evolving Inter-firm Relations*, London: Routledge, 1–26.

Commons JR (1934) *Institutional Economics*, Madison, WI: University of Wisconsin Press.

Conner KR (1991) 'An historical comparison of resource-based theory and five schools of thought within industrial organisation economics: do we have a new theory of the firm?', *Journal of Management*, 17: 121–154.

Conner M (2001) 'Developing network-based services in the NHS', *International Journal of Health Care Quality Assurance*, 14, 6, 237–244.

Conrad D and Shortell S (1996) 'Integrated health systems: promise and performance', *Frontiers of Health Service Management*, 13, 1: 3–40.

Conway S (1997) 'Strategic personal links in successful innovation: link-pins, bridges and liaisons', *Creativity and Innovation Management*, 6, 4: 226–233.

Coulson A, ed. (1998) *Trust and Contracts: Relationships in Local Government, Health and Public Services*, Bristol: Policy Press.

Coyle DJ (1994) 'The theory that would be king', in Coyle DJ and Ellis RJ, eds, *Politics, Policy and Culture*, Boulder, CO: Westview Press, 219–239.

—— (1997) 'A cultural theory of organisations', in Ellis RJ and Thompson M, eds, *Culture Matters: Essays in Honour of Aaron Wildavsky*, Boulder, CO: Westview Press, 59–78.

Coyle DJ and Ellis RJ, eds (1994) *Politics, Policy and Culture*, Boulder, CO: Westview Press.

Crawford A (1995) 'Appeals to community and crime prevention', *Crime, Law and Social Change*, 22: 97–126.

—— (1998) 'Community safety partnerships', *Criminal Justice Matters*, 33: 4–5.

—— (1994) 'The community approach to crime prevention: corporatism at the local level', *Social and Legal Studies*, 3: 497–519.

Crawford A and Jones M (1995) 'Inter-agency co-operation and community-based crime prevention: some reflections on the work of Person and colleagues', *British Journal of Criminology*, 35, 1: 17–33.

Creasy, P (1988) 'European Defence Agreements in Cooperation Agreements', in Creasy P and May S, eds, *The European Armaments Market and Procurement Cooperation*, London: Macmillan.

Creasy P and May S (1988) 'Political and economic background', in Creasy P and May S, eds, *The European Armaments Market and Procurement Cooperation*, London: Macmillan.

Cropper S, Hopper A and Spencer S (2002) 'Managed clinical networks', 87, 1: 1–4.

Cross B (1997) 'Partnership in practice: the experience of two probation services', *Howard Journal*, 36, 1: 62–79.

Cross R and Prusak L (2002) 'The people who make organisations go – or stop', *Harvard Business Review*, June: 105–112.

Crow G and Allan G (1994) *Community Life: an Introduction to Local Social Relationships*, Hemel Hemstead: Harvester Wheatsheaf (Prentice-Hall).

Crump J (1993) 'Sectoral composition and spatial distribution of department of defense services procurement', *Professional Geographer*, 45, 3: 286–296.

Currall SC and Inkpen AC (2000) 'Joint venture trust: interpersonal, inter-group and inter-firm levels', in Faulkner DO and de Rond M, eds, *Cooperative Strategy: Economic, Business and Organisational Issues*, Oxford: Oxford University Press, 324–340.

Curtin L, Tilley N, Owen M and Pease K (2001) *Developing Crime Reduction Plans: Some Examples from the Reducing Burglary Initiative*. Crime Reduction Research Series Paper 7, London: Home Office.

Cvetkovich G and Löfstedt RE, eds (1999) *Social Trust and the Management of Risk*, London: Earthscan.

Cyert RM and March JG (1963) *A Behavioural Theory of the Firm*, Englewood Cliffs, NJ: Prentice-Hall.

Dahl RA (1957) *Who governs? Democracy and Power in an American City*, New Haven, CT: Yale University Press.

Dahlstrom R and Nygaard A (1995) 'An exploratory investigation of interpersonal trust in new and mature market economies', *Journal of retailing*, 71, 4: 339–361.

Das TK and Teng B-S (2000) 'Instabilities of strategic alliances: an internal tensions perspective', *Organisation Science*, 11: 77–101.

Dasborough M and Sue-Chan C (2002) 'The role of transaction costs and institutional forces in the outsourcing of recruitment', *Asia Pacific Journal of Human Resources*, 40, 3: 306–321.

Dasgupta P (1988) 'Trust as a commodity', in Gambetta D, ed., *Trust: Making and Breaking Cooperative Social Relations*, Oxford: Blackwell, 49–72.

David PA (1985) 'Clio and the economics of QWERTY', *American Economic Review*, 75: 332–337.

Day M, Burnett JMV and Forrester PL (2001) 'Supply network management in the UK tableware industry: empirical results of a three years study', *British Ceramic Transactions*, 100, 2: 86–89.

De Bruijn JA and ten Heuvelhof EF (1998) 'Instruments for network management', in Kickert WJM, Klijn E-H and Koppenjan JFM, eds, *Managing Complex Networks: Strategies for the Public Sector*, London: Sage, 119–136.

Deeds DL and Hill CWL (1996) 'Strategic alliances and the rate of new product development: an empirical study of entrepreneurial biotechnology firms', *Journal of Business Venturing*, 11: 41–55.

Delapierre M and Mytelka LK (1998) 'Blurring boundaries: new inter-firm relationships and the emergence of networked, knowledge-based oligopolies, in Colombo MG, ed., *The Changing Boundaries of the Firm: Explaining Evolving Inter-firm Relations*, London: Routledge, 73–94.

Department for Transport (2003) *Evaluation of Local Strategic Partnerships: Report of a Survey of all English LSPs*, London: Department for Transport.

Department of Health (1997) *Substance misuse and young people: the social services response. A Social Services Inspectorate study of young people looked after by Local Authorities*, London: The Stationery Office.

Deutsch K (1963) *The Nerves of Government: Models of Political Communication and Control*, New York: Free Press.

DiMaggio PJ, ed. (2001) *The Twenty First Century Firm: Changing Economic Organisation in International Perspective*, Princeton, NJ: Princeton University Press.

DiMaggio PJ and Powell WW (1983) 'The iron cage revisited: institutional isomorphism and collective rationality in organisational fields', *American Sociological Review*, 48: 147–160.

Domingues JM (2002) 'Modernity, complexity and mixed articulation', *Social Science Information*, 41, 3: 383–404.

Dopson S, Locock L, Chambers D and Gabbay J (2001) 'Implementation of evidence-based medicine: evaluation of the promoting action on clinical effectiveness programme', *Journal of Health Services Research and Policy*, 6: 23–31.

Doreian P and Woodward KL (1999) 'Local and global institutional processes', in Andrews SB and Knoke D, eds, 1999, *Research in the Sociology of Organisations, vol 16 – Networks in an Around Organisations*, series ed. Baharach SB, Stanford, CT: JAI Press, 59–83.

Doucette WR and Wiederholt JB (1997) 'Cooperation in pharmacy-drug wholesaler relations', *Pharmaceutical Research*, 14, 8: 976–983.

Douglas M (1970) *Natural Symbols: Explorations in Cosmology*, London: Routledge.

—— ed. (1982a) *Essays in the Sociology of Perception*, London: Routledge and Kegan Paul.

—— (1982b) [1978], 'Cultural bias', in Douglas M, *In the Active Voice*, London: Routledge and Kegan Paul, 183–254.

—— (1982c) 'Passive voice theories in religious sociology', in Douglas M, *In the Active Voice*, London: Routledge and Kegan Paul, 1–15.

—— (1986) *How Institutions Think*, London: Routledge and Kegan Paul.

—— (1996) 'Prospects for asceticism', in Douglas M, *Thought Styles: Critical Essays on Good Taste*, London: Sage, 161–192.

Douglas M and Mars G (2003), 'Terrorism: A Positive Feedback Game', *Human relations*, 56, 7: 763–786.

Douglas M and Ney S (1998) *Missing Persons: a Critique of Personhood in the Social Sciences*, Berkeley, CA: University of California Press and New York: Russell Sage Foundation.

Dowding K (1995) 'Model or metaphor? A critical review of the policy network approach', *Political Studies*, 43, 1: 136–158.

Dowding KM (1991) *Rational Choice and Political Power*, Edward Elgar, Aldershot.

Doz YL and Baburoglu O (2000) 'From competition to collaboration: the emergence and evolution of R&D cooperatives', in Faulkner DO and de Rond M, eds, *Cooperative Strategy: Economic, Business and Organisational Issues*, Oxford: Oxford University Press, 173–192.

Doz YL and Hamel G (1998) *Alliance Advantage: the Art of Creating Value through Partnering*, Boston, MA: Harvard Business School Press.

Draper A (1990) *European Defence Equipment Collaboration*, Basingstoke: Macmillan.

Drucker F (1991) 'The new productivity challenge', *Harvard Business Review*, November–December: 69–79.

Dubbs N, Bazzoli G, Shortell S and Kralovec P (2004) 'Reexamining organizational configurations: an update, validation, and expansion of the taxonomy of health networks and systems', *Health Services Research*, 39, 1: 207–220.

Dukes EF (1996) *Resolving Public Conflict: Transforming Community and Governance*, Manchester: University of Manchester Press.

Dumont L (1980) [1966], *Homo Hierarchicus: the Caste System and its Implications*, tr. Sainsbury M, Dumont L and Gulati B, Chicago: University of Chicago Press.

Dunsire A (1993) 'Modes of governance', in Kooiman J, ed., *Modern Governance: New Government-Society Interactions*, London: Sage, 21–34.

Durkheim É (1951) [1897], *Suicide: a Study in Sociology*, tr. Spaulding JA and Simpson G, London: Routledge.

—— (1961) [1925; lectures: 1902–03] *Moral education: a Study in the Theory and Application of the Sociology of Education*, tr. Wilson EK and Schnurer H, New York: Free Press.

—— (1984) [1893], *The Division of Labour in Society*, tr. Halls WD, MacMillan, Basingstoke.

—— (1995) [1912], *Elementary Forms of Religious Life*, tr. Field KE, New York: Free Press.

Dussauge P and Garrette B (1993) 'Industrial alliances in aerospace and defence: an empirical study of strategic and organizational patterns', *Defence Economics*, 4: 45–62.

Eccles RG and Nohria N with Berkley JD, 1992, *Beyond the Hype: Rediscovering the Essence of Management*, Boston, MA: Harvard Business School Press.

Edwards N (2002) 'Clinical networks. Advantages include flexibility, strength, speed, and focus on clinical issues', *British Medical Journey*, 324, 7329: 63.

Eisenstadt SN and LeMarchand R eds, 1981, *Political Clientelism, Patronage and Development*, London: Sage.

Eisenstadt SN and Roniger L (1984), *Patrons, Clients and Friends: Interpersonal Relations and the Structure of Trust in Society*, Cambridge: Cambridge University Press.

Elster J (1983) *Explaining Technical Change: a Case Study in the Philosophy of Science*, Cambridge: Cambridge University Press.

—— (1989) *The Cement of Society: a Study of Social Order*, Cambridge: University of Cambridge Press.

Emerson RM (1972a) 'Exchange theory, Part I: a psychological basis for exchange', in Berger J, Zelditch M jnr and Anderson B, eds, *Sociological Theories in Progress: Volume Two*, Boston, MA: Houghton Mifflin, 38–57.

—— (1972b) 'Exchange theory, Part II, exchange relations and networks', in Berger J, Zelditch M jnr and Anderson B, eds, *Sociological Theories in Progress: Volume Two*, Boston, MA: Houghton Mifflin, 58–87.

Eng C, Pedulla J Eleazer P, McCann R and Fox N (1997) 'Progam of all-inclusive care for the elderly [PACE]: an innovative model of integrated geriatric care and financing', *Journal of the American Geriatric Society*, 45: 223–232.

Etzioni A (1961) *A Comparative Analysis of Complex Organisations: on Power, Involvement and their Correlates*, New York: Free Press.

Fama E (1980) 'Agency problems and the theory of the firm', *Journal of Political Economy*, 88: 288–307, excerpted in Putterman L, ed., 1986, *The Economic Nature of the Firm: a Reader*, Cambridge: Cambridge University Press, 196–208.

Faulkner DO (2000) 'Trust and control: opposing or complementary functions?', in Faulkner DO and De Rond M, eds, *Cooperative Strategy: Economic, Business and Organisational Issues*, Oxford: Oxford University Press, 341–361.

Faulkner DO and De Rond M (2000) 'Perspectives on cooperative strategy', in Faulkner DO and De Rond M, eds, *Cooperative Strategy: Economic, Business and Organisational Issues*, Oxford: Oxford University Press, 3–39.

Ferlie E, Gabbay J, Fitzgerald L, Locock L and Dopson S (2001) 'Evidence-based medicine and organisational change: an overview of some recent qualitative research', in Ashburner L, ed., *Organisational Behaviour and Organisational Studies in Health Care: Reflections on the Future*, Basingstoke: Palgrave.

Ferlie E and Pettigrew A (1996) 'Managing through networks: some issues and implications for the NHS', *British Journal of Management*, 7: S81–S99.

Fineman S (2000) *Emotion in Organisations*, London: Sage.

Fiske AS (1991) *Structures of Social Life: the Four Elementary Forms of Human Relations*, New York: Free Press.

Fisman R and Khanna T (1999) 'Is trust a historical residue? Information flows and trust levels', *Journal of Economic Behaviour and Organisation*, 38, 1: 79–92.

Fligstein N (2001) *The Architecture of Markets: an Economic Sociology of Twenty-first Century Capitalist Societies*, Princeton, NJ: Princeton University Press.

Foucaud P, Rault G, Sautegeau A and Navarro J (2002) 'Clinical networks and cystic fibrosis', *Archives of Pediatrics and Adolescent Medicine*, 3 Suppl 1: 312s–314s.

Fountain JE (2001) *Building the Virtual State: Information Technology and Institutional Change*, Washington DC: Brookings Institution Press.

Fox A (1976) *Beyond Contract: Work, Power and Trust Relations*, London: Faber and Faber.

Frater A and Gill M (2002) 'Clinical networks. Sum of the parts', *Health Services Journal*, 112, 5827: 24–25.

French JRP jnr and Raven B (1959) 'The bases of social power', in Cartwright DP, ed., *Studies in Social Power*, Institute for Social Research, Ann Arbor, MI: University of Michigan, 150–167, repr. in excerpted form in Shafritz JM and Ott JS, eds, 2001, *Classics of organisation Theory*, 5th edn, Fort Worth: Harcourt College Publishers, 319–328.

Friend JK, Power JM and Yewlett CJL (1974) *Public Planning: the Inter-corporate Dimension*, London: Tavistock.

Fukuyama F (1995) *Trust: the Social Virtues and the Creation of Prosperity*, Harmondsworth: Penguin.

Fulcher H (2000) 'Partners in crime reduction', *Police Review*, 28: 19–20.

Fulk J, DeSanctis G (1998) *Shaping Organisational Form: Communication, Connection and Community*, California: Sage.

Galbraith J (1973) *Designing Complex Organisations*, Reading, MA: Addison-Wesley.

Gambetta D (1988) 'Can we trust trust?', in Gambetta D, ed., *Trust: Making and Breaking Co-operative Relations*, Cambridge: Cambridge University Press, 213–237.

Gansler J (1992) 'Restructuring the Defense Industrial Base', *Issues in Science and Technology*, Spring: 50–58.

—— (1995) 'Defense conversion: transforming the arsenal of democracy', Cambridge, MA: Massachusetts Institute of Technology Press.

Garcia-Pont C and Nohria N (2002) 'Local versus global mimetism: the dynamics of alliance formation in the automobile industry', *Strategic Management Journal*, 23: 307–321.

Garfinkel H (1967) *Studies in Ethnomethodology*, Englewood Cliffs, NJ: Prentice-Hall.

Garland D (1996) 'The limits of the sovereign state: strategies of crime control in contemporary society', *British Journal of Criminology*, 36, 4: 445–471.

—— (1997) 'The social and political context', in Burnett R ed., *The Probation Service: Responding to Change. Proceedings of the Probation Studies Unit First Annual Colloquium*, Oxford: Centre for Criminological Research.

Geertz C (1973) 'Thick description: toward an interpretive theory of culture', in Geertz C, ed., *The Interpretation of Cultures*, London: Fontana, 3–32.

Gemser G, Leenders MAAM and Wijnberg NM (1996) 'The dynamics of inter-firm networks in the course of the industry life-cycle: the role of appropriability', *Technology Analysis and Strategic Management*, 8, 4: 439–453.

Gendreau P and Ross RR (1979) 'Effective correctional treatment: Bibliotherapy for cynics', *Crime and Delinquency*, 25: 463–489.

Gendreau P, Little T and Goggin C (1996) 'A meta-analysis of the predictors of adult offender recidivism: what works?' *Criminology* 34: 575–607.

George G, Zahra SA, Wheatley KK and Khan R (2001) 'The effects of alliance portfolio characteristics and absorptive capacity on performance: a study of biotechnology firms', *Journal of High Technology Management Research*, 12, 2: 205–226.

Gerritsen H, Linschoten H van, Nies H and Romijn C (2001) *Netwerken in de gespecialiseerde gezondheidszorg voor ouderen*. Nijmegen: ITS.

Gersony N (1996) 'Sectoral effects on strategic alliance performance for new technology firms', *Journal of High Technology Management Research*, 7, 2: 175–189.

Geyskens I, Steenkamp J-BEM, Scheer LK and Kuman N (1996) 'The effects of trust and interdependence on relationship commitment: a trans-Atlantic study', *International Journal of Research in Marketing*, 13, 4: 303–317.

Ghoshal S and Mora P (1996) 'Bad for practice: a critique of transaction cost theory', *Academy of Management Review*, 21, 1: 13–47.

Gibbs A (1998) *Probation Partnerships: a Study of Roles, Relationships and Meanings*. Probation Studies Unit Report No. 7, Oxford: Probation Studies Unit.

Gibbs A (2001) 'Partnerships between the probation service and voluntary sector organisations', *British Journal of Social Work*, 31: 15–27.

Giddens A (1991) *Modernity and Self-identity: Self and Society in the Late Modern Age*, Cambridge: Polity Press.

Gilling D (1993) 'Crime prevention Discourses and the multi-agency approach', *International Journal of the Sociology of Law*, 21: 145–157.

Gilling D (1994) 'Multi-agency crime prevention: some barriers to collaboration', *The Howard Journal* 33, 3: 246–257.
—— (1996) 'Policing, crime prevention and partnerships', in Leishman F *et al.*, eds., *Core Issues in Policing*. London: Longman.
—— (2000) 'Surfing the crime net: UK Home Office guidance on the Crime & Disorder Act 1998', *Crime Prevention and Community Safety: An International Journal*, 2, 1: 51–54.
Glückler J and Armbrüster T (2003) 'Bridging uncertainty in management consulting: the mechanisms of trust an networked reputation', *Organisation Studies*, 24, 2: 269–297.
Goldblatt P and Lewis C, eds (1998) *Reducing Offending: an Assessment of Research Evidence on Ways of Dealing with Offending Behaviour*, Home Office Research Study 187, London: Home Office.
Goldstein H, *Problem-oriented Policing*, New York: McGraw-Hill, 1990.
Gonzalez R and Mehay S (1991) 'Burden sharing in the NATO alliance: an empirical test of alternative views', *Public Choice*, 68, 1–3 107–116.
Goodwin N (1998) 'Leadership in the UK NHS: where are we now?', *Journal of Management in Medicine*, 12: 121–132.
—— (2004) 'Networks in health and social care', in 6 P, Goodwin N, Peck E, Freeman T and Posaner R, *Managing Across Diverse Networks of Care: Lessons from Other Sectors*, HSMC, University of Birmingham, 299–366.
Gouldner AW (1960) 'The norm of reciprocity: a preliminary statement', *American Sociological Review*, 25, 161–178.
Grabher G (1993) 'Rediscovering the social in the economics of interfirm relations', in Grabher G, ed., 1993, *The Embedded Firm: on the Socioeconomics of Industrial Networks*, London: Routledge, 1–32.
—— ed. (1993) *The Embedded Firm: on the Socioeconomics of Industrial Networks*, London: Routledge.
Grandori A (1997) 'An organisational assessment of interfirm coordination modes', *Organisation Studies*, 18, 6: 897–925.
Grandori A and Soda (1995) 'Inter-firm networks: antecedents, mechanism and forms', *Organisation Studies*, 16, 2: 183–214.
Granovetter M (1985) 'Economic action and social structure: the problem of embeddedness', *American Journal of Sociology*, 81, 3: 43–63.
Granovetter MS (1973) 'The strength of weak ties', *American Journal of Sociology*, 78: 1360–1380.
—— (1985) 'Economic action and social structure: the problem of embeddedness', *American Journal of Sociology*, 91: 481–510, reprinted in Granovetter MS and Swedberg R, eds, 1992, *The Sociology of Economic Life*, Boulder, CO: Westview Press, 53–80.
—— (1994) 'Business groups', in Smelser NJ and Swedberg R, eds, *The Handbook of Economic Sociology*, Princeton, NJ: Princeton University Press and New York: Russell Sage Foundation, 453–475.
—— (1995) [1974], *Getting a Job: a Study of Contacts and Careers*, 2nd edn, Chicago, IL: University of Chicago Press.
Gray B (1996) 'Cross-sectoral partners: collaborative alliances among business, government and communities', in Huxham C, ed., *Creating Collaborative Advantage*, London: Sage, 57–79.
Greer P (1994) *Transforming Central Government: the Next Steps Initiative*, Buckingham: Open University Press.
Greig R and Poxton R (2001) 'From joint commissioning to partnership working: will the new policy framework make a difference?', *Managing Community Care*, 9, 4: 32–38.

Gröne O and Garcia-Barbero M (2002) *Trends in Integrated Care – Reflections on Conceptual Issues*. World Health Organisation, Copenhagen, EUR/02/5037864. http://www.euro.who.int/ihb

Gross J and Rayner S (1985) *Measuring Culture: a Paradigm for the Analysis of Social Organisation*, New York: Columbia University Press.

Gulati R (1995a) 'Social structure and alliance formation patterns: a longitudinal analysis', *Administrative Science Quarterly*, 40: 619–652.

—— (1995b) 'Does familiarity breed trust? The implications of repeated ties for contractual choice in alliances', *Academy of Management Journal*, 38, 1: 85–112.

—— (1998) 'Alliances and networks', *Strategic Management Journal*, 19: 293–317.

Gulati R and Singh H (1998) 'The architecture of cooperation: managing coordination costs and appropriation concerns in strategic alliances', *Administrative Sciences Quarterly*, 43: 781–814.

Gulick L and Gulick L (1937) 'Notes on the theory of organisation', in Gulick L and Gulick L, eds, *Papers in the Science of Administration*, New York: Institute of Public Administration, 3–13.

Hagedoorn J (1995). 'Strategic Technology Partnering in the 1980s: trends, networks, and corporate paterns in non-core technologies', *Research Policy*, 24, 207–231.

Hague G and Malos E (1998) 'Inter-agency approaches to domestic violence and the role of social services', *British Journal of Social Work*, 28: 369–386

Hakansson H and Lind J (2004) 'Accounting and network coordination', *Accounting, Organisations and Society*, 29, 1: 51–72.

Halpern D (2005) *Social Capital*, Cambridge: Polity Press.

Ham C, Smith J and Temple J (1998) *Hubs, Spokes and Policy Cycles*, Health Services Management Centre: University of Birmingham.

Hammer M (1996) *Beyond Reengineering: How Process-centred Organization is Changing our Work and our Lives*, New York: Harper Business.

Hammer M and Champy J (1993) *Reengineering the Corporation: a Manifesto for Business Revolution*, London: HarperCollins.

Hannan MT and Freeman J (1989) *Organisational Ecology*, Cambridge, MA: Harvard University Press.

Hardin R (1993) 'The street-level epistemology of trust', *Politics and Society*, 21, 4: 505–529.

—— (2000) 'Trust and society', in Galeotti G, Salmon P and Wintrobe R, eds, *Competition and Structure: the Political Economy of Collective Decisions – Essays in Honour of Albert Breton*, Cambridge: Cambridge University Press, 17–46.

—— (2002) *Trust and Trustworthiness*, New York: Russell Sage Foundation.

Hardy C, Phillips N and Lawrence T (1998) 'Distinguishing trust and power in interorganisational relations: forms and facades of trust', in Lane C and Bachmann R, eds, *Trust Within and Between Organisations: Conceptual Issues and Empirical Applications*, Oxford: Oxford University Press, 64–87.

Hargreaves D (2003) *Education Epidemic: Transforming Secondary Schools through Innovation Networks*, London: Demos.

Harrison B, Kelley M and Gant J (1996) 'Innovative firm behaviour and local milieu: exploring the intersection of agglomeration, firm effects and technological change', *Economic Geography*, 233–258.

Hart K (1988) 'Kinship, contract and trust: economic organisation of migrants in an African slum city', in Gambetta D, ed., *Trust: Making and Breaking Cooperative Relations*, Oxford: Blackwell, 176–193.

Hartley K (1998) 'Defence procurement in the UK', *Defence and Peace Economics*, 9: 39–61.

Hartley K and Martin S (1993) 'Evaluating collaborative programmes', *Defence Economics*, 4: 195–211.

Hay C (2004) 'Theory, stylized heuristic or self-fulfilling prophecy? the status of rational choice theory in public administration', *Public Administration*, 82, 1: 39–62.

Health Services Management Centre (HSMC) (2003) The West Highland Project, HSMC, University of Birmingham.

Hebert R, Durand P, Dubuc N and Tourigny A (2003) PRISMA: a new model of integrated service delivery for frail older people in Canada, *International Journal of Integrated Care*, 3: 1–10.

Heckathorn D (1984) 'Mathematical theory construction in sociology: analytic power, scope and descriptive accuracy as trade-offs', *Journal of Mathematic Sociology*, 10: 295–323.

Heifetz RA (1994) *Leadership Without Easy Answers*, Cambridge, MA: Belknap Press of the Harvard University Press.

Heimer CA (1992) 'Doing your job *and* helping your friends: universalistic norms about obligations to particular others in networks', in Nohria N and Eccles RG, eds, *Networks and Organisations: Structure, Form and Action*, Boston, MA: Harvard Business School Press, 143–164.

Heisbourg F (1988) 'Public policy and the creation of a European arms market', in Creasy P and May S, eds, *The European Armaments Market and Procurement Cooperation*, London: Macmillan.

Hendriks F (2004) 'The poison is the dose', *Innovation: the European Journal of Social Science Research*, 17, 4: 349–361.

Hennart (1993) 'Explaining the "swollen middle": why most transactions are a mix of "market" and "hierarchy" ', *Organisation Science*, 4: 529–547.

Hicks D and Katz JS (1996) 'Science policy for a highly collaborative science system', *Science and Public Policy*, 23, 1: 39–44.

Hill S (1975) *The Dockers: Class and Tradition in London*, London: Heinemann.

Hirschman AO (1985) 'Against parsimony: three easy ways of complicating some categories of economic discourse', reprinted in Hirschman AO, ed., *Rival Views of Market Society and Other Recent Essays*, Cambridge, MA: Harvard University Press, 142–160.

Hite JM and Hesterly WS (2001) 'The evolution of firm networks: from emergence to early growth of the firm', *Strategic Management Journal*, 22: 275–286.

HMIC (2000) *Calling Time on Crime*, London: Her Majesties Inspectorate of Constabulary and the Home Office.

Hochschild AR (1983) *The Managed Heart: Commercialisation of Human Feeling*, Berkeley, CA: University of California Press.

Hoffman AM (2002) 'A conceptualisation of trust in international relations', *European Journal of International Relations*, 8, 3: 375–401.

Hofstede G (1991) *Cultures and Organisations – Software of the Mind: Intercultural Cooperation and its Importance for Survival*, London: HarperCollins.

Holt GD, Love PED and Li H (2000) 'The learning organisation: toward a paradigm for mutually beneficial strategic construction alliances', *International Journal of Project Management*, 18, 6: 415–421.

Home Office (1990) *Partnership in Dealing with Offenders in the Community*, London: HMSO.

—— (1992) *Partnership in Dealing with Offenders in the Community: a Decision Document*, London: HMSO.

—— (1999) *Statutory Partnerships: Pathfinder Series Report*. London: Home Office.

Hood C (1991) 'A public management for all seasons', *Public Administration*, 69: 3–19.
Hood CC (1976) *The Limits of Administration*, London: Wiley.
—— (1983) *The Tools of Government*, Basingstoke: MacMillan.
—— (1998) *The Art of the State: Culture, Rhetoric and Public Management*, Oxford: Oxford University Press.
Hosking D-M and Morley IE (1991) *A Social Psychology of Organising*, Hemel Hempstead: Harvester Wheatsheaf.
Hosmer LT (1995) 'Trust: the connecting link between organisation theory and philosophical ethics', *Academy of Management Review*, 20, 2: 379–403.
Huang J-M, Berlin CI, Lin S-T, Keats BJB and Buskens V (1998) 'The social structure of trust', *Social Networks*, 20, 3: 265–289.
Hudson B (2002) 'The net worth of networks', *Health Services Journal*, January: 16.
—— (2004) 'Analysing network partnerships: Benson revisited', *Public Management Review*, 6, 1: 75–91.
Huxham C, ed. (1996) *Creating Collaborative Advantage*, London: Sage.
Huxham C and Vangen S (2000) 'Leadership in the shaping and implementation of collaborative agendas: how things happen in (not quite) joined up world', *Academy of Management Journal*, 43, 6: 1159–1175.
Ingham M and Mothe C (1998) 'How to learn in R&D partnerships?', *R&D Management*, 28, 4: 249–261.
International Defense Review (1991) 'Defense and the Single Market: the outlook for collaborative ventures', 9: 949–963.
James A and Raine (1998) *The New Politics of Criminal Justice*, London: Longman.
Jensen MC and Meckling WH (1976) 'Theory of the firm: managerial behaviour, agency costs and ownership structure', *Journal of Financial Economics*, 3: 305–360, excerpted in Putterman L, ed., *The Economic Nature of the Firm: a Reader*, Cambridge: Cambridge University Press, 209–229.
Jepperson RL (1991) 'Institutions, institutional effects and institutionalism', in Powell WW and DiMaggio PJ, eds, *The New Institutionalism in Organisational Analysis*, Chicago, IL: University of Chicago Press, 143–163.
Jervis R (1997) *System Effects: Complexity in Political and Social Life*, Princeton, NJ: Princeton University Press.
John P (1998) *Analysing Public Policy*, London: Pinter.
Johnson S (1997) *Pathways of Care*, Oxford: Blackwell Science.
Jones C, Hesterly W and Borgatti S (1997) 'A general theory of network governance: exchange conditions and social mechanisms', *Academy of Management Review*, 22, 4: 911–945.
Kane RL, Kane RA, Finch M, Harrington C, Newcomer R, Miller N and Hulbert M (1997) 'S/HMOs, the second generation: building on the experience of the first social health maintenance demonstrations', *Journal of the American Geriatrics Society*, 45, 1: 101–107.
Kapstein E (2002) 'Allies and armaments', *Survival*, 44, 2: 141–155.
Katz D and Kahn RL (1966) *The Social Psychology of Organisations*, New York: Wiley.
Katz JS (1994) 'Geographical proximity and scientific collaboration', *Sociometrics*, 31, 1: 31–43.
Kaufmann D, Schwartz D, Frenkel A and Shefer D (2003) 'The role of location and regional networks for biotechnology firms in Israel', *European Planning Studies*, 11, 7: 823–840.
Kaufmann S (1995) *At Home in the Universe: the Search for the Laws of Self-Organisation and Complexity*, Harmondsworth: Penguin.
Kelley M and Watkins T (1995) 'In from the cold: prospects for conversion of the defence industrial base', *Science*, 268: 525–532.

Kelley M and Watkins T (1998) 'Are defense and non-defense manufacturing practices all that different?', in Susman G and O'Keefe S, eds, *The Defense Industry in the Post-Cold War Era*, New York: Pergamon, 251–280.

Kemshall H and Ross L (2000) 'Partners in evaluation: modelling quality in partnership projects', *Social Policy and Administration* 34, 5: 551–566.

Kendrick S (1996) 'The patterns of increase in emergency hospital admissions in Scotland', *Health Bulletin*, 54: 169–183

Kenney M (1986) *Biotechnology: the University-Industrial Complex*, New Haven, CT: Yale University Press.

Kickert WJM, Klijn E-H and Koppenjan JFM, eds (1997) *Managing Complex Networks: Strategies for the Public Sector*, London: Sage.

Kim K (2000) 'On interfirm power, channel climate and solidarity in industrial distributor–supplier dyads', *Journal of the Academy of Marketing Science*, 28, 3: 388–405.

King G, Keohane R and Verba A (1994) *Designing Social Inquiry*, Princeton, NJ: Princeton University Press.

Knight J (1992) *Institutions and Social Conflict*, Cambridge: Cambridge University Press.

Knoke D (1990) *Political Networks: the Structural Perspective*, Cambridge: Cambridge University Press.

Kodner D (1994) *The Social/Health Maintenance Organisation – Results and Lessons of an Experiment in Integrated Care for the Elderly*, presentation at SYSTED 94, Geneva, Switzerland, 2 May.

Kodner D (1999) *Integrated Long Term Care Systems in the New Millennium – Fact Or Fiction?* Presentation at the American Society on Ageing, Summer Series on Ageing, 26 July 1999.

Kodner D and Kyriacou C (2000) 'Fully integrated care for the frail elderly: two American models', *International Journal of Integrated Care*, 1, 1: 1–21.

Kogut B (1989) 'The stability of joint ventures: reciprocity and competitive rivalry', *Journal of Industrial Economics*, 38, 2: 183–198.

Kogut B, Shan W and Walker G (1992) The make-or-cooperate decision in the context of an industry network, in Nohria N and Eccles RG, eds, *Networks and Organisations: Structure, Form and Action*, Boston, MA: Harvard Business School Press, 348–365.

—— (1993) 'Knowledge in the network and the network as knowledge, in Grabher G, ed., *The Embedded Firm: on the Socioeconomics of Industrial Networks*, London: Routledge, 67–94.

Korb L (1996) 'Merger Mania', *The Brookings Review*, Summer: 22–25.

Kornai J (1992) *The Socialist System: the Political Economy of Communism*, Oxford: Oxford University Press.

Kosh M and Williams B (1995) *The Probation Service and Victims of Crime: a Pilot Study*, Keele: Keele University Press.

Kraakman R (2001) 'The durability of the corporate form', in DiMaggio PJ, ed., *The Twenty first Century Firm: Changing Economic Organisation in International Perspective*, Princeton, NJ: Princeton University Press, 147–160.

Kramer RM and Tyler TR, eds (1996) *Trust in Organisations: Frontiers of Theory and Research*, London: Sage.

Kuhn T (1970) [1962], *The Structure of Scientific Revolutions*, 2nd edn Chicago, IL: University of Chicago Press.

Kuldeep K and van Dissel H (1996) 'Sustainable collaboration: managing conflict and cooperation in interorganisational systems', *MIS Quarterly*, 20, 3: 279–300.

Kümpers S, Van Raak A, Hardy B and Muir I (2002) 'The influence of institutions and culture on health policies: different approaches to integrated care in England and the Netherlands', *Public Administration*, 80, 2: 339–358.

Kunkler I (2000) 'Managed clinical networks: a new paradigm for clinical medicine', *Journal of the Royal College of Physicians*, 34, 3: 230–233.

Kyläheiko K, Sandstrom J and Virkkunen V (2002) 'Dynamic capability view in terms of real options', *International Journal of Production Economics*, 80, 1: 65–83.

La Porte T (1996) 'Shifting vantage points and conceptual puzzles in understanding public organisation networks', *Journal of Public Administration Research and Theory*, 6, 1: 49–74.

La Porte TR and Consolini PM (1991) 'Working in practice but not in theory: theoretical challenges of high reliability organizations', *Journal of Public Administration Research and Theory*, 1, 1: 19–47.

Lane C (1998) 'Introduction: theories and issues in the study of trust', in Lane C and Bachmann R, eds, *Trust Within and Between Organisations: Conceptual Issues and Empirical Applications*, Oxford: Oxford University Press, 1–30.

Lane C and Bachman R, eds (1998) *Trust Within and Between Organisations: Conceptual Issues and Empirical Applications*, Oxford: Oxford University Press.

Lane PJ and Lubatkin M (1998) 'Relative absorptive capacity and interorganisational learning', *Strategic Management Journal*, 19: 461–477.

LaPalombara J (1964) *Interest Groups in Italian Politics*, Princeton, NJ: Princeton University Press.

Larson A (1992) 'Network dyads in entrepreneurial settings: a study of the governance of exchange relationships', *Administrative Science Quarterly*, 37: 76–104.

Latour B (1987) *Science in Action: How to Follow Scientists and Engineers through Society*, Cambridge, MA: Harvard University Press.

Law J and Hassard J (1999) *Actor Network Theory and After*, London: Sage.

Lawrence PR and Lorsch JW (1967) *Organisation and Management: Managing Differentiation and Integration*, Graduate School of Business Administration Press, Cambridge, MA: Harvard University Press.

Lee C, Lee K and Pennings JM (2001) 'Internal capabilities, external networks and performance: a study of technology-based ventures', *Strategic Management Journal*, 22: 6–7, 615–40.

Leggat S (2000) 'From the bottom up and other lessons from down under', *Healthcare Papers*, 1, 2: 37–47.

Leigh A, Read T and Tilley N (1996) *Problem-oriented Policing: Brit Pop*. Crime Detection and Prevention Series Paper 75, London: Home Office.

Leitzel J (1992) 'Competition in Procurement', *Policy Sciences*, 25: 43–56.

Lerner J, Shane H and Tsai A (2003) 'Do equity financing cycles matter? Evidence from biotechnology alliances', *Journal of Financial Economics*, 67, 3: 411–446.

Lesser EL, ed. (2000) *Knowledge and Social Capital: Foundations and Applications*, London: Butterworth Heinemann.

Leutz W (1999) 'Five laws for integrating medical and social services: lessons from the United States and the United Kingdom', *The Milbank Quarterly*, 77, 1: 77–110.

Leutz W, Greenberg J, Abrahams R, Prottas J, Diamond L and Gruenberg L (1985) *Changing Health Care for an Aging Society: Planning for the Social Health Maintenance Organisation*, Lexington, MA: Lexington Books.

Lewicki RJ and Bunker BB (1996) 'Developing and maintaining trust in work relationships', in Kramer RM and Tyler TR, eds, *Trust in Organisations: Frontiers of Theory and Research*, London: Sage, 114–139.

Lewis JD and Weisgert A (1985) 'Trust as a social reality', *Social Forces*, 43, 4: 967–485.

Liddle M and Gelsthorpe L (1994a) *Inter-agency crime prevention: further issues*, Police Research Group Supplementary Paper to Crime Prevention Unit Series No 53, London: Home Office.

Liebenhuft R (1996) *Antitrust Analysis of Hospital Networks and Shared Services Arrangements*. Paper presented to the American Hospital Association, Sixth Annual Conference, New York, 10 October, www.ftc.gov/speeches

Liebeskind JP, Oliver AL Zucker LG and Brewer MB (1996) 'Social networks, learning and flexibility; sourcing scientific knowledge in new biotechnology firms', *Organisation Science*, 7, 4: 428–443.

Lin N (2001) *Social Capital: A Theory of Social Structure and Action*, Cambridge: Cambridge University Press.

Lin Y and Wan T (1999) 'Analysis of integrated healthcare networks' performance: a contingency-strategic management perspective', *Journal of Medical Systems*, 23, 6: 477–495.

Lipton D, Martinson R and Wilkes J (1975) *The Effectiveness of Correctional Treatment: a Survey of Treatment Evaluation Studies*, New York: Praeger.

Livingston M and Woods K (2003) *Evaluating Managed Clinical Networks for Cancer Services in Scotland*, paper presented to the WHO/IJIC International Conference on New Research and Developments in Integrated Care, Barcelona, 21–22 February, www.ijic.org

Local Government Association (2001) *All Together Now? A Survey of Local Authority Approaches to Social Inclusion and Anti-poverty*, London: LGA.

Locke T (1990) *New Approaches to Crime in the 1990s*, Harlow: Longman.

Lorenz EH (1988) 'Neither friends nor strangers: informal networks of subcontracting in French industry', in Gambetta D, ed., 1988, *Trust: Making and Breaking Cooperative Relations*, Oxford: Blackwell, 194–210.

Lorenzoni G and Lipparini A (1999) 'The leveraging of interfirm relationships as a distinctive organisational capability: a longitudinal study', *Strategic Management Journal*, 20: 317–338.

Luhmann N (1979) *Trust and Power*, ed., Burns T and Poggi G, New York: Wiley.

—— (1988) Familiarity, confidence, trust: problems and alternatives, in Gambetta D, ed., *Trust: Making and Breaking Co-operative Relations*, Oxford: Basil Blackwell, 94–107.

Luke JS (1997) *Catalytic Leadership: Strategies for an Interconnected World*, San Francisco, CA: Jossey-Bass.

Luke R and Begun J (1988) 'The management of strategy', in Shortell S and Kaluzny A, eds, *Healthcare Management: a Text in Organisational Theory and Behaviour*, New York: Wiley.

Lukes S (1973) *Émile Durkeim: His Life and Work – an Historical and Critical Study*, Harmondsworth: Penguin.

—— (1974) *Power: a Radical View*, Basingstoke: MacMillan.

Macaulay S (1963) 'Non-contractual relations in business', *American Sociological Review*, 28, 1: 55–67.

Macneil IR (1974) 'The many futures of contracts', *Southern California Law Review*, 47: 691–816.

—— (1980) *The New Social Contract: an Inquiry into Modern Contractual Relations*, New Haven, CT: Yale University Press.

—— (1985) 'Reflections on relational contract', *Journal of Institutional and Theoretical Economics*, 141: 541–546.

Madhavan R, Koka BR and Prescott JE (1998) 'Networks in transition: how industry events (re)shape interfirm relationships', *Strategic Management Journal*, 19: 439–459.

Mahoney J (2001) 'Review essay: beyond correlational analysis: recent innovations in theory and method', *Sociaological Forum*, 16, 3: 575–593.

Mann M (1986) *The Sources of Social Power, Volume 1: a History of Power from the Beginning to AD 1760*, Cambridge: Cambridge University Press.

March JG (1991) 'Exploration and exploitation in organisational learning', *Organisation Science*, 2, 1: 1–13.

Mantzavinos C (2001) *Individuals, Institutions and Markets*, Cambridge: Cambridge University Press.

—— (1999) [1991], 'Exploration and exploitation in organisational learning', *Organisation Science*, 2: 71–87, repr. in March JG, *The Pursuit of Organisational Intelligence*, Oxford: Blackwell, 114–136.

March JG and Olsen J-P (1976) *Ambiguity and Choice in Organisations*, Bergen: Universitetsforlaget.

—— (1989) *Rediscovering Institutions: the Organisational Basis of Politics*, New York: Free Press.

Markowski S and Hall P (1998) 'Challenges of defence procurement', *Defence and Peace Economics*, 9: 3–37.

Marks SR (1998) 'The gendered contexts of inclusive intimacy: the Hawthorne women at work and home', in Adams RG and Allan G, eds, *Placing Friendship in Context*, Cambridge: Cambridge University Press, 43–70.

Markusen A and Costigan S (1999a) 'The military industrial challenge', in Markusen A and Costigan S, eds, *Arming for the Future: a Defense Industry for the 21st Century*, New York: Council on Foreign Relations Press, 3–34.

—— (1999b) 'Policy choices', in Markusen A and Costigan S, eds, *Arming for the Future: a Defense Industry for the 21st Century*, New York: Council on Foreign Relations Press, 409–424.

Mars G (1982) *Cheats at Work: an Anthropology of Workplace Crime*, 3rd edn, Aldershot, Hampshire: Ashgate (Dartmouth Publishing Company).

—— (1999) 'Criminal social organisation, cultures and vulnerability: an approach from cultural theory', in Canter D and Alison L, eds, *The Social Psychology of Crime: Criminal Groups, Teams and Networks*, Aldershot: Ashgate, 21–50.

Marsden D (1998) 'Understanding the role of interfirm institutions in sustaining trust within the employment relationship', in Lane C and Bachmann R, eds, *Trust Within and Between Organisations: Conceptual Issues and Empirical Applications*, Oxford: Oxford University Press, 173–202.

Martin J (1992) *Cultures in Organisations: Three Perspectives*, Oxford: Oxford University Press.

Martin S, White R and Hartley K (1996) 'Defence and firm performance in the UK', *Defence and Peace Studies*, 7: 325–337.

Martinson R (1974) 'What works? Questions and answers about prison reform', *The Public Interest*, 35: 22–54.

Mayntz R (1999) 'Organisational coping, failure and success: academies of sciences in central and eastern Europe', in Anheier HK, ed., *When Things Go Wrong: Organisational Failures and Breakdowns*, London: Sage, 71–88.

McGregor D (1960) *The Human Side of Enterprise*, New York: McGraw-Hill.

McGuire J, ed. (1995) *What Works: Reducing Offending Guidelines from Research and Practice*, Chichester: Wiley.

McGuire M (2002) 'Managing networks: propositions on what managers do and why they do it', *Public Administration Review*, 62, 5: 599–609.

McKee M and Healy J (2002) *Hospitals in a Changing Europe*, Buckingham: Open University Press.

McKelvey M, Alm H and Riccaboni M (2003) 'Does co-location matter for formal knowledge collaboration in the Swedish biotechnology-pharmaceutical sector?', *Research Policy*, 32: 483–501.

McLaughlin V, Leatherman S, Fletcher M and Wyn-Owen J (2001) 'Improving performance using indicators. Recent experiences in the Unites States, the United Kingdom, and Australia', *International Journal for Quality in Health Care*, 13, 6: 455–462.

McLeay E (1998) 'Policing policy and policy networks in Britain and New Zealand', in Marsh D, ed., *Comparing Policy Networks*, Buckingham: Open University Press, 110–131.

McNulty T (2002) 'Reengineering as knowledge management: a case of change in UK healthcare', *Management Learning*, 33, 4: 439–458.

Meggitt MJ (1967) 'The pattern of leadership among the Mae-Enga of New Guinea', *Anthropological Forum*, 2, 1: 20–35.

Merton RK (1968) [1949], *Social Science and Social Structure*, New York: Free Press.

Merton RK and Barber E (1976) 'Sociological ambivalence', in Merton RK, ed., *Sociological Ambivalence and Other Essays*, New York: Free Press, 3–31.

Meyer JW and Rowan B (1977) 'Institutionalised organisations: formal structure as myth and ceremony', *American Journal of Sociology*, 83: 340–363.

Meyer MW and Zucker LG (1989) *Permanently Failing Organisations*, Newbury Park, CA: Sage.

Miles RE and Snow CC (1984) 'Fit, failure and the hall of fame', *California Management Review*, 26, 3: 10–28.

—— (1992) 'Causes of failure in network organisations', *California Management Review*, 34, 4: 53–72.

Milward HB and Provan KG (2000) 'Governing the hollow state', *Journal of Public Administration Research and Theory*, 10, 2: 359–379.

Mintzberg H (1983) *Power in and Around Organisations*, Englewood Cliffs, NJ: Prentice-Hall.

—— (1983) *Structure in Fives: Designing Effective Organizations*. Englewood Cliffs, NJ: Prentice Hall.

Mintzberg H and Waters JA (1994) [1985], 'Of strategies, deliberate and emergent', *Strategic Management Journal*, 6: 257–272, repr. in Tsoukas H, ed., *New Thinking in Organisational Behaviour: From Social Engineering to Reflective Action*, Oxford: Butterworth-Heinemann, 188–208.

Misztal B (1996) *Trust in Modern Societies: the Search for the Bases of Social Order*, Cambridge: Polity Press.

—— (2000) *Informality: Social Theory and Contemporary Practice*, London: Routledge.

Mohr J and Spekman R (1994) 'Characteristics of partnership success: partnership attributes, communication behaviour and conflict resolution techniques', *Strategic Management Journal*, 15: 135–152.

Moir D, Campbell H, Wrench J and Miller S (2001) 'First steps in developing a managed clinical network for vascular services in Lanarkshire', *Health Bulletin (Edin)*, 59, 6: 405–411.

Morgan G (1986) *Images of Organisations*, London: Sage.

Morgan J (1991) *Safer Communities: the Local Delivery of Crime Prevention through the Partnership Approach*, ('The Morgan Report') London: Home Office.

Mounteney J (1996) 'One year on: DATs: how have they measured up?', *Druglink*, July/August: 8–9.

Mundt M (1997) 'A model for clinical learning experiences in integrated health care networks', *Journal of Nursing Education*, 36, 7: 309–316.

Murphy JT (2003) 'Social space and industrial development in east Africa: deconstructing the logics of industry networks in Mwanza, Tanzania', *Journal of Economic Geography*, 3: 173–198.

Murray F (2002) 'Innovation as co-evolution of scientific and technological networks: exploring tissue engineering', *Research Policy*, 31, 8: 1389–1403.

National Treatment Agency (NTA) for substance misuse (2002) *Key Findings on Drug Treatment: Drug Action Teams Template Analysis*, London: NTA.

Nee V (1998) 'Sources of the new institutionalism', in Brinton MC and Nee V, eds, *The New Institutionalism in Sociology*, Stanford, CA: Stanford University Press, 1–16.

Neef D, ed. (1998) *The Knowledge Economy*, Boston, MA: Butterworth-Heinemann.

Nelkin D (1982) 'Blunders in the business of risk', *Nature*, 298: 775–776.

Nelson RR and Winter SG (1982) *An Evolutionary Theory of Economic Change*, Cambridge, MA: Belknap Press of the Harvard University Press.

Newman J (2000) 'Beyond the new public management? Modernising public services', in Clarke J, Gewirtz S and McLaughlin E, eds, *New Managerialism, New Welfare?*, London: Sage, 45–61.

NHS Management Executive (1999) *Introduction of Managed Clinical Networks in Scotland*, Edinburgh: NHS Management Executive (MEL, 1999, 10).

Nies H, van Linschoten P, Plaisier A and Romijn C (2003) 'Networks as regional structures for collaboration in integrated care', *International Journal of Integrated Care*, paper presented to the *IJIC*/WHO Conference, Barcelona.

Niskanen WA (1994) *Bureaucracy and Public Economics*, Aldershot: Edward Elgar.

North DC (1990) *Institutions, Institutional Change and Economic Performance*, Cambridge: Cambridge University Press.

—— (1998) 'Economic performance through time', in Brinton MC and Nee V, eds, *The New Institutionalism in Sociology*, Stanford, CA: Stanford University Press, 247–257.

Noteboom B (2004) *Inter-firm Collaboration, Learning and Networks: an Integrated Approach*, London: Routledge.

O'Neill O (1996) *Towards Justice and Virtue: a Constructive Account of Practical Reasoning*, Oxford: Oxford University Press.

O'Toole LJ jnr (1988) 'Strategies for intergovernmental management: implementing programs in interorganisational network', *Journal of Public Administration*, 25, 1: 43–57.

—— (1993) 'Interorganisational policy studies: lessons drawn from implementation research', *Journal of Public Administration Research and Theory*, 3, 2: 232–251.

—— (1998) 'The implications for democracy in a networked bureaucratic world', *Journal of Public Administration Research and Theory*, 7, 3: 443–459.

O'Toole LJ, jnr and Meier KJ (1999) 'Modelling the impact of public management: implications of structural context', *Journal of Public Administration Research and Theory*, 9, 4: 505–26.

Oden M (1998) 'Defense mega-mergers and alternative strategies: the hidden costs of post cold-war defense restructuring', in Susman G and O'Keefe S, eds, *The Defense Industry in the Post-Cold War Era*, New York: Pergamon, 3–20.

—— (1999) 'Cashing in, cashing out and converting: restructuring of the defense industrial base', in Markusen A and Costigan S, eds, *Arming for the Future: a Defense Industry for the 21st Century*, New York: Council on Foreign Relations Press, 75–105.

Office for Public Management (2002), 'NetWorks: resolving the collateral issues associated with managed clinical networks', Office for Public Management and NHS South Eastern Regional Office.

Okely J (1983) *The Traveller-gypsies*, Cambridge: Cambridge University Press.

Oliver AL (2001) 'Strategic alliances and the learning life-cycle of biotechnology firms', *Organisation Studies*, 22, 3: 467–489.

Olson M and Zeckhauser R (1966) 'An economic theory of alliances', *Review of Economics and Statistics*, 48: 266–279.

Orrú M, Biggart NW and Hamilton GG (1991) 'Organisational isomorphism in east Asia', in Powell WW and DiMaggio PJ, eds, *The New Institutionalism in Organisational Analysis*, Chicago, IL: University of Chicago Press, 361–389.

Orsenigo L, Pammolli F, Riccaboni M, Bonaccorsi A and Turchetti G (1997) 'The evolution of knowledge and the dynamics of an industry network', *Journal of Management and Governance*, 1, 2: 147–175.

Ostrom E (1990) *Governing the Commons: the Evolution of Institutions for Collective Action*, Cambridge: Cambridge University Press.

—— (1998) 'A behavioural approach to the rational choice theory of collective action', *American Political Science Review*, 92, 1: 1–22.

Ouchi WG (1980) 'Markets, bureaucracies and clans', *Administrative Science Quarterly*, 25: 129–141.

Owen-Smith J and Powell WW (2003) 'The role of university patenting in the life sciences: assessing the importance of experience and connectivity', *Research Policy*, 32: 1695–1711.

Owen-Smith J, Riccaboni M, Pammolli F and Powell WW (2002) 'A comparison of US and European university-industry relations in the life sciences', *Management Science*, 48, 1: 24–43.

Pages E (1999) 'Defense mergers: weapons, cost, innovation and international arms industry cooperation', in Markusen A and Costigan S, eds, *Arming for the Future: a Defense Industry for the 21st Century*, New York: Council on Foreign Relations Press, 207–223.

Pahl RE, 1975, *Whose City? And Further Essays on Urban Society*, 2nd edn, Harmondsworth: Penguin.

Parsons T (1969) *Politics and Social Structure*, New York: Free Press.

Peck E, ed. (2005) *Organisational Development in Healthcare*, Oxford: Radcliffe.

Peck E and 6 P (2006). *Beyond delivery: policy implementation as sense-making and settlement basing stoke*, Palgrave MacMillan

Peck E, 6 P, Gulliver P and Towell D (2004) 'Why do we keep on meeting like this? The board as ritual in health and social care', *Health Services Management Research*, 17, 3: 100–109.

Peck E, Towell D and Gulliver P (2001) 'The meanings of culture in Health and Social Care: a study of the combined Trust in Somerset', *Journal of Interprofessional Care*, 15, 4: 319–327.

Peck M and Scherer F (1962) *The Weapons Acquisition Process: an Economic Analysis*, Cambridge, MA: Harvard University Press.

Pennings JM and Harianto F (1992a) 'The diffusion of technological innovation in the commercial banking industry', *Strategic Management Journal*, 13, 1: 29–46.

Pennings JM and Harianto F (1992b) 'Technological networking and innovation implementation', *Organisation Science*, 3: 356–382.

Penrose E (1959) *The Theory of the Growth of the Firm*, Oxford: Blackwell.

Perrow C (1986) [1972], *Complex Organisations: a Critical Essay*, 3rd edn, New York: McGraw-Hill.

—— (1992) 'Small firm networks', in Nohria N and Eccles RG, eds, *Networks and Organisations: Structure, Form and Action*, Boston, MA: Harvard Business School Press, 445–470.

Perrow C (1999) [1984], *Normal Accidents: Living with High Risk Technologies*, 2nd edn, Princeton, NJ: Princeton University Press.

Peters BG (1999) *Institutional Theory in Political Science: the 'New Institutionalism'*, London: Pinter.

Peters L, Groenwegen P and Fiebelkorn N (1998) 'A comparison of networks between industry and public sector research in materials technology and biotechnology', *Research Policy*, 27: 255–271.

Pfeffer J (1981) *Power in Organisations*, Marshfield, MA: Pitman.

Pfeffer J and Salancik GR (1978) *The External Control of Organisations: a Resource Dependence Perspective*, New York: Harper and Row.

Phillips C, Jacobson J, Prime R, Carter M and Considine M (2002) *Crime and Disorder Reduction Partnerships: Round One Progress*. Police research series paper no. 151 London: Policing and Reducing Crime Unit.

Phillips C and Sampson A (1998) 'Preventing repeated racial victimisation: an action research project', *British Journal of Criminology* 38, 1: 124–144.

Pinelli Beauline Associates Ltd (1998) *CHOICE Evaluation Project: Evaluation Summary, Final Report*. Pinelli Beauline Associates Ltd, 26 November.

Piore M and Sabel C (1984) *The Second Industrial Divide: Possibilities for Prosperity*, New York: Basic Books.

Plogman P, Pine M, Reed D *et al.* (1998) 'Anthem Blue Cross and Blue Shield's coronary services network: a managed organization's approach to improving the quality of cardiac care for its members', *American Journal of Managed Care*, 4, 12: 1679–1686.

Podolny JM and Page KL (1998) 'Network forms of organisation', *American Review of Sociology*, 24, 57–76.

Polanyi M (1962) [1958], *Personal Knowledge: Towards a Post-critical Philosophy*, London: Routledge and Kegan Paul.

Polivka, Robinson-Anderson (1999) *Managed Care for the Elderly and the Role of the Ageing Network: Volume IV*. Commission on Long-Term Care in Florida, The Florida Policy Exchange Center on Aging, University of South Florida, Tampa, June 1999.

Pollitt C (2004) 'Strategic steering and performance management: agencies – beautiful form or weak variable?', paper given at the ESRC international expert colloquium, Governance and performance: how do modes of governance affect public service performance?, 15–16 March 2004, School of Public Policy, University of Birmingham.

Pollitt C and Bouckaert G (2000) *Public Management Reform: a Comparative Analysis*, Oxford: Oxford University Press.

Porter ME (1998) *The Competitive Advantage: Creating and Sustaining Superior Performance*, New York: Simon and Schuster.

Portus R (1995) 'Process control: clinical pathways analysis', in Bakker H, Holzeimer W, Tallbey M and Grobe S, eds, *Informatics: The Infrastructure for Quality Assessment Improving in Nursing*. San Francisco, CA: VC Nursing Press, 68–76.

Powell WW (1990) 'Neither market nor hierarchy: network forms of organisation', in Cummings LL and Staw B, eds, *Research in organisational behaviour*, vol 12, series ed. Bacharach B, Greenwich, CT: JAI Press, 295–336.

Powell WW (1996) 'Trust based forms of governance', in Kramer RM and Tyler TR, eds., *Trust in Organisation: Frontiers of Theory and Research*, London: Sage, 51–67.

—— (2001) 'The capitalist firm in the twenty first century: emerging patterns in western enterprise', in DiMaggio PJ, ed., *The Twenty First Century Firm: Changing Economic Organisation in International Perspective*, Princeton, NJ: Princeton University Press, 33–68.

Powell WW and Brantley P (1992), 'Competitive cooperation in biotechnology: learning through networks', in Nohria N and Eccles RG, eds, *Networks and Organisations: Structure, Form and Action*, Boston, MA: Harvard Business School Press, 366–394.
Powell WW and DiMaggio PJ, eds, (1991) *The New Institutionalism in Organisational Analysis*, Chicago, IL: University of Chicago Press.
Powell WW, Koput KW and Smith-Doerr L (1996) 'Interorganisational collaboration and the locus of innovation: networks of learning in biotechnology', *Administrative Science Quarterly*, 41: 116–145.
Powell WW, Koput KW, Smith-Doerr L and Owen-Smith J (1999) 'Network position and firm performance: organisational returns to collaboration in the biotechnology industry', in Andrews S and Knoke D, eds, *Networks in and Around Organisations, Research in the Sociology of Organisations*, Greenwich, CT: JAI Press, 16, 129–159.
Powell WW and Smith-Doerr L (1994) 'Networks and economics life', in Smelser NJ and Swedberg RJ, eds, *The Handbook of Economic Sociology*, Princeton, NJ: Princeton University press and New York: Russell Sage Foundation, 368–402.
Powell WW, White DR, Koput KW and Owen-Smith J (2005), 'Network dynamics and field evolution: the growth of interorganisational collaboration in the life sciences', *American Journal of Sociology*, 110, 4: 1132–1205.
Power M (1997) *The Audit Society: Rituals of Verification*, Oxford: Oxford University Press.
Poza EJ and Hanlon S and Kishida P (2004) 'Does the family business interaction factor represent a resource or a cost?', *Family Business Review*, 17, 2: 99–118.
Prahalad CK and Hamel G (1990) 'The core competence of the corporation', *Harvard Business Review*, May–June, 89–91.
Pratt MG and Doucet L (2000) 'Ambivalent feelings in organisational relationships', in Fineman S, ed., *Emotion in Organisations*, 2nd edn, London: Sage, 204–226.
Prevezer M (2001) 'Ingredients in the early development of the US biotechnology industry', *Small Business Economics*, 17, 1/2: 17–29.
Provan K and Milward H (2001) 'Do networks really work? A framework for evaluating public sector organisational networks', *Public Administration Review*, 61, July/August: 414–423.
Provan KG and Milward HB (1995) 'A preliminary theory of network effectiveness: a comparative study of four mental health systems', *Administrative Science Quarterly*, 40, 1: 1–33.
Przeworski A and Teune H (1970) *The Logic of Comparative Social Inquiry*, New York: John Wiley & Son.
Putnam RD (2000) *Bowling Alone: the Collapse and Revival of American Community*, New York: Simon and Schuster.
Putnam RD with Leonardi R and Nanetti Y (1993) *Making Democracy Work: Civic Traditions in Modern Italy*, Princeton, NJ: Princeton University Press.
Quinn J, Anderson P and Finkelstein S (1996) 'Leverage intellect', *The Academy of Management Executive*, 10, 3: 7–27.
Ragin CC (2000) *Fuzzy Set Social Science*, Chicago, IL: University of Chicago Press.
Rappaport RA (1967) *Pigs for the Ancestors: Ritual in the Ecology of a New Guinea People*, New Haven, CT: Yale University Press.
Rayner S (1992) 'Cultural theory and risk analysis', in Krimsky S and Golding D, eds, *Social Theories of Risk*, Westport, CT: Praeger Publishing, 83–116.
Rayner S (1982) 'The perceptions of time and space in egalitarian sects: a millenarian cosmology', in Douglas M, ed., *Essays in the Sociology of Perception*, London: Routledge and Kegan Paul, 247–274.

Rayner S (1988) 'The rules that keep us equal: complexity and the costs of egalitarian organisation', in Flanagan JG and Rayner S, eds, *Rules, Decisions and Inequality in Egalitarian Societies*, Aldershot: Avebury, 20–42.

Regnér P (2000) 'Strategy in the periphery: the role of external linkages in strategy creation', in Birkinshaw J and Hagström P, eds, *The Flexible Firm: Capability Management in Network Organisations*, Oxford: Oxford University Press, 82–105.

Renn O (1992) 'Concepts of risk: a classification', in Krimsky S and Golding D, eds, *Social Theories of Risk*, Westport, CT: Praeger Publishing, 53–79.

Reuer JJ and Koza MP (2000) 'International joint venture instability and corporate strategy', in Faulkner DO and De Rond M, eds. *Cooperative Strategy: Economic, Business and Organisational Issues*, Oxford: Oxford University Press, 261–280.

Reuer JJ and Zollo M (2000) 'Managing governance adaptations in strategic alliances', *European Management Journal*, 18, 2: 164–172.

Reuer JJ, Zollo M and Singh H (2002) 'Post-formation dynamics in strategic alliances', *Strategic Management Journal*, 23, 135–151.

Rhodes RAW and Marsh D (1992) 'New directions in the study of policy networks', *European Journal of Political Research*, 21, 1–2: 181–205.

Rhodes RAW (1997) *Understanding Governance: Policy Networks, Governance, Reflexivity and Accountability*, Buckingham: Open University Press.

Richards M and De Carolis DM (2003) 'Joint venture research and development activity: an analysis of the international biotechnology industry', *Journal of International Management*, 9: 33–49.

Richards P (1996) *Fighting for the Rain Forest: War, Youth and Resources in Sierra Leone*, Oxford: James Currey.

Richards S, Barnes M, Coulson A, Gaster L, Leach B and Sullivan H (1999) 'Cross-cutting issues in public policy and public services', London: Department for the Environment, Transport and the Regions.

Ricketts M (2001) 'Trust and economic organisation', *Economic Affairs*, March: 18–22.

Rindfleisch A (2000) 'Organisational trust and interfirm cooperation: an examination of horizontal versus vertical alliances', *Marketing Letters*, 11, 1: 81–95.

Ring PS and Van de ven AH (1992) 'Structuring cooperative relationships between organisation', *Strategic Management Journal*, 3: 483–498.

Roberts KH (1993) *New Challenges to Organisation Research: High Reliability Organisations*, New York: MacMillan.

Roberts KH, Rousseau DM and La Porte TR (1994) 'The culture of high reliability: quantitative and qualitative assessment aboard nuclear powered aircraft carriers', *Journal of High Technology Management Research*, 5, 1: 141–161.

Robertson PJ (1995) 'Involvement in boundary-spanning activity: mitigating the relationship between work setting and behaviour', *Journal of Public Administration Research and Theory*, 5, 1: 73–98.

Robinson J and Casalino J (1996) 'Vertical integration and organisational networks in health care', *Health Affairs*, 15, 1: 7–23.

Robinson R and Steiner A (1998) *Managed Health Care: US Evidence and Lessons for the National Health Service*, Buckingham: Open University Press.

Rochlin GI, ed. (1996) 'Reliable organisations: present research and future directions', *Journal of Crisis Contingency Management*, 4, 2: 55–59.

Roethlisberger FJ and Dickson WJ (1939) *Management and the Worker*, Cambridge, MA: Harvard University Press.

Roger Howard Associates (1994) *Across the Divide: Building Community Partnerships to Tackle Drug Misuse* London: Department of Health.

Roninger L (1998) 'Civil society, patronage and democracy', in Alexander JC, ed., *Real Civil Societies: Dilemmas of Institutionalisation*, London: Sage.

Rooks G, Raub W, Selten R and Tazalaar F (2000) 'How inter-firm co-operation depends on social embeddedness: a vignette study', *Acta Sociologica*, 43, 2: 123–137.

Rothaermel FT (2001) 'Complementary assets, strategic alliances, and the incumbent's advantage: an empirical study of industry and firm effects in the biopharmaceutical industry', *Research Policy*, 30, 8: 1235–1251.

Rothstein B (2000) 'Trust, social dilemmas and collective memories', *Journal of Theoretical Politics*, 12, 4: 477–501.

Rotter J (1980) 'Interpersonal trust, trustworthiness and gullibility', *American Psychologist*, 35, 1: 1–7.

Rudberg M and Olhager J (2003) 'Manufacturing networks and supply chains: an operations strategy perspective', *Omega*, 31: 29–39.

Rugman AM and D'Cruz JR (2000a) 'The theory of the flagship firm', in Faulkner D and De Rond M, eds, *Cooperative Strategy: Economic, Business and Organisational Studies*, Oxford: Oxford University Press, 57–73.

—— and D'Cruz JR (2000b) *Multinationals as Flagship Firms: Regional Business Networks*, Oxford: Oxford University Press.

Rumgay J and Cowan S (1998) 'Pitfalls and prospects in partnership: probation programmes for substance misusing offenders', *The Howard Journal*, 37, 2: 124–136.

Russell J, Greenhalgh T, Boynton P and Rigby M (2004) 'Soft networks for bridging the gap between research and practice: illuminative evaluation of CHAIN', *British Medical Journal*, 328.

Sabel CF (1982) *Work and Politics: the Division of Labour in Industry*, Cambridge: Cambridge University Press.

—— (1992) 'Studied trust: building new forms of cooperation in a volatile economy', in Pyke F and Sengenberger W, eds, *Industrial Districts and Local Economic Regeneration*, Geneva: IILS, 215–250.

—— (2001) 'Diversity, not specialisation: the ties that bind the (new) industrial districts, paper presented at the conference', *Complexity and Industrial Clusters: Dynamics and Models in Theory and Practice*, Milan, 19–20.6.01.

Sako M (1992) *Prices, Quality and Trust: Inter-Firm Relations in Britain and Japan*, Cambridge: Cambridge University Press.

Sako M and Helper S (1998) 'Determinants of trust in supplier relations: evidence from the automotive industry in Japan and the United States', *Journal of Economic Behaviour and Organisation*, 34: 387–417.

Salamon LM (1987) 'Partners in public service: the scope and theory of government-nonprofit relations', in Powell WW, ed., *The Nonprofit Sector: a Research Handbook*, New Haven, CT: Yale University Press, 99–117.

Sandler T and Hartley K (1995) *The Economics of Defense*, Cambridge: Cambridge University Press.

Sardell A (1996) 'Clinical networks and clinician retention: the case of CDN', *Journal of Community Health*, 21, 6: 437–451.

Sassen S (1991) *The Global City: New York, London, Tokyo*, Princeton, NJ: Princeton University Press.

—— (1997) 'Cities in the global economy', *International Journal of Urban Sciences*, 1, 1: 11–31.

Schapiro M (1988) 'Judicial selection and the design of clumsy institutions', *Southern California Law Review*, 61: 1555–1569.

Schein EH (1992) *Organisational Culture and Leadership*, 2nd edn, San Francisco, CA: Jossey-Bass.

Schluchter W (1981) *The rise of Western Rationalism: Max Weber's Developmental History*, tr. Roth G, Berkeley, CA: University of California Press.

Schön DA (1983) *The Reflective Practitioner*, New York: Basic Books.

Schotter A (1981) *The Economic Theory of Social Institutions*, Cambridge: Cambridge University Press.

—— (1986) 'The evolution of rules', in Langlois RN, ed., *Economics as a Process: Essays in the New Institutional Economics*, Cambridge: Cambridge University Press, 117–134.

Schroeder R and Swedberg R (2002) 'Weberian perspectives on science, technology and the economy', *British Journal of Sociology*, 53, 3: 383–401.

Schulman PR (1993) 'Negotiated order of organizational reliability', *Administration and Society*, 25, 3: 356–372.

Schumpeter J (1934) *The Theory of Economic Development*, Cambridge, MA: Harvard University Press.

Schurr PH and Osanne JL (1985) 'Influence on exchange processes: buyer's perceptions of a seller's trustworthiness and bargaining toughness', *Journal of Consumer Behaviour*, 11: 939–953.

Scott J (1991) *Social Network Analysis: a Handbook*, London: Sage.

—— (2003) 'Absorptive capacity and the efficiency of research partnerships', *Technology Analysis and Strategic Management*, 15, 2: 247–253.

Scott WR (1992) *Organisations: Rational, Natural and Open Systems*, 3rd edn, Englewood Cliffs, NJ: Prentice-Hall.

—— (1993) 'The organisation of medical care services: toward an integrated theoretical model', *Medical Care Review*, 50, 3: 271–302.

Scott WR, Meyer JW and associates (1994) *Institutional Environments and Organisations*, London: Sage.

Seibel W (1989) 'The function of mellow weakness: nonprofit organisations as problem nonsolvers in Germany', in James E, ed., *The Nonprofit Sector in International Perspective: Studies in Comparative Culture and Policy*, New York: Oxford University Press, 177–192.

Seibel W (1999) 'Successful failure: an alternative view of organisational coping', in Anheier HK, ed., *When Things go Wrong: Organisational Failures and Breakdowns*, London: Sage, 91–104.

Seligman A (1997) *The Problem of Trust*, Princeton, NJ: Princeton University Press.

Selznick P (1980) [1949], *The TVA and the Grass Roots: a Study of Politics and Organisation*, Berkeley' CA: University of California Press.

Senge P (1990) *The Fifth Discipline: the Act and Practice of the Leading Organisation*, New York: Doubleday/Currency.

Sermeus W, Vanhaecht K and Vleugels A (2001) 'The Belgian–Dutch Clinical Pathway Network', *Journal of Integrated Care Pathways*, 5, 1: 10–14.

Shan W, Walker G and Kogut B (1994) 'Interfirm cooperation and startup innovation in the biotechnology industry', *Strategic Management Journal*, 15: 387–394.

Shapiro SP (1987) 'The social control of impersonal trust', *American Journal of Sociology*, 93, 3: 623–658.

Sheaff R (2000) 'A problematic transition from networks to organisations: the case of English primary care groups', in Ashburner L, ed., *Organisational Behaviour and Organisational Studies in Health Care*, Basingstoke: Palgrave.

Sheaff R Marshall M Rogers A Roland M Sibbald B and Pickard S (2004) 'Governmentality by Network in English Primary Healthcare', *Social Science and Administration*, 38, 1: 89–103.

Shortell S, Bazzoli G, Dubbs N and Kralovec P (2000) 'Classifying health networks and systems: managerial and policy implications', *Health Care Management Review*, 25 4: 9–17.

Silverman D (1970) *The Theory of Organisations: a Sociological Framework*, Aldershot: Gower.

—— (1984) 'Going private: ceremonial forms in a private oncology clinic', *Sociology*, 18, 2: 191–204.

Simmel G (1971) [1907], 'Exchange', from Simmel G, *The philosophy of money* tr. Levine DN, in Levine DN, ed., *George Simmel on Individuality and Social Forms*, Chicago, IL: University of Chicago Press, 43–69.

Simon HA (1955) 'A behavioural model of rational choice', *Quarterly Journal of Economics*, 69: 129–138.

—— (1997) [1945], *Administrative Behaviour: a Study of Decision-Making Processes in Administrative Organisations*, 4th edn, New York: Free Press.

Sitkin SB and Roth NL (1993) 'Explaining the limited effectiveness of legalistic remedies for trust/distrust', *Organisation Science*, 4, 3: 367–392.

Sitkin SB and Stickel D (1996) 'The road to hell: the dynamics of distrust in an era of quality', in Kramer M and Tyler TR, eds, *Trust in Organisations: Frontiers of Theory and Research*, London: Sage, 196–215.

Sjöberg M (1999) 'Resistance against networking: Chain of Care' (in Swedish), The Department of Social Science, Mid Sweden University.

Sjöberg L (1997) 'Explaining risk perception: an empirical and quantitative evaluation of cultural theory', *Risk, Decision and Policy*, 2: 113–130.

—— (2003) 'Distal factors in risk perception', *Journal of Risk Research*, 6: 187–212.

Skelcher C (2000) 'Changing images of the state: overloaded, hollowed-out, congested'. *Public Policy and Administration* 15, 2: 3–19.

Lowndes V and Skelcher C (1998) 'The dynamics of multi-organisational partnerships: an analysis of the changing forms of governance', *Public Administration*, 76: 313–333.

Slovic P (1993) 'Perceived risk, trust and democracy', *Risk Analysis*, 13, 6: 675–682, repr. in Slovic P, 2000, *The Perception of Risk*, London: Earthscan, 316–326.

Smith-Doerr L, Owen-Smith L, Koput KW and Powell WW (1998) 'Network and knowledge production: collaboration and patenting in biotechnology', in Leenders RTAJ and Gabbay SM, ed., *Corporate Social Capital and Liability*, Boston, Kluwer: MA, 390–408.

Snyder-Halpern R and Chervany N (2000) A clinical information system strategic planning model for integrated healthcare delivery networks. *Journal of Nursing Administration*, 30, 12: 583–591.

Stacey R (1999) *Strategic Management and Organisational Dynamics: the Challenge of Complexity*, London: Routledge.

Steier L and Greenwood R (2000) 'Entrepreneurship and the evolution of angel financial networks', *Organisation Studies*, 21, 1: 163–192.

Steinmo S, Thelen K and Longstreth F, eds (1992) *Structuring Politics: Historical Institutionalism in Comparative Perspective*, Cambridge: Cambridge University Press.

Stewart R, 1996 [1989], *Leading in the NHS: a Practical Guide*, 2nd edn, Basingstoke: MacMillan.

Stinchcombe AL (1986) 'Rationality and social structure: an introduction', in Stinchcombe AL, ed., *Stratification and Organisation: Selected Papers*, Cambridge: Cambridge University Press, 1–32.

—— (1990) *Information and Organisations*, Berkeley, CA: University of California Press.

—— (2001) *When Formality Works: Authority and Abstraction in Law and Organisations*, Chicago, IL: University of Chicago Press.

Stinchcombe AL and Heimer CA (1985) *Organisation Theory and Project Management: Administering Uncertainty in Norwegian Offshore Oil*, Oslo: Norwegian University Press.

Streeck W (1992) *Social Institutions and Economic Performance: Studies of Industrial Relations in Advanced Capitalist Economies*, London: Sage.

Stuart TE, Hoang H and Hybels RC (1999) 'Interorganisational endorsements and the performance of entrepreneurial enterprises', *Administrative Science Quarterly*, 44: 315–349.

Sugden R (1989) 'Spontaneous order', *Journal of Economic Perspectives*, 3: 85–97.

Sullivan H and Skelcher C (2002) *Working Across Boundaries: Collaboration in Public Services*, Basingstoke: Palgrave.

Susman G and O'Keefe S (1998) 'Introduction: post-cold war challenges for government and industry', in Susman G and O'Keefe S, eds, *The Defense Industry in the Post-Cold War Era*, New York: Pergamon, 3–20.

Swan JA, Scarbrough H and Robertson M (2002) 'The construction of "communities of practice" in the management of innovation', *Management Learning*, 33, 4: 477–496.

Swedberg R (1998) *Max Weber and the Idea of Economic Sociology*, Princeton, NJ: Princeton University Press.

Swift T (2001) 'Trust, reputation and corporate accountability to stakeholders', *Business Ethics: a European Review*, 10, 1: 16–26.

Sydow J (1998a) 'Understanding the constitution of interorganisational trust', in Lane C and Bachman, eds, *'Trust Within and Between Organisations: Conceptual Issues and Empirical Applications*, Oxford: Oxford University Press, 31–63.

—— (1998b) 'Franchise systems as strategic networks: studying network leadership in the services sector', *Asia Pacific Journal of Marketing and Logistics*, 10, 2: 108–120.

Sztompka P (1999) *Trust: a Sociological Theory*, Cambridge: Cambridge University Press.

Tait J and Baxter J (2002) 'A managed clinical network for home perenatal nutrition', *Nursing Times*, 98, 10: 49–50.

Tallman S (2000) 'Forming and managing shared organisation ventures: resources and transaction costs', in Faulkner DO and De Rond M, eds, *Cooperative Strategy: Economic, Business and Organisational Issues*, Oxford: Oxford University Press, 96–116.

Talmud I and Mesch GS (1997) 'Market embeddedness and corporate instability: the ecology of inter-industrial networks', *Social Science Research*, 26: 419–441.

Tanriverdi H and Venkataraman N (1999) *Creation of Professional Networks: an Emergent Model Using Telemedicine as a Case*. Boston University, School of Management, Proceedings of the 32nd Hawaii International Conference on System Science.

Taylor M (2000a). 'Maintaining community involvement in regeneration: What are the issues?' *Local Economy*, 15: 251–255.

—— (2000b) 'Communities in the lead: power, organisational capacity and social capital'. *Urban Studies*, 37: 1019–1035.

Teich I (1998) 'Clinical information systems for integrated healthcare networks', *Proceedings of the Annual Symposium of the American Medical Association*, 19–28.

Thomas H (2003) 'Improving the doctor–manager relationship. Clinical networks for doctors and managers', *British Medical Journal*, 326, 7390: 655.

Thompson G (2003) *Between Hierarchies and Markets: the Logic and Limits of Network Forms of Organisation*, Oxford: Oxford University Press.

Thompson G, Frances J, Levačić R and Mitchell J, eds (1991) *Markets, Hierarchies and Networks: the Coordination of Social Life*, London: Sage.

Thompson GF (2003) *Between Hierarchies and Markets: the Logic and Limits of Network Forms of Organisation*, Oxford: Oxford University Press.

Thompson JD (1967) *Organisations in Action: Social Science Bases of Administrative Theory*, New York: McGraw-Hill.

Thompson M (1979) *Rubbish Theory: the Creation and Destruction of Value*, Oxford: Oxford University Press.

—— (1982a) 'A three dimensional model, in Douglas M, ed., *Essays in the Sociology of Perception*, London: Routledge and Kegan Paul, 31–63.

—— (1982b) 'The problem of the center: an autonomous cosmology', in Douglas M, ed., *Essays in the Sociology of Perception*, London: Routledge and Kegan Paul, 302–328.

—— (1992) 'The dynamics of cultural theory and implications for the enterprise culture', in Hargreaves Heap S and Ross A, eds, *Understanding the Enterprise Culture: Themes in the Work of Mary Douglas*, Edinburgh: Edinburgh University Press, 182–202.

—— (1996) *Inherent Relationality: an Anti-dualist Approach to Institutions*, Bergen: Los Senteret (Norwegian Research Centre in Organisation and Management).

—— (1997a) 'Rewriting the precepts of policy analysis', in Ellis RJ and Thompson M, eds. *Culture Matters: Essays in Honour of Aaron Wildavsky*, Boulder, CO: Westview Press, 201–216.

—— (1997b) 'Cultural theory and technology assessment', in Fischer F and Hajer M, eds., *Living with Nature: Environmental Discourse as Cultural Politics*, Oxford: Oxford University Press.

—— (1997c) 'Cultural theory and integrated assessment', *Environmental Modelling and Assessment*, 2: 139–150.

—— (2003) 'Technology and how to think about it, paper presented at the conference, '*Democratic Governance of Technological Change in an Era of Globalisation*', Lisbon, 23–26 February.

Thompson M, Ellis RJ and Wildavsky A (1990) *Cultural Theory*, Boulder, CO: Westview press.

Thompson M, Grendstad G and Selle P, eds (1999) *Cultural Theory as Political Science*, London: Routledge.

Thompson M and Wildavsky A (1986) 'A cultural theory of information bias in organisations', *Journal of Management Studies*, 23, 3: 273–286.

Tilley N and Laycock G (2002) *Working out What to do: Evidence-based Crime Reduction*, Crime Reduction Research Series Paper 11, London: Home Office.

Tilley N (1993) 'Crime prevention and the safer cities story'. *The Howard Journal* 32, 1: 40–52.

Tilly C (1998) *Durable Inequality*, Berkeley, CA: University of California Press.

Tomkins C (2001) 'Interdependencies, trust and information in relationships, alliances and networks', *Accounting, Organisations and Society*, 26, 2: 161–191.

Traill WB and Duffield CE (2002) 'The structure of the European agro-food biotechnology industry: are strategic alliances here to stay?', in Santaniello V, Evenson RE and Zilberman, eds, *Market Development for Genetically Modified Foods*, Wallingford: CAB International, 283–290.

True JS, Jones BD and Baumgartner FR (1999) 'Punctuated-equilibrium theory: explaining stability and change in American policy making, in Sabatier PA, ed., *Theories of the Policy Process*, Boulder, CO: Westview Press, 97–116.

Tsoukas H (2002) 'Introduction: knowledge-based perspectives on organisations: situated knowledge, novelty and communities of practice', *Management Learning*, 33, 4: 419–426.

Turnbull C (1972) *The Mountain People*, New York: Simon and Schuster.

Ugolini C and Nobilio L (2003) 'Vertical integration and contractual networks in cardiovascular sector: the experience of the Italian region of Emilia Romagna', *International Journal of Integrated Care*, 3: 2 16–35.

Uslaner E (2002) *The Moral Foundations of Trust*, Cambridge: Cambridge University Press.
Uzzi B (1997) 'Social structure and competition in interfirm networks: the paradox of embeddedness', *Administrative Science Quarterly*, 42: 35–67.
Van de Ven AH (1992) 'Suggestions for studying strategy process: a research note', *Strategic Management Journal*, 7, 1: 37–51.
Vanhaverbeke W and Noorderhaven NG (2001) 'Competition between alliance blocks: the case of the RISC microprocessor technology', *Organisation Studies*, 22, 1: 1–30.
Verweij M and Thompson M, eds (2006) *Clumsy Solutions for a Complex World*, Earthscan, London.
Veugelers R (1997) 'Internal R & D expenditures and external technology sourcing', *Research Policy*, 26, 3: 303–315.
Vickers I and Cordey-Hayes M (1999) 'Cleaner production and organizational learning', *Technology, Analysis and Strategic Management*, 11, 1: 75–94.
Volkoff O, Chan YE and Newson PEF (1999) 'Leading the development and implementation of collaborative interorganisational systems', *Information and Management*, 35, 2: 63–75.
Wagner E (1998) 'Chronic disease management: What will it take to improve care for chronic illness?', *Effective Clinical Practice*, 1: 2–4.
Walker G, Kogut B and Shan W (1997) 'Social capital, structural holes and the formation of an industry network', *Organisation Science*, 8, 2.
Walker W and Willett S (1993) 'Restructuring the European defence industrial base', *Defence Economics*, 4: 141–160.
Walsh V, Niosi J and Mustar P (1995) 'Small-firm formation in biotechnology: a comparison for France, Britain and Canada', *Technovation*, 15, 5: 303–327.
Walshok ML, Furtek E, Lee CWB and Windham PH (2002) 'Building regional innovation capacity: the San Diego experience', *Industry and Higher Education*, 16, 1: 27–42.
Waltz K (1979) *Theory of International Politics*, Reading, MA: Addison Wesley.
Wan T, Allen M and Blossom Y (2001) 'Integration and the performance of healthcare networks. Do integrated strategies enhance efficiency, profitability, and image?' *International Journal of Integrated Care*, June 2001, www.ijic.org
Wasserman S and Faust K (1994) *Social Network Analysis: Methods and Applications*, Cambridge: Cambridge University Press
Webb A (1991) 'Coordination: a problem in public sector management', *Policy and Politics*, 19, 4: 229–241.
Weber M, 1978/1968 [1922], *Economy and Society*, tr. Roth G and Wittich C, 2nd edn, Berkeley, CA: University of California Press.
—— (1976) *The Protestant Ethic and the Spirit of Capitalism*, tr. Parsons T, London: Allen and Unwin.
Weick KE (1995) *Sensemaking in Organizations*, London: Sage.
—— (2001) *Making Sense of the Organisation*, Oxford: Blackwell Business.
Weick KE and Roberts KH (1993) 'Collective mind and organizational reliability: the case of flight operations on an aircraft carrier deck', *Administrative Science Quarterly*. 38, 3: 357–381.
Weidenbaum M (1967) 'Defense Expenditure and the Domestic Economy', in Enke S, ed., Defense Management, New Jersey: Prentice Hall.
Weil T (2001) *Health Networks, Can they be a Solution?*, University of Michigan Press.
Weisenfeld U, Reeves JC and Hunck-Meiswinckel A (2001) 'Technology management and collaboration profile: virtual companies and industrial platforms in the high-tech biotechnology industries', *R & D Management*, 31, 1: 91–100.
Wenger E (1998) *Communities of Practice*, Cambridge: Cambridge University Press.

Wenger E (2000) 'Communities of practice and social learning systems', *Organisation*, 7: 2, 225–246.

West E, Barron D, Dowsett J and Newton J (1999) 'Hierarchies and cliques in the social networks of health care professionals: implications for dissemination and implementation', *Social Science and Medicine*, 48, 5: 633–646.

Westney DE (2001) 'Japanese enterprise faces the twenty first century', in DiMaggio PJ, ed., *The Twenty-first-century Firms: Changing Economic Organisation in International Perspective*, Princeton, NJ: Princeton University Press, 105–144.

White HC (1981) 'Where do markets come from?', *American Journal of Sociology*, 87: 517–547.

—— (2001) *Markets from Networks: Socioeconomic Models of Production*, Princeton, NJ: Princeton University Press.

Wildavsky A (1993) 'Democracy as a coalition of cultures', *Society* 31, 1: 80–83.

—— (1998) *Culture and Social Theory*, ed., Chai S-K and Swedlow B, New Brunswick, NJ: Transaction Publishers.

Wildavsky A and Caiden N (2001) *The New Politics of the Budgetary Process*, 4th edn, New York: Addison Wesley Longman.

Wilkinson RG (2000) *Mind the Gap: Hierarchies, Health and Human Evolution*, London: Weidenfeld and Nicholson.

Williams B (1999) 'Youth Offending Teams and partnerships', *The British Criminology Conference: Selected Proceedings. Volume 3. Papers for the British Society of Criminology Conference, Liverpool*, July 1999.

Williams P (2002) 'The competent boundary spanner', *Public Administration*, 80, 1: 103–124.

Williams T (2000) 'The defence supply chain: linkage patterns in the south west of England', *Defence and Peace Economics*, 11: 313–328.

Williamson OE (1975) *Markets and Hierarchies: Analysis and Antitrust Implications*, New York: Free Press.

—— (1985) *The Economic Institutions of Capitalism: Firms, Markets, Relational Contracting*, New York: Free Press.

—— (1994) 'Transaction cost economics and organisation theory', in Smelser NJ and Swedberg R, eds (1996), *The Handbook of Economic Sociology*, Princeton, NJ: Princeton University Press and New York: Russell Sage Foundation, 77–107.

Wilson WJ (1996) 'When Work Disappears: The New World of the Urban Poor', New York: Alfred A. Knopf.

—— (1998) 'Integrated care management', *British Journal of Nursing*, 74: 201–202.

Wolf C, jnr (1988) *Markets or Governments: Choosing between Imperfect Alternatives*, Cambridge, MA: Massachusetts Institute of Technology Press.

Woods K (2001) 'The development of integrated health care models in Scotland'. *International Journal of Integrated Care*, 1: 1.

Yordi C and Waldman J (1985) 'A consolidated model of long-term care: service utilization and cost impacts', *Gerontologist*, 25, 4: 389–397.

Young M and Willmott P (1957) *Family and Kinship in East London*, London: Routledge and Kegan Paul.

Young S, Kennedy C, Davidson C and Rayment K (2002) 'Implementation of an integrated care pathway for acute myocardial infarction: turning a concept into reality', *Journal of Integrated Care Pathways*, 6: 77–81.

Zander K (2002) 'Integrated care pathways: eleven international trends', *Journal of Integrated Care Pathways*, 6: 101–107.

Zander K and McGill R (1994) 'Critical and anticipated recovery paths: only the beginning', *Nursing Management*, 25: 34–40.

Zimmerman Y, Pemberton D and Thomas L (1998) 'Evaluation of the program of all-inclusive care for the elderly (PACE). Factors contributing to care management and decision-making in the PACE model', *Health Care Financing Administration.*

Zucker LG (1986) 'Production of trust: institutional sources of economic structure, 1840–1920', in Bacharach S, ed., *Research in Organisational Behaviour,* JAI Press, Greenwich, CT, 53–111.

Zucker LG and Darby MT (1997) 'Present at the biotechnological revolution: transformation of technological identity for a large incumbent pharmaceutical firm', *Research Policy,* 26: 429–446.

Zucker LG, Darby MR and Brewer MB (1998) 'Intellectual human capital and the birth of US biotechnology enterprises', *American Economic Review,* 88, 1: 290–306.

Zucker LG, Darby MR, Brewer MB and Peng Y (1996) 'Collaboration structure and information dilemmas in biotechnology: organisational boundaries as trust production', in Kramer RM and Tyler TR, eds, *Trust in Organisations: Frontiers of Theory and Research,* London: Sage, 90–113.

Index